The
New Socialist
Revolution

Michael P. Lerner

The
New Socialist
Revolution

AN INTRODUCTION TO ITS
THEORY AND STRATEGY

Delacorte Press/New York

Library of Congress Cataloging in Publication Data
Lerner, Michael P.   1943-
    The new socialist revolution.

    Includes bibliographies.
    1. Socialism in the United States.   2. Radicalism—
United States.   I. Title.
HX86.L36   335'.00973   72-10372

Dedicated to
THIERRIE
*and to my sisters and brothers who died in
the Nazi concentration camps, and in the
bombing and napalming and torture by the
American invaders of the country of Vietnam.*

"The demand to abandon illusions about
our condition is a demand to abandon
a condition which requires illusions."

KARL MARX

Contents

Introduction

THE SEEMING harmony and quiet of the 1950s and early 1960s in American society has been shattered for all time. Despite the frantic smiles and slippery phrases of political leaders, despite the "new hope" that commentators proclaim whenever a liberal politician enters the arena or gets elected, almost everyone senses the crisis. Even President Nixon talked about "a revolution" and called for "power to the people" in his 1971 State of the Union address—as if by coopting words he could destroy what they represented. Lindsay, McGovern, McCarthy, Kennedy, and a host of other liberal politicians have done their best to revive the declining faith in the American political system. But they have not accomplished this. The New American Revolution is not the creation of a Madison Avenue adman or a television commentator looking for a catchy phrase. Rather, it is the result of social forces that have been gathering for over a century, forces that include the majority of the peoples of the world. People may be dazzled for a while by the fanfare of a media campaign offering up some new liberal as the embodiment of all that is good. But the media image soon fades—and the reality remains. Only programs that actually change American *reality* will matter in the not-too-long run.

This book is an attempt to explain why the only changes that will make sense in America are those that will move this country to socialism, a socialism that will be a far cry both from the "welfare statism" of Sweden and the bureaucratic regimes of Eastern Europe. And I hope also to show why that socialism cannot be achieved by relying on the political system to move slowly in the direction of socialism but can be realized in this country only through revolutionary struggle.

The three sections of the book correspond to three basic questions:

1. How are the problems of American society rooted in the basic structure of capitalism?

2. Which forces in American society can bring about a socialist revolution and what tactics can they use?

3. What will the New Socialism be like?

These questions encompass large areas and require considerable research. It would be impossible to cover them fully in this short book. Instead, I have attempted to synthesize some of the basic work in this area and present a simplified account. My hope is that my readers will realize that there *is* a coherent revolutionary socialist position (something they would never know from the fragmented articles that appear in the establishment press, the underground newspapers, and even in books by the media-made New Left superstars), and will want to pursue further each topic I have touched upon. In presenting my synthesis, then, I have constructed a model through which one can view the American reality. But I caution the reader that the model needs to be filled in with a great deal more empirical research. By itself, no single book can hope to present convincing arguments on each point, but it may show how those points form a coherent whole.

Fortunately, some research has already been done. Each chapter concludes with a suggested set of readings, some of which have been used in building the argument of the chapter and some of which offer a more careful development of the empirical data. If you think my model makes any sense at all, I beg you to read this more specialized material.

The claims made in this book are meant to be empirical, not empty and rhetorical. Too often people think that the Left uses words such as *imperialism* and *racism* simply to get an emotional response—to emphasize that things aren't merely bad, but *really* bad. This is not our intent. If what I say is false, discard it: the Left must not be allowed to lie to you and if it does lie, its claims must be refuted. But if what I say is true, it will affect your life profoundly. And the Left is not lying. It is telling the truth: It is providing the only analysis that can make sense of your own experiences; and it is making predictions that will be verified within the next thirty years. So check it out carefully. Read the sources, reflect on your own life, find out for yourself.

Reality is always more complex than a model, of course, and different historical periods may require me to stress different aspects of reality. Moreover, reality is constantly changing and being transformed (e.g., the forms that imperialism may take in the late 1970s may be quite different from the forms it took in the early 1960s). If this book is not prophetic enough to cover every important transformation in the ways capitalism exploits people, that does not disprove its thesis. But this book should be discarded (and the whole Left should be repudiated) if it turns out that capitalism is reformed in such a way as to make available to everyone a meaningful, creative, and humane life—a life in which the basic social institutions are democratically controlled. This book claims that such a development will never occur under capitalism, and that to achieve a better, freer society nothing short of socialist revolution will be necessary.

It would be a mistake to assert that talking about social reality is simply a matter of "describing what is really there." Any account necessarily makes decisions about what to select and what analytical tools to use, and those decisions in turn are based on value-laden criteria. Therefore, let me state my underlying value assumptions. I believe that every human being has a self which gives that person the capacity for freedom, reason, creativity, love, and sympathy. I believe that, because each person has such a self, we ought to respect him and create situations in which he can develop his capacities.* I look at social reality from the standpoint of this belief, asking to what extent it has been realized in current institutional arrangements and to what extent we can find ways of viewing reality which will help us to transform it in such a fashion that this belief becomes the foundation of human affairs.

But there is no bible in a revolution. The fundamental procedural injunction is: Make a serious scientific study of society to see how it can be transformed. Any American revolutionary movement is bound to come to grief if it substitutes slogans for thought or the experience of revolutionary movements in different historical and economic circumstances for a concrete study of the American reality. Unless we understand the reality in which we live, we will never change it in the ways we desire.

Understanding does not, however, emerge simply from abstract detached study. It emerges precisely in the struggle to transform reality. Not every socialist must be a political leader, but without the existence of a socialist movement oriented toward struggle, even the greatest socialist intellects will find their work less meaningful and less revealing of the true nature of this society and how to transform it. For that reason, this book is an invitation to action. It invites you to participate in the struggle to rebuild our world in such a way that human values and individual self-realization become an integral part of our daily lives.

The struggle to overthrow capitalism is also, in part, a struggle to re-

* I want to explain a troublesome word usage in this book. In several places I will use the words *he, him,* or *his* when of course I am referring to both sexes. At first, I used *he or she* and *his or her* in every case but this formulation became so cumbersome that I reverted back to the ordinary usages even though I am very uncomfortable with their male orientation. I sincerely hope that the women's movement will soon come forward with an alternative style that can be used intelligibly in this connection.

make ourselves as human beings. In writing this book, I do not put myself forward as someone who has succeeded in this effort, but as a person who—like every other American—has been badly marred by growing up in a society that thrives on competition and mutual exploitation. Those who advocate the socialist revolution in America do not say that they are good and everyone else is bad. Rather, they are ordinary people who have come to understand that they can only fully be what they want to be as human beings when the impediments to their own and everyone else's self-development are overthrown.

The attempted suicide of the New Left over the past few years now makes possible the development of a revolutionary movement in the United States that can synthesize the best in the old and new Lefts, and can go beyond them to speak to emerging realities. Throughout this book you will find an implicit critique of the most devastating failures of the New Left. The socialist revolutionary movement of the period ahead will start with a rejection, for instance, of the New Left's anti-intellectualism and its refusal to make a serious study of American capitalism. It will reject the overglorification of the Third World that finally led New Leftists to think that China or Cuba provided an adequate model for American revolutionary strategy and revolutionary goals. It will reject the cults of spontaneity and inwardness that led people to believe they could transform themselves into full socialist human beings long before there was a corresponding transformation of the society as a whole. It will reject the antileadership tendencies that too often were used as a cover for personal jealousies and feelings of inadequacy. And it will reject the anti-organization attitudes that made it possible for the New Left to emerge from a period of tremendous upsurge in this country without a single strong national organization.

As this book goes to press, some elements in the revolutionary movement have already begun to move beyond the mistakes of the past. Ultimately, sectarian and centrifugal tendencies will have to be overcome so that we can build the organization necessary to play a central role in American politics. Because the deepening crisis in American life will not be solved by the liberals (no matter how glamorous, sincere, or intelligent they be), the possibility of socialism in the 1970s can be raised as a serious question. The key statement of the 1960s was "What you are saying is wrong." The key statement of the 70s will be "What's your alternative?" Socialism is our alternative. The immediate goal of a revolutionary movement for the 70s is to place socialism on the agenda. If we build a political organization and strategy that combines vision, daring, and intelligence, we can make socialism the central political issue in the

American political arena by the late 70s and early 80s. And we *can* build such an organization.

The next thirty years could mark the beginning of *human* history: the emergence of human life from the kingdom of necessity—which had to be centered around producing enough goods so that people could live—to the kingdom of freedom—which can be centered around the creation of beauty and pleasure, human self-realization, love, and wisdom. Only when one fully appreciates what human life can become does he become fully committed to overthrowing those vestiges of the past that have kept human beings from realizing their potentialities. Those vestiges, institutionalized as the capitalist system, not only keep us from our potentialities but simultaneously threaten the whole world with extinction in the process of maintaining an oppressive rule. Both our humanity and our reason demand that we engage ourselves in the struggle for socialist revolution.

Because this book is in part a call to further intellectual work and to political activity, I would be happy to hear from readers who agree with its basic thesis and want to be part of the process of building the intellectual and organizational activity of the future. I can be reached at Trinity College, Hartford, Conn. 06106. One immediate project I would like to start is a theoretical magazine where some of the questions raised in this book could be debated and explored in greater detail. The absence of such a magazine has been one factor in the general low level of intellectual understanding on the left. The rub, as in so many areas, is the absence of money. I know of people throughout America who would gladly write for such a magazine. I'd be happy to hear from anyone who knew where we could get the initial capital.

I want to express my deep thanks to those who have helped and guided me in the preparation of this book. Ray Barglow and David Kolodney made helpful suggestions for the chapter on Powerlessness; Roger Harris and Neil Thomason did the same for the chapter on Racism and Sexism; as did Robert Fitch, David Smith, and David Danning for the chapter on Imperialism. Important comments and suggestions for the whole manuscript came from Richard Arneson, Diana Adams, and Marian Fish. And Thierrie Cook gave valuable advice and suggestions at every stage in the development of the book (as well as painstakingly compiling the index) and convinced me to rewrite sections with which she had disagreements. More generally, I should mention the intellectual guidance I have received from Richard Lichtman, David Horowitz, and Abraham Joshua Heschel and the more general contribution of the entire Marxist tradition and the tradition of struggle of the New Left, both of which have played a crucial part in developing the ideas I have tried to simplify and synthesize in this book. And finally, my love and thanks to my parents, whose constant guidance and love shielded me from some of the worst aspects of capitalist conditioning and oppression.

Trinity College
Hartford, Connecticut
August, 1972

The
New Socialist
Revolution

part 1
Analysis of American Society

1
Powerlessness

ON JULY 22, 1971, the *Wall Street Journal* carried a report that captures the flavor of the situation of American workers today. Consider some excerpts from that story:

> It was 1940 when Elmer Novak walked out of his sophomore year in high school and into the coal mines, just as his brothers had before him and father before them. Thirty-one years later, Elmer Novak has a mortgage, 10 kids and black lung. Looking back, he says he would never have gone down to the mines if he hadn't felt he had to. But there was not then—and there is not now—much else to do around Edensburg, Pa., a tiny town on the western slopes of the Allegheny mountains. As a 100 pound, 17-year-old, Elmer Novak started as a track layer's helper at $6.75 a day and graduated in a few months to pick-and-shovel miner at 65¢ a ton. . . . Today Elmer Novak is a member of the rock crew at Number 32 mine of Bethlehem Mines Corp., where he timbers walls. He takes home $120 a week, often works in water up to his ankles, never has a coffee break, takes half an hour to eat lunch from a tin bucket and works a rotating shift. After three decades, he is still not used to the danger or the coal dust or the chill in a mine shaft 1000 feet under ground. At home, he never talks about his job, and his wife never asks. He has never had a new car or a savings account, and he says there is "no way I could raise $100 in an emergency." Elmer Novak has 14 years to go before he can retire on a union pension that currently is $150 a month—unless his illness worsens before that time and he can apply for black lung benefits. . . . Why does Elmer Novak con-

tinue to work at a job that has cost him his health and paid him a wage that he had to struggle on all his grown life? "There aren't many jobs around here for a high school dropout," he says. "I'd leave in a minute, but where would I go?" That is the dilemma of millions of relatively unskilled manual laborers across the country. They mine coal, shovel steel slag, gut animal carcasses, sort mail, clean hotel rooms, bend over sewing machines and perform a thousand other grueling or mind-deadening tasks. . . . And when they are asked, as several dozen of them recently were by *Wall Street Journal* reporters, why they keep at it, most of them echo Elmer Novak: Where else could I go? . . . Most of them know they are not on the very bottom of the economic heap: they are *not* among the 17 million workers in the country—over 30% of the work force—who earn less than $5000 a year. But for the privilege of escaping poverty they have paid the price of accepting labor that ranges from grinding to merely monotonous, under conditions that range from uncomfortable to miserable. Few of them hope anymore for anything better. All of them say they learned long ago to simply stop thinking about the way things might have been. . . . Many of them hate every minute on the job. But a surprising number of them take a measure of pride in performing well jobs that can only be described as either back-breaking or deadly dull. . . .

Marvin Conyers works the 3:30 to midnight shift on "the line"—the assembly line at Chrysler Corporation's Jefferson Avenue plant in Detroit. Mr. Conyers, 34 years old and the father of five, has been on the line for seven years now, and he says bluntly and with considerable despair, that it is brutal. Mr. Conyers' job involves physical effort and strain, but unlike Elmer Novak . . . he doesn't lift heavy loads all day long. What he does is perform a job so monotonous and bleak that it drives him into a mental trance daily. . . . For eight years, he worked selling insurance or as a helper at his aunt's restaurant. He says he enjoyed that, but with a growing family he decided in 1964 to return to the line. Mr. Conyers is better off now than he was then. At first, "I had to climb over into the trunk, weld in the back window, climb down, and get ready for the next car. I did that eight or nine hours a day, about one car every fifty seconds. . . . I think about everything, just everything, to keep my mind occupied. The day goes by real slow. It seems like 16 hours." . . . Alcohol and drugs are rampant, and Mr. Conyers admits he once or twice has been

4

drunk on the job himself. Nearly 6% of the workers at the Jefferson plant don't show up on any given day, and nearly 30% of the work force turns over every year. But for most, the alternatives are worse. Money brought them to the line, and it keeps them there.

Mrs. Malindia Boykin, age 53, is a worker in a Los Angeles laundry and has been for 21 years. Until recently she was a press operator—a job that involves working in heat over 100 degrees and keeping a swift pace, turning out 250 pieces an hour on a cuff and collar press, 225 shirts an hour on a "body press" or 150 pairs of pants an hour on the pants press. Like all laundry workers, Mrs. Boykin is among the lowest paid of manual workers, earning a meager $2.19 an hour. That's $87.60 a week—gross. . . . Mrs. Boykin claims no sense of pride. She has found a better way to endure the job. She simply accepts it; like the sun rising in the morning and setting at night, the job, to her, is just "there," a fact of life that is unpleasant but uncontrovertible. When she is questioned about the job, Mrs. Boykin is sunny, cooperative, and says, yes, the pay is terrible and the work is dangerous and the routine monotonous—in much the manner one might comment on the weather. . . . Malindia Boykin has no complaints. And no hopes. . . . The kind of resignation Malindia Boykin has learned may be the best defense against the drudgery of a mindless job. It is a defense many have learned.[1]

This report highlights a central claim of the radical analysis of American society: the most important feature of the internal life of America is the total powerlessness of the overwhelming majority of people to control the circumstances of their lives. And this powerlessness stems not from "the human condition" or from the inevitable circumstances of a complex society, but from the specific form of economic-social-political organization that develops in an advanced industrial capitalist society.

To prove my point this chapter documents three facts: (1) a small number of Americans have vast economic power while the overwhelming majority have almost no power in the economic realm; (2) economic power gives the small group that wields it a huge amount of political power while, for most Americans, political power is very limited and exists within a very narrow framework; and (3) powerlessness in the economic and political spheres affects people's daily lives in a large

[1] "News Roundup," *Wall Street Journal,* 22 July 1971, p. 1.

number of ways, permitting the development of a society in which the human needs of most people are largely ignored so that the wealthy and powerful can benefit. Additionally, I argue that most of the problems Americans think of as individual are in fact shared by most other people and are rooted in the nature of the system itself.

CAPITALISM AND CLASSES

What exactly is capitalism? We can define it as an economic system in which small numbers of people, through their ownership and control of the means of production (e.g., factories, farms, mines), are able to buy the labor power of most other people and to direct that labor power into the production of goods to be sold for the profit of the owners. Typically, capitalism involves competition among the capitalists for a share of the market, though in the present advanced stages of capitalism several areas of production are governed by large monopolies that try to limit competition so that they can rationalize their production over long periods of time and control prices and profits. As was the case with previous forms of social organization, capitalist society is divided into classes: the very small ruling class owns and controls the means of production and the very large working class sells its labor power. Ownership of the means of production and the vast wealth that it brings provides the class of owners with a vastly disproportionate amount of political power which they use to sustain their own privileged position and to govern the lives of everyone else.

You may want to stop right here. I know I did when I first heard these ideas presented. I had recently graduated from Columbia College at the time and was proud to be an intellectual and a liberal. I had heard all these "tired old Marxist ideas" before, and had taken several classes in which they had been "disproved." Moreover, to accept them would lead me to conclusions that would upset the pleasant plans I had for myself as a detached scholar. Nevertheless, my own experience over the next several years, and the intellectual work that accompanied it, forced me to rethink these ideas in light of the empirical evidence. And so I ask the reader: Read on. See if you, too, will find that these ideas make sense of your own experience in a way that high school civics courses or *Time* magazine or liberal college professors never did.

America is a class society. The two fundamental classes are the owners of the means of production—variously referred to as the bourgeoisie or the ruling class—and the wage laborers—usually called the working class

6

or the proletariat—who use the productive apparatus to create material or service goods. Within each class is a high degree of differentiation between sections or strata.

The ruling class can be differentiated from the working class in two important ways. First, there is a crucial structural fact: a small group of people have control over the banks and corporations, and that control gives them a huge amount of power over the lives of nearly everyone else. Second, these people do not have to sell their labor power to someone else, as does almost everyone else. The working class *has* to work—otherwise its members would literally starve (unemployment and welfare benefits do run out, and people are slowly starving in the United States even as you are reading this book). The "free" marketplace has always had this ambiguity: It is free in the sense that no one is required by law to take any particular job, as, for instance, the feudal serf was required by law to work the land on which he was born. But there are only a limited number of jobs available (in the United States in 1972, nearly 6 percent of the work force could not get jobs); and if you do not get a job you will shortly get very hungry and live pretty miserably. If you are confused about which of the two fundamental classes you belong to, try the following test: Lie in bed and just listen to music for the next two months. If you start getting hungry during that time you're a worker. On the other hand, if two months of recumbent music listening does not interfere with your ability to live comfortably and feed yourself and your family adequately, you're probably not a member of the working class.

In addition to the two fundamental classes, a few other groups have interests that sometimes put them on the side of the working class and sometimes on the side of the ruling class. For example, there is a group called the lumpen proletariat, composed of those who do not seek employment—petty crooks, gamblers, "bums," etc. And there is the petite bourgeoisie—small-time entrepreneurs such as independent artisans, small farmers, small shopkeepers, and self-employed providers of services, selling some skill or service or product directly to the public.

One reason people hesitate to talk about class structure is that they see so many obvious differences among workers with regard to pay, status, and the like. Another is that many recently developed jobs require skilled, college-educated personnel, and it seems difficult to assimilate such workers as engineers and scientists into a category reserved for the hardcore industrial workers on the assembly lines and in the mines. Many American workers like to describe themselves as middle class, and in some ways their life styles are similar to those of the "middle-class" elements—such as lawyers and doctors, for example. After all, at least some American workers live in expensive suburbs, own big, expensive cars and other trappings of luxury. But this similarity is often exaggerated. In 1969 the average union scale in the building trades, generally considered the "aristocracy of labor," was $5.67 an hour, which would yield an income of $11,794 a year for a full year's employment—and a full year's employment is a rare occurrence for most workers in the building trades. Nevertheless, it points to an important fact: large differences exist among the standards of living of members of the working class. The person who sells his labor power at $15,000 a year can have quite a different kind of life from the person who sells it at half that much. Over 80 percent of U.S. families earned less than $15,000 a year in 1971, and in most of the families that did earn $15,000 two people were working. The differences in income that exist mean a lot to the people involved. In the main, it is these differences that give rise to the popular notion that some workers are "middle class": some are able to sell their labor power at a higher price than others.

It is understandable why so much attention is paid to the differences in price at which people sell their labor power. After all, ordinary workers or professionals do not have much basis on which to compare their lives to the lives of the Rockefellers or Duponts. But they *can* compare their lives with one another's. And as long as people focus their attention on these gradations of wealth between the lower paid workers and higher paid workers or small entrepreneurs, they miss the really crucial differences between themselves and the rulers, whose vast wealth and power remain outside public scrutiny.

Another cause for confusion is the existence of a small percentage of the population that has to work and has no control over the means of production but nevertheless makes a great deal of money. A wealthy doctor or lawyer is not usually a member of the ruling class in the strict sense. But by and large, doctors and lawyers identify with the ruling class and its interests. And this could also be true of a medium-size store owner who nets $20,000 a year, or a worker who wins a large sum in the sweepstakes and retires from work, or a hard-working adviser to the president, etc. It is a mistake to assume that because the boundary lines for a concept are hard to draw, the concept is meaningless. This kind of reasoning misses the "open-texture" nature of our language: often a concept is perfectly workable even when borderline cases exist. Consider the concept of baldness. It is often difficult to decide whether or not to call a given man "bald"; there are, after all, no agreed-upon criteria—as, for example, counting his hairs individually. But we would not on those grounds toss out the concept, because it points to a fundamental reality.

8

Similarly, in talking about the differences between David Rockefeller or Ted Kennedy on the one hand and a bus driver or a store clerk on the other, the notion of working class makes a lot of sense. We may be puzzled about what to call the owner of a small or medium-size farm or business, and we may want to make it clear that teachers and mine workers perceive themselves differently. But the notion of classes *does* help to unravel many of the apparent mysteries of American political and economic life.

Just as there is much stratification within the working class (which I shall discuss further in the second part of this book), so the ruling class has a series of differentiated strata and interests. Some people have much more wealth and, consequently, much more power than others. Nor is the ruling class organized democratically: those with more wealth have much more power than those with less. Moreover, wealth and power are greatly concentrated in one small section of the ruling class. In 1969, the latest year for which figures are presently available, a very large number of small corporations in the United States (906,458, or 59 percent of the total number of corporations) held only a tiny portion of corporate assets ($31 billion, or 1.5 percent of the total), while at the top a few giant corporations (958, or 0.06 percent of the total) held a majority of all corporate assets ($1.07 trillion, or 53.2 percent of the total).[2]

Is there really a class in the United States that has disproportionate amounts of wealth and power? Yes. Let us consider, for example, income distributions. As G. William Domhoff points out, "The top 0.1% were 45,000 families who received an average of $110,000 per year, or 15 times as much as their numbers would warrant if income were equally distributed under conditions of equality."[3] The government no longer makes available information about personal wealth, but for 1953, the last year when such figures were published, the top 1.04 percent of the population owned 28.5 percent of all the wealth, while the bottom 20 percent of the population owned less than 2.5 percent (actually a slight reduction from its percentage fifty years before).

According to the 1970 census data, the poorest fifth of families in the United States received 5.5 percent of the total money income. The second poorest fifth received 12 percent of the total money income, so together the poorest 40 percent of American families in 1970 received 17.5 per-

[2] Figures cited in Howard Sherman, *Radical Political Economy* (New York: Basic Books, 1972).

[3] G. William Domhoff, *Who Rules America?* (Englewood Cliffs, N.J.: Prentice-Hall, 1967), p. 41.

9

cent of money income. On the other hand, the richest fifth of American families received 41.6 percent of all money income. In money terms, the average income of the 10.4 million families in the bottom fifth in 1970 was $3,054; the average income of the 10.4 million families in the top fifth was $23,100. (Had money income been divided equally among families, the average income for each family would have been over $11,000.) And this picture has remained relatively constant since World War II, despite much-heralded fair deals, great societies, and poverty programs. In 1947, for example, the poorest fifth received 5 percent and the richest fifth received 43 percent of the total money income, very slight fluctuations from the picture twenty-three years later.[4]

John Kenneth Galbraith's famous celebration of American capitalism, *The Affluent Society,* together with a barrage of magazine and newspaper propaganda, has created the popular notion that in America we live in an "affluent society" where almost everybody has become "middle class." But, for most working people, the reality is quite different. According to the 1962 Conference on Economic Progress in the United States, 38 million Americans were living in poverty, as defined by the U.S. Labor Department's standards. Another 37 million were living in conditions of "deprivation" (defined as living above the stark poverty level but below the Labor Department's description of a "modest but adequate" family budget). In 1969 the median income of all families in the United States,

---

[4] Data compiled here from the U.S. Bureau of the Census. *Current Population Reports,* 4 October 1971, is latest available. Information has been compiled on these matters by Letitia Upton and Nancy Lyons of the Cambridge Institute and issued as a pamphlet entitled "Basic Facts: Distribution of Personal Income and Wealth in the United States," available by writing to the Cambridge Institute, 1878 Massachusetts Avenue, Cambridge, Massachusetts.

A key point about all these figures: they show a general trend and overall configuration. Obviously, they will change somewhat from year to year. Incomes will rise, but often not as fast as inflation. A liberal Democrat may be elected president and submit plans for slightly revising the total distribution picture. What is interesting about the proposals made by even the most liberal Democrats is that they make only slight alterations in the total picture and would not change the basic class structure, but only smooth off some of its more piercing edges. McGovern, for example, has repudiated the National Welfare Rights Organization's plan for a minimum income of $6,500 for a family of four and is embarrassed that his income assistance plan is seen as too radical. But even the minimal programs that liberal politicians promise will be much scaled down by the time they emerge from congressional committees. The likely prognosis is for much fanfare about income redistribution and tax reform, with conservatives yelling that the vastly inadequate programs of the liberals constitute outright socialism, but the basic picture will not be altered to the degree that it would make sense to drop the categories of "class" that have been central to an understanding of capitalist societies for the past few hundred years.

based on the income of all wage earners in the family, was $8,632. While in that same year the U.S. Bureau of Labor Statistics estimated that a family of four needed $10,077 a year to live in an urban area at a "moderate living standard." Tens of millions of Americans that year could not even claim a moderate living standard. Furthermore, more than one person in the family usually has to work to achieve even a below-moderate living standard. In 1967, for example, more than 60 percent of white families needed two or more earners to reach an income of $5,000 or more a year. The so-called middle-class worker may read accolades to his new status in *Time* magazine or his children's sociology textbooks, but the words do not correspond to the reality. In 1967 the median income of craftsmen—skilled workers—was only $7,227; in 1968 the average auto worker made $7,280; and in 1969 the U.S. Department of Agriculture estimated that over 12 million Americans were severely undernourished and hungry. In 1965 there were 12 million workers (in farm, domestic, retail trade, restaurant, laundry, factory, and hospital jobs) whose hourly wages were less than $1.50: if these men and women managed to work 50 weeks of the year they would still have earned only $3,000.

And things have not been getting more equal. Despite all the claims about the effects of the New Deal and the Progressive Era before it, the basic contours of wealth distribution in America have remained largely constant throughout the past fifty years. The relative inequalities still exist. True, over the past thirty years things have been getting better in material terms for many people. Part of the reason is that, although each class's share of the pie has remained about the same, the pie as a whole has grown considerably (because of factors we shall explore in the chapter on imperialism). But there has been no "democratization of wealth," as the apologists for American capitalism like to pretend.

But what about taxes? Don't they change all that by redistributing income from the wealthy to the poor? No. Despite all the rhetoric, the percentages of wealth distribution after income tax are virtually the same as before. And most taxes hit hardest at those least able to pay. A 1960 income study showed that those who made under $2,000 per year paid 38 percent of their income in all types of taxes; those who made from $2,000 to $5,000 paid from 38 percent to more than 41 percent; and those who made above $10,000 paid only 31.6 percent. And, typically, those who made over $750,000 a year paid a percentage of their income to income taxes not much greater than the percentage paid by the average wage earner. Moreover, large corporations are permitted to spend millions of dollars each year that are not reported as income but are written off as business expenses. In fact, the tax system actually works to redistribute wealth from the poor to the rich, because the wealthy control the state legislatures, the Congress, and the governmental bodies. The rich are often able to use tax money to subsidize their own business ventures or to defend their investments abroad.[5]

Every few years there is some talk about reforming the tax system, and occasionally an obvious abuse is modified. But in the process, other benefits are arranged for the rich. There can be no clearer testimony to the powerlessness of most working people in America than the fact that it is *their* taxes, rather than corporate and wealth taxes, that are raised to fund vitally needed social services. And when taxes are lowered, it is the corporation that benefits most. Consider the 1971 tax relief passed by the Democratic Congress. According to political scientist James Ridgeway, the measure gives an estimated $7.5 *billion* to corporations. The bill grants a $500 million tax subsidy to the big international corporations that do most of U.S. trading abroad, by setting up dummy corporations called Domestic International Sales Corporations, through which sales can be channeled. The bill was driven through Congress not by conservative Republicans but by the Democratic leadership, specifically by Wilbur Mills in the House and Russell Long in the Senate, both of whom describe themselves as "populists." It is not impossible that in the future, reformers will be elected who will reverse this latest subsidy to the corporations, but that is not the point. What is important is that tax law is written by and for the rich, and hence is not likely to have any effect on changing the concentration of wealth in the hands of a very few.

DEMOCRACY IN THE ECONOMY?

There is an argument that runs somewhat along these lines: "Sure, a few people have a great deal of wealth, but isn't that really irrelevant? After all, the key institutions in capitalism are the corporations, so the question of corporate control is the real key. And ownership of these corporations is itself becoming more democratic." It is true that many

[5] See Joseph A. Pechman, "The Rich, the Poor, and the Taxes They Pay," *Public Interest,* no. 17 (Fall 1969). Pechman points out that "the effective rate of tax paid in 1967 by the top 1% was only 26% of their total reported income, including all of their realized capital gains." Now, obviously, 26 percent of $125,000 a year leaves quite a healthy share for the rich person, whereas the same or even a lesser percentage of taxes paid on an income of $11,000 or less is really going to hurt the struggling-to-make-ends-meet working person.

millions of people in the United States own stock, but it is also true that most of them own very little of it. According to Gabriel Kolko,[6] less than 1 percent of American families own 80 percent of all publicly held industrial stocks, and approximately 0.2 percent of the "spending units" own 65 to 71 percent of the publicly held stock. In 1968 about 41 percent of all people with large stockholdings ($25,000 or more) inherited either all or part of these stocks from relatives. So the facts about stock ownership confirm, rather than deny, the picture of vast concentration of wealth.

To these facts, John Kenneth Galbraith and other apologists for capitalism have devised a clever retort. Ownership, they tell us, is unimportant, because the real control of the corporations has slipped out of the hands of the owners: a new group of professional managers has arisen whose sole interest is in good management of the corporation. These managers have made the issue of "capitalism" irrelevant, since the problem in America is not to redistribute power away from the class of owners, but rather to influence the corporation managers to be more concerned with the public interest. The fact is (1) that the claim that managers have some new power is false; and (2) that even if it were true, it would not prove anything significant.

First, for many firms the claim is flatly false because (a) among the hundred largest industrial corporations in the country, at least ten are family controlled; and (b) among the largest 500 family-named companies, approximately 75 are still directed by the founding family.

And what about the rest? There is no reason to believe that manager-controlled firms act against the interests of their wealthy owners and for the interests of the majority of Americans. On the contrary, managers usually possess substantial holdings themselves (through special stock options that give them part ownership in the company, for example). Even if they are not members of the owning class by birth, their high salaries, dependent on the company's high profits, lead them to identify with the owners' interests. Managerial groups in corporations are "the largest single group in the stockholding population, and a greater proportion of this class owns stocks than any other." [7] Further, according to Ralph Miliband, "of 900 top American executives studied by Fortune magazine, 80% were found to earn more than $50,000 annually, excluding shares, pensions, and retirement provisions, expense accounts, etc." [8] No group of managers with these interests is likely to act in a way

[6] Gabriel Kolko, *Wealth and Power in America* (New York: Frederick A. Praeger, 1962).

[7] *Ibid.*, p. 67.

[8] Ralph Miliband, *The State in Capitalist Society* (New York: Basic Books, 1969).

qualitatively different from the owners. Both groups have the same goals—to build the company and reap corporate profits.

Precisely because managers have demonstrated some ability to do these things, they are able to acquire and keep their posts. Nor is this a simple question of "selfishness" in the souls of individual managers: the rationale of the system requires them to act in this manner in order to avert failure in corporate competition with other firms. In terms of the internal logic of the capitalist market, it would be irrational and possibly immoral for the managers to act in any other way than to maximize profits; they would be betraying the trust of all those who had bought stock in their company with the expectation that the company would act to maximize returns. So while there may be some short-run disputes between owners and managers (e.g., stockholders may feel that managers are insufficiently dividend-conscious while managers may feel that shareholders are sometimes short-sighted and not sufficiently worried about long-range profit making), the disputes occur within a context of fundamental agreement: the corporation should be run to maximize profits. And, of course, these profits go mainly into the pockets of that miniscule percentage of the population that owns the greatest number of stocks.

In a series of articles entitled "Who Rules the Corporations," Robert Fitch and Mary Oppenheimer recently challenged the notion that corporations are now governed internally by managers.[9] In their study, Fitch and Oppenheimer show that banks exercise significant power in corporate decision making. This power is often used to maximize the profits of financial institutions even at the expense of the particular corporation with which the bank may be connected. For instance, a bank may use its power on the board of directors of one corporation to get it to do business with another corporation with which the bank also does business, particularly if the second corporation is in financial trouble and might default on its bank loans. Or financial interests may decide to gut a less profitable corporation for a more profitable one, regardless of how this affects the vital social services the gutted corporation provides.[10] Or a bank might convince a corporation to take out loans for unneeded investments in order to increase the bank's wealth. Fitch and Oppenheimer cite one startling example: the control by financial institutions of the major airlines. "The First National City Bank's executive vice president announced

9 Now published in *Who Rules the Corporations?* (New York: Random House, forthcoming).

10 A good example is how the Pennsylvania Railroad was bilked of some of its assets by directors who placed priority on making profits from some of their other investments.

14

recently that 'after the Russian and American government, we have the biggest air force in the world.' Citibank, the leader in aircraft leasing, owns more than a hundred planes valued at over a billion dollars. Bank control over the airlines is so heavy-handed that, even though airlines are suffering from considerable overcapacity, they continue to buy more giant planes." Banks are willing to finance the production and sale of unneeded aircraft because they make an estimated 56 percent profit on their aircraft-leasing activity. And, "for that kind of profit, the risk of bankrupting an airline or two is quite sensible, especially since the amounts of the bank equity involved in the airlines is comparatively small. And in the event of bankruptcy, the banks take over all the rest of the planes, anyway." [11] So what is good for the industry may not be good for financial profit at the bank, and often it is the latter that wins out in corporate decision making. The interests of the few, their desire to maximize profits, guide the life of corporations; if there is any kind of internal struggle, it is not between managers who are looking out for the social good and capitalists who want to make profits, but rather between different groups of capitalists (some of whom may also be managers) arguing about how to maximize their own profits. They key consideration in these disputes is not some imagined social good, but who has what investments where and what policies will maximize the sum of these investments, producing the greatest profits. The actual operations of the corporations simply confirm the importance of the power wielded by the small percentage of people with vast economic resources.

EARNED WEALTH

Someone may now concede, "Sure, there are social and economic classes, and the upper class has a vastly disproportionate amount of wealth and power, but don't the members of that class deserve their great wealth and power because they worked harder, and isn't there a great deal of social mobility today among classes?" No, on both counts. Most people with large fortunes in America today did not achieve their fortunes because they worked hard—although this is more likely to be true of the upper-middle-class professionals and small entrepreneurs than of the upper 0.5 percent of the population that controls the banks, corporations, and industries. But even if they were hard workers, they were not the only ones. What distinguishes them from the large numbers of

---

[11] Robert Fitch, "Reply to James O'Connor," *Socialist Revolution,* no. 7, p. 169.

people with equally high (or higher) intelligence who worked equally hard (or harder) is some combination of the following factors: (1) access to large sums of capital which they could use to invest, either through familial wealth or through special access to credit institutions; (2) access to educational opportunity often unavailable to people from working-class families; (3) influence with businessmen and politicians needed to initiate their own business ventures; (4) ruthlessness in competition; (5) exploitation of their workers in order to maximize their own profits. Most wealthy people today either inherited their wealth or depended on family or bank connections for large sums of initial capital. This money was available to their families and to banks because previous generations had managed to accumulate surplus wealth through a variety of tactics, important among which were enslaving black men and women; importing Irish, Italian, Chinese, and other immigrant groups as sources of cheap labor; and profiting from the labor of those they employed. If anybody "deserves" to have wealth either because of previous family accomplishments or because of work done earlier in life, it is clearly the working people of this country whose back-breaking, tedious, and insipid labor in this and previous generations has built and sustained modern America.

SOCIAL MOBILITY AND COMPETITION

At this point you may object, "At least our children can make it out of the working class if they try hard enough." But the facts do not support your thesis. "Studies on the basis of data up to 1960 have found that the number of sons of manual workers who were able to make . . . 'the big leap' into higher business and independent professional occupations . . . was nearly 8% for the United States. It may not be essential, in order to achieve material or professional success, to be born of wealth, or even of well-to-do parents; but it is certainly an enormous advantage, rather like joining a select club, membership of which offers unrivaled opportunities for the consolidation and enhancement of the advantages which it in any case confers." [12] True, a higher level of education is now available to working-class children than in the past, but this is largely because advanced capitalism requires more highly trained personnel. We now have junior or community colleges to train working-class people, state universities and college systems to train business and professional men, and a

[12] Miliband, *The State in Capitalist Society*, pp. 39–40.

small group of elite universities that still provide "recruits for the command posts of society." The university system as presently constructed reinforces the pattern of class structure.

None of this denies that a small percentage of working people *do* make it, *do* switch classes in a real sense. But these switches, far from undermining the class system, actually strengthen it by assuring that the most highly competitive and ambitious people will not be operating against the interests of the ruling class, but in concert with them. These individual advances are made against a background of general class stability in which the system of maldistribution of wealth and power remains intact. This is true at virtually every level of the class system. When an economic system has a level of involuntary unemployment approaching 6 percent, three out of every fifty people simply cannot get a job. In fact, the government officially considers an unemployment rate of 4 percent to be "full employment." The individual's ability to be employed depends at least in part on the fact that someone else is unemployed. In short, whenever any particular person makes it, other people necessarily lose out. Hence, from childhood on, Americans are carefully indoctrinated by the family, school, and media to compete with other people and to see others as impediments to their own success. Nor is this view of others the product of some irrational "urge to evil" in human nature. In the context of capitalist society it is quite rational. For you really *do* have to compete in order to survive, and you really *do* have to beat out others in the process. In such a context, being sly, scheming, deceptive, self-protective, guarded, self-centered, and distrustful all become quite rational. What is irrational is the context.

The best clue to human relationships in capitalist society is to understand how the basic economic institutions function and then see how these institutions affect the rest of human life. Consider the way the individual is treated by the large corporations: as a means to make profit for the few. Capitalists use everybody for their own personal gain. When they can no longer use a person as a worker, they simply throw him out of work. When he is too old to be used, he is dismissed as irrelevant. (Hence the "tragedy of old age." Death is a problem for any society, but old age is a "tragedy" only because a capitalist society measures human worth in terms of the individual's usefulness to the ruling class for its own ends.) Human needs are important only to the extent that they help create a workforce capable of producing more wealth for the capitalists.

Needless to say, if people are formed, and form themselves, in order to succeed and survive in this context, they become unsuited for human

17

relationships which require precisely the opposite kinds of qualities. If you have been pushed to compete in school, in seeking employment, and in advancing yourself at your job, you are ill prepared to see others as ends in themselves, as individuals to be respected because they are human beings. It often becomes extremely difficult to establish friendships. You may find a few friends and perhaps a sexual partner with whom you can become a single economic unit (and hence enhance each other's buying power), but most of the outside world is likely to appear indifferent or even hostile to you. This is not paranoia—the rest of the world really is indifferent or even hostile to you. Why? Because you stand in its way. You have to stop caring about others, because if you get too involved with them you yourself won't survive. As theologian A. J. Heschel points out, "Suspect your neighbor as yourself" has become the motto of the present age. What could be a greater indictment of a social system than this: it makes humane and loving relationships between people less likely and more difficult?

POLITICAL DEMOCRACY?

"Granted that there are economic classes in society and that some have vastly more power than others. But this can't really be as bad for the people as you say, because otherwise they would simply vote and change things. So people obviously like things the way they are!" The critical assumption in this statement is that we live in a society in which the people have the political power to make basic decisions. But this is not true. In fact, most citizens are never asked to make decisions of any importance to them except which of two candidates who agree on almost everything shall represent them. When the people look at the men in power from one administration to the next, they see basically the same men and the same policies. No wonder many people end up by not voting at all or by treating the elections as a spectator sport. In 1968 about 38 percent of eligible citizens failed to vote in the presidential election and about 44 percent failed to vote in the congressional election. The folk wisdom embodied in the notion that things will not change no matter who wins any particular election is an insightful reflection on the actual limits of power that most people have.

One way in which the wealthy minority exercises disproportionate political power is by dominating the key decision-making posts in the state. This is demonstrated by G. William Domhoff: "Of the 13 men who have been Secretary of War since 1932, eight have been listed in the Social Register. The others are bankers and corporation executives, and clearly members of the power elite." [13] Gabriel Kolko studied the key American foreign policy decision makers from 1944 through 1960—234 individuals who held 678 posts in a 16-year period, nearly all of them high-level and policy-making posts. Kolko writes:

> The net result of this study, however imperfect, revealed that foreign policy decision-makers are in reality a highly mobile sector of the American corporate structure, a group of men who frequently assume and define high level policy tasks in government, rather than routinely administer it, and then return to business. Their firms and connections are large enough to afford them the time to straighten out or formulate government policy while maintaining their vital ties with giant corporate law, banking or industry. . . . Of the 234 officials examined, 35.8% . . . held 63.4% of the posts. Thirty men from law, banking and investment firms accounted for 22% of all the posts which we studied, and another 57 from this background held an additional 14.1% or a total 36.1% of the key posts. Certain key firms predominated among this group: members of Sullivan & Cromwell or Carter, Ledyard & Milburn, and Coudert Brothers [all large corporate law firms serving the giant corporations], in that order among law firms, held twenty-nine posts, with other giant corporate-oriented law firms accounting for most of the remainder. Dillon, Read & Co. [one of the largest investment firms] with four men, and the Detroit Bank, with only Joseph M. Dodge, accounted for eighteen and ten posts, respectively, and two men from Brown Brothers, Harriman [another huge investment firm] held twelve posts—or forty posts for three firms. . . .[14]

In all, men who came from big business, investment firms, and the law firms that serve these interests held 59.6 percent of all posts.

But what about elective offices? Certainly the wealthy do not play such an important role here. The evidence, however, is to the contrary. The wealthy do not always serve in the chief elective positions, but the people

[13] Domhoff, *Who Rules America?*, p. 99.

[14] Gabriel Kolko, *The Roots of American Foreign Policy* (Boston: Beacon Press, 1970), pp. 17–19.

who get elected are almost always those who are acceptable to the wealth and power elites and who have been able, thereby, to accumulate sufficient capital to run an election campaign. Needless to say, if all wealthy owners of newspapers have decided to ignore you, and the media in general consider your candidacy irrelevant because you are "irresponsible," you have only a very slight chance of getting the large sums of money an election campaign requires. And the key to being "responsible" is to accept the basic contours of the distribution of wealth and power in this society and the basic requirements of American imperialism abroad.

"Well, maybe it's hard for the organized Left," one may counter, "but if individuals are dissatisfied, why don't they run for office as independents or reformers? If they don't take advantage of their opportunities, they have only themselves to blame." This may be a theoretical possibility, but even for the mildly reformist working person, the actual task of breaking into the political arena is monumental. Where is he supposed to get the time off from his job to run around to the endless meetings in which people make themselves known? Where is he to get the money to print and distribute even a few thousand leaflets? How is he to catch the attention of the press? How is he to prove that he really is "responsible" without undercutting the thrust of his criticism of the established order? These and similar problems make it simply unimaginable to the average worker that he could participate in electoral politics in any sustained way, except through his labor union. And more likely than not, his union's political alliances are formed at the top by labor bureaucrats almost as hard to challenge as the rest of the system. If by some miracle a worker such as we have just discussed did manage to overcome these problems and run and win, what would his position be as a congressman? Essentially powerless. One might argue that if enough people could run and at the same time, things would change. True. But what I have been explaining throughout this chapter is why enough people will not decide to do this at the same time, given the distribution of power, campaign funds, and control of the media. In practice, the formal mechanisms of democracy function to conceal the actual operations of a system that operates often *by,* and always *for,* the interests of the wealth and power elites.

The United States now has a two-party system, but there is no reason to believe the system could not be flexible enough to accept other parties, as long as they are "responsible." Thus, in 1968 the candidacy of right-wing racist George Wallace received much play and much financial backing, while the candidacy of Black Panther Eldridge Cleaver went virtually unmentioned: Cleaver could garnish neither the publicity nor the money for advertising that would have made him known.[15] Moreover, the actions and messages of the left are distorted whenever the media pay any attention to it. The media decide which of the Left's spokesmen to publicize, often choosing the most colorful or controversial figures rather than the most representative or intelligent ones. And they will never report the actions or statements of the Left unless those actions or statements are presented in an explosive manner. As a result, many people know that the Left *exists*, but they do not know *the content* of its programs, the rationale for its actions. It is almost impossible to learn the message of the Left through the media. Neither the Right nor the Center has to demonstrate to get its message across; the message is drummed into people from an early age in public schools, editorials in newspapers and on radio and television, and in the public speeches of the ruling parties (which are often given free prime time on television in mutual gestures of "fairness" set up by the FCC which never extend to any groups that have basic disagreements with the system).

Liberal newsmen are likely to take offense at this argument. "After all," they will tell you, "the Right criticizes us for giving too much of a leftist slant to the news." And that is true—the powers that be readily label as "Left" anything that has a tendency to raise questions about the established order. Hence, the media are denounced if they report that masses of civilians were massacred at My Lai or that Greek dictators torture their own people with American arms or that the Pentagon spends huge sums on pro-military propaganda or that there are people in America who are hungry. These denunciations tend to intimidate newsmen, so that they think themselves daring when they are simply reporting the truth. But this does not mean that the Left is getting a hearing in the media: the message of the Left is not simply that there are many problems in America (a message that many a liberal Democrat puts forward in order to get himself elected), but that these problems are mutually related and rooted in the capitalist structure. If you want any further evidence, look at the editorial page of any major newspaper. You will find a smattering of conservative, reactionary, and liberal columnists, but nary a new leftist or revolutionary socialist.

"Well, at least you got to publish this book, so what are you complaining about?" This book will not reach millions of people. The media will

15 In early 1968 both Wallace's party (American Independent) and Cleaver's party (Peace and Freedom) qualified for the California ballot with 100,000 registrants each. So, in terms of potential base, Cleaver's was as large and deserved as much attention.

21

not discover in me some explosive character or clown who can be made into a media star. Precisely because this book is both relatively sober and reasoned, and yet markedly radical, it will be largely ignored or denounced. If it were more offensive to people and hence less persuasive, much more attention would be paid to it.

Not only are serious challenges to the system ignored or distorted. Once they begin to pick up any sizable support, the dissenters are defined as criminals and are brutally suppressed. American history is replete with periods when those who held power felt sufficiently challenged to use the full coercive mechanism of the state against its critics—from the employment of national guards at factories or college campuses to the use of legal mechanisms like "conspiracy" or "criminal anarchy" charges, or by stirring up racist and chauvinistic sentiments among the people, who proceed to take vigilante action on their own. Dissenters are fired from their jobs, jailed, and sometimes murdered. Normally these kinds of suppression are reserved for the most radical elements, but the government is prepared to terrorize everyone even vaguely associated with a movement for social change in periods when the radicals seem to offer a serious challenge. So in the late 1940s and early 1950s anyone who challenged the developing "cold war" mentality or who questioned the suppression of free speech by the House Un-American Activities Committee and Joe McCarthy was labeled a "pinko" and faced with the loss of his job and social ostracism.[16] The current antiwar movement faces an even higher level of suppression. Newspapers are attacked for reporting the news and liberal legislators are intimidated by administration charges that they are either dupes or unpatriotic. The ordinary citizen fares even worse: police riots are now an established practice as a way of dealing with demonstrators. Young people have faced police assaults on their communities (e.g., in Isla Vista, Berkeley, and Madison) while black people face an accelerated racism in the community as a whole as well as police who roam through their communities ready to shoot at the slightest hint that their "black boys" are misbehaving. Firings from factories, stores, and universities for rejecting the politics and behavior of modern America have become so commonplace that even the Left has begun to treat this kind of repression as "normal" and spends its time focusing on more dramatic instances—the murder of college students, the assaults on the Panther headquarters around the country, or the conspiracy trials.

[16] Moreover, the history of people's revolts and their suppression has been kept from pupils in the schools, so that each generation thinks it is the first and can't learn from the struggles of the past.

22

Unions, with all their potential money and support, should provide an alternative way for people to get into politics. Yet they do not. When they are involved in politics, they usually support candidates who favor limited reforms, but are not critical of the capitalist system. This is frequently offered up as proof that the workers are "naturally conservative" and that there is some kind of harmony of interests in the United States. In fact, throughout the twentieth century, and particularly in periods of war, labor leaders who have been identified as radicals have been hounded out of their positions by the combined forces of government prosecution and media denigration. In the "Red Raids" of January 1920 thousands of militant workers were arrested and hundreds were deported. Entire unions were expelled from trade union associations when they failed to cooperate with the McCarthy-era witch hunts, including the ILWU, United Electrical Workers (UE), and the Mine, Mill & Smelting Union.[17] And the bosses could always intervene to keep the unions "moderate" by conceding to the demands of the more conservative elements while ignoring those of the radicals. The union leader who asked for nothing more than higher pay for the workers could demonstrate his ability to produce results, while the radical leader who wanted more power for the workers in their jobs and a society geared to serving human needs rather than corporate profit could show nothing but a bruised head and a legislative investigation for his trouble. And, of course, the ruling class could manipulate in this way because it had the additional financial latitude provided by imperialism (more on this in the next chapter).

I ought to mention the disastrous role of the Communist party in all this. The CP was almost always dominated by Stalinist elements who thought it more important to defend socialism (sic) in one country (the Soviet Union) than to make a revolution elsewhere. The initial respect for the Soviet Union was understandable—where else had a revolution succeeded in throwing off the old ruling class and attempting to build a workers' state? But when the Stalinist terror became known and it was impossible to claim that workers had real power in the U.S.S.R., the American CP should have gone its own way and attempted to build revolutionary consciousness in America. Instead, locked into its desire to defend the Soviet Union, the CP feared antagonizing the ruling class in the United States lest it join with Germany in a worldwide fascist crusade against the Soviet Union. So, while the CP gained extensive recruits among the workers, aided by the depression that gripped this country in

[17] A fuller picture of the constraints on labor emerges from reading Len De Caux, *Labor Radical* (Boston: Beacon Press, 1971).

23

the 1930s, it pushed a basically reformist line and called for more material goods, scarcely realizing that the system would shortly be able to deliver the goods by expanding its imperialist ventures and producing an anti-Communist mania that would justify its huge military postwar expenditures. Many workers heard the Old Left talk about material goods. But who needs the Left when the conservatives and liberals can provide the goods the Left can only talk about? And the CP's constant glorification of the Soviet Union in the face of evidence of the horrors of Stalin convinced many people of the truth of the capitalist's claim that the CP was a foreign agent, not concerned with the conditions of the American workers. Who needs socialism if socialism is what Russia had under Stalin?

POWER IN CONGRESS?

Recent years have shown another side of the problem: the highest elective legislative offices have little power to effect any serious change in the system. Imagine the surprise of U.S. Senator Fulbright, Chairman of the Foreign Relations Committee of the Senate, when he found that he could not affect foreign policy in Southeast Asia one whit. Beginning in 1967 he attempted unsuccessfully to change U.S. policy in Vietnam. He found that the only power he had was the power to protest the decisions that had been made by the administration. In 1971 the Congress passed a resolution calling upon the president to withdraw all troops from Vietnam on the condition that prisoners of war be released (a condition to which the North Vietnamese had previously publicly agreed). The president baldly told the country that he had no intention of following the mandate of Congress. Year after year, good people spend much time running good left liberals in congressional elections, some of whom actually win, and thinking that something will change thereby. But the basic dimensions of American society remain impervious to these assaults, and are actually strengthened by the continued channeling of potentially disruptive energy into so easily coopted directions.

This does not mean that elected representatives and the people who elect them have no power. What people lack is *significant* power—power to alter basic features of American society. There is real power at the polls and in the halls of Congress when situations arise (and there are many) in which there is no consensus about which path is in the best interests of the established order. In such situations the people and their

24

elected representatives have real power, and what they decide makes a difference. For the American ruling class is not united except with regard to the most basic questions. It *is* united on its support for the preservation of the capitalist system and hence in its commitment to imperialism. But it is divided on precisely *how* to attain its ends and which industries should receive most benefit from government support. After all, capitalism is based on competition. While it is true that devices such as "price leadership" (one company announces prices and the other companies in the same field follow its lead and announce similar prices) decrease price competition almost to zero, much competition still exists among firms for the consumer market. Similarly, different sectors of the economy compete with each other for government support. The automobile industry wants increased funding of public highways, while airplane manufacturers want bigger and better airports and planes. Many conflicts are fought out in the economic marketplace, but many more become public issues because private firms have increasingly been looking to the government to help them out. In cases like this, "representatives" of the people do have real power: power to decide which sections of the ruling class will benefit and which will lose out.

One of the most striking examples of this kind of feud came in late 1971 when Lockheed sought to get bailed out of its financial mess by asking for a $200 million loan from the federal government. The splits that competition has caused within the ruling class were suddenly revealed: the Nixon Administration backed the loan, legislators from areas with firms competing with Lockheed or its subcontractors opposed it. The issue was so fierce that David Packard, the deputy secretary of Defense, broke with the administration and opposed the loan out of loyalty to General Dynamics, a Lockheed competitor, of which he is a director. Not only did Lockheed's competitors have an immediate stake in seeing Lockheed fail. They were worried, as Robert Fitch pointed out in *Ramparts* magazine, that "once the U.S. government gets involved as a major creditor of a corporation, it develops a vested interest in its well-being. McDonnell, Douglas and G.E. which are manufacturing the DC10, and Boeing and United Aircraft, which have combined to produce the 747, have reason to fear the influence that the government can bring to bear in arm-twisting foreign governments to buy the (Lockheed) Tri-Star." [18] Needless to say, some of the strongest supporters of the loan were people who are outraged when payments to welfare re-

[18] Robert Fitch, "How the U.S. (and Britain & Germany) Got Involved in Lockheed," *Ramparts* 10, no. 3 (September 1971): 44–49.

cipients are raised a few dollars or when it is suggested that the federal government use its resources to end hunger in the United States.

More and more firms have come to believe that the people, through taxes, should absorb some of the most important side-costs of production —building transportation facilities and training personnel through business and engineering schools. At times, the need of one sector of the economy becomes so pressing that it is willing to challenge the hegemony of the military-industrial complex and demand a larger share of the budget for itself. Hence, recent developments in which some firms with a large investment in the cities, realizing the dangers with which their interests were faced unless substantial sums were spent to ease racial tensions and to rebuild decaying urban areas, began to support efforts to get the United States out of Vietnam so that the money spent on the war could be used to bolster their own investments. Formation of the Urban Coalition and Common Cause by elements of the corporate elite reflects attempts on the part of these interests to mobilize political power—including a willingness to involve the people themselves in the struggle among capitalist interests. So in the case of the Vietnam war, at least part of the corporate elite tried to take their case directly to the people. This would have been a very important decision but the only reason the people might have been allowed to make this choice was the split that existed among the capitalists about the best way to maintain capitalism and at the same time maximize their own interests. The peace candidates took great pains to assure us of their loyalty to capitalism: for example, Senator McGovern's television campaign ads stressed the need for the U.S. to invest more resources in the competition with Japan and Eastern Europe. The minimal reductions in defense spending that he was willing to stand by, McGovern assured the critics from the military-industrial complex, would still allow America to remain the Number One military power.

But most disputes between sections of the ruling class are fought out in the governmental arena and are never put to the people as issues during election time. During the 1960 elections, very few people knew which corporate interests Nixon represented and which ones Kennedy represented. Nor would it have been easy to find out. Although the people made a choice between these two candidates—a choice that had advanced the interests of one sector of the corporate ruling class over another—few voters knew the specific meaning of that choice in terms of any particular policy options. But it would be a mistake to think of candidates as the servants of particular industries. True, almost all candidates for Congress and the presidency have special ties to the big industries in their home states, but on most other economic clashes they are committed to the preservation of the corporate system as a whole and will often risk antagonizing the short-run interests of even very large firms to ensure that preservation. Hence, although President Kennedy attacked U.S. Steel's price increases, he expressed his anger when he was accused of being antibusiness. Couldn't the business community see that he was acting in its long-term best interests by trying to fight inflation? Many shortsighted elements in the business community do not in fact always appreciate the long-range help the federal government gives them, and sometimes feel genuinely antagonistic. But this *perceived* antagonism between government and these sections of the business community in no way means that a *real* antagonism exists between them. Although decisions are sometimes made which genuinely impinge on the interests of one section of the economy and aid another, the general picture is one of close cooperation between government and most sections of the corporate community, with *both* political parties receiving much financial support from the same big industries.

CONSPIRACY THEORIES

The Left's analysis of the ruling class is often misunderstood. Leftists do not believe there is a conscious conspiracy going on, with groups of men meeting secretly to determine the governmental and economic policies they will support. The ruling class is too big for such a meeting; anyway, no such meeting would be necessary. Indeed, even if there were very little contact between the heads of the big industries and the heads of the big financial institutions, they would know how to act to preserve their corporate interests and profit. The interlocking directorates between the large financial institutions and business and industrial firms may greatly facilitate communication and provide for the possibility of coordination of many economic policies, but this coordination can easily be worked out without direct contact, when the firms are left to operate according to the dictates of the marketplace. The same holds true in the government. A disproportionate number of people in government may come from the corporate economy and may be in constant touch with the interests of big business. But most people in government do not need to be told what to do by the president of ITT or General Motors or U.S. Steel or Standard Oil. Their ability to act on their own and their demonstrated loyalty to the interests of the established order were necessary conditions for their having obtained high governmental positions in the first place. And what is of greatest importance, most high governmental positions are filled by people who genuinely believe no conflict of interest exists between government and the corporate economy and that it is in the best interest of all to protect the capitalist marketplace. They do not need secret meetings with the representatives of industry.

But such meetings do take place. In September 1969, in San Francisco, the International Industrialist Conference held a session at which the heads of most of the large corporations and financial institutions met to discuss a variety of corporate issues. President Johnson met with a delegation from Wall Street to discuss Vietnam just before making the decision to stop the bombing in Vietnam. A host of lobbyists daily confront congressmen and senators with a host of requests. And the executive branch is packed with people from industry or business who are tapped to do a part-time policy task. The 1972 ITT scandals revealed a high degree of contact between government and corporate leaders which was seen to be unusual only in the blatant way by which ITT attempted to secure its private ends.

Contact between the corporations and the government is particularly intimate in the regulatory agencies. As James Ridgeway points out in "The Antipopulists," oilmen set prices at the Federal Power Commission; at the Civil Aeronautics Board, airline presidents call secret meetings and direct the members how to proceed. The big industries that are supposed to be regulated have representatives on the regulating boards supposedly as impartial representatives of the public! Lobbyists spend huge sums of money on junior officials in the agencies, almost always succeeding in getting them to see problems primarily from the standpoint of the industry. And when an occasional maverick slips through to some position of power, he is quickly removed, as was Walter Hickel, Nixon's first secretary of the interior, or, as in the case of Nicholas Johnson at the Federal Communications Commission, isolated.

Corporate leaders and the people in government who serve them do not believe they are harming everyone else to serve the interests of the ruling class. On the contrary. They believe they are maintaining a system that provides the greatest possible benefits for all. They recognize an occasional problem here or there within the system, but they attribute this to isolated deficiencies that can be remedied within the confines of the system as a whole. Nor are these ideas completely irrational: within the context of a capitalist society, it certainly *is* more rational to serve the interests of the ruling class: after all, the well-being of millions of people depends on the well-being of capitalism. If there is a depression many people will lose their jobs, and many more will be hungry and homeless. Within the context of capitalist society, there is a genuine coincidence of interests between the government and the ruling class. When the economy is doing well, many people within it are also doing relatively well (though tens of millions are not). People want prosperity, and in the context of capitalist society, this requires prosperity first for the capitalists. If business were to cut back on employment there would be a lot of unemployed people who might want a different form of government. Any government official can thus justify his support for the interests of the ruling class on the grounds of his commitment to democracy. The problem is, of course, that this rationality masks a higher irrationality.

GOVERNMENT INTERVENTION
IN THE ECONOMY

It is this seeming identity between the national interests and the interests of the corporate economy that allows the government to intervene so freely in the economic life of the country. For, despite all the rhetoric, the most persistent and successful applicants for public assistance in the American "welfare state" have not been the poor. They have been the corporate giants of the private enterprise system—whether for tariff aid in protecting American markets from foreign products; military aid to protect foreign markets and sources of raw material; emergency funds to keep the railroads operating at a profit; oil depletion allowances to protect the oil companies from paying their share of taxes; military contracts to keep profit levels high; transportation facilities to lower the company's distribution costs; and social services that workers would demand of the corporations were they not provided for by the government (and paid for, through taxes, by the people as a whole rather than by the corporations).

In the "national interest" the government has traditionally stepped in to defeat strikes, either by the application of the indirect pressure of disapproval or by the use of injunctions, police, and troops. The ILWU dock strike of 1972 is a good example. After the Taft-Hartley injunctions had expired, dockworkers struck for a variety of wage and fringe benefits. Because it was hurting some trade interests and farmers, Congress passed legislation to coercively end the strike and the dockworkers capitulated. As Ralph Miliband points, the government attempts to place

inhibitions upon organized labor in order to prevent it from exercising what pressures it can on employers (and on the state as a major employer) in the matter of wage claims. What they tend to achieve, by such means as an "incomes policy," or by deflationary policies which reduce the demand for labor, is a general weakening of the bargaining position of wage-earners. Here too, the policies adopted are proclaimed to be essential to the national interest, the health of the economy, the defense of the currency, the good of the workers, and so on. And there are always trade union leaders who can be found to endorse both the claims and the policies. But this does not change the fact that the main effect of these policies is to leave wage-earners in a weaker position vis-à-vis employers than would otherwise be the case. The purpose, in the eyes of political officeholders, may be all that it is said to be; but the result, with unfailing regularity, is to the detriment of the subordinate classes. This is why the latter, in this as in most other instances, have good reason to beware when the political leaders of advanced capitalist countries invoke the national interest in defense of their policies— more likely than not they, the subordinate classes, are about to be done.[19]

Conservatives never opposed this kind of governmental intervention, and only became adamant about the principle of government neutrality when it appeared to them (quite mistakenly) that New Deal liberals might attempt to use government as a means of redistributing wealth and power on a more equal basis.

Probably the most dramatic instance of this was the series of economic moves introduced by the Nixon Administration in 1971 to deal with the inflationary crisis. In one blow, these moves demonstrated how limited, in fact, are the freedoms of the free marketplace. Nixon set up a freeze, and then sharp controls on wages and much less forceful controls on prices. As always, the working class and the poor were asked to pay the price for the ruling class's extravaganza. The cause of the inflation was military spending to defend America's economic empire, but the measures introduced neither ended the war nor reduced military spending. Nor did they create needed social goods. Instead, wages were frozen. Supposedly, prices were frozen as well, although the big industries were given some exceptions. Rents were allowed to rise by 2.5 percent plus all of the additional taxes that could be passed back to renters (and

[19] Miliband, *The State in Capitalist Society,* p. 81.

many rents were quickly unfrozen), and food prices were unchecked and continued to soar. Nor were there any controls imposed on corporate profits or profits from stocks and bonds. Some very large unions achieved wage increases for their members while the members of the smaller unions and unrepresented working people were worse off. There was virtually no mechanism for consumer control of prices, which could rise in a variety of covert ways. Does all this seem to be against the interests of the working man? Well, the policy was dreamed up by the Democratic party, which had been attacking Nixon's handling of the problem and urging him to adopt its ideas. Which, surprising everybody but the radicals, he did. Do controls seem to be the height of government intervention, unlikely to be endorsed by conservative Republicans? Well, Nixon's policy was so endorsed, even by Wall Street. All the talk about freedom of contract, about people being able to set their own prices for their labor power, is thrown out the window the minute intervention seems to be clearly in the interests of the ruling class. Needless to say, this most startling suspension of the "free" capitalist market was never put to the people for approval, nor were they asked to elect representatives to the Pay Board and Price Board. These controls may be lifted or changed when that seems a better course for capitalist interests. But the crucial fact is that the government shows no reluctance to use all the powers of the state to intervene directly in the economy when intervention seems to be in the interests of the ruling class.

HAPPINESS AND IDEOLOGY

"But if Americans are so powerless in both the economic and political sphere, why don't they seem more unhappy about the system as a whole?" The answer to this problem is complicated and an attempt to unfold it will take place throughout the next few chapters. For one thing, it is not quite true to suggest that people are happy with the current arrangements in America. In the late 1950s, there did not seem to be any basic discontent. But the 1960s changed all that. Moreover, people who feel discontent find it difficult to express their feelings in ways that make any difference. Sometimes, in desperation, they turn to a George Wallace or to other political figures who seem to be speaking to some of their anxieties. But many people take no social action at all. Americans have been heavily indoctrinated to believe that the problems they feel are not social, but personal, and reflect their own inner difficulties. When they sense something wrong with their lives, they are instructed to look

31

inward, whether through the old forms of religion or psychoanalysis, or the more hip version of encounter groups. Besides, people are able to acquire at least some of the material things they need, and are constantly reminded of how much more they have than those below them and those in other countries. Finally, the system validates itself by setting forth a persuasive ideological line about the virtues of American society. Not only does American society institutionalize democracy, we are told, but also liberty: men are free to do as they will. So why complain since you are free to do whatever you want?

It is only later that we learn through experience that the alternatives are chosen by someone else, and that, in fact, we are free to sell our labor power or starve. We are told that all men are equal, though it is conceded this equality does not exist in any real, material sense but only in the formal sense that we all have equal rights before the law. Even if we did have formal equality (though any black person can show how false that claim is) it would mean something quite different than what we originally thought was embodied in the notion of a society based on equality. Equality before the law now can be seen to mean that the beggar and Rockefeller are both prohibited from sleeping under the bridge when they are homeless, from trespassing on another's property to pick berries if they are hungry, from shoplifting from a department store when they need clothes, from forcibly keeping scabs from taking their jobs when they are on strike for higher wages. But Rockefeller does not have to do any of these things since he has inherited enough money to sustain him for his entire life. So, in practice, the law works against the poor, protecting those who have made it against those who have not. Any society needs some safeguards. The point is that in this society the people who are really protected are the rich. Crime runs rampant against working people and the poor. And most of that crime is motivated by economic need generated by the capitalist maldistribution of wealth. Law and order maintain stability, but in America that stability is a *class*-oriented stability, a stability that favors the wealthy and oppresses the downtrodden.

One of the greatest ideological myths in the United States is the myth of free speech. Free speech is granted only as long as it has no significant effect. Thus, in the late 50s and early 60s nearly everyone could criticize freely, without fear of being called a "kook" or "bum" by the president. When speech was used simply to express dissent, freedom of speech was acceptable—it was, in fact, a key tool in the ideological struggle against the Left. The U.S. Information Service took movies of protest demonstrations, sent them around the world, and proclaimed "This is what we are fighting for in Vietnam—the right to have differing points of view and to be able to express them freely." While the Left was obeying the polite rules of the game, the government was ordering greater escalations of the war or more efficient bombings or intensified pacification programs. *Our* speech was being used to pacify us while *their* speech was used to mask a policy of murder. But when free speech was used to organize, as it was in the late 60s, the Left faced outright oppression: the use of naked violence against demonstrators and the use of conspiracy and criminal anarchy charges to imprison organizers. Formal freedoms quickly disappear when anyone threatens to use them effectively against the interests of the ruling class. The irony is that civil liberties have been withdrawn just at those times when they are most necessary: when there is serious political conflict about the direction of American society. True, in some cases an appeals court may later reverse a conviction. But the years spent in jail or in litigation have a markedly restraining effect. The government often succeeds in intimidating people from participating in activity that is theoretically protected by the Constitution. A vindication years later in the courts really doesn't change the reality of repression.

CONSEQUENCES FOR DAILY LIFE

The distribution of power in the economic and political spheres affects our daily lives in a myriad of ways. Consider the millions of people who work in factories. Marx described them as alienated in the sense that they have no control over the circumstances of their work, and this Marxian thesis still applies today. Marx was not talking about psychology: he was not saying that workers are necessarily *unhappy*. Indeed, many slaves in ancient Rome or Greece or in this country in the nineteenth century would have said they were happy with their lot. It is the structural, sociological phenomenon that Marx was stressing: in a capitalist society the worker is powerless to control his own life. Powerlessness on the part of the worker is a defining characteristic of capitalist society. (One important reason the New Left cannot consider the Soviet Union a socialist society is that the relations between workers and managers there still leave the worker basically powerless.)

The worker is powerless to affect what he is going to produce. He has, for example, no say in General Motors' decision to produce cars that will pollute the environment and fall apart after a few years. He must produce inferior goods when it is technologically feasible to produce goods of superior quality, durability, and safety—both for the environment and for human health. In addition to feeling no pride in what he produces, the worker also ends up hurting himself: he too will have to consume the shoddy goods. Needless to say, it is a much greater burden on someone making $8,500 a year than on someone making $20,000 a year to buy a new car every three or four years, or to spend extravagant amounts in repairs and replacement of defective parts. As long as the main purpose of production is corporate profit, American industry will produce shoddy goods. The longer a product lasts—whether it is a car or a light bulb or a television set—the smaller the demand for it, and hence the smaller the corporate profit. If goods lasted longer, workers could spend less time replenishing them and more time producing goods and services for those who cannot now obtain them. And if the goods and services to live humanly were available to everyone, people could turn their attention to fulfilling other needs. If our economy were restructured to serve human needs rather than the needs of large corporations and banks, it could produce enough to satisfy the basic material needs of everyone in this country and help in the development of the Third World, while still allowing for a dramatic reduction in the amount of time spent on production.

Just as he has no control over the quality of the goods produced, the worker has no say over the *kinds* of goods produced. For example, it is reasonable to ask whether there ought to be any cars in our cities. It is conceivable that people might prefer an extensive underground mass transit system with the streets replaced by parks and malls. But the two largest industries in the country—oil and automobile—would never allow democratic consideration of any serious proposal to shift the transportation system to one that rested primarily on mass transit powered by sources other than gas and oil. Workers may realize that the things they are producing create many of the problems they face in their everyday life: air pollution, ugly cities, plastic housing, weapons of destruction. But they are not consulted about what they are producing. They are faced with a rather simple choice: here are the available jobs—either take one or be unable to feed, clothe, and house your family adequately. Indeed, they may even fight to continue production of cars or munitions when they know that the alternative for them in the capitalist system might be sustained unemployment.

In a capitalist economy, every important decision about the use of resources is decided by profit potential for the owners of the corporations. Huge productive capacities go unused, factories work at two-thirds capacity because using them fully would not produce more profits for the owners. Goods are needed, but people do not have the money to buy

34

them. So they are not produced. Meanwhile, workers are idle, looking in vain for jobs. Imagine an economy so irrational that in order to deal with its problems it must consciously plan to induce higher levels of unemployment in order to fight inflation, only to find that while unemployment increased more than had been planned, inflation was still growing wildly. This is precisely what happened in the United States in late 1969. The smug and self-satisfied like to talk about those who refuse to work. (Undoubtedly there are some, though I often wonder how many of those who talk this way would be willing to accept the jobs that would be available to them if they had to switch places—would they be willing to work as night watchmen? delivery men? domestics?) But the majority of the unemployed simply cannot get jobs, and the capitalists actually attempt to raise that number at various points in order to deal with other problems of the economy.

Consider the over $16 billion a year that is wasted in advertising—advertising directed not toward informing people of the nature of the products available to them, but toward convincing them to buy one brand name rather than another. Advertising adds nothing to the product's value; its sole worth is to increase profits. Imagine the creative talents wasted in this socially useless task! Consider the waste of talent and resources involved in our vast military expenditures, to produce goods that will quickly become obsolete or (hopefully) will never be used—and certainly will never be needed. Consider the wasted work hours that come through duplication of efforts in merchandising systems: the stores that compete with each other selling similar merchandise at slightly different prices. Aside from the duplication, there is the waste: in such situations the store's facilities are never fully used. Consider the proliferation of small retail outlets, such as gas stations, that are only partially used because someone across the street has another gas station, selling another brand of gasoline. The duplication and waste is astounding, and the people who have to work in these operations become cynical about their jobs and about their own creative possibilities and worth. They are often the most conservative workers, because they are so unsure of their worth that they fear any kind of social change might render them useless.

CONSUMER'S POWER?

"But the industries only produce what the people want, otherwise they couldn't sell their products!" This argument reflects a conceptual con-

35

fusion. True, no one is literally forced to buy any product. But coercion may work in more subtle ways. Aldous Huxley's famous novel *Brave New World* describes a society with four basic classes (alphas, betas, gammas, and deltas) each with highly differentiated powers and responsibilities. The alphas have been conditioned from birth to want what alphas are supposed to want, the betas have been conditioned to want what betas are supposed to want, etc. Would anyone say that such a society is free? Yet, in many ways, American society is like Huxley's science fiction world. From birth Americans are subjected to an intensive indoctrination to make them believe that the good life requires extravagant consumption of every possible consumer good. This indoctrination is transmitted directly or indirectly through the school system, the movies, television, and through a massive advertising campaign costing billions of dollars each year. The goal of this advertising is twofold: to sell a particular product and to reinforce the concept that the good life requires people to buy more and more and to have the latest model if they are to be real and equal members in American society.

In such a situation, people come to experience needs they would never otherwise have felt: needs for products they themselves produce under extremely alienating factory conditions. And they spend their salaries for the satisfaction of these conditioned needs! So, increasingly people's desires are shaped to meet the needs of capitalist production: they learn to buy what is produced, instead of producing goods to fill human needs. Of course, this conditioning is not yet completely successful, and some people do reject the consumer mentality. But many more see themselves and their lives inadequate because they do not make enough money to buy the goods advertised in the media, and many feel personally guilty or think themselves failures. Still others work themselves silly, elbowing everyone who might possibly get in their way, so they can achieve the "good life," as defined for them by capitalism.

The few who own and control the means of production decide what to produce, although their decisions affect the lives of everyone. You as an individual have no control in this area. "Free competition" is a myth. It would take hundreds and millions of dollars to start an automobile company producing nonpolluting and long-lasting cars. Where would any individual get such a sum? Certainly not from the banks, whose interests are closely tied, through interlocking directorships and investments, to the interests of the automobile companies. Nor could you and a thousand friends pool enough surplus resources to come up with the required amount. Most people simply do not have the resources to start their own firms. This is part of the reason why hippie and black capitalism always end up being indistinguishable from regular capitalism: the hippies and the blacks simply become new intermediaries between those who control the major industries and the people.

The ideology of consumerism manifests itself in the passivity and isolation of American life. If people found fulfillment in their work, they would feel a need to relate to the people with whom they worked and to provide for mutual self-realization. But when one's attention is focused on consumption, when work is considered a wasteful distraction from what life is really supposed to be about (the getting of more and more goods), the privatized realm becomes dominant.

Capitalism teaches us to compete with each other not merely in seeking employment but also in consuming. Indeed, the good life seems to be defined on terms of having more than the next person. The emphasis is on what a person possesses rather than on what kind of human being he is. Competitive consumption, like the competitive search for employment, separates people from one another, making them mutually suspicious and distrustful and defining as "malcontents," "bums," "freaks," or "communists" those who try to overcome their passivity and reestablish a genuine productive community. The capitalist uses the word "community" to describe fragmented human beings alienated from one another in a class-structured social organization.

Many things that the capitalist market sells are needed only because of the destruction of the natural environment caused by unplanned industrialization and industrial growth. Because capitalism mindlessly rapes the natural environment to provide raw materials for its productive operations, people become increasingly dependent on the social environment to fill their needs. As Andre Gorz points out in *Strategy for Labor,* the need for air becomes the need for vacations from the factory or office, for public gardens, for city planning, for escape from the city; the need for rest every night becomes the need for comfortable housing protected against noise; the need to eat becomes the need for food to be consumed immediately after work, and therefore the need for cafeterias, restaurants, canned and frozen foods and foods that require a minimum of preparation time. The impoverishment of man's relation to nature and the exhaustion or destruction of resources that were once taken for granted (air, water, silence, light, space) have forced people to satisfy their needs in ways that require money and the consumption of consumer goods.

While the development of capitalism has created many new needs, some entirely superficial and some elaborations or refinements of more basic needs, the capitalist economy only satisfies those needs from which it can make a profit. It will sell back air, light, space, and water according to one's ability to pay, but it will not provide a means for satisfying collective needs that cannot be met through the sale of commodities to individuals. People need an urban landscape and environment that furthers their own creativity and self-development, but it is not profitable to provide areas of green and parks for those with little money. People need services such as transportation, laundries, day care centers, and nursery schools, but capitalists can make more money selling cars and washing machines, so these needed services are not available to those who desperately need them. There is little or no profit to be made on schools, libraries, concert halls, swimming pools, stadiums, or hospitals, so these facilities are in short supply in most areas of the country.[20] Sometimes, in response to massive public pressure (often involving civil disobedience and always involving attacks on the mobilizers of such pressure) a particular locality will introduce some public benefit. When this is done, it is paid for by raising taxes, the burden of which falls most heavily on those who most need the services and are least able to pay. Higher sales taxes are particularly hard for the poor to bear, and even property taxes are immediately shifted back to the poorer consumer in the form of higher rents.

Advertising and indoctrination do not fully explain the patterns of consumption in modern America. For, within the context of the contemporary capitalist system, people *do* need certain consumer goods in order to survive. Given that the interests of the oil and auto companies in the continuation of private transportation make the expansion of mass transit extremely unlikely, many workers *do* need cars if they are to get to work. As long as it is difficult for women to find employment, they are required to compete with each other to sell their bodies and talents to a man, and so they *do* need flashy outfits and makeup. Without public facilities for cooking, washing clothes, storing food, raising children, people *do* need their own stoves, washing machines, refrigerators, children's toys, and clothing, etc. So people don't consume just because of false needs, but because of needs peculiar to a capitalist form of social organization.

CONDITIONS OF WORK

Another key respect in which the worker is powerless is his inability to control the conditions under which he must work. Owners choose managers, who supervise the productive operations and decide what can and

---

[20] See Andre Gorz, *Strategy for Labor* (Boston: Beacon Press, 1968), p. 93.

cannot be done on the job. The managers' solution to the problem of decreasing profits is very often to speed up production. In order to maximize efficiency, the worker increasingly is turned into a machine, executing a few small tasks with complete regularity in a short period of time. This requires men and women who are

> mutilated, stunted in knowledge and responsibility. The dream of large industry is to absorb the worker from the cradle to grave . . . so as to narrow his horizon to that of his job. It is important to begin with not to give the worker (and not to permit him to acquire) skills superior to those which his specialized job requires. The worker must not be permitted to understand the overall production process, nor to understand work as an essentially creative act; for such thoughts might lead him to reflect, to take the initiative, and to make a decision—as for example the decision to go sell his labor power elsewhere. For its repetitive tasks, whether those of clerks in the banks and insurance houses or those of soldering in electronics, industry requires passive and ignorant manpower.[21]

The basic pattern remains the same even for the more highly skilled laborer and technician: increased technical responsibility does not bring the worker greater control over the conditions of work or the product he is making.

Perhaps this is easy to see with respect to factory workers, but does it apply to white-collar occupations? Consider a few examples. The average office worker types or files or makes purchases or handles a payroll or engages in one of a number of other tasks, all of which are set by the bosses and over which the worker has no control. Whether as a part of a large bureaucracy or a small office, the worker still finds virtually no room to express creativity. The frustrations of working in such a situation maximize irritability and pettiness, internal power struggles, intrigues, affairs, and anything else that can possibly keep one's mind off the work's drudgery.

Consider the teacher in a grade school or high school. Originally motivated by a passion to improve things and to help people, the teacher quickly finds that the school administration has placed decisive limitations on experimentation and creativity. Sometimes the reason for this

21 *Ibid.*, p. 35.

will be arbitrary and sometimes sensible, but the end result is that the creative teacher must either seriously restrict his area of creativity or get fired. The state has a set goal in mind: producing cogs that will fit in well with the corporate machine. The precise type of cog differs from class to class, and the range of alternatives is much wider for middle-class than for working-class students: the former will become professionals, while the latter must be prepared for the rigid discipline of factories and offices. But even in the most enlightened and progressive middle-class high schools, the teacher's creativity must be channeled within a rigid framework that never leads the students to ask basic questions about their society and then to *act* on the basis of their answers. Moreover, most students do not go to progressive schools, but to schools where teachers feed them a predigested curriculum that deadens interest and suppresses individuality and personal creativity.

Or consider the social worker. He tries his best to be sensitive to his clients, but he is so overloaded with cases that any sustained personal contact is impossible. Within a context rigidly set by the state he may allow certain benefits and sometimes make a decision in favor of his clients. But he has no way of dealing with the root causes of the problems he handles: he cannot affect poverty; the maldistribution of incomes, wealth, and power; poor housing; inadequate food supplies. He can maneuver to improve things somewhat for a particular client, but that usually only reenforces the client's passivity and willingness to be part of a system that degrades him. As the representative of the system that has so often treated people shabbily, the social worker is rarely dealt with honestly, and hence is isolated both from the system and from the people.

Or consider the lawyer. If he is self-employed, he *does* have considerable flexibility with regard to his work conditions. But he is still basically powerless to affect the product of his work. He is skilled in maneuvering within the legal framework, perhaps even in accomplishing minor modifications within the law. But the legal framework as a whole is out of his control. That framework, which combines a sacrosanct attitude toward private property with an inhuman penal system, always works to strengthen the capitalist order and hence to minimize the possibility of serious structural changes. Occasionally, there are victories for liberalization, but they are always insignificant in comparison with the monumentally conservative thrust of the law. Nor are the liberalizations cumulative: the "liberal" Warren Supreme Court is undermined by the later reactionary Burger court. And the liberal lawyer must always accept the rationality of the system and play the game lest he lose the case for his client, and face disbarment or jail (contempt of court à la the Chicago conspiracy trial).

Of course, the lawyer is much less likely to experience his powerlessness than the worker. For the lawyer, as for the teacher, the social worker, the government employee, and a host of other professionals, powerlessness is a structural fact that only emerges to consciousness when the professional no longer accepts the ideological framework imposed from above. And when there are high material compensations, many professionals often end up too personally comfortable to risk anything by starting to question the framework.

In all these cases, we have been considering the problem of powerlessness from the standpoint of the group reputed to have the most power in the society: white males. Other groups—women, young people, minorities —are even more powerless.

CONSEQUENCES OF POWERLESSNESS

Every important social problem and most important individual problems become intelligible against the background of powerlessness that pervades the economic and political life of capitalist society. There was an obvious reason for Marx to stress the relations that exist between people in production as the key to understanding all the rest of the things that happen during any historical epoch: the relations that obtain between people during the greatest number of their hours of peak consciousness—the hours when they are engaged in making a living—must inevitably have an effect on the quality of their lives and their consciousness during the few hours when they are neither working, commuting to work, sleeping, nor relaxing in exhaustion from the work activity.

The combined effects of a competitive marketplace and the daily powerlessness of people to affect their world is shown most dramatically in the relations between men and women. The man, frustrated and made to feel insignificant by the outside world, finds his opportunity to seem important and powerful by dominating and controlling a woman. The hierarchy of the outside world is re-created in the family, with the mother often finding her sole power in being able to make her children dependent on her in some way. Human relations are treated as if they were relations between marketable things: the chief criteria being How much can I get out of him (her)? and What's in it for me? How else are people to react to other people when their whole lives and the entire structure of society combines to make them view one another as threats to survival, and as objects to be manipulated? We shall deal with this in more detail in Chapter 3.

The neuroses afflicting so many people (and which keep psychiatrists

41

rich) are a direct consequence of a society in which people are forced to compete with each other, and in which they perceive the utter impossibility of controlling their own lives and the utter waste of so much of their time in useless or even destructive production. To be "normal" in a society that exploits people all around the world, that suppresses people at home, that renders human beings into mere objects for manipulation and control—requires a human being so insensitive that his very humanity may be in question. Whoever is not abnormal in such a society has either no feelings or no mind. Insanity is one possible response to these conditions. Another is to ape the characteristics of the system in your own life by finding some group—be it Vietnamese, blacks, women, children—over whom you can play out the inhumanities that have been inflicted upon you.

The vast majority of crimes committed in this society stem from the economic structure. Crime is almost nonexistent in the pseudo-socialist societies of Eastern Europe or in Cuba, North Vietnam and the Israeli kibbutz, which are somewhat closer to socialism. In addition to the crimes that shouldn't be crimes even by capitalist standards (e.g., smoking marijuana), there are those that stem from people's needs for more money (hence the petty ripoffs, bank robberies, grocery store holdups, etc.) or from their feelings of frustration in society (from which so many crimes of passion derive). The biggest criminals are the ones who have managed to rob whole classes and whole countries—the people who sit on the boards of corporations, banks, and universities and who administer the federal government. Perhaps cognizant of the fact that any attack on the big criminals might lead to embarrassing questions, the FBI and other law enforcement agencies bend over backward not to attack the Mafia and other centers of organized crime: the "most wanted" become the small-time bankrobbers, the muggers and the political organizers. Honor among thieves.

Nor are the crimes of the rich without danger to the rest of the population. In their frenzy for profits, the rich are willing to go to any lengths of destructiveness, from bombing the Vietnamese to building unsafe industrial plants. In 1968 a total of 14,300 Americans died in industrial accidents; between 1961 and 1969, 126,000 Americans were killed this way. In 1968, 90,000 workers suffered permanent impairments and a total of 2,100,000 suffered total but temporary disability. Minimal precautions could have prevented most of these accidents and deaths. But such precautions would have required capital outlays and hence cut into corporate profit, so they were often deemed not worth it. Congress made a great fanfare of passing an industrial health and safety bill in 1970, but it has been virtually unenforced. In any sane society the men who run factories and mines and who knowingly refuse to provide adequate safety controls would be treated as the worst of criminals. But in capitalist America, they become the secretaries of defense and state, or advisers to governmental agencies. And, ironically, they are the ones who cry most loudly for "law and order."

Even those who do not turn to crime or racism or insanity or neuroses are plagued with an overriding sense of the meaninglessness of their lives. Existentialism describes this as a general problem, built into the structure of human existence. But in fact it is societal in origin and is true for a certain historical period. Within a society in which men cannot control their own lives, there is no way for them to introduce any meaning into their daily affairs. In a society in which the criterion of production is profitability, when people's talents can never be developed but only "exploited" by the large corporations, when people's human potentialities are stunted and underdeveloped unless someone can "use" them, it is inevitable that people will feel dissatisfied and unfulfilled. The task of religion or patriotism or chauvinism or psychoanalysis is to channel this feeling in a direction that does not challenge its fundamental source: the capitalist economic structure.

In the face of these conditions, the worker protests in the only way he can: by demanding more money for the time he is wasting in production. The worker must sell his skin, so why not sell it at the highest price possible? This direction of protest is taken because it is only with regard to wages that management seems willing to bargain at all. But the price the worker gets will never be high enough to compensate for a lost life, and his willingness to accept this channel plays directly into the hands of management, which (while imperialism is still functioning well) can often afford to raise pay and then raise prices.

Powerlessness is not merely an insignificant fact about the economy or the political realm. It pervades every area of people's lives, ensuring that their human potential for creativity, freedom, rationality, love, and human sympathy will not be realized.

EDUCATION

The educational system provides a particularly dramatic example of the way in which American capitalism destroys the possibility of human self-realization. The people are basically powerless to affect what they are being taught and to prevent themselves from being shaped by the system to meet the system's needs. And the primary need of the system is for narrow and obedient robots who are willing not to think for themselves, but to take orders, to see problems in the narrowest possible perspective, and to see themselves as isolated from everyone else. The schools do a marvelous job on all counts.

Through "tracking" programs youngsters are selected out at an early age and if they are not deemed "college material" (usually determined by criteria heavily culturally biased in favor of the upper middle class) are given skill training which prepares them for manual or secretarial work and leaves them unaware of human accomplishments in literature, science, and a host of other fields. Even those who are offered college preparation study little in the junior high and high school curriculum that stimulates creativity or self-mastery. History courses distort the facts of America's past, seeking to instill blind loyalty for flag and country. In every area the premium is on memorization and dutiful repetition of what text and teacher say. The high schools teach respect for constituted authority and the sense of powerlessness—and they teach these very well. The school day is filled with busywork, designed to keep the students out of trouble, to teach them that if they behave and follow the rules of the game (no matter how absurd those rules) they can make it to the next higher stage. What better preparation for the mental degradation of the assembly line or for most junior colleges and many universities?

The colleges and universities are often ideal fulfillments of the previous preparation. Here, too, the student is taught that if he follows the rules and does what he is told he can make it. True, one learns more facts in college than in high school, but the fragmented structure of college education makes it highly unlikely that anyone will emerge with any coherent understanding of his world.

Colleges are like intellectual supermarkets: a little bit of this and a little bit of that ("Try it, you'll like it") but never any attempt to organize knowledge coherently or to relate it to the problems most people will face in their later lives. "Knowledge" becomes a matter of adding up credits in various fields, and the "major requirement" pushes most students into specializing almost as soon as they have completed their required courses.

Each department jealously guards its own subject, and very little intellectual communication takes place between members of different departments. Within each department there is a preponderance of specialists who have often managed to narrow their field of interest to such an extent that they can honestly claim to be one of the five or ten leading authorities on their subject in the country. Rarely do these academics have an overview of their own academic discipline, let alone an interest in anything outside it. These men, greatly respected by their opposite numbers at other institutions of "higher learning," are often profoundly anti-intellectual and uninterested in any attempts to make their field relevant to the needs of their students. Often these professors are completely unaware of the intellectual traditions that have integrated knowledge and action. Incapable of seeing any larger context even within their own discipline, they equate rationality with piecemeal solutions and so can never understand the impetus to radicalism and substantive change among their students. And when they do understand it, they are often so tied to the system—either by the comforts of middle-class living or by the fear of losing their jobs (a not unfounded fear since they have radical colleagues who have been thrown out of universities even when they had tenure)—that their only response to national crises is "How do I save myself and how do I save the university?"

As a whole, the university has three functions: (1) to train narrow specialists who can run the complicated machinery of an advanced industrial society, from building its bridges to servicing its legal, psychological, and physical needs; (2) to reinforce the ideological belief system that supports capitalism; and (3) to provide intellectual busywork for the millions of young people who might otherwise be looking for jobs in an overcrowded labor market. In these tasks, different departments fill somewhat different functions. Most of the money at universities and colleges goes into specialty training: engineering, business, science, mathematics, and other fields in which people are trained to service the needs of the ruling class. Small wonder: it is precisely the magnates of big business who dominate the boards of regents of the various universities. When applied, the advances made in the "pure" sciences, such as physics and chemistry, serve the interests of the rulers. Who else can afford to purchase the machinery and equipment needed to put discoveries in these fields into use? Sometimes the benefits trickle down to the people: a better cure for a disease or a more comfortable airplane (assuming that some company decides they are marketable and can be sold at a good profit). But more often research is geared to the needs of its sponsors and potential users: the corporate ruling class. Billions of dollars are poured into war-related research, and the man who can bring in lucrative research grants becomes an indispensable and much-honored faculty member in his school.

The chief ideologists of capitalism dominate the political science, history, sociology, anthropology, and economics departments—men who refuse to see American imperialism and racism, who accept the narrow conceptions of bourgeois thought (from conceptions about human nature to methodological assumptions that the only way to understand things is to examine them in isolation from their context) and who actively support the present system of wealth and power. The Vietnam war has exposed this crew of intellectual charlatans for the apologists they are. For each new escalation, for each new evasion of the democratic procedures, these men worked out some new explanation and justification, finally settling on the most effective one: America's problems are caused by the dissenters; if students were not so unreasonable, we could patch everything up. These social scientists have already given up hope of using reason to alter the shape of American power; the most they can expect is to derive some satisfaction from America's power by serving it. Since America has already achieved the good life, all that reason can do is maintain the current structure, making an occasional necessary minor correction or adjustment. Most social scientists cannot see that a particular social defect or social benefit is rooted in a larger pattern; they can be critical of the Vietnam war but fail to understand how that war is connected with the invasion of the Dominican Republic or with the internal operations of the capitalist system. They can applaud the increase in average working-class wages and gross national product but cannot recognize the ways these increases are rooted in the larger system of exploitation by which the United States deals with the underdeveloped world.

Those few political scientists who sense the need for a larger vision often retreat into a romantic view of the academic past—the good old days of political theory, for example, before the behaviorists took over. But in the social science departments, as in the pure science departments, the most desired men are those who can bring in the research grants. And research grants come increasingly from the federal government and from large foundations (Ford, Rockefeller, Mellon) whose main interest is to control intellectual research and the dissemination of ideas. The proof is in the studies that actually get funded. The subjects of study are usually the people about whom the rulers want to know things: Third Worlders, students, blacks, women, laborers, criminals, and any other elements that might cause disruption of the established order. Almost no research is done on the subject about which a majority of Americans need to know most: the ruling class. As a result, we can find out almost nothing about how the leading corporations have interacted with the government or with one another, what policies have been pursued by what interests, etc. Radicals have to start virtually from scratch when they want to find out in detail who has what power and how it is used. Anyone who objects to this corporate control (exercised indirectly through the foundations) of research is written off as a narrow "ideologue" trying to impose his views on others. After all, the argument goes, shouldn't there be freedom of inquiry at the university? The fact that the goals of research are thus defined from the outside by those who are willing to fund some projects but not others is not seen as interference with freedom. Those who suggest

46

that the foundations and the government should not be allowed to fund specific projects but rather should be required to give money to a general university fund (after which the academic community itself would select research projects) are denounced as starry-eyed idealists: after all, wouldn't that have the effect of drying up the sources of money? Indeed it would—because the money isn't given for research for humane knowledge but rather to find out specific information that will be useful to those who have the money to give. So the freedom-of-inquiry issue becomes big every time someone objects to a particular department doing counterinsurgency work for the State or Defense Departments. The freedom within the university is the freedom to teach and to do research that either directly aids the owners and financial backers of the university or at least does not seriously challenge them. Social scientists who bring in these grants are themselves elevated to high status, eventually becoming department chairmen, deans, heads of special institutes connected with the university, and even university presidents. They help make the university an ideological institution—for an ideology that the social scientists live in their courses, their research, and their government consultations.

If the social sciences provide ideological cover, and the physical and biological sciences serve established power by developing weapons systems, instruments for biological and chemical warfare, and technological innovations that can be marketed by the giant corporations, the humanities serve the established order in more subtle ways. Philosophy, literature, the arts were vehicles through which human beings attempted to step back from their daily struggles for survival and survey their world and their own lives. To do this in a society in which deep alienation and a pervasive sense of powerlessness prevail would be subversive to the established order. So increasingly these disciplines have narrowed their scope to focus on highly technical and specialized questions about word usages, formal argumentation, internal coherence and structure. The deep philosophical questions are dismissed as "meaningless," the use of literature and art as vehicles for reexperiencing ourselves and our world, the whole enterprise of self-reflection and reconstruction are all ruled out of these disciplines. The questions that are dealt with have an intrinsic interest, and with much more time, would be worth considering along with inquiries which try to integrate knowledge, put it in a social context, and evaluate it. But time is the rub and the university makes sure that the student does not have enough of it, through a heavy course schedule, large amounts of required reading, term papers, quarters or semesters so short that the course is over before the student has had sufficient exposure to the material to be able seriously to challenge the instructor about the structure or content of his course.

47

Not that most instructors could answer those challenges if they were offered: trained as they are in very narrow spheres, they often find a student's question irrelevant, unintelligible, or personally threatening.

So just at the moment in world history when we most need integrated knowledge of the relationship among the economic, political, sociological, psychological and philosophical aspects of our world, our society and our intellectual traditions, the university becomes dominated by professors, courses, and concepts that are increasingly narrow and specialized. The men of reason serve the men of power, while that power in turn is used against American workers, blacks, and students, against Third Worlders, and against all those around the world who challenge American domination.

When students begin to challenge the way in which the university is being run, the ways in which they are being mass produced and misshaped to fill the needs of the society, the university itself becomes another battleground for the rulers, and professors begin to justify the use against their students of the same naked force that was previously reserved for Vietnamese and blacks. Students are suspended, dismissed, and finally shot down on their own campuses. If the campuses are quieter and less confrontation-oriented in the 1970s, it will not be because the university has changed, but because the tremendous force and violence used in the late 1960s against students has led many of them to see dissent as leading nowhere but literally to their own destruction. When ten thousand troops occupy Berkeley and helicopters indiscriminately spray tear gas on the population below, when students are killed at Kent and Jackson State— students elsewhere get the message. Protest leads to violence. So protest must be curtailed.

Any faculty member who does not go along with the capitalist world view is quietly denied employment or tenure, and if charges of discrimination are raised the rare professor whose tenure predated his awakening to political reality is used as proof that the university is flexible and open-minded. Some young faculty members are fired explicitly for their politics, but more often the excuse is that they are academically incompetent. And, indeed, if the criteria of competence center around the ability so to narrow one's interests that they are irrelevant to the social problems of one's time, then one can see why many radical thinkers choose to be "incompetent." The very fact that a radical intellectual may write articles or teach courses that do not neatly fit into one established academic discipline is held against him as a sign that he must be "fuzzy-minded" or lack rigor in his thinking. The large industrialists who first established most colleges (and sat on the board of regents of state colleges) carefully selected people to fill academic departments who could be counted on to define academic competence in such a way that those involved in fundamental critiques of society would be ruled out.

The university becomes a training ground for cynicism. Its corruption and deification of the established power, its contempt for wisdom and deep understanding, undermine the idealism of many young people. A few clever students may manage to find the few decent professors and work out a college career that is not destructive to their human capacities. But the overwhelming thrust of the university is to turn people away from any serious thinking about their world and to make them believe that except for minor problems things are basically all right in America. The university reinforces people's feelings of powerlessness and their obedience to senseless rules.

Education in modern America reflects capitalist society at large. It is no surprise that people who have emerged from twelve or sixteen years in such institutions should be so unsure of themselves and so cut off from an understanding of their own psychological and social circumstances that they are willing to accept the society they enter. Pacified and shaped by years of schooling, Americans are now ready for a life dominated by television, the boss, the husband, or what they are told is "public opinion." Nor have the few moments of radical political activity on campus, the participation perhaps in an antiwar demonstration, significantly changed the massive feelings of powerlessness and lack of direction.

Real possibilities exist, particularly at the university and community college level, to break through all this and revive, at least for some students, the life of critical intellect. When students reach the age when they are breaking away from parental ties and are trying to define themselves independently of their past, they are open to genuine growth and learning. It was a tragedy of the Left during the 1960s that although it spoke to students' gut feelings, it did not have a serious core of scholarship that could be counterposed to the pseudo-scholarship they were imbibing in classes every day. Developing the serious intellectual work and radical scholarship that will provide some kind of alternative to contemporary education is an important task in the period ahead.

The cynicism that prevailed on the campuses in the 1950s and that may be returning in the 1970s emphasizes another point. Because people think that powerlessness is built into the very structure of their lives, they are not inclined to struggle against the things they do not like. And their reluctance to fight leads to even more powerlessness: each potential fighter looks around, sees that he is alone, and decides there is no point in becoming a martyr. Powerlessness corrupts, because even the people who recognize that they are involved in a net of ugly and immoral situations feel they have no alternative but to accept these situations and make the best of them.

ECOLOGY AND HEALTH

Perhaps the most striking example of the powerlessness of most people in modern American society is their lack of influence over their own natural environment. The organization of production to promote corporate profit has left a scorched earth, not only in Vietnam, where food production may be damaged for decades in the future, but also over all the world. In the past, the capitalist refused to think about the needs of future generations as he roamed the earth extracting its raw materials, overworking its land, exploiting its people, polluting its air and water, and ravishing its forests. But we are the future generation and even now the rape of the earth proceeds apace.

The ecological crisis has gone far beyond the possibility of solution by such measures as cleaning up a few dirty ponds or returning used bottles. What we are talking about is the ability of the earth to sustain human life. "As a result of industrial and domestic combustion activities, the quantity of carbon dioxide in the atmosphere has increased by roughly 25% in the past 100 years, a figure that may well double again by the end of the century. . . . Eventually, it is supposed, the gas will inhibit the dissipation of the earth's heat into space, causing a rise in overall temperatures which will melt the polar ice caps and result in an inundation of vast coastal areas." [22] Studies by ecologists reveal that within forty years the earth may become uninhabitable unless the ecological disaster is dealt with in a decade. But the corporate elite, which has already placed the world on the brink of nuclear destruction several times during the past twenty years, is not likely to be frightened by scientific predictions that are a decade away from fruition. Instead, we are told that the fault is with the consumer, that man is an natural polluter. In the January 1972 issue of *Harper's*, Peter F. Drucker, a leading apologist for the established order, wrote: "Today every one of us—in the underdeveloped countries almost as much as in the developed ones—is a polluter. . . . We face an environmental crisis because for too long we have disregarded genuine costs. . . . The expense must be borne, eventually, by the great mass of people as consumers and

[22] Murray Bookchin, "Toward Ecological Solution," *Ramparts* 8, no. 11 (May 1970): 8.

producers. The only choice we have is which of the costs will be borne by the consumer in the form of higher prices, and which by the taxpayer in the form of higher taxes." Statements like this appear in the rhetoric of the newspapers and political leaders almost every day. But who exactly is this "we" who made the decisions to disregard genuine costs? Do you remember being consulted when General Motors refused to use available technological knowledge and skills to create a nonpolluting car? Did the coal companies ask you if they should use strip-mining techniques? Did Standard Oil ask you whether to dig for oil in the Santa Barbara channel? You and I enter the picture only when the time comes to pay the costs. (The disregard for the ecological effects of production that characterizes many of the decisions of the ruling class in the Soviet Union is another indication of the people's powerlessness there, and of the fact that it is not truly a socialist society.)

Equally insidious is the suggestion that the Third World's real problem is not underdevelopment but overpopulation. This approach obscures the fact that the American economy, serving 15 percent of the world's population, uses more than 50 percent of the world's resources. The place where population control should be instituted—from the point of view of pollution at least—is the United States (one American consumes the same amount of raw material as fifty citizens of India).

The notion that we are all equally polluters is similarly ridiculous. Although every human being to some small extent does inevitably pollute the environment, the creators of the ecological crisis are the huge corporations which have consistently viewed the resources of the planet as tickets to corporate wealth. The damage done to the environment by General Motors, Ford, Chrysler, Standard Oil, Shell Oil, and Union Oil is so far out of proportion to the damage done by all the millions of Americans taken together [23] that the comparison makes no sense whatsoever. Nor are our problems going to be solved by ecological do-gooders whose response to the crisis is to pick up litter in their neighborhood parks, while refusing to confront the corporate powers that are driving us to worldwide destruction.

Matters are not likely to get much better now that ecology has become a political football for the major political parties, which have been using it in an attempt to deflect attention from the failure of the president and Congress to end the war in Vietnam. But the young did not abandon their concern for the Vietnamese. A week and a half after "Earth Day" in the

[23] A common gauge of pollution is biological oxygen demand (BOD), the amount of oxygen required to sustain decomposition of waste. There are 8.5 trillion pounds of human BOD per year and 30 trillion pounds for industry in America.

spring of 1970, the invasion of Cambodia inspired strikes and militant demonstrations on campuses around the country. Nevertheless, ecological consciousness among the people has been raised to such a point that candidates from each party vie with one another in expressions of concern for the environment (just as, in 1968, the key question was Who could talk more convincingly about ending the war). But their proposals are always inadequate for dealing with the problem. Thus, for example, in 1967 Senator Muskie proposed "ambient" air standards on a regional basis. The plan was to establish criteria for the amount of pollutants a particular geographical region should be permitted to have in its air. The proposal may have seemed like an important step, but it was, in fact, a very small one. It was not feasible as proposed, and did not set emission standards for such stationary sources of pollution as smokestacks. We are likely to see much similar legislation—too little, too late—in the next several years, along with speedy patch-ups and pious words as the ecological crisis steadily deepens and people remain powerless to affect the industries that cause and sustain it.

The ecological crisis affects the very foods Americans eat. In order to ensure a high level of profits, the food industry has introduced 3,000 different synthetic flavors, colors, thickeners, acidifiers, bleaches, preservatives, package contaminants, antibiotics, and poison pesticides. As Daniel Zwerdling pointed out in a recent article: "Virtually no food on the grocery shelves is free from chemical additives which have no nutritive value, are probably harmful, and whose main purpose is to make eaters think they're eating something they aren't." [24] The effects of these additives are not immediately determinable; nevertheless, the government, instead of requiring long-term testing, permits them to be used. Zwerdling quotes Marvin Legator, chief biochemist at the Food and Drug Administration, who admits: "We never know for sure whether additives are safe or not. Long-term usage of additives can in no way be rated with safety. We have so many cases of common diseases like mental retardation and cancer, which we can't account for through epidemiological studies, for which we can't find a cause and effect." And, Legator goes on, "The only reason we ever pinpointed Thalidomide poisoning was because its effects were such gross abnormalities which are so darn rare. And even then it took us five years to find out."

According to Zwerdling, food industry sales amounted to $130.6 billion in 1971—a 63 percent growth since 1960—and food is the biggest and fastest growing business in the country. *Food Engineering,* a leading

[24] Daniel Zwerdling, "Food Pollution," *Ramparts* 9, no. 11 (June 1971): 30.

trade journal, points out that the more additives, "the higher the potential profit-margin." Most produce is grown on lands that have been seeped with chemical poisons, and some of the pesticides still remain on the finished product. Chickens and cows are fattened by a variety of antibiotics and synthetic growth hormones. Food wrappings are treated with chemicals that seep into the food itself. Many food additives do nothing to enhance food quality or freshness—they are there only to enhance the "aesthetic value." The variety of foods on the shelves of a modern supermarket may give one the impression that Americans have real freedom of choice about what they are going to put inside them. But in reality, the choice is between one set of additives and another. A small number of people with plenty of free time, energy, and information may be able to avoid the worst aspects of food pollution by buying at such places as natural food coops. But for most Americans, this is another area of powerlessness directly caused by the capitalist structure.

When food pollution, ecological pollution, and "natural" causes begin to take their toll on the health of the ordinary American, he has to cope with the exorbitant costs of medical care. In this country, access to a health system—doctors, hospitals, medical schools, drug companies—is a privilege of money and not a human right. Like every other industry in America, the health industry is in business to make money. The American Medical Association does its best to ensure that free or low-cost health care is not made available by the government, in order to protect the privileged position of doctors. Physicians are a very wealthy group. In 1971 the median (reported) income of doctors in the United States was $40,550. The wealth of the average doctor in his mid-forties was estimated by the National Bureau of Economic Research in 1963 at between $100,000 and $120,000. This compares with $490 for the average family. During the 1960s medical costs rose faster than any other part of the Consumer Price Index. The average cost per patient stay for hospital care was almost $100 a day in 1969, over three times what it was ten years before. In 1972, 125 million Americans were not covered by hospital insurance at all. And those who had it paid, on the average, $460 per year. And health plans pay, on the average, a mere 36 percent of subscribers' health care costs. Medicare, a relatively high-paying plan, pays only 45 percent of the health care costs of the aged. As Harold Jacobs points out in "Live!!," [25] the monthly newsletter on health and ecology: "It is easy to see why most poor people are in constant fear of becoming seriously ill and why for three out of four American families, one major illness or

[25] Available by subscription by writing to Box 152, West Hurley, New York 12491.

accident can turn into a financial disaster." Nor has the American medical system been provided increasingly better care. Since 1952, Jacobs points out, the life expectancy of an American man over sixty-five has decreased, while health costs have been skyrocketing. The United States ranks 18th in infant mortality and 22nd in male life expectancy in the world. Poverty and malnutrition are major causes of the widespread and preventable chronic diseases that attack the 30 to 40 million Americans who in 1972 were poorly nourished, housed, and educated. And the health care that is available follows the most narrow definitions of medicine: concern with nutrition, chiropractic, acupuncture, or other new methods is restricted as long as the American Medical Association fears they may cut into medical profits.

Profits are the key to health care. Proposals for assistance, through medical insurance or extended hospitals, always require the people to bear the burden through additional taxes. An article in *Ramparts* for November 1971 shows how Ross Perot, Texas multimillionaire, made his fortune through high costs to publicly supported health projects on data processing. And many of the key proposals for reform currently being considered in Congress are at the same time proposals to make private insurance companies even richer by using public taxes to pay the premiums.

Among the greatest beneficiaries of the current health arrangements are the drug companies. The Kefauver hearings on drugs in the 1950s showed that mark-up rates of several hundred percent were not uncommon. Nothing has changed. Well over three quarters of a billion dollars a year is spent by the drug industry in advertising and promotional material aimed exclusively at persuading doctors to specify brand names in the prescriptions they write. Drug companies are often forced to admit that many of these drugs have side effects more harmful than the diseases they were supposed to cure. According to *The New York Times* of April 17, 1970, three leading drug companies offered a package of $105 million to settle damage claims by forty-three states, hundreds of cities, and thousands of individual consumers. Instead of testing drugs extensively before putting them on the market, the drug companies test them by persuading doctors to prescribe them to patients who do not know they are guinea pigs. Only if the results prove bad are the companies forced to remove the drug from circulation. Need we go on? Virtually every American of moderate means knows how difficult it is to get this basic necessity—decent health care—at a tolerable cost. We are powerless to control our very own bodies.

CONCLUSION

Until now, we have been talking about the material, psychological, and social powerlessness that has become an ingredient of American life during a period when the American economy was doing relatively well, and when the richest country in the world was able to set conditions of trade and investment for itself around the globe. Even in that period of unrivaled prosperity, the problem of powerlessness was extremely acute. But now we are entering a new period, one in which American imperial domination is being severely challenged. The results of those challenges are now being felt on the domestic economy. Perhaps the worst shocks of the transition will be assimilated. But the basic condition that caused President Nixon to eliminate the "free" marketplace will remain: and with it, an intensification of the country's economic problems. In the coming period, then, one of the rulers' key weapons—the ability to give in without too much trouble to demands for higher wages while ignoring all other kinds of demands—will be increasingly curtailed. For example, between 1965 and 1970 the spendable weekly earnings (take-home pay) of manufacturing workers with three dependents declined from an average of $102.41 to an average of $99.66.[26] With growing limitations on the maneuverability of the rulers in the economic sphere there will be a growing awareness of the multi-dimensions of powerlessness herein outlined.

It is not unlikely that in the years ahead some of the forms of powerlessness may change. A liberal president might patch up a few areas, and a *climate* of change could certainly be established. This was the case during the New Deal; many otherwise intelligent people thought that basic changes were being made in their society. Some problems *do* get solved or alleviated, but always in the context in which other problems grow worse and new problems emerge from the same basic cause. As long as the capitalists control the financial and industrial corporations of America, no liberal will be allowed to make much of a dent in anything. Even the capitalists (or at least a majority of them) can be convinced that some changes will be necessary to preserve the system, so these changes might be made even by a more conservative president. But the basic dimensions of powerlessness will persist. People will remain powerless as producers and as consumers and they will have little opportunity to hear the arguments and analyses of socialists who offer a real alternative. As a result, the breakdown of American society will continue apace.

[26] *Monthly Labor Review,* August 1971.

SUGGESTED READINGS

Armstrong, Gregory. *Life at the Bottom*. New York: Bantam Books, 1971.

Domhoff, G. William. *Who Rules America?* Englewood Cliffs, N.J.: Prentice-Hall, 1967.

Fitch, Robert. *Who Rules the Corporations?* New York: Random House, forthcoming.

Gorz, Andre. *Strategy for Labor*. Boston: Beacon Press, 1968.

Horowitz, David. *Radical Sociology*. San Francisco: Canfield Press, 1971.

Kaufman, Richard F. *The War Profiteers*. New York: Doubleday Anchor, 1972.

Kolko, Gabriel. *Wealth and Power in America*. New York: Praeger, 1962.

Longgood, William. *The Poisons in Your Food*. New York: Pyramid Books, 1969.

Marcuse, Herbert. *One-Dimensional Man*. Boston: Beacon Press, 1965.

Marx, Karl. *Early Writings*. Edited by T. B. Bottomore. New York: McGraw-Hill Paperbacks, 1964.

Miliband, Ralph. *The State in Capitalist Society*. New York: Basic Books, 1969.

Mintz, Morton, and Cohen, Jerry. *America, Inc*. New York: Dial Press, 1971.

Ridgeway, James. *The Politics of Ecology*. New York: Dutton, 1970.

Sexton, Patricia and Brendon. *Blue Collars and Hard Hats*. New York: Random House, 1971.

Sherman, Howard. *Radical Political Economy*. New York: Basic Books, 1972.

Zeitlin, Maurice, ed. *American Society, Inc. Studies of the Social Structure and Political Economy of the United States*. Chicago: Markham, 1970.

2
Imperialism

THROUGHOUT the world the United States is recognized as a major imperialist country. Yet most Americans find it difficult to apply the concept of "imperialism" to their own country, and are sure the Left is exaggerating when it uses the term. They may be willing to admit that America acted like an imperialist country in the early part of this century, when it took the Philippines and used "gunboat" diplomacy in the Caribbean; and to agree that our intervention in Vietnam was a terrible tragedy both for us and for the Vietnamese. To the liberal, however, these are matters of the past: "We are getting out of Vietnam. We have learned from our mistakes." The radical position is very different. It asserts that the United States' relationship to the rest of the world is primarily exploitative, and that exploitation is made necessary by the internal workings of the capitalist system.

First, let's get the record straight about the United States' role around the world. Before World War II, the United States had intervened militarily in the Philippines, Puerto Rico, Panama, Haiti, Honduras, Colombia, Peru, the Dominican Republic, Costa Rica, Nicaragua, China, Mexico and most of the Caribbean countries. Since World War II, the United States has intervened militarily in Guatemala, Cuba, China, Korea, Indonesia, Laos, Bolivia, the Congo, Lebanon, Venezuela, the Dominican Republic, Vietnam, and Cambodia. Nor do these overt instances of American imperialism tell the whole story. The full story of imperialism in its modern form is the story of the way the corporate structure of the United States and its supportive political-military institutions dominate the economic and political life of countries around the world. It is this story, which includes military intervention but goes far beyond it, that we refer to when we talk about imperialism. The purpose of this chapter is to show that imperialism is

57

rooted in the basic structure of capitalism, and that it is therefore misleading for liberal politicians to promise to end America's global role when they are unprepared to alter the capitalist system itself.

SOME EXAMPLES FROM
THE LAST DECADES

Let us begin with a few examples of the role of the United States in influencing the political and economic directions of other countries. Consider the case of Brazil.[1] Between 1961 and 1964 Brazil was governed by the liberal millionaire J. Goulart. Goulart was no great crusader. In the early part of his administration he used troops to break up popular demonstrations calling for the implementation of his own liberal program and he granted concessions to American mineral and oil firms. But by 1964, Goulart started to strengthen Brazil's economic life. He committed the crime of attacking American investments, by proposing a limit on the amount of profits that could be taken out of Brazil in any given year. Thereafter, according to Philip Siekman,[2] a coterie of Brazilian businessmen approached U.S. Ambassador Lincoln Gordon to ask what the U.S. position would be if civil war were to break out in Brazil. Gordon gave them the impression that if a new government could hold out for forty-eight hours, the United States would give it recognition and aid. On March 18, Assistant Secretary of State for Inter-American Affairs Thomas C. Mann was reported to have developed a major modification of Kennedy Administration policy: the United States would abandon its efforts to deter Latin American dictators. On March 19, a State Department spokesman explained that U.S. policy toward unconstitutional governments would be guided by the national interest (rather than by the formal pledge the government had made to discourage any more coups d'état). On April 1 Goulart was removed from office by a military coup sponsored by the business coterie. Less than twenty-four hours after the news reached Washington the new regime was recognized. As Carl Oglesby reports: "By November 1964 the United States had dramatized its enthusiasm for the new regime by a loan of $400 million over and above already programed Alliance for Progress funds. . . . Four months later, a new law made possible the lengthy imprisonment of individuals without declara-

[1] This account follows that compiled by Carl Oglesby in *Containment and Change* (New York: Crowell, Collier—Macmillan, 1967).
[2] In "When Executives Turned Revolutionaries," *Fortune,* September 1964.

tion of offense or pressing of charges. . . . On October 27, 1965, Institutional Act No. 2 was promulgated, banning all 13 existing political parties and creating two new ones, one to serve as 'loyal opposition.' . . . On January 27, 1966, all ports were declared national security zones, which automatically made all dock strikes and slowdowns military crimes." [3] The change in government produced golden opportunities for the capitalists. The new regime cut short the construction of new steel mills and started to sell back to private capital industries that had been nationalized years before. One of the greatest beneficiaries was the Hanna Mining Company of Cleveland, Ohio, which had lost some of its Brazilian concessions in 1958. Shortly after the new dictator took power he was visited by U.S. Ambassador Gordon and former U.S. High Commissioner in Germany John J. McCloy, representing Hanna Mining Company, and a while later he promulgated a new presidential decree calling for private competitive development of Brazil's vast iron-ore reserves and discouraging any monopoly by the state or other enterprises.

Now consider the U.S. attempt to overthrow the Castro regime. In 1959, when Castro came to power, U.S. economic interests dominated Cuban life, controlling 80 percent of the country's utilities, 90 percent of the mines, 90 percent of the cattle ranches, 50 percent of the public railways, close to 100 percent of the oil refining industry, 50 percent of the public railways, 40 percent of the sugar industry, and 25 percent of all bank deposits. Castro found a Cuba which, in David Horowitz's words, "was in the throes of a social disaster, the direct result of decades of corrupt tyrannical regimes under U.S. tutelage. 600,000 Cubans were unemployed, as many proportionally as were unemployed in the U.S. during the great depression. Half the population did not have electricity, and three and a half million Cubans lived in huts, shacks and slums without sanitary facilities. In the cities, rents represented almost one-third of family income. Almost 40 percent of the population was illiterate; 100,000 persons suffered from tuberculosis and 95 percent of the children in rural areas were affected by parasites. Only 1½ percent of the landowners controlled 46 percent of the total area of the nation, while 85 percent of the small farmers paid out almost a third of their incomes in rent." [4] Castro sought aid from the United States in the form of a loan, but failed to get it: the U.S.-controlled International Monetary Fund insisted on conditions that would have prevented him from introducing any serious reforms of the Cuban economy. Thwarted by the United States, Castro proceeded to

[3] *Containment and Change*, p. 88.
[4] David Horowitz, *Free World Colossus* (New York: Hill & Wang, 1965), p. 203.

develop his Agrarian Reform Law, which hit hard at large landowners. In response, the United States became extremely hostile. On July 7, 1960, President Eisenhower cut the quota of Cuba's vital export, sugar. (In the secret councils of the government, Vice President Nixon proposed an invasion of Cuba. He was later to denounce John F. Kennedy in a presidential campaign television debate for proposing the same plan, and to claim thereafter that *this* was just a ruse to fool people and provide a cover for the Eisenhower invasion plan then in process.) President Kennedy made fine pronouncements about freedom in Latin America. But his administration gave covert aid to the abortive Bay of Pigs invasion—the attempt by Cuban refugees to invade Cuba and retake it with military force. The CIA helped purge the leadership of the refugees' left wing which supported Castro's nationalization of foreign-owned utilities to assure that those who took control of the reconquered colony would be committed to returning all nationalized assets to U.S. corporations. An explicit element of the CIA plan for the invasion was "Operation Forty," which included the assassination, by a hand-picked task force of professional killers, of political leaders who stood in the way of the proposed new regime, and of any other obdurate elements that might oppose a return to the good old days. It was hoped that in the confusion of battle, such killings would go unnoticed and the victims could be depicted as Communists.[5] Luckily for the Cuban people, the U.S. plan for a full-scale counterrevolution was defeated. Since that time, the United States has tried a variety of lower-level moves designed to weaken the Castro regime—from supporting acts of CIA-financed sabotage and terrorism to promoting an economic boycott of Cuba designed to make the Cuban people dissatisfied with their government. The major provocation for this treatment was the determination of the Castro regime to make Cuba's resources serve her own people, instead of the interests of U.S. investors.

U.S. interests in Greece center around strategic access to Middle East oil, domestic refining, interest payments on the Greek national debt, and using Greece as the center for propaganda and intelligence operations in the Mediterranean. The Center Union Party, under the leadership of Andreas Papandreas, threatened these interests. An election was scheduled for 1967 in which it appeared that the Center Union Party would win. A few weeks before the election a right-wing coup was staged which eliminated democracy in Greece. The dictatorship restored the American business community's confidence in the Greek political situation and American

[5] Such a program was carried out by the CIA in Vietnam, but failed to destroy the Vietcong political infrastructure in South Vietnam.

military aid increased. A recent article on Greece by Robert Fitch [6] points out that one of the key beneficiaries of the new regime is Thomas Pappas, a key fund-raiser for the Republican party who has extensive shipping and oil-refining interests in Greece. The Esso-Pappas enterprise in Greece is one of the key economic units in the country—and both Pappas and Nelson Rockefeller (of the Rockefellers who own Esso) were among the coterie that picked Greek-American Spiro Agnew to be part of the Nixon ticket. And after Nixon and Agnew were elected, Pappas accompanied the latter to Greece for a series of private talks with the dictatorship which did much to prop up its image with the Greek people. The dictatorship responded to this help by raising tariffs around Pappas's iron and steel products to protect them from world competition. And, Fitch continues, "over angry opposition from Greece's citrus farmers, the government has allowed Pappas to establish Coca-Cola bottling plants in Athens, Salonika and Patras." All this maneuvering is in the service not of individuals, but of corporations— Standard Oil, Pepsi-Cola, and other firms that benefit from an economic climate in which business is king. The sufferers are the Greek people, whose civil liberties have been suspended and who have seen suspected dissenters jailed and tortured. This kind of thing could not happen and could not be sustained without U.S. support of every sort—and that's precisely what the U.S. investor expects from his government.

The examples could be multiplied endlessly. Only space prevents us from detailing how in country after country around the world the United States supports regimes and policies that are supportive of U.S. economic interests but destructive of the native people. I implore the reader neither to reject this claim as some kind of exaggeration nor to take it on faith, but to read carefully some of the books listed in the bibliography at the end of this chapter, which detail and conclusively prove this claim. It is crucial to be clear about the magnitude of U.S. imperialism, because in the period ahead, as the United States begins to play down its troop involvement in the Vietnam war, apologists for American capitalism will be claiming that this war is the last vestige of imperialism and that a new era has begun.

A LIBERAL HYPOTHESIS

Some liberals agree that America's continued interventions in the internal affairs of other countries are too systematic to be matters of chance or poor judgment alone. Chance or poor judgment cannot account for the inva-

[6] "Greece," *Ramparts* 10, no. 8 (January 1972): 38.

sions of the Dominican Republic, Cambodia, and Vietnam; the CIA war in Laos; the CIA roles in overthrowing the governments of Iran, Guatemala, and Indonesia; and American support for dictatorships around the world. So these liberals lay the blame on the fervent hatred of communism that has plagued American foreign policy since World War II. Nor is this explanation entirely wrong: anticommunism has played an important role in moving people in power to adopt repressive policies and in getting acceptance from the people for these policies. But the explanation is not adequate.

In the first place, American domination of other countries did not begin in response to the 1917 Russian Revolution; it was well underway by 1900. Until the closing of the frontier in 1890, the expansionary needs built into the U.S. economy could be met by the inexorable drive westward. But the closing of the frontier forced the business and industrial community to look abroad, and the period that followed was characterized not only by the conquest of Cuba and the Philippines, but also by renewal of the Monroe Doctrine in a form that meant complete U.S. domination of Latin America. While the period since World War II has seen a vast expansion of the number of areas dominated by the United States, nothing in the basic policy of economic expansion is qualitatively new and can be attributed simply to a fearful response to a newly powerful Communist "threat."

Moreover, anticommunism is not a spontaneous eruption on the part of the masses. On the contrary, it has been systematically indoctrinated into American minds by a long, intensive campaign. Millions of workers were close to Communist ideas and organizations in the 1930s, and during World War II the Soviet Union was an ally and a key element in the defeat of Nazism. The emergence of strong anticommunism must itself be explained. Who fostered it? Why was it fostered? Whose interests did it serve? Many Americans undoubtedly developed an antipathy to communism based on what they knew of Stalin and his activity.[7] But why did the government

[7] The Nazi-Soviet pact certainly disillusioned many Americans. Many people could understand why the pact was necessary, given the failure of Britain or the United States to agree at that time to any mutual defense agreement with the Soviet Union. In fact, many capitalist policy makers were still considering siding with Germany in any struggle against the Communists, while others actively urged neutrality and quietly hoped that both sides would be destroyed—the best of all possible worlds for the capitalist regimes of the United States and Britain. But while many could understand the necessity of the pact as a short-term solution to the immediate threat of war, it was much harder to understand the complete turnabout in the American Communist party's line on fascism. Instead of explaining the pact as the product of a difficult necessity, the American CP totally changed its emphasis from antifascist

and business leaders spend so much time building up the "Communist threat," circulating and strengthening accounts they knew to be false (that, for example, Russia would take over the world unless stopped, or that Moscow-based Communists were about to take over the U.S. government), unless some deeper interest was involved? George Kennan, Dean Acheson, Averell Harriman, Dean Rusk, Walter Rostow, Robert McNamara, and Henry Kissinger are among the most brilliant men the business and academic communities could loan to the government. Their policies are not products of mindless confusions or muddled thinking, but rather represent their views of the best way to serve both their class and the business community whose economic interests they identify with the general interest of all Americans. It is a bit disingenuous for liberals to explain U.S. foreign policy in terms of anti-Communist myths (or as Senator Fulbright suggests, in terms of an "arrogance of power") without explaining why these myths arise and what their function is for a particular class in America. At the very least, such an explanation obscures precisely what needs to be explained.

Finally, anticommunism is totally inadequate for explaining the relations between the USSR and the U.S. in the 1960s or between China and the U.S. in the early 1970s. In both cases, the supposed hard-nosed opposition to communism was modified to fit more immediate American economic interests.[8] Indeed, despite the protests of the many genuinely ideological anti-Communists in Congress, policy makers have been remarkably flexible in distinguishing between Communist countries that have been willing to accommodate themselves to American imperialism and those that have refused to do so. This reached a point of absurdity when President Nixon visited China while continuing to bomb the Vietnamese, in continuation of a war that had been justified on the grounds that China was trying to expand its influence in Southeast Asia. If the conclusion of the Vietnam war is accompanied by a resurgence of anti-Russian or anti-Chinese propaganda, we can be sure that new military "gaps" will be invented to explain an increase in U.S. military spending. Or perhaps we will rediscover that Cuba is a military threat.

The liberal explanation of the world met its most severe challenge with

united front to a new anticapitalist militancy. And once the United States came into the war on Russia's side in 1942, the CP shifted back again. A policy bound to support the mistrust of Communists and the suspicion that they are inherently dishonest.

[8] In the case of China, for instance, the policy was influenced more by the need to offset growing Japanese economic power in the Pacific than to achieve any significant exploitation of Chinese markets.

the war in Vietnam. It seemed more than a bit implausible that men as intelligent as McNamara or Rostow or Kissinger really believed we were fighting for democracy, when the dictatorial and repressive nature of South Vietnam under Diem, Ky, and Thieu was obvious. Nor was it plausible to believe—as so many liberals intimated in their pleas to the antiwar movement to enter Democratic party politics—that the problem was the evil or stupid men who had gained power while we weren't looking. Much more plausible were the actual words of these policy makers: the United States had global interests and the loss of Vietnam would adversely affect our hold on other parts of the "free world."

THE FREE WORLD

What are these global interests and why must the United States fight for them? In attempting to answer this, let us begin by discovering common characteristics of these "free world" countries that enable us to list them under one rubric. There is no common political feature. The "free world," after all, includes countries with parliamentary governments (e.g., Britain, Italy and Germany); and dictatorships (e.g., Spain, Portugal, Thailand, Saudi Arabia, Greece, Taiwan, South Korea, and a host of others in Latin America). Some of these countries allow a "free" press, but most do not. Some have elections, most do not. Some have formal guarantees of political equality for all people and some have racism built into their legal structure. Nor are all the countries in the "free world" solid allies with the United States in its political struggles with the USSR and China. What, then, do the countries of the "free world" have in common? In what sense are the countries within that world "free"? The common feature is economic: all countries in the "free world" are free for American economic penetration and exploitation. It was precisely this loss of markets and sources of investment in China, Eastern Europe, and Cuba that so infuriated the rulers of this country about the "Communist takeovers." It is certainly a bit hypocritical for people who are "upset" about the loss of civil liberties in the "communist" countries of Eastern Europe to be oblivious to the absence of these same liberties in most of the "free world." But the rulers of this country are not being hypocritical when they talk about a country being lost to the "free world." They have in mind something very real and concrete: their ability to exploit the country economically.

Talk about economic exploitation may seem a bit strong, and since we use the term exploitation a great deal we should state what we mean by it. Exploitation involves an unfair advantage to one party in a relationship with another. This unfair advantage derives from some structural feature of the relationship (e.g., that he's the boss while I'm the worker; not that he happened to get in line for the limited number of seats at this movie before me), and allows the exploiter to benefit materially at the expense of the other person or group. Our notions of fairness, by the way, usually imply that each party to an arrangement has an equal opportunity to achieve his or her goals. Moreover, the goals must be genuinely open— i.e., people's views and expectations must not be so conditioned by those who benefit from the system that they do not seek goals that would conflict with the rulers' benefits.

Imperialism is not a uniquely American phenomenon. On the contrary, it is only since World War II that the United States has emerged as the world's leading imperialist power. Before then, Britain, France, Germany, Italy, and Japan, as the leading capitalist powers, had all played an imperialist role, and it was only after the war had crippled them economically and militarily that the United States was able to begin to take over their former colonies. It would be hard to argue that imperialism emerged in each of these countries for some mysterious psychological reason ("lust for power" or "stupid and evil leadership") rather than as the result of the need for economic expansion. And indeed, it was precisely the conflict among the economic interests of these imperialist countries that led to both world wars.

One reason it is more difficult to recognize modern imperialism than the older varieties is that imperialism takes different forms at different historical moments. The traditional form was colonialism, in which the mother country actually ran the political and economic life of the imperialized country, directly choosing its rulers and having formal political sovereignty over its political life. More recently, a new form of imperialism has developed in which the mother country dominates not through formal legal mechanisms, but through a de facto control over the economic life of the imperialized country combined with a readiness to intervene in its political life (e.g., through coups d'état or direct military invasions) when the mother country's investments are threatened. Since America entered imperialist circles very late, it never acquired many political colonies (although Hawaii and Puerto Rico are nothing to sneeze at) and had to rely primarily on the second form of imperialism. It was expedient for the United States to denounce the "colonialism" that allowed its rivals to dominate the economic markets U.S. businessmen coveted. But once a vacuum had been created by the weakening of the other capitalist countries, the United States was quick to step in with its smoother and less obvious forms of economic and political domination.

The radical analysis of American society holds that American imperialism is not the result of stupidity or evil in the men in power, but rather that it flows from the necessities of capitalism. What is it about capitalism that forces it to adopt an imperialist policy? The answer is complex, and I will not attempt here either to give an exhaustive account nor to rank the factors in the order of their importance.

FOREIGN MARKETS

The need for foreign markets has been a recurrent theme in American history, iterated by the highest officeholders and policy makers. Consider, for example, Dean Acheson's testimony before the special Congressional Committee on Post-War Economic Policy and Planning, in which he warned that the only way to avoid another depression would be to ensure adequate foreign markets. "You don't have a problem of production. The United States has unlimited creative energy. The important thing is markets. . . . We could argue for quite a while that under a different system in this country you could use the entire production of the country in the United States . . . you find you must look to other markets and those markets are abroad. . . . If I am wrong about that, then all the argument falls by the wayside, but my contention is that we cannot have full employment and prosperity in the United States without foreign markets." [9]

Why do we need foreign markets? Well, beyond the obvious—that they produce increased profits—another theory has been put forward. The United States produces more goods than it can consume and therefore must find markets for them abroad. Several qualifications must be stated immediately if this formulation is to make sense. The United States is a class-stratified society in which vast differentials exist in the distribution of wealth and income. The statement that some goods cannot be consumed within the country does not mean that no one could use them, but that not enough people have the money to buy them. A simple rule of thumb in a capitalist society is that not everyone can afford to buy what he needs, much less what he wants. "Why is this a problem?" you might ask. "Why don't the owners of the factories just produce fewer goods?" Some do, and cut employment. But decreased production means a cutback both on profits

[9] Hearing Before the Committee on Post-War Economic Policy and Planning, House of Representatives, 78th Congress, 2nd Session (1944) cited in William Appleman Williams, *The Tragedy of American Diplomacy* (New York: Delta, 1959), pp. 235–36.

and on employment, neither of which is acceptable to the capitalist class. Capitalists do not want to cut back on profits both because they risked investment in the first place precisely to maximize their profits, and because they continually need more money invested in their firms if they are to be able to modernize their equipment to enable their goods to compete with other goods. Nor do they want to cut down on employment if they can avoid it since, in the United States, large-scale unemployment has traditionally been accompanied by a militant labor movement that can ask some very embarrassing questions of the capitalists. Why, then, don't the capitalists redistribute the wealth of the country internally so that more people can afford to buy their goods? Because the wealth would have to be redistributed *away* from someone, and that someone would be precisely the owners of the industries seeking to maximize their wealth. And since it is these very people who have control over the political system, redistribution is not considered seriously as a possible solution. The obvious solution is to try to find new markets that will allow the industrialists to sell their goods without cutting either profits or employment—and these markets are to be found abroad—in Europe, Japan, and in the Third World.

One Marxist objection to this account is that it is much too abstract: it talks about the capitalist class as a whole trying to determine what is in its interest, and then acting accordingly. In fact, one group has this function—the government. It does try to decide what is in the best interest of the capitalist class as a whole, and then act on it. And perhaps it was from this standpoint that Dean Acheson was talking. But in real life very few private businesses make investment decisions on the basis of the interest of their class as a whole. Rather, their concern is to make more profits for their own firms. And the goods produced in the United States for world trade are only a small part of the imperialist picture.

"But even if we do need foreign markets, so what? Isn't it to the advantage of the Third World that we sell them goods they can't produce themselves?" Yes, but we first have to ensure that there *is* a market for the goods, and this involves on the one hand creating a need for goods that people previously lived without (e.g., private automobiles or women's cosmetics) and on the other hand forcibly preventing them from industrializing their own countries so that they can produce their own goods. If they did that, the American goods, which would have to bear the cost of transport, would have to sell for a higher price and hence would be unable to compete. Moreover, since the cost of labor is lower in the Third World than in the United States, goods could be produced more cheaply there. Consequently, the imperialist country must ensure that the imperialized country does not industrialize, at least not in the fields in which the imperialist country's industries predominate. At different stages in history this has been accomplished by different means. In the early 1800s, England actually dismantled factories in India and sent them back to England. As Charles Bettelheim points out, "India, still an exporter of manufactured products at the end of the 18th century, became an importer. From 1815 to 1832 India's cotton exports dropped by 92%. In 1850 India was buying one quarter of Britain's cotton exports. All industrial products shared this fate. The ruin of the traditional trades and crafts was the result of British commercial policy." [10]

At other times, the mother country has been content to ensure that the dominated country keeps its economy on a few-crop basis rather than attempting to industrialize. Thus the colony supplies raw materials to the mother country and other industrialized countries and then has to buy back the finished products. A worldwide division of labor develops in which the underdeveloped countries are compelled to remain as suppliers and consumers to the developed countries' factories. So Cuba was directed to develop reliance on sugar; Bolivia on tin; Egypt, Sudan, and Uganda on cotton; Venezuela, Iraq, Saudi Arabia, Kuwait on oil; Guatemala and Colombia on coffee; Honduras, Costa Rica, Ecuador on coffee and bananas; Senegal on ground nuts and products derived from them, and so on. Since the natural resources of England, Canada, Silesia, the Ruhr, and similar areas did not lead to monoproduction in these countries, we cannot argue that monoproduction is the result of "natural" conditions. Rather, many of the monocultures have been introduced from abroad (e.g., natural rubber in Southeast Asia; coffee in Java, Ceylon, and Brazil; cotton in Egypt and the Sudan; sugar cane in Cuba; etc.).

RAW MATERIALS

If Third World industrialization were to progress sufficiently to enable its nations to use a large part of their own raw materials, the prices of these materials would rise considerably for U.S. corporations. Getting these raw materials cheaply is one of the chief needs of American industry. As Gabriel Kolko points out, the significance of raw materials is qualitative rather than quantitative: the absence of even a small quantity of a needed raw material may have drastic consequences. "The steel industry must add approximately 13 pounds of manganese to each ton of steel and though

10 Charles Bettelheim, *India Independent*, trans. W. A. Caswell (London: Mac-Gibbon & Kee, Ltd., 1968).

the weight and value of the increase is a tiny fraction of the total, a modern diversified steel industry *must* have manganese. . . ." [11] In 1960 a greater percentage of many of these vitally necessary raw materials was coming from the Third World than ever before: the trend in the United States was not toward more self-reliance, but toward more dependence on obtaining these materials abroad. The United States imported 32 percent of its iron ore, 98 percent of its bauxite, 35 percent of its lead, 60 percent of its zinc, and 46 percent of its copper. It was importing almost 60 percent of its wool, all of its cocoa, coffee, and bananas, and well over half of its sugar supply. Moreover, much of what we need comes from the Third World countries the United States strives to dominate.

> Over half of U.S. iron ore imports in 1960 came from Venezuela and three equally precarious Latin American countries. Over half the known world reserves of manganese are in Russia and China, and most of the remainder is in Brazil, India, Gabon and South Africa. South Africa and Rhodesia account for nearly all of the world's chromium reserves, Cuba and New Caledonia for half the nickel, China for over $2/3$ the tungsten, Northern Rhodesia, Congo and Peru for well over $2/3$ of the foreign copper reserves. Guyana has about six times the American reserves of bauxite, and Chican has three times, while Malaya, Indonesia and Thailand alone have $2/3$ of the world tin reserves, with Bolivia and the Congo possessing most of the balance. Only zinc and lead, among the major metals, are in politically stable regions, from the American viewpoint. [12]

Nor are American companies interested in raw materials only for domestic use. Many of the raw materials are sold to foreign markets. The key consideration for American firms is to have control over the sources of raw materials. Control allows industries to expand with relative confidence that the raw materials will still be available. Control also guarantees that no other country will have access to the same raw materials and undersell you in the world market. This explains why capitalist countries compete so vigorously for control of raw materials: even if a country cannot use a particular raw material now or cannot use more than a certain percentage of it, they must be sure that another country does not get hold of it and start selling it for less, hence forcing the first country to sell for less (and

[11] Gabriel Kolko, *The Roots of American Foreign Policy* (Boston: Beacon Press, 1969), p. 50.
[12] *Ibid.*, p. 53.

hence lower its profit). This leads to the need to hoard raw materials that may not even be needed.

"What's wrong with a country using raw materials from some other country? The steel industry will need manganese even under socialism, won't it?" Yes. The problem is not that the capitalist countries get raw materials from the Third World, but that the profit motive forces them to take away as much as possible in exchange for as little as possible. Thus, instead of paying for the raw material, the capitalist country often owns the fields or the mines from which it comes, paying the host country only a minimal export tax, plus a percentage of royalties on some exports. If the Venezuelan people owned and controlled their own oil, for example, they could sell it on the world market for its full price. In addition, they might decide to reduce the quantity of oil they *did* sell, since Venezuela's known oil reserves will be exhausted in about twelve years if the high annual production rate is maintained. But at the moment the decision is out of the hands of the Venezuelans: outside firms decide, and they decide in the knowledge that their concessions are scheduled to expire in 1984.

PROFITS FROM INVESTMENTS

The main spur to imperialism is the fundamental law of capitalist enterprise: capitalist firms must expand or die. You have to keep growing, so that you can get more money, so that you can reinvest that money to perfect your technology, so that you can produce your goods more cheaply and efficiently. If you do not, your competition will undersell you and you will have to go out of business. At the same time, you need to have a high profit return to investors, otherwise they will stop investing in your firm. Moreover, once the price of your stock starts to decline on the market, you are less likely to get the loans and credits that will give you capital for expansion. So it is crucial to keep profits high and total income expanding.

In the present monopoly stage of capitalism, a few large corporations dominate the domestic economy. Consequently some aspects of competition have been somewhat alleviated. IBM, for example, simply has no effective competitors, and its main reason for selling abroad is the vast potential market for profits. But many firms which are virtual monopolies in the domestic economy are still threatened by foreign competition. American auto and steel companies, for example, face competition from Germany and Japan. So do many other important industries. Unless they continue to expand, or unless there are available other mechanisms, such

70

as direct government aid in the form of subsidies or tariffs, they will eventually be in serious trouble.

One reason many investors found the Third World a good place to accrue profits is that labor can be exploited there to a higher degree than in the large industrial countries. This reflects several factors in the underdeveloped countries: the very low level of wages; the long working day; the persistence of child labor; the absence of social legislation giving workers minimum protections; the widespread use of forced labor or labor paid in kind. In 1947–48, the first year of India's political independence, the hourly wage in India's textile industry was 9.4 to 12 American cents as compared with $1.04 to $1.06 in the United States. Nor can lower wages be explained by a lower level of needs: the workers in these countries live in conditions of extreme poverty and hunger. The result is that the U.S. firms' rate of profit on direct investment in the Third World is even higher than their rate of profit in Europe. In 1967 the rate of profit amounted to 12.3 percent in Latin America, 14 percent in Asia, and 19.7 percent in Africa, as against 10.1 percent on direct investment in Canada, Western Europe, and Australia.[13]

Foreign investments are sometimes claimed to improve the conditions of the people in the country in which the investments are made. A few factors should be kept in mind:

1. More money leaves the backward nations than is invested in them currently by the developed nations. U.S. Department of Commerce figures show that in the period 1950–65 U.S. corporations made investments in Europe of $8.1 billion and brought back an income of $5.5 billion for a net flow of $2.6 billion to Europe. But in Latin America, U.S. corporations invested $3.8 billion and extracted an income of $11.3 billion, for a net flow of $7.9 billion to the United States.

2. Much of the profit that U.S. companies make from the Third World comes from extractive industries, not from goods manufactured for consumption in the Third World. Thus, even in an earlier period, when U.S. investments in the Third World may have been higher than the amounts taken out in profits, the investment was primarily in industries that provided no new source of needed goods for the people of the area. Many of the goods produced in the Third World for domestic consumption are small consumer items (e.g., transistor radios, television sets, Pepsi-Cola, etc.) which the people do not need and, before extensive advertising, did not want.

13 *Survey of Current Business* 18, no. 10 (1968): 24–25.

3. Investments create jobs, but it does not follow that there would be no jobs without them. If, the Third World people were to nationalize their raw materials and sell them on the open market, the same jobs would still be available, but higher wages could be paid for them.

If these countries could do it alone, why don't they? Why don't they industrialize and employ their own labor? Why do they depend on the United States? Part of the answer is that at least some of the investing firms have influence with the U.S. government, and persuaded it to ensure that no political group will come to power that would nationalize resources and begin to industrialize in fields in which the United States predominates. Gunboat diplomacy, whether in Vietnam or in Latin America, does tend to limit a country's alternatives.

But even if the Third World countries could get out from under the direct political-military influence of the United States and other capitalist countries, they still would not be able to industrialize easily. They do not have the wealth, the accumulated capital, to begin this costly venture. Why not, if they are so rich in raw materials? Because for the past four hundred years their wealth has been robbed, sometimes "legally" and sometimes not, by the countries of Western Europe and by the United States. Many Western European countries depended on the pillage of the Third World to amass the wealth that allowed them to finance their industrial revolutions. For instance, the total amount of gold and silver exported from Latin America between 1503 and 1660 has been estimated at over 500 million gold pesos. Between 1650 and 1780 the Dutch East India Company made over 600 million gold florins on what it took out of Indonesia. And the profits made from the labor of blacks in the British West Indies amounted to over 200 million pounds sterling. Between 1750 and 1800 British plunder from India has been estimated at between 100 and 150 million pounds sterling. As Ernest Mandel points out, "for the period 1760–1780 the profits from India and the West Indies alone more than doubled the accumulation of money available for rising industry. . . . The chief victims of primitive accumulation were, more than the yeomen driven from their farms by sheepraising or the journeymen of the crafts left without work in the towns and forced to work for a miserable pittance in poor-relief workshops, the indios condemned to mita (forced labor), the Bantus sold as slaves, the wretched inhabitants of the Hongy islands, exterminated by the expeditions of the Dutch East India Company, the people of the Mogul Empire, pitilessly plundered by the agents of the British East India Company. It was this systematic plundering of four continents during the commercial expansion of the 16th to 18th centuries that created the conditions for the decisive lead acquired by Europe from the industrial revolution onward." [14] And it is almost impossible to evaluate the economic damage done to Africa through the theft of millions of black people dragged away to serve as slaves to build up the economy of the newly emerging American capitalism.

So if the Third World now faces problems in the accumulation of capital, this must be understood in the historical context in which the capitalist world has for centuries robbed it of the necessary capital. The predominance of America and Western Europe over the Third World is a testimony to acquisitiveness and ruthlessness, not to special intelligence or wisdom.

It is sometimes thought that along with investment comes foreign aid, and that this aid has substantially bettered the conditions of the Third World. It is important to note, however, that this aid (usually far less than 1 percent of the industrial nations' GNP) has for the most part gone to undertakings referred to as the "industrial infrastructure"—road construction or the building of the dams, canals, harbors, and railroads necessary for the economic penetration of the underdeveloped countries. The primary users of these facilities are the foreign firms that extract raw materials to ship them abroad. Needless to say, the average peasant needs a new road or railroad far less than he needs more food and health care, and whereas the railroad or the port could be used to transport those necessities to him, they are in fact used primarily to strengthen the economic stranglehold of the imperialist country. The cost of developing this infrastructure might well be prohibitive for a private firm, but that is not who pays for the foreign aid. It is the working people of the imperialist country. Their taxes go to increase imperialist profits.

A tremendous amount of what is called foreign aid is in fact military aid aimed at stabilizing political regimes that give advantages to American industry. This military aid does not in any way benefit the average foreign citizen. Moreover, increasingly the aid is taking the form of long-term loans which must be spent on U.S. products, hence creating markets for our goods. Further, the loans must be repaid in dollars, which forces the developing nation to export goods that the developed nations need. And since developed nations do not need finished goods as much as raw materials, the loans tend to force the developing nations back into the pattern of dependency and monoproduction from which the developed countries benefit. Finally, when the aid takes the form of directly needed goods, e.g., food, it has often been tied with the most vulgar of political devices de-

[14] Ernest Mandel, *Marxist Economic Theory* (New York: Monthly Review Press, 1968), p. 45.

signed to advance American economic domination. During a recent famine in India, the United States refused to commit itself to shipping badly needed wheat until India promised not to develop her own fertilizer factories but to allow U.S. fertilizer plants there to retain control of the market.

We have already cited figures which show that from 1950–65 investment in Europe was much larger than in the Third World, although profits from the Third World were much greater. This may suggest that the Third World is unimportant in the imperialist picture. But some of the profit from investment in Europe comes from American-owned European firms, or firms in which there are heavy investments. And these firms make profits in the Third World. Moreover, while Third World investments and markets may not be of crucial importance to the entire ruling class, they are extremely important to some of the more important elements of that class. The Rockefellers' interests in Standard Oil give them a very strong interest in Third World developments: and a representative of the Rockefeller brothers' interests has served either as secretary of state, assistant secretary of state, or special adviser to the President on foreign affairs in every administration for the past 30 years. The importance of Third World domination to the United States must not be judged by asking how it affects lesser powers in the ruling class. The ruling class of the United States is not run democratically.

U.S. investments in Europe and Japan are a different story. They were made possible by the blows that the European and Japanese economies suffered in World War II. American investors were able to rebuild the European economies, and simultaneously to avoid the tariffs that were being thrown up by the Europeans to protect themselves as recovery began by investing in firms within the walls of the tariffs. American economic penetration of Europe and Japan was extremely ingenious. Robert Fitch, editor of *Ramparts* magazine, gives the following lively account of how it all happened:

> Let's consider the postwar trade and monetary system . . . as a gigantic poker game between the U.S. and the other capitalist countries. The U.S., because it had most of the world's gold and real resources, set itself up as the house. Any country wanting to get in the game had to play with dollar chips. . . . As the game started out, the U.S. began to "lose" the first few hands. It lost in the sense that it ran balance of payments deficits. Generally speaking, the Europeans and the Japanese won. Because they kept on winning it was easy for them to exchange their domestic currencies

for house money—the dollar chips. . . . There was a big difference though in the consequences of a loss for the U.S. and the other losers. A balance of payment deficit on the part of an ordinary player meant a loss of foreign exchange—goods. But since the U.S. paper money served as house money—since it doubled as the capitalist world's trading and reserve currency—a balance of payments deficit created no such hardship for the U.S. Nothing the printing press couldn't take care of in a few days. . . .

Gradually the European players' attitude towards this rich American who kept on losing began to change. At first it was nice simply to take his chips. Now however they worried about what to do with their surplus hoards. How could they cash in? At the same time, they began to notice that the American "loser" had been running another game on the side. With the same dollars that he'd been bringing into the game in nearly unlimited quantities, he'd been buying up the mortgages of their businesses. . . . The Americans had lots of debts, in the form of dollar chips held by Europeans, but they'd accumulated an enormous swag in the form of holdings in European business.[15]

U.S. investments in Europe thus grew tremendously. In 1960 they amounted to $6.7 billion; in 1970, about $24.5 billion. The effect on Europeans is profound. They resent the fact that their economy is permeated by U.S.-dominated firms. But this domination ties them to the United States and thus makes them fearful of a collapse in the U.S. economy that might hurt them as well. Similarly, many U.S. multinational corporations have conflicting interests. Their domestic investments may benefit from greater American economic nationalism, but since they also have investments in the economies of other countries they do not want to cause economic strains that would reduce their foreign profits. And they certainly do not want to see foreign governments emerge that might nationalize their investments.

At least fifty major U.S. corporations now derive over $400 million, or 40 percent of their total revenues, overseas. Included in this list are not only the big oil companies, but also manufacturing corporations such as IBM, ITT, Ford, GM, Eastman Kodak, Proctor & Gamble, Dow Chemical, Dupont. Typically, a multinational corporation makes a higher rate of profit on foreign sales than on domestic sales. To believe, as liberals seem to, that the U.S. role in trying to control the economic and political life

---

[15] Unpublished manuscript on Imperialism by Robert Fitch.

of foreign countries could be changed by the election of liberal Democrats, is to miss the whole context in which the powerhouses of the U.S. economy demand a stable international situation so that they can rationally plan their profitable investments.

THE MILITARY

The growth of the military is partly a result of the other sources of imperialism, and partly an independent fact in its own right. The unique role of the military in the structure of imperialism can be seen once we realize that it is not simply a service arm but a major business in its own right. Each year a huge amount of money—roughly about 10 percent of the GNP and well over 40 percent of the national budget—is sunk into military and military-related expenditures. These expenditures have one feature that makes them very desirable for manufacturers: no firm or individual has to buy them. They are bought by the government, and hence paid for by everybody. So military expenditures are a partial and important way of dealing with the problem of surplus. The people are taxed heavily to permit the corporations to produce goods no one can use. This production-for-waste meets spendidly the basic requirements of capitalist production. The owners of the factories make big profits, written into their contracts, and are able to ensure high levels of domestic employment: 1 out of every 11 persons in the work force is employed in "defense" or defense related activity.

But if the government is willing to spend money to create profits and employment, one might ask, why does it not spend it to produce socially necessary goods instead of military hardware that is often outdated before it comes off the assembly line? Because this would require the government to compete with the corporations and thus would cause havoc in the existing economic arrangements. If the government started to provide mass transportation it would hurt not only the auto makers but also the gas and oil industry. The ideal solution would be for the government to pay existing corporations to do what they are doing and expand their operations, thus ensuring high profits for the corporations, high employment, and a high level of goods. Here an ideological problem emerges: the government would be taking money from the people and giving it to corporations, which would thereby get a high level of profit. But the people have been led to believe that the whole justification for corporate profit is the fact that corporations take some risk with their investments. As the percentage of his income used to subsidize corporation profit went up, the taxpayer would become more concerned about why he has to spend his money to ensure corporate profits rather than for his personal purposes. The government does try to get away with this use of tax money on a small scale (e.g., in developing the communications satellite and then giving it to ITT), but the huge expenditures we are talking about require some kind of justification. Defense it is.

Virtually anyone can be convinced that it is proper to spend tens of billions on all sorts of production ventures to defend the country against aggression. The problem is to convince people that a threat to the country does exist. This is no small trick for the only country to have emerged from World War II unscathed, with a dazzling industrial and military capacity, and with sole ownership of the atomic bomb. Nevertheless, an intensive campaign of indoctrination enabled U.S. leaders to paint the "spheres of influence" privately negotiated for the United States, France, and Britain as reasonable extensions of "free world" influence and the "sphere of influence" obtained by Russia as a naked grab for power. By stirring up mania against communism, by making people feel that they were threatened both from without (the war-devastated Soviet Union) and from within (anyone who was in favor of socialism or who questioned the intelligence of a blind anticommunism abroad), the business interests were able to provide the popular base for the Truman Doctrine, the Marshall Plan, the Korean war, and the huge defense expenditures that have followed. Some of the fears of the business community were justified: communism was spreading as more and more people began to question the rationality of capitalism. So the rebuilding of Europe vastly helped the U.S. economy at the same time that it prevented Communists from winning greater popular support in European elections. The Communist threat could deflect attention from the problems of a class-stratified society that had never successfully dealt with the legacy of its prewar depression at the same time it provided a rationale for sufficient government spending to make a serious impact on employment and surplus problems. The consequence of these military expenditures is the growth of a huge military establishment charged with the task of protecting us from "threat," and more importantly, with providing the kind of stable world atmosphere that permits American corporations to flourish. To do this, armies must be prepared to move against any force that threatens a potential or actual U.S. market or source of raw materials.

One problem that develops for the corporate rulers when they rely on a military strategy and the building of a military-industrial complex is that the ideology they use to defend these ventures may begin to take on a life of its own. Thus, anticommunism may originate in the need of the

corporations, but as an idea it cannot be controlled at will, and may sometimes yield unexpected results that are not completely desired or con-
trollable by the ruling class which fostered the idea in the first place. The
idea of anticommunism may be introduced because it is functional for the
ruling class at a particular historical moment, but the people who accept
it—from preachers to congressmen to generals—do so because they think
it is right, not because they think it is expedient. And so the idea itself
becomes a partial political force which has to be reckoned with, even
when it limits the flexibility of those who introduced it. Hence the odd
spectacle of the early 1960s, when liberal members of the ruling class were
faced with popular and congressional disapproval of economic deals with
Eastern European countries. Some modifications of the ideology was
needed if businessmen were to continue to make profits: this was the
function of "détente" and the political scientists' contention that we could
distinguish between good and bad Communists on the basis of their willingness to trade with us and to cool down anticapitalist struggles.

Much persuasive research work has been written to show that the leaders
of the military, both civilian and military, have always shared the class
ends of the rulers of the economy. When they retire, military leaders often
find jobs in defense industries. Military extremists are often relieved of
their jobs, and there have been no coups or even any serious antigovern-
ment alliances between political and military forces.

Nevertheless, the military has a limited autonomy that can be used as a
serious pressure toward imperialist adventures. That the policies pursued
do not conflict with established economic interests does not tell the whole
story. When a variety of possible actions are available that do not conflict
with the interests of the economic rulers, the one chosen may be determined
by the pressure of the military. And sometimes the decisions commit the
government to long-term conflicts previously unanticipated. For example,
the war in Vietnam may be completely consistent with America's general
policy of dominating the world and its particular interest in preserving
existing markets and sources of raw material in Southeast Asia and keeping
it open for further economic penetration. Also, the first escalations of the
war may have helped our sagging economy and provided a boost at a
crucial moment. But the escalation of the war in late 1964 and early 1965
might not have occurred without strong pressure from the military and
the possible falsification of information about the incidents in Tonkin Bay.
Similarly, strong pressure from the military may have been the final
factor in the escalation of the war into Cambodia, with all that may
portend for a wider Southeast Asia war. Although the general content of

American foreign policy is set by the requirements of capitalism, a variety of separate forces may move us at any particular moment in one direction or another. One such important force is the hugely swollen military establishment, which was created in response to the needs of capital but is not at every moment simply a passive receptor of Wall Street's messages.

PAX AMERICANA

America is not a militaristic society in the sense that it places stress on the active use of the military. For capitalists' purposes it would be adequate for the military to exist as a source of employment and as a profit generator. America does not seek wars: it seeks a Pax Americana, a peace imposed on the world by American might which ensures to America's businesses the continued right to exploit people around the globe. The government's basic policies are not produced by pressure from the military, but by the requirements of a capitalist economy. If America is at war, the ultimate responsibility cannot be placed with the military but with the economy the military serves. Liberal establishment ideologues such as John Kenneth Galbraith may try to focus our attention on ways of getting control over the military, but in fact the problem for the majority of Americans is how to get the economy working in the interests of all people instead of a select elite.

There is no Pax Americana for most people. American power is feared and hated. Imperialism is not just an abstract economic term: it has real consequences for the lives of the people in the countries it affects. When the people of India have their factories dismantled, when the Venezuelans sell their oil at less than one-third its worth, when the Jamaicans lose their bauxite, when scores of countries are prevented from industrializing and then find the prices of their crops sliding on the world market at the whim of a commodities exchange magnate, the result is untold suffering for the peoples of these countries. This suffering manifests itself not only in a relatively short life expectancy, but also by physical and emotional suffering throughout life. The most prevalent and obvious effect is the wide-scale hunger and starvation that occurs when the Third World country cannot get enough money to buy adequate food, or is forced to sell its food, or to grow nonfood crops. Because poor countries do not have adequate health care facilities, even those not destroyed by hunger spend much of their lives suffering from diseases that could have been prevented or cured or alleviated had more money been available for medicine, hospitals, and training of personnel. Then there is the suffering that comes from inadequate housing, clothing, and heating. Less quantifiable but equally outrageous is the suffering that comes from ignorance and fear, from the dehumanization of virtual slavery, and from the setting of brother against brother in local wars and antagonisms that the imperialist countries fan to turn the attention of the exploited away from their real enemies. I have attempted a dispassionate analytic account of the functioning of imperialism, but it would be inhuman not to be infuriated at the pain and suffering this system causes. It is a system that has declared war on the majority of the world's people. The one million-plus Vietnamese civilians who have been murdered by U.S. imperialism are only the latest victims of an economy built on the murder and enslavement of tens of millions of blacks and on the domination of ever larger numbers of people.

To understand the significance of the Vietnamese struggle, we must look at the prevalent forms of political life in the Third World. Why do the exploited countries allow this exploitation to continue? When they break their colonial ties, why do they remain in the imperialist orbit? Because their governments are responsive not to the needs of their own people, but to the interests of a small ruling elite. Many of these countries are made up of a very small upper class, often less than 0.5 percent of the population, which owns most of the land and which controls the government; a middle class of some 3 to 8 percent of the population, made up of traditional merchants plus newer elements that have grown up around government service and servicing the interests of the foreign corporations; and a huge peasantry that lives by working the soil and paying out of its crops for rent and tax to the upper class. The vast wealth the upper class has expropriated from the labor of the peasants is protected by the colonialists and imperialists. In exchange for their right to exploit the raw materials of the country and to prohibit industrialization, the imperialists provide the ruling class with material aid, military aid, and, if necessary, with military intervention to preserve class dominance. Sometimes, the ruling circle seeks to strengthen its position by dispossessing some of the large landholders and by creating a new class of landholding peasants who in turn exploit the majority of the peasant population. This is the liberal plan for land reform.

In this situation, the middle classes often split between those who side with the ruling group and those who feel that the price of continued economic exploitation by the imperialist country is too high to pay. This latter group often sides with the peasantry and even leads fights for national liberation, though its interest in so doing may only be to set itself up as the new ruling class. Sometimes, however, it becomes engulfed in the tide of the revolutionary goal of withdrawing the country altogether from the sphere of capitalist investment and economic penetration. This is what happened in China, for example.

Under normal circumstances, the ruling class, aided by its U.S.-financed, trained and equipped army, can deal with local peasant insurgence before it involves masses of people. But when it cannot, as in the case of Vietnam, the U.S. Army can be counted on to maintain the ruling class in power. In the future the mechanism may be more subtle: the United States may succeed in creating regional counterinsurgency forces, such as the inter-American force to be composed of joint armies from all the dictatorships the United States supports in Latin America that has been proposed by the Pentagon. Originally, the United States had hoped that the United Nations would serve this purpose of camouflaging U.S. imperial ambitions and preserving the Pax Americana. But the United Nations, though it took this role in Korea late, refused when more Third World countries began to have a say in its voting.

It is in this context that we must understand the domino theory which has been advanced to explain our involvement in the war in Vietnam. Its more sophisticated rendition tells us that if the peasants succeed in Vietnam, their message—that one can struggle successfully against American imperialism—will spread and will encourage peasants around the world to struggle against American exploitation in their countries. Faced with the cutting off of raw materials and markets, the United States would face a monumental economic crisis that would threaten the very existence of capitalism. So the message must be stopped. Moreover, if we were to abandon Vietnam, it would cause great fear among the large landowners who are our allies in the Third World. They would rightly ask themselves if they could count on the United States to fight to the end against their own insurgent forces. If not, they might perhaps feel compelled to make a better accommodation with their own people—by raising the tax on some of the raw materials U.S. corporations are taking out of the country, by nationalizing some U.S.-owned companies, by setting up domestically owned factories. It is to the advantage of the United States to head off such developments by showing that it is in fact loyal to the ruling elite of Vietnam, no matter how corrupt and unpopular it is. On the other hand, as the liberals argue, if you can't win in Vietnam, better give it up and make your stand in some area more vital to U.S. economy.

One of the peculiar characteristics of capitalism in its imperialist stage is that the class struggle, previously fought out primarily in national terms, becomes an international struggle between what might be termed bourgeois countries (the colonialist and imperialist countries) and proletarian ones (the underdeveloped countries of the Third World). In this sense, the history of the past fifty years might be viewed as the slow victory of the proletarian countries over the bourgeois, as literally hundreds of millions of people have opted out of the arena of capitalist exploitation. Putting the class struggle on an international plane, however, has had peculiar consequences for the internal class struggles, which have been severely modified and sometimes completely submerged in the larger international struggle. In the proletarian countries this has meant that large sections of the bourgeoisie have joined the peasantry in fighting the common enemy: the colonial or imperial power.

IMPERIALISM AND
THE DOMESTIC ECONOMY

In bourgeois countries such as the United States the development of imperialism has had conflicting effects on the internal development of the economy. On the one hand, the profits some corporations have earned in their foreign investments have made it easier for them to deal with workers' demands for higher pay at home. Additionally, defense spending has created many jobs. For a small number of labor union bureaucrats, U.S. imperialism has meant a great windfall as the CIA and State departments spent many millions of dollars encouraging the establishment of conservative trade union organizations in other parts of the world. This has made it easier for a small but vocal section of the trade union movement to support imperialist adventures.

On the other hand, as multinational corporations have increasingly sent money abroad to set up manufacturing operations, the working class has been severely pinched by the closing down of U.S. plants. Multinational corporations have sought large pools of cheap labor abroad to manufacture goods to be sent back to the United States for consumption. Some elements in the labor movement are beginning to see the disastrous consequences this form of imperialism can have for domestic employment. Moreover, the kind of domestic employment generated by military spending creates very insecure economic conditions. Since many companies depend on military expenditures, even slight cutbacks may mean the closing of plants with hundreds and sometimes thousands of employees. It becomes crucial for companies to sell the government hardware—no matter how useless—and to channel the talents of engineers and scientists into a production that would have no market were it not for continued governmental support. If a company manufacturing such products in a particular area loses government contracts to a lower bidder, that whole area's economy may be ruined. Further, the channeling of talents, resources, and scientific research into narrow military concerns impoverishes the American economy. The people are told there are no resources to create needed housing, transportation, health care, etc., and that even heavier taxes will be necessary to produce minimal benefits in these important fields. The reason is simple: their tax dollars are being spent to subsidize the American corporate elite—directly through handouts to produce useless goods, and indirectly through the creation of military and economic apparatuses vital for their profit-making ventures abroad.

REFORMING IMPERIALISM?

The Vietnam war and the antiwar movement it created have stimulated thinking about how to deal with imperialism. Many liberals, failing to understand the nature of the problem, assume that the election of a "liberal" president and liberal congressmen will change the course of American policy. When it is pointed out to them that it was the liberal John F. Kennedy who got us militarily involved in Vietnam, that liberal Adlai Stevenson was an apologist for the war, and that virtually every liberal candidate for the presidency supported it for years, they will tell you that these mistakes will never recur. When their political heroes swear allegiance to American capitalism, and argue that the war in Vietnam was a mistake because it diverted our attention from our really vital interests in Europe and Latin America, they do not hear. Instead, they persist in the motion that imperialism can be reformed.

"Capitalism doesn't really need imperialism," they say, "because employment and high profits could be guaranteed through Keynesian spending at home." This objection misses several key points. First, Keynesian spending has already been instituted in the United States, but only in the field of the military. Capitalists do not spend in other fields for fear that they would create competition for existing firms and hence generate economic chaos. Nor would people agree to taxes for nonvital production. Some of the money now being spent for defense could be spent to create some social services that do not compete directly with private businesses as McGovern and others have suggested. But this would deal with only a small part of the problem. There is no way to supplant the full amount of U.S. investments in the world and the U.S. stakes in foreign markets and raw materials by internal spending.

More important, the abstract question of whether imperialism can be reformed misses the dynamic of the system as it operates in the real world. It is much like asking, "Could capitalism give up Texas to the Chicanos or give back Manhattan to the Indians?" [16] In the abstract, it probably could, but anyone who tried to base a political program on this abstraction does not understand much about the way political power operates in the United States. This country is not a "democracy" in any meaningful sense. The small number of men whose economic power gives them political power would lose a tremendous amount if the system were transformed. And they would do everything they could to prevent that from happening; i.e., to stop proponents of imperialism from being taken seriously as candidates, much less being elected to office.

But imagine that someone is elected who holds anti-imperialist views (not just the view that a particular war was not in the U.S. interest). As soon as the new president made his intentions clear, the bankers would stop buying government bonds, the stock market would crash, and millions of workers would be thrown out of work as the capitalists scurried to get their capital out of the country. The economy would be brought to the point of crisis. Unless the president and his supporters were prepared to take the next step—nationalizing the factories and financial institutions that were closing down or severely curtailing their operations—unless, in other words, he was prepared for socialism, he would find that the ruling class had outmaneuvered him. But if he had only run on a reform program, how could he expect the people to support a more revolutionary one whose implications and problems he had never outlined? Moreover, in any kind of showdown, he could not count on the loyalty of the military, which would be opposed to his anti-imperialism. He would be quickly isolated and find himself powerless—if not dead.

It is entirely possible that reforms and amendments in the ways in which imperialism operates lie ahead. But the basic dynamic of American capitalism exploiting other countries will not change until capitalism itself is replaced.

INTRACAPITALIST RIVALRIES

In the period immediately following World War II, which profoundly shook most of the world's capitalist societies, it was natural to think of

---

[16] Harry Magdoff, one of the leading authorities on imperialism, makes this point in "Is Imperialism Really Necessary?" *Monthly Review* (November 1970).

imperialism basically in terms of the relationship between the United States and the Third World. It was possible to believe with former Chinese leader Lin Piao that the key contradiction was the one between the advanced capitalist societies that needed to dominate the Third World, and the emerging countries of the Third World yearning for freedom and self-determination. But in the past decades Germany, Japan, and Western Europe were able to rebuild their economies and begin to compete with the United States again for markets—including the domestic U.S. market, which is being sought by a number of competent European and Japanese firms. In critical high-technology fields Japan and Germany are regaining their competitive position. As a result, American capitalism may be facing more serious challenges from the advanced capitalist countries than from the Third World.

How did this happen? In part, because the United States government was so interested in rebuilding the capitalist economies of these countries, in order to ensure that their domestic Communist movements would not gain support, that it ignored the possibility they might eventually become competitors. In part, because the United States has dedicated so much of its energy to weapons research that it has underplayed civilian research (we spend less of our GNP on research than either Germany or Japan). And in part because the United States became so involved in defending the stability of its Third World empire that it paid inadequate attention to the other developed nations.

The result is likely to be increasing strife in the 1970s. Many of the large corporations that control our political system have much to fear from the competition of revivified Japanese and European economies. These corporations will be pushing for increasingly aggressive policies to defend U.S. interests against Japan and Europe. This is not the first time in this century that there has been intraimperialist strife, and the results have almost always been catastrophic. We may well see an attempt by corporations to revive a militant anti-Japanese and anti-European spirit. People who are put out of work by the export of capital will be told that their real enemies are the Japanese and European competitors. Labor almost certainly will be told to accept fewer wage increases if U.S. corporations are to stay competitive. This could lead only to an intensification of strife. And even if this strife is resolved by some new arrangement dividing the world between imperialists, the resolution is not likely to be permanent. Capitalist money-seekers have a way of being irrational and of trying to maximize their own profits at the expense of everyone else. As long as capitalism remains the form of economic organization we live under, there will be little ground for optimism about world peace.

SUGGESTED READINGS

Baran, Paul A., and Sweezy, Paul M. *Monopoly Capital.* New York: Monthly Review Press, 1966.

Horowitz, David. *Corporations and the Cold War.* New York: Monthly Review Press, 1969.

————. *Empire and Revolution.* New York: Random House, 1969.

————. *Free World Colossus.* New York: Hill & Wang, 1965.

Kolko, Gabriel. *The Politics of War.* Boston: Beacon Press, 1970.

————. *The Roots of American Foreign Policy.* Boston: Beacon Press, 1969.

Magdoff, Harry. *The Age of Imperialism.* New York: Monthly Review Press, 1969.

Mandel, Ernest. *Marxist Economic Theory.* New York: Monthly Review Press, 1969.

Mattick, Paul. *Marx and Keynes.* Boston: Porter Sargent, 1969.

Oglesby, Carl. *Containment and Change.* New York: Crowell, Collier— Macmillan, 1967.

3
Racism and Sexism

T HE TENSION between liberal ideals and the actual practice of the American order under capitalism is graphically demonstrated in the treatment of women, blacks, Chicanos, American Indians, and other minorities. Nor are racism and sexism perversions subsequently foisted on a society that began as equalitarian. The Declaration of Independence proclaimed "All men are created equal," but its authors had no intention of including women or blacks in this proclamation. Eleven years later, the framers of the U.S. Constitution explicitly excluded most blacks from political rights (counting slaves as three fifths of a person for purposes of apportioning congressional seats). Women were denied the vote until 1920. America was founded on racism and sexism, and any celebration of the American revolutionary tradition should recognize this critical limitation.

Throughout American history, racism and sexism have been used by those in power to maintain their own economic and political positions and to divide their opposition. Racist assumptions were crucial in convincing large numbers of people to acquiesce in the genocide of the American Indian. The country's expansion westward served in part as a safety valve to class conflict. But that land belonged to someone else: the American Indian and, in the Southwest, the Chicanos. The capitalist solution was to paint these groups as inferior and to encourage the destruction of "redskin savages" in order to advance progress and civilization.

In the eastern United States, another economic arrangement, slavery, helped to nourish a racist consciousness. The capitalist ideology depended on the notion of the "free" marketplace, in which those who needed food, clothing, and shelter "freely" sold their labor power to those who had the money to buy it. Because slavery was a denial of this concept, those whose

87

wealth depended on slave labor were forced to justify their position by nourishing and intensifying racism among the white population.

Slavery was not accepted by the developing manufacturing interests of the Northeast, who manipulated abolitionist sentiments in the North as a tool in their struggle with southern land interests. But (after the Civil War had guaranteed their own supremacy in national economic decision making), when it became clear that racism could be used as a tool against dissident workers in the North, the monied interests were quick to support and encourage it. Unemployed black freed men were used as strike-breakers. Poor whites were encouraged to compare themselves with even poorer blacks as a way of keeping them from thinking about class questions. Sexism played a similar role: it offered even the most oppressed male worker someone he could oppress and who would serve him.

Racism and sexism were not created by capitalism, though capitalism is their chief sustainer. They have their roots in a more primitive period. The evidence now available about this period is not adequate to answer definitely the question of why these forms of domination arose. Nor is their primitive origin the real problem for us today. What we need to know is what sustains them and how to eliminate them.

The question is complicated. Blacks, Indians, Chicanos, and women are exploited not only because of their race and/or sex, but also as workers, and the oppression that is practiced against them generally puts them in the lowest categories in the working class. Hence the demand of the socialist movement for women's liberation and for black liberation, includes not only emancipation from racism and sexism but from all the economic, political, and social constraints that prevent human self-realization.

Over the last few years much attention has been given to racism in America and more recently to the women's struggle. Liberals are quick to admit the reality of these problems, but because they do not relate them to the economic and political order, they believe they can be solved by reforms achieved through the existing political system. But the evidence is against them: these problems are as old as America, and despite generations of liberal reformers they have intensified. What is more, things are getting worse—not better, but worse. This becomes clear when we look more carefully at the problems.

RACISM

Many people think of racism as a strictly psychological phenomenon—a problem of hatred. But in fact racism is primarily a structural fact: the economic, political, and social structures of capitalism operate to oppress minority races far more than whites. The psychological and structural facts are intimately related. For example, the last decade has seen a considerable growth in antiblack sentiment in the northern states, where previously there had been some tolerance and even support for southern desegregation; and this growth of antiblack feeling is directly tied to the blacks' struggle for improvements in their economic and political position. As long as blacks accepted their subordinate position, psychological racism was almost completely discredited in the North.

The civil rights movement that grew out of the overt political and social discrimination against blacks in the South had a profound effect on black people throughout the country. Liberal reformers such as Martin Luther King promised a better social order for blacks if they slowly struggled to achieve change through the system. But the passage of several major civil rights bills did nothing to lessen oppression of blacks in the North, and resentment in the ghettos grew. The result was a series of spontaneous rebellions and riots. After a few years of black rioting, the government decided to look into the causes of what it termed "civil disorders," and appointed the Kerner Commission to investigate the problem. The Commission's report was notable for its depth of perception in depicting black oppression, but it was totally unable to supply any kind of programs to deal with the problem because it could only see symptoms and not the underlying cause. The minimal steps it recommended in terms of increasing employment, housing, and health care were greeted with great fanfare and applause, and then were abandoned. It talked about "white racism" and many liberals responded with breast-beating and self-flagellation. But it nowhere showed who benefits from racism or how capitalist institutions sustain it. Instead, racism seemed to be just an ideological matter—its solution was to get our heads straight.

The Kerner Commission report explains the formation of racial ghettos as a consequence of the mass migration of blacks from the South to the North and West. The migration reflected both the expectation that jobs were available for unskilled workers in the North and the shift to mechanized farming in the South, as a result of which, a large number of black farmworkers had been displaced. But unlike previous immigrant groups, black people in the cities did not rise quickly on the economic

89

ladder to success. True, the move to the city constituted an upward step in itself, in the sense that even the lowest economic rungs of the urban ladder were higher than those to which most blacks could aspire in the rural South. But once in the city, black upward mobility became relatively slight. Blacks were the last great migration to the cities, so they inherited the worst jobs and living conditions. Moreover, unlike Europeans who were assimilated within a few generations, blacks were easily identifiable. As the class system rigidified, someone had to be at the bottom, and most bosses found it easy to convince white workers that it might as well be the blacks.

The first result was the creation of large ghettos in northern and western cities. Whereas the vast majority of white population growth is occurring in the suburban portions of metropolitan areas, almost all black population growth is occurring within metropolitan areas, primarily within central cities. Since 1960, white central-city population has declined by 1.3 million. And as wealthier whites move outside the city, the tax base decreases just at the moment when the need for social services is most pressing—both to handle the increasing number of poor blacks and to cure some of the more obvious sores the capitalist economy has helped to develop. In 1960 urban segregation was already so severe that 86 percent of all blacks would have had to change their place of residence within the city to create an integrated population distribution.

Life for many blacks is highly oppressive. The Kerner Commission reports that between 16 to 20 percent of the total black population of all central cities live in squalor and deprivation. In 1967 the unemployment rate for blacks was more than double that for whites. And the available jobs are often extremely undesirable. Black men are more than three times as likely as white men to be in low-paying, unskilled, or service jobs. The report goes on, "Employment problems have drastic social impact in the ghetto. Men who are chronically unemployed or employed in the lowest status jobs are often unable or unwilling to remain in their families. The handicap imposed on children growing up without fathers in an atmosphere of poverty and deprivation is increased as mothers are forced to work to provide support. . . . The culture of poverty that results from unemployment and family breakup generates a system of ruthless, exploitative relationships within the ghetto. Prostitution, dope addiction and crime create an environmental 'jungle' characterized by personal insecurity and tension." As to conditions of life in the ghetto: "Poor health and sanitation conditions in the ghetto result in higher mortality rates, a higher incidence of major diseases and lower availability and utilization of medical services. The infant mortality rate for nonwhite babies under the age of one month is 58 percent higher than for whites; for one to 12 months it is almost three times as high. The level of sanitation in the ghetto is far below that in high income areas. Garbage collection is often inadequate. Of an estimated 14,000 cases of rat bite in the United States in 1965, most were in ghetto neighborhoods. . . . Ghetto residents believe they are 'exploited' by local merchants; and evidence substantiates some of these beliefs." In fact ghetto residents often pay more for food and consumer goods than do people in higher income areas.[1]

Despite all the attention given to the Kerner report, the overall picture has changed little and there is little prospect of the massive programs of spending that would be necessary to begin needed reforms. The myth of black political and economic progress in the last few years is based on a combination of misleading information and wishful thinking well described in "The Myth of Black Economic Progress" by Dick Roberts in the magazine, *International Socialist Review*, June 1970. According to the Bureau of Labor Statistics, the median income of nonwhite families increased from $3,794 to $5,590 from 1960 to 1968, while the median income of white families rose from $6,857 to $8,937. The difference between white and nonwhite family median incomes was $3,063 in 1960; in 1968 it was $3,347. Even these figures conceal important features. For example, nonwhite families are on the average larger than white families; the gap between individual incomes is therefore even greater than the gap between family incomes. The Bureau of Labor Statistics estimated that in 1968 the median income of black families with three wage earners was not significantly different from that of white families with one working member. Thirty-nine percent of nonwhite families earned $7,000 a year or higher, while 66 percent of white families earned $7,000 or higher. The minimal gains made in employment through retraining programs have been more than offset by the increased number of young blacks entering the workforce and by the 1969–72 recession. Indeed, the period from 1951 to 1953 had a lower rate of unemployment for nonwhites than any year since then. And the reason for that lower rate of unemployment was the Korean war. This points out another crucial factor: progress in all fields is limited by the fact of the capitalist business cycle. When things are going well for the capitalists, large numbers of people are employed, which makes it appear that we are making progress on our race problems.

[1] These ghetto problems are not the cause of oppression: it is the oppression of blacks under capitalism that is the cause of the conditions. The white power structure has created the conditions in which decent housing, sanitation, and health care are not available for blacks, just as it has created the conditions for black unemployment and the inability of many blacks to survive except through welfare.

91

But when the system hits one of its inevitable downturns, the blacks are the first to feel the impact. Thus, blacks in Detroit who did not find jobs until the very peak of the war boom in 1968, had already lost their jobs by the spring of 1970; their share in the prosperity lasted about eighteen months out of an eight-year period.

Nor has black capitalism been particularly successful in bringing black people into a significantly higher economic bracket. "The essential purpose for putting Black power into business," Robert L. Allen suggests in *Black Awakening in Capitalist America,* is "the creation of a stabilizing Black buffer class which will make possible indirect white control (or neocolonial administration) of the ghettos. . . . At the apex of the new hierarchical structure being created in the ghettos is to stand the Black capitalist and managerial class. This is the class that will have the closest contact with corporate America and which is to act as conduit for its wishes." [2] But even this goal is hard to fulfill under conditions of advanced capitalism. Since 1950 the number of black-owned businesses has been declining. The number of restaurants declined 33 percent; other retail business more than 33 percent; even funeral parlors and barber shops were affected by the trend, declining 6 percent and 16 percent respectively. The decline of small business is a general phenomenon, not restricted to the black community, but it indicates that unless blacks are given sufficient capital to start large corporations, black capitalism will ultimately be helpless to create a new social-economic class within the black community. As the magazine *The Black Scholar* puts it in the April 1970 issue, "A layer of Blacks is increasingly filling certain strata of administrative, professional and technical jobs, in overwhelmingly white-owned and managed corporations. This is the kind of 'job upgrading' that is really taking place. It corresponds to the technological advance of American industry as a whole particularly during a time of economic boom. This economic progress, such as it is, is clearly enclosed within the racist and capitalist property owning structure handed down by the 19th century. It does not even create a sufficient number of Black businessmen to run a few of the larger businesses in the Afro-American community."

Black capitalism would have real meaning only if it gave blacks ownership and control of the means of production in some key financial institutions and industrial corporations, and then only if those in control oriented their businesses toward the needs of the black communities and not toward

[2] Cited by Dick Roberts in "The Fraud of Black Capitalism," *International Socialist Review* (July 1970). This article is the source for much of the information that follows.

keeping their firms solvent as competitive enterprises in a capitalist market. Needless to say, no steps have been taken in this direction.

One development did affect the ghetto somewhat: the trickling of limited funds into the War on Poverty. This created a new group of black technocrats, often culled from the most articulate protest spokesmen and spokeswomen. It was a classical cooptation technique: give some jobs to the leaders of black militancy, but do not give them either authority enough or money enough to do anything substantial. The new technocrats take militant poses, and conservatives in Congress complain about this "hideaway and seedbed of revolution," but the actual effect on most blacks is negligible. The best-known antipoverty programs were job-retraining programs. But the blacks who were retrained discovered that the new jobs simply did not exist. The problem was not inferior black preparedness, but the fact that capitalism cannot employ all workers, no matter how well trained.

It is not my contention that American capitalism could not make things much better for black people. It is certainly economically possible for capitalists to create crash programs to raise the standard of living materially for blacks. But such programs might involve serious economic dislocations for some white workers and would certainly involve a shift away from the pattern of spending characteristic of the federal budget in the past twenty-five years. And if such programs were to be introduced under capitalism, it would only be after the people had been so conditioned that they believed themselves primarily responsible for the problem and that they should therefore bear the financial burden by accepting higher unemployment and higher taxes.

It is possible for a reformer to come along who manages to put together a political alliance based on the interests of those who have large domestic investments and those who oppose the war, and such a reformer (operating either through the Democratic party or through a new third capitalist party) would begin to spread money around the black community through a variety of job programs and antipoverty agencies. It is almost inconceivable, however, that such a reformer, acting within the boundaries of a capitalist framework, would be permitted to alter the *relative* balance of wealth and power between blacks and whites. Some of the misery might be eliminated, but not the racist structures that keep black people "in their place." As Baran and Sweezy point out in *Monopoly Capital*,[3] racism serves the interests of the rulers in a very direct way. The existence of a

[3] Paul A. Baran and Paul M. Sweezy, *Monopoly Capital* (New York: Monthly Review Press, 1966).

segregated subproletariat allows employers to play one group off against another, weakening all.

In the past, much black migration to the North came about because blacks, who did not have an adequate share of jobs and were hungry for food, clothing, and decent shelter, were recruited as strikebreakers. Often white bosses recruited southern blacks who were completely ignorant either of the strike or the issues involved. When they got to the job, often at the owner's expense, they were in debt to the bosses and friendless in a strange town. They therefore felt compelled to take any job even if it meant strikebreaking. The workers feared and hated the blacks who had taken their jobs, and it was easy to generalize this hatred to all blacks, just as previously hatred had been generalized to all Irish, Italian, and East European immigrants, some of whom had been used in this way. With the close of immigration blacks were used more consistently in this manner than any other group and hence aroused greater fear and hate among the white workers. The fear that blacks would be introduced to break a strike often kept white working people from striking against intolerable conditions, and their hostility toward their bosses was sometimes in part deflected toward blacks. Unions reacted with anger to the new labor supply, and most unions kept blacks out. This only complicated the problem, because it ensured the existence of a large number of blacks without union consciousness who would hence be willing to take jobs as strikebreakers.

It is precisely because economic equality would provide a basis for political unity that the capitalist system can never give equality to the blacks. Nor is this because of the simple fact of their color. If Jews or Italians or Poles had been the last immigrant group into the big cities, they would have been able to play the same role.

An oppressed minority serves a number of other important functions for the capitalist system. "Owners of ghetto real estate are able to overcrowd and overcharge. . . . Middle and upper income groups benefit from having at their disposal a large supply of cheap domestic labor. . . . Many small marginal businesses, especially in the service trades, can operate profitably only if cheap labor is available to them. . . . White workers benefit by being protected from Negro competition for the most desirable and higher paid jobs. Hence the customary distinction, especially in the South, between 'white' and 'Negro' jobs, the exclusion of Negroes from apprentice programs, the refusal of many unions to admit Negroes, and so on." [4]

4 *Ibid.*, p. 264.

With the institutionalization of business unionism in major sectors of the economy and the growth of accommodations between big business and the union bureaucrats, blacks as a reserve labor force and as potential strikebreakers have declined in importance. The role of the black as union-breaker may have helped create the conditions in which the ideology of racism first flourished, but it no longer acts as its key sustainer. Today, the mechanisms are much subtler. There are only a limited number of jobs, and unemployment fluctuates from 4 to 7 percent of the workforce. So a minimum of 4 percent are going to be unemployed, and the power structure ensures that blacks face much higher rates of unemployment than whites. But the very fact of those unemployed blacks serves as a warning to whites that things could be much worse for them, and hence as a damper on militancy. Someone has to be unemployed, and many white workers are willing to agree with the bosses that if it has to be someone. better it should be the blacks. But whites are then faced with another problem: the entire welfare system which keeps the unemployed from simply starving to death. Welfare taxes fall heavily on white working people, who consequently resent them. Logically this resentment should be directed against those who set up the tax structure so that the rich and the corporations get away with murder. Instead, since the same people who set the tax structure have extraordinary power over the media and means of forming public opinion, working people are encouraged to turn their resentment against the welfare recipients. And since these welfare recipients are often black, it is easy to play on previously established racism to convince people that those who receive welfare don't want to work. This cynical game is played by many legislators who will give hundreds of millions, even billions, of dollars to corporations in outrageous giveaways, then turn around and scream about the high cost of welfare, hoping thereby to create the impression that high taxes are really going to subsidize those who simply refuse to work, who are (it is implied) those nasty black people.

But although white racism serves many purposes for the rulers, it is directly counter to the best interests of most white people. For it is precisely through this kind of racism that the majority of people are manipulated into focusing their attention away from their own oppression and exploitation. The participation of many white people directly and indirectly in racist practices and institutions earns them the antipathy of many blacks, and the antipathy is often expressed in ways which reinforce white fears and hatreds. So the spiral continues downward toward overt race war, restrained only by the powerlessness of the minority black population.

That spiral can be broken only when white people come to understand the racism of the system of which they are a part, and struggle to change it.

This will not come about through speeches by whites against racism. One key part of breaking through the spiral is black activity in opposition to racism. Another is the general level of activity of the working class. When most white workers see themselves as part of a large struggle to change the society, they will be able to see blacks as a potential source of support. One of the important steps in breaking racism is, then, to help foster conditions in which whites will move from their general passivity about the system and begin to struggle for the things they need.

It is a tribute to the dominance of capitalist assumptions that even when large numbers of white people become sensitized to some aspects of the problem of racism, they persist in interpreting it on a psychological level. The establishment liberal line is as pervasive as it is malicious: "We are all responsible for racism, so we must all change our attitudes and then everything will be all right." We are told that *we* have oppressed the black people, and if *we* want to deal with this problem—even on a minimal basis—*we* will have to bear the burden of higher taxes and make many sacrifices. Many whites have indeed participated in the exploitation and have themselves adopted racist attitudes, and this fact should neither be excused nor glossed over. But neither should we be allowed to fall so deep into the liberal celebration of guilt that we forget the fact that many of us have fought racist attitudes wherever we were conscious of them, and that even those who have not fought racism cannot be held responsible for its existence in institutions over which they have no control.

Each of us must work on his consciousness and try to transform it, but the sources of racist consciousness cannot be separated from the racist institutions that are the immediate stumbling block to the emergence of any new consciousness. And we are not all equally guilty for racist institutions: factory owners and managers who use blacks as strikebreakers, who hire blacks last and fire blacks first, are in quite a different situation from workers whose jobs are threatened by black men. It may be irrational for the worker to get angry at the black man instead of the system that does not provide enough jobs, but he is not responsible for creating that system.

In emphasizing the structural sources of racism, we must not overlook the obvious fact that psychological oppression is indeed one of its important dimensions. But it has been given so much attention in recent literature that one tends to forget the economic and political sources. Neither should we deny the important role ideas play in demeaning black people and filling their lives with suffering and anguish. The militants' proud proclamation that "Black is beautiful" can easily be understood in the context of a culture that equates blackness with evil. The myth of black inferiority has been accepted by almost all Americans, black and white. "Black is beautiful" and other attempts at reviving pride in black culture are part of the blacks' attempt to free themselves from that self-destructive myth. The cultural models by which we judge ourselves are the product of white-controlled schools and white-controlled media. These cultural models are oppressive to almost everybody, but particularly so to black children. Establishment newspapers and television stations talk from the standpoint of "us white males" and history books from the standpoint of whites looking at the "black problem." What is more, personal contacts between whites and blacks have been so influenced by sexual stereotyping that blacks must learn early a whole mythology about themselves if they are to know the safe way to act in school or in seeking a job with "Whitey's" children.

It is impossible for a white fully to appreciate or understand what it means to be black in racist America. It means you are one of a group that is the special target of oppression by large numbers of whites and the object of derision among an even larger number. A rational appraisal of your chances gives you little grounds for hope. Your life will be filled with disappointed promises and personal frustration, and your future will be in the hands of a system in which racism has been a major, constant factor. You are feared by the great majority of Americans. Almost every week you can read about a fellow black being shot and killed without reason by policemen who are then acquitted by investigating commissions or grand juries as having engaged in "justifiable homicide." And you know that almost any member of your group who attempts to realize his creative talents and uniqueness will be beaten down.

The forms of oppression of other minority groups vary. In the Southwest and West states, Chicanos play the same role as blacks in other parts of the country. Throughout the country, all Latins face tremendous economic and political discrimination, and Spanish-speaking people are forced to renounce their cultural identity in order to be accepted on even the more peripheral levels in the society. Spanish teachers are often forbidden to teach in Spanish, resulting in functional illiteracy rates among Spanish-speaking students in the Southwest that are often twice as high as blacks and seven times as high as Anglos. Since IQ tests are given in English, it is no surprise that Chicanos are classified as 27 percent of the "mentally retarded" although they make up only 14 percent of the students. Unemployment among Chicanos is 70 percent higher than among Anglos.

American Indians must choose between living on reservations whose resources have been progressively depleted by the federal government and the large corporations or going to the cities where they find themselves grossly discriminated against in employment and education. Raised in a society that glorifies the annihilation of their grandparents and which identifies "redskin" with "savage," the American Indian is another oppressed minority group. Chicanos and American Indians find their history distorted, their culture denied. From childhood, they are urged to become assimilated into a society that will not assimilate them. Racism is so deep that no matter how "white" their souls, their physical appearance compels them to face unrestrained discrimination. The list goes on and on. But the point is clear: racism is an integral part of American society, and has been fostered and used by the capitalist order to sustain itself.

SEXISM

Awareness of racism in America has been a constant theme in American history. This awareness was fostered primarily by self-satisfied northerners who could easily point a finger at the South. But the story is quite different when it comes to the oppression of women. There were women throughout the country, in the families of capitalists as well as workers. So it was intolerable to admit that women were oppressed in any real sense. If they were oppressed, men were oppressing them; such a thought was intolerable for the men. This is undoubtedly why many people even today find it difficult to take the exploitation and oppression of women seriously: to do so would mean to raise fundamental questions about the most intimate areas of their lives—their families, and their sexual and social relations. Yet, precisely in these areas capitalism manifests itself in its most perverse form, turning human relations into struggles for domination and control. If the question of the oppression of women is difficult or threatening to most men and women, it is even more threatening to the rulers of American society, whose control over the society is greatly strengthened by sexist institutions and practices.

Capitalist society defines men in terms of their relation to the means of production, and women in terms of their relation to men and in terms of their reproductive functions. Men are viewed in terms of how much the rulers can use them to make a profit. Women also are assigned definite roles: they must serve their husbands when they are not serving their bosses. A woman's life prospects are delimited by her body, which gives her defined tasks and ensures that her work will reinforce her subordinate position. Accompanying the enslavement of women is an ideology that parallels the myths of the inferiority of nonwhite races—the myth that women's roles are "natural." The argument goes like this: only women can give birth to and nurse children, so it is only "natural" that a woman's place is in the home; or, if she does work, she should be protected from the harsher aspect of society.

But when one looks at the matter more closely, the "natural place" of women turns out to be a carefully nurtured consequence of our social organization. In primitive times and even until quite recently, much of a woman's life was centered on her reproductive role. Constant pregnancies and the necessity to breast-feed children consumed much of her time and caused a severe deterioration of health. But these physical facts were not, in themselves, responsible for the inferior status and finally the complete subjugation of women. Women's physical weakness may have played an important role in enabling men to subjugate them, but did not require that subjugation, as has been shown by the anthropological evidence that not all primitive societies hold women in subjugation. Scarcity of food and basic necessities was the background in which societies were formed. Accumulation of food and other goods became essential. The development of agriculture as a way of dealing with scarcity saw the emergence of the family as a valuable work unit, and also as a means of laying claim to whatever surplus existed. Control over women and children was certainly functional for the physically tougher men, who could use women and children to do needed work and could then hand on the accumulated material surplus to their children. In short, the same dynamic that led men to fight against and enslave one another was the dynamic that led them to enslave women: material scarcity.

But does not the statement that male domination is rooted in natural physical superiority support the male supremist argument? No. For there is no reason to allow physical infirmities to govern social life, and precisely what distinguishes man from the animals is man's ability to overcome and transcend many of the limitations of the natural world. Even as we would find it ridiculous to say that one should let the sick suffer and die because disease and pain are "natural," so it is silly to argue that we should allow differences in physical strength to become the justification for oppressing half the human race.

WOMEN WORKERS

The notion that women have a "natural" role is very convenient for the rulers of this society when women are actually required to enter the workforce. A woman worker is considered a woman first. She is still

99

expected to fulfill her sex-defined tasks, such as raising children and taking care of the household. She is still supposed to be subordinate to her husband, with all that this entails, from washing his underwear to soothing his ego. At the same time, the woman is often the sole support of a family, and equally often, her income is crucial to keeping the family's standard of living above the poverty level. According to 1968 U.S. Bureau of Statistics figures, 75 percent of all married women workers come from families in which the husbands earn less than $7,000 per year; the majority from families in which the husbands are making less than $5,000. In 1965 the median income for families in which only the man worked was $6,592, in families where both the man and the woman worked it was $8,597.

Because placing some women in the workforce has enabled many families to get along financially, work for women has been viewed by the ruling class as an acceptable alternative to an increase in working-class militancy. At the same time, it has subjected women to labor that is unsatisfying and to conditions of employment that are far worse than men's. Women usually get less satisfying jobs, and are paid less for the same work than men. Thirty-two percent of all employed women are clerical workers engaged in typing and other rote work. Women are 42 percent of all sales workers and 58 percent of all retail sales workers. But women rarely get the sales jobs that pay high commissions, such as appliance and auto sales. Women are kept down in the professions in a variety of ways,[5] most of them taking advantage of the fact that in a society that considers children the responsibility of the individual woman, her possible motherhood can be used against every woman. Because women leave work for a while when they have young children, it is harder for them to accumulate seniority, and they are therefore more likely than men to be laid off and less likely to be promoted. Employers who assume that women will be absent more frequently because of their children will often hire men instead. The proportion of women in professional jobs has decreased in this country, from 40 percent in 1950, to 37 percent in 1966. Nearly half of all women professionals are teachers, mainly below the college level. Women comprise 8 percent of all scientists, 7 percent of all physicians, 3 percent of all lawyers, 1 percent of all engineers. In fact, women employees are in the majority only in service work, which is almost entirely unskilled,

[5] Some of these figures will change over the next few years, particularly as government and universities try to accommodate demands for better opportunities for women. By and large the changes will affect only a narrow section of upper- and upper-middle-class women and the picture will remain relatively constant. Much fanfare, naturally, will be given to any small advances.

usually very low paying, and mostly nonunionized. For instance, 72 percent of all waiters/waitresses, cooks, and bartenders are women. And women make up 98 percent of all private household workers.

In a society in which almost all work is alienating and money is all the worker can show for his labor, women get lower-paying jobs than men, and often less pay than men for the same work (although this fact is frequently hidden by giving different names to the same work when it is done by different sexes). In 1955, the median income of full-time women workers was 64 percent of men's; by 1965 their median income in relation to men's had dropped to slightly under 60 percent. Black women, who face both sex and race oppression, make only two-thirds as much as white women.[6] Among salesworkers, full-time women workers make 40.4 percent the salaries of men. Although twenty-five states have laws requiring equal pay for equal work, these laws are seldom enforced. Nor does greater education bring greater equality of income. Recent studies showed that women chemists holding doctorates made less than men with BAs; and that a year after graduation from law school the average man earned 20 percent more than the average woman, and ten years later he earned 200 percent more.[7]

Nor are these conditions applicable only to a few women who want to work. Today, 90 percent of American women will work at some time in their lives, and most will work because they must. They will find themselves used in traditional ways by employers: last hired, first fired, least organized, and shunted into the least-skilled jobs. Take only one example. In 1971, the Federal Equal Employment Opportunity Commission charged that AT&T violated the law by discriminating against women, blacks, and Spanish-surnamed workers. AT&T employs a great many women. But women are tracked into the lowest-paying jobs where the work is intolerable and the possibility of promotion slim. Almost all jobs at the phone company are totally sex-segregated, with the better-paying and more creative jobs going to men and the boring clerical and operator jobs going to women. The average yearly wage for "entry-level jobs" for men is $8,613; for women it is $6,114. Almost half of all phone workers earn less than $7,000 annually, but only 4 percent of white males employed by AT&T are in this group, while 80 percent of all females are. The 16 percent balance is made up of blacks and Chicanos, who, as one AT&T

---

[6] A complete discussion of this problem is available in a pamphlet by Irene Winkler called "Women Workers" published by International Socialists, 874 Broadway, New York, New York 10003.

[7] For further documentation see *1965 Handbook on Women Workers* (Washington, D.C.: U.S. Department of Labor, Women's Bureau, 1966).

vice-president explained, are hired because the phone company needs a steady supply of people "available for work paying as little as $4,000 to $5,000 a year." On the job, women are hemmed in by petty and restrictive work rules and by overbearing supervisors who hover over employees at the rate of one supervisor to every four operators. One indication of Ma Bell's bad working conditions is the incredibly high turnover rate. And AT&T is only one of many employers who use and abuse women in the workforce.

THE FAMILY

The central oppressive institution for most women is the nuclear family. Women raise the children and impart to them the entire set of social mores. Given no other outlet for their intelligence, sensitivity, and creativity, many women become overly dependent on this role as a way of ensuring their own self-worth. Since a woman's fulfillment is seen in terms of her children, her life is virtually over when her children grow up.

Women are expected to put in a full day's labor (or more) on household duties, which are particularly onerous during the early years of child rearing. This is a socially necessary labor, but because the ideology of sexism holds it to be women's "natural work," society does not pay for it. The nuclear family, charged with full responsibility for the care of its members, provides society with a mechanism through which to avoid many human responsibilities. The rearing of children, the provision of clothing, food, and shelter, care for the sick and aged—these are not society's tasks but the individual's. It is precisely for these reasons that the family is filled with tensions: whether because of the enormous financial pressure introduced by sickness, or the costs of education, or of getting a child's teeth straightened. In an agricultural society, the family had some function as an economic unit. The father was not concerned to educate his children; he could use their labor on the farm. But this has become less possible since the family moved from the farm to the cities, and industrial life imposed minimal restrictions on some forms of exploitation.

Respect for authority, responsibility, and loyalty at all times are the key values of the nuclear family; but they are built up artificially, demanded as an obligation rather than flowing from the natural development of the individual's feelings. Love becomes another instrument of control and domination. How can real love exist between people so unequally situated as husband and wife, or father and children? Even the love of a mother for her children is often perverted by the mother's need to find all her meaning in life through her children.

102

The central love relationship is supposed to be the one between man and wife. Yet the woman is so undermined in her socially conferred roles that it is hard to imagine how love is possible. When the husband comes home from work, he is supposed to find his wife fresh and expectant. But she, too, has spent the day working. Nevertheless, she must soothe him as he complains about his work and she must continually mend his wounded ego. At the same time she must put up with his sexist definitions, under the terms of which she is weak, unimportant, uninteresting, and obliged to serve him. And if this is not enough, she must continue to be a satisfactory sex object, able to hold her man's attention away from all other possible sex objects in the outside world. With all the vital services she performs, the woman is still often seen as expendable and replaceable. The man has an outside work world, and therefore the thought of re-arranging his home life is not the greatest terror. But many women have nothing else, and the loss of their home is the end of their world.

Nor are women mistaken in this assessment because the family is the social unit of identification and interaction in virtually every community. For a woman to support herself demands that she face an extremely discriminatory job market. And this becomes more difficult as the woman becomes older and hence less marketable—not merely as a worker but as a sexual object. Of course, these conditions differ for different social classes. A woman who is independently wealthy, or one who has upper-middle-class parents or a husband who can afford high alimony, does not face the same trouble as does a working-class woman. For the latter, loss of her husband means being thrown into the workforce with the least possibility of earning decent pay and the greatest possibility of being given extremely unpleasant work to do. Even so, many women seek divorce—testimony to the oppression they find in their home situations.

That love becomes increasingly difficult in a nuclear family is one more irony of male chauvinist life. To men in capitalist society, a home of their own is a place in which to escape the dog-eat-dog world of capitalist social relations. But those same relations are then re-created at home, under the guise of love and care. For at home the man often becomes the boss and the wife the worker, with the added problem that the wife is required to enjoy her exploitation rather than to form unions to combat it. The strong feelings that can exist between man and woman sometimes impede them from noticing the conditions of their relationship. And women who find this area the only one in which they have any ability to exercise choice are not likely to be abandoned. But as Shulamith Firestone points out, provoking a man's interest, and ensnaring his commitment once he has expressed that interest, is not exactly self-determination.[8] And once a relationship has been finalized in the form of a nuclear family, the one thing that gave the woman equality—her freedom to end the relationship—disappears. It is difficult to perceive a household slave as a full human being. The very structure of dependence and domination built into the nuclear family in male chauvinist society makes any real love impossible.

So strong is the human urge toward love that, despite all these factors, many relationships are still able to sustain love between man and woman for a few years. But how many really loving relationships do any of us know that have lasted for any length of time? Men dominate women in an attempt to ensure that they will get a certain kind of love that very domination makes impossible. And all this is intensified by the fact that most men return to their homes from a work world structured to deny their own worth and creativity, so that most men believe very little in their own worth, while demanding to be told by their wives that they are great. (And if the wife really believes her praise of her husband, the man loses respect for her; after all, she is so easily duped.)

The family is not just a random happening in our society—it is greatly encouraged by legal arrangements. A woman faces a host of problems if she is not married and a host of benefits if she is. But even when she is married, the law does not grant her full control over her own body. Birth control devices are not always easily available, and in some places their sale is restricted. Abortion laws prohibit a woman from deciding whether she will have a child or not.

Yet we cannot say that the decline of the nuclear family is very good for women either, as long as an exploitative capitalist society remains. For women may be freed of the family only to be more freely available as a sexual object to a male population that increasingly demands sexual gratification as a means of forgetting its lost life at work.

SEXUAL OBJECTS AND SEX ROLES

Because women are defined in terms of their men, it is crucial that they get a man for themselves. If women must sell themselves into familial subjugation, they ought to get themselves the best possible deal. And most women know that they have a far better chance of getting the mate they want if they are considered sexually attractive and sensitive to the current fashions. One should not be fooled by the appearance of a "hip" crowd, or by the culture that surrounds the college campuses and youth

[8] Shulamith Firestone, *The Dialectics of Sex* (New York: Bantam Books, 1971).

ghettos. The fashions may be different from those of the middle class, but these cultures too have their appropriate look, dress, and hair style, and they are just as coercive as is the culture of the middle class.

This is a situation ripe for exploitation by individual men, and by the economic structures that promote and benefit from it. Individual men are able to take advantage of women's insecurities and need for a stable relationship by promising the possibility of such a relationship in return for sexual conquest. Moreover, since the sexual revolution began to define women as "uptight" and "neurotic" if they did not sleep with everyone, things have become even worse. Women are perfect targets for manipulation by the mass media. The significant men in a woman's life (prospective bosses, friends, husband) are likely to measure her appearance against that of the models used to sell cigarettes or cosmetics or clothes. At the same time, the media play on those themes in a woman's life likely to move her: her loneliness, her dependence, her desire to be creative. Advertisements attempt to show how their product will make it possible for a woman to find self-expression even within the context of her confining life. Or they will promise to get things done more quickly, with the implied promise that more time will enable her to do something meaningful with her life. Or the product will promise relief from pain and nervous tension. All the ads are based on an acceptance of the subjugated place of women. And the products that use "hip" advertisements, describing themselves as the essence of the revolution ("You've come a long way, baby") offer choices only between useless products. Advertising also sells useful products, but frequently their usefulness is a function of the social organization of capitalist society. Take, for example, the dishwasher. Obviously one can sell many more dishwashers in a society in which nuclear families live and eat in isolation from one another than in a society in which people live communally.

Many businessmen depend for their success on the isolated consumer, willing to change his needs as the media changes its styles, and willing to develop new needs when the media announce them. That businessmen take advantage of this situation and help to sustain it is not attributable to any inherent evil, but rather to need for new and expanded markets. Domestic imperialism is the logical correlate of foreign imperialism, and has as its consequence the continual search for new ways to make people discontented with what they have and to instill in them the need for more and more things. Any attempt that people might make to re-create their lives so that they no longer need more and newer material things would be an unmitigated disaster for the capitalist. Because they can make large profits from the special consumer needs that a sexist society creates for women, because they can use women as a reserve force in the labor market to take low-paying jobs, because they can use women to provide socially necessary labor in the home without demanding compensation, and to provide sexual and ego gratifications that deflect workers' attentions from their alienation at work, most capitalists will fight the basic thrust of women's liberation even as they pay lip service to it.

Besides all the other advantages that accrue to the capitalists from a sexist societal framework, the exploitation of women has an additional dimension: the female body can be used to sell products—to eroticize the business environment so that it becomes more pleasant for the male customer. The most blatant examples of this are the television commercials that use young women to promote airlines, shaving creams, etc., but the same phenomenon is repeated every time a receptionist or salesgirl is hired. Thus, a woman's body can become an economic liability if it does not meet the requirements set by the fashion leaders. For this reason, the working woman must pay careful attention to her clothes and her makeup; there is no question but that the media try to condition women to want useless items. But this does not mean that the women who buy these items are irrational dupes. Any woman who has sought a job knows that she has a far better chance of getting one if she is sexually attractive and if she follows the current fashion fads.

What does it take to get human beings to accept this treatment and these limitations on their possibilities? Massive indoctrination—which, ironically, women then transmit to their children. Women are told that it is natural for them to have certain character traits—traits that make them passive and accepting and unable to act in the world. As Jo Freeman points out,[9] the female image is characterized as anxious, nervous, hasty, careless, fearful, dull, childish, helpless, sorry, timid, clumsy, stupid, silly and domestic. On the more positive side, women are understanding, tender, sympathetic, pure, generous, affectionate, loving, moral, kind, grateful and patient. All of these characterizations fit in well with the passive, accepting, and giving role that a male chauvinist society assigns to women.

The process begins long before puberty. As Freeman points out,

> It begins with the kind of toys young children are given to play with, with the roles they see their parents in, with the studies in their early reading books, and the kind of ambitions they express or actions they engage in that receive rewards from their parents and

[9] Jo Freeman, "The Building of the Gilded Cage," in Ann Koedt, ed., *Notes from the 3rd Year* (P.O. Box AA, Chelsea Station, New York, N.Y. 10011, n.d.).

other adults. . . . Girls receive more affection, more protective-ness, more control and more restrictions. Boys are subjected to more achievement demands and higher expectations. In short, while girls are not always encouraged to be dependent per se, they are usually not encouraged to be independent and physically active.[10]

At every stage in her training and socialization the woman is taught to curtail her intelligence. In the first place, it is unlikely she will find any place to use it in the employment world. Second, if she is intelligent she is likely to offend the men in her life, who are looking for someone to flatter their egos rather than for someone stimulating who may be superior to them intellectually. Finally, she is encouraged to be passive and accept-ing, to wait for the world to act on her rather than to become an active agent determining her own future. Even with the vogue of sexual libera-tion, the man usually makes the first approach to the woman: few women will phone a man and ask him out or over for sexual fun. Eventually, the mask becomes the face—and women actually become less interesting and less able to act for themselves—hence all the stereotypes that at once describe, reinforce, and re-create the conditioning of history. And since all the institutions of capitalist society are built to reinforce this passivity and to oppose women's self-development and self-control, the woman who refuses to give in to it may well end up being unhappy—not because she is fighting her "natural role" but because the struggle against sexist institu-tions is too difficult and frustrating.

Just as whites "benefit" in the short run from racism, so do men "benefit" from sexism. But the benefit exists only in the context of a society based on private property and exploitation, and it would truly benefit all humans if that context were changed. We have already mentioned one of the numerous ways in which the "benefits" to men of sexism undercut them-selves: that men cannot find any lasting and satisfying love relationships. Love becomes an endless game of conquests in which the conquered person loses precisely what the conquerer loved. What could be a more serious indictment of a society than that it makes real human relationships im-possible? Yet that is precisely what a sexist society does.

Moreover, sexism defines men's sex roles also, and persuades them that they must live up to them or feel inferior. These roles integrate them into capitalism's competitiveness by teaching them that their success in com-petition with everyone else for money, status, prestige, and women is a sign of their own masculinity. So, to be "real men" they must deny their

10 *Ibid.*

feelings of camaraderie and view others as opponents. Life is a series of "challenges"; and the more the man wins, the more he fulfills his masculinity. As Meredith Tax explains it, men

> are taught that to be masculine is to be physically and verbally aggressive, hyper-active sexually, authoritarian in manner, and capable of abstract thought. Being observant of the ordinary details of daily life is not considered part of being masculine. Men are taught to chart the stars in their courses, but not to notice when someone in the room has been crying. Or, if they are forced to notice, to regard it as a threat and act aggressively or condescendingly or helplessly. Sensitivity to other people's needs is considered, in our society, to be feminine. So is vulnerability to other people. The ideal American male, in terms of the dominant values of our society, is a competitive machine, competent, hard-driving, achieving, and soulless, with a sexual life, but no personal life. Fortunately, most men can't live up to this ideal; but the strain of trying is considerable. . . .[11]

In short, the ideology and practice of sexism sets up goals for men that make them unhappy and dehumanize them.

It is no wonder that this culture finds homosexuality so threatening. The homosexual, male or female, has rejected the conditioned sexual role, and no longer gears his or her sexuality toward achieving such societal goals as reproduction of the workforce or supplying a stable atomized economic unit of consumption. Instead, the homosexual lets himself or herself love another human being for what that person is. If homosexuals have been forced to abandon physical relationships with people of the opposite sex because so many relations are defined in stereotypic ways, we should question the society that creates those stereotypes and not the individual who responds to them in this way.[12] The homosexual role should not be idolized either: too often the homosexual roles themselves become defined in exploitative ways. But they seem to have a reasonable case for claiming that homosexual relationships do not depend on definitions of "how to act" that have been inculcated from childhood, and hence often have more of a possibility of genuine freedom and creativity. That homosexuals are perceived as a threat is testified to by the extreme reactions they provoke

[11] Meredith Tax, "Woman and Her Mind: The Story of Everyday Life," in *Notes From the Second Year* (Radical Feminism, P.O. Box AA, Old Chelsea Station, New York, N.Y. 10011, n.d.).

[12] Of course, many homosexuals are not responding to anything social, but merely living and feeling as their bodies and minds dictate.

from the rest of society, which does everything from ridicule them to jail them. In the end, behind sexual roles stands the power of the state.

What makes racism and sexism so difficult to deal with is that these phenomena touch on people's lives both through the impersonal institutions of capitalist society and also through the actions of ordinary human beings. The oppressed and exploited worker in turn oppresses and exploits others, at once becoming tied to the system of exploitation and deflecting the attention of those he exploits away from the system and onto himself. The racism and sexism that pervade American life are disasters not only because of their destructive effect on the individual, but also because they create conflicts between groups of the oppressed and so make more difficult a unified struggle against the oppressors. For the rulers this is ideal: "Let blacks fight with whites, and men with women, and we will continue to rake in the profits." No small group of men consciously plans this out, behind closed doors and gleefully peeking out at the havoc they have wrought. But this is how the system functions, and the rulers who benefit from it will do all they can to oppose any substantial change—often under the rubric of "maintaining our sacred traditions," "upholding the sanctity of the individual," "protecting the people from the interference of the government in their personal affairs."

As long as capitalist society remains fundamentally intact, the sexist structures will continue to deform us all. And we, in turn, will deform our children. Indeed, the oppression of children is yet another legacy of sexism in capitalist society. In a society in which all human activity, from working to loving, is misshapen and alienated, it becomes necessary to create the myth that there is at least one happy period in life. Hence what Shulamith Firestone calls the myth of childhood.[13] Children *must* be happy. To ensure this, capitalism has produced a host of industries that feed off parents' needs about childhood—producing everything from special toys, games, food, books, candy and gum, to television and movies, child psychology, pediatrics and compulsory education.

In fact, childhood is an especially oppressive period, accentuated by the economic and physical dependence of the child on his parents. Some of this is the result of the natural physical inequalities between children and adults. But much of it is the product of societal arrangements. Children are "minors" under the law, without civil rights, the property of their parents. Economic dependence is one key—the adolescent has to please his parents in order to get money, or the car, or permission to go out at night.

[13] Firestone, *Dialectics of Sex.*

Children are taught their parents' sexual repressions, forced to deny their own sexuality and to appear "pure," to become estranged from their bodies and to restrain their sensual desires in conformity with what the society considers "acceptable" sexual behavior. Indeed the full range of neuroses that plague the parents are almost always absorbed, though sometimes in inverted forms, into the psychic structures of the children. That is why the subtle psychological pressures of family life, like the requirement of family loyalty and denial of one's own identity, can be so detrimental to children's individuality and development. The nuclear family intensifies the effects of parental neuroses. This effect could be widely diffused if the child were able to relate to more than one man and one woman on a close emotional basis, as is demonstrated by the lower incidence of neuroses among the children who grow up on an Israeli kibbutz.

Though woman's oppression has a longer history than racism, and hence may seem more "natural" and harder to fight, women have, through the years, engaged in many struggles against their oppression. And these struggles, like the struggles of workers against alienated social relations, take on added force and meaning at this period in history, when it is possible to eliminate scarcity for all human beings. But these struggles will not be won as long as capitalism remains in power. This is well illustrated by the history of the women's struggle in the early part of this century. Women won the right to vote, but found that as long as the capitalists controlled the electoral arena, the vote could not eliminate sexist institutions. It seems increasingly likely that some jobs will be opened up for upper-middle-class women in the relatively near future, while most working-class women will face the same old problems. Reformers must be conscious of the class divisions that exist among women. Reformist demands can be won, but as long as it serves the interests of the rulers to use women against men, the fundamental structures that oppress women will not be altered in significant respects. But the reforms that can be won are *not* insignificant: anything that eliminates the worst aspects of the oppression of women is good in itself and has the advantage of releasing women's energies to engage in the struggle for other fundamental changes.

SUGGESTED READINGS

RACISM

Allen, Robert. *Black Awakening in Capitalist America.* New York: Vintage, 1970.

Boggs, James. *Racism and Class Struggle*. New York: Monthly Review Press, 1970.

Cruse, Harold. *Crisis of the Negro Intellectual*. New York: Apollo, 1967.

Foner, Philip, ed. *Black Panthers Speak*. New York: Lippincott, 1970.

Hayden, Tom. *The Love of Possession Is a Disease with Them*. New York: Holt, Rinehart & Winston, 1972.

Jacobs, Paul; Landau, Saul; and Pell, Eve. *To Serve the Devil*. New York: Vintage, 1971.

Ludwig, Ed, and Santibaney, James, eds. *The Chicanos*. New York: Pelican, 1972.

Ofari, Earl. *The Myth of Black Capitalism*. New York: Monthly Review Press, 1970.

Steiner, Stan. *The New Indians*. New York: Delta, 1971.

———. *La Raza*. New York: Harper & Row, 1971.

SEXISM

Greer, Germaine. *The Female Eunuch*. New York: Bantam, 1971.

Koedt, Ann, and Firestone, Shulamith, eds. *Notes*. A yearly journal available from Radical Feminism, P.O. Box AA, Chelsea Station, New York, N.Y. 10011.

Millet, Kate. *Sexual Politics*. New York: Avon, 1970.

Mitchell, Juliet. *Women's Estate*. London: Penguin, 1971.

Morgan, Robin. *Sisterhood Is Powerful*. New York: Random House, 1970.

Nin, Anais. *Diary of Anais Nin*. New York: Harvest, 1967.

Reed, Evelyn. *Problems of Women's Liberation*. New York: Pathfinder Press, 1971.

Thompson, Mary Lou, ed. *Voices of the New Feminism*. Boston: Beacon Press, 1971.

part 2

The Revolutionary Strategy to Change America

4

The Liberal Alternative

THE AMERICAN people are noted for their boundless optimism. "Everything will work out for the best. After all, America is an exception in so many respects. We've had all kinds of crises in the past and we've always managed to pull out of them. In the depression, for example, along came the New Deal and saved the system. Why shouldn't the same thing happen again?" One thing is wrong with this argument: it is ahistorical. It refuses to look closely at the factors that bailed America out in the past—or more precisely, that bailed out America's ruling clique—and why these factors are no longer operative.

American history is the history of capitalist expansion. As long as there was a frontier to conquer, it was always possible to alleviate the worst aspects of the growth of capitalism by extracting new wealth and by finding new markets farther to the west. When the frontier closed down, in the latter part of the nineteenth century, expansion continued into the Pacific. It reached its height after the Second World War, when the United States emerged as the world's leading economic power, dominating markets around the globe. People often forget that it was not the New Deal that stopped the Great Depression. In 1939, 17.2 percent of the workforce was unemployed, and 1.4 percent of the workforce was employed as a consequence of the military budget; these workers, together with the unemployed, thus represented 18.6 percent of the workforce. In 1961, the unemployment rate was 6.7 percent and 9.4 percent of the workforce was employed through the military (before the monumental buildup in war expenditures, first justified to close the nonexistent missile gap and then to fight the Vietnamese). In other words, a total of 16.1 percent of the workforce was either unemployed or dependent for employment on military spending. The war machine, and not the liberals' solutions, ended the crisis in the economy. Moreover, the economic crisis that now faces the country cannot be solved through a military buildup. The American empire is more likely to shrink than grow, both because of the increasing challenges to its imperialism and because the avenue of military expenditures is already utilized to the maximum.

Finally, the current crisis is not simply economic. It is political as well. New Deals cannot solve the fundamental political crisis; it derives from the fact that capitalism makes life intolerable for the vast majority of the world's people, makes most Americans totally powerless to control their own lives, sustains racism and sexism, and makes likely the continued and possibly irreversible destruction of the environment.

In the face of all this, American optimism still offers the liberals as a last-gasp hope. This belief in liberalism, which has kept many people from joining a political movement that really could deal with current problems, has an almost unshakable tenacity in some people's minds.

The term liberal has become so muddled that it is often more confusing than helpful. In part, this happened because liberals who became more conservative nevertheless retained the "liberal" label, so that the term now refers to everyone from Hubert Humphrey and Jacob Javits to Benjamin Spock and Ralph Abernathy. There is a certain justification for the current usage: it is meant to include everyone who thinks that there are serious problems in the functioning of American political and economic life, and who feels that the main problems facing Americans are not, as conservatives seem to hold, those of how to control the people. But this leaves room for many extremely important differences. Let me describe the major positions and discuss some of the concomitant problems—both the problems that are common to all the liberals' positions and those that are unique to one or another of them.

I'll call liberal A the person who holds that some serious problems exist in American society, but that these problems are isolated from each other and can be dealt with through piecemeal reform within the system. Liberal A sees problems here or there, and is willing to concede that they should be dealt with as soon as possible. But A doesn't see any really serious structural problems, and believes that if there were more rational people in government, they would solve the problems that less rational people have created.

Liberal B is a little more upset than A. He believes that certain problems are rooted in basic institutional arrangements of American life. He sees that the war in Vietnam is related to the power of the American military establishment, and that the entire militarized economy has to be challenged in some way if there is to be peace. Hubert Humphrey's work in the late 1950s as chairman of the Senate subcommittee on disarmament showed an understanding of this kind of relationship. But although B sees the need for changing particular structures, he does not see any connection between the different struggles to change different structures—between the struggle to save the ecology from disaster or the struggle against male supremacy and racism, for example. He may sympathize with all of them, but he sees no real connection between them other than the general idea that things should be better for everybody. And he believes that the necessary changes can be accomplished within the present political structure.

Liberal C agrees with B that some institutions are at fault, but does not believe that the problems can be solved simply by using the established mechanisms for change. He feels, for example, that the way to deal with the army is to hold demonstrations designed to pressure existing political officeholders or parties to respond. The extremists of this position are those who think about forming third parties (e.g., John Gardner and Ramsey Clark and Eugene McCarthy) and those who go to jail as moral witnesses in order to mobilize people against a particular institution or set of institutions.

Liberals A, B, and C have one thing in common. None of them recognizes that the various institutional problems have a single common root—the structure of capitalism—and cannot be dealt with short of eliminating capitalism itself. Liberal D, on the other hand, does see this. Nevertheless, he holds that everything will be changed when he and his friends are elected to office. Relatively few people hold this position: once they come to see that the problem is capitalism, they usually also see that capitalists have too much control over the political arena to permit liberal D and his friends to be elected. Position D comes closest to the radical position, and we will investigate it in more detail below. But, for the moment, consider the defects in positions A–C.

The most obvious problem with the liberal position is that it provides a mistaken analysis of the problems and hence cannot provide a solution. For example, suppose that you thought, as many liberals do, that racism arose because of some bad psychological attitudes, or because some employers were not *diligent* enough in their hiring of blacks. Then you'd be tempted to base your approach to the problem, as many liberals do, on the hope that through education about racism and efforts to get legislation passed against job discrimination, the problem would begin to go away. Imagine the surprise of many people who held these attitudes in the 1950s when, by the late 1960s, the problem had not gone away but had intensified—

117

despite the best efforts of a generation of liberal teachers in northern schools and despite antidiscrimination legislation embodied in a host of "civil rights" legislation. When their liberal approach did not seem to work, many people were even tempted to accept the conservative explanation of things: "People just *are racists,* and you can't legislate it away." In fact, the conservative position is at least half right: legislation aimed at racism that leaves intact the capitalist structures that make racism necessary and attractive is unlikely to change anything but the forms in which racism will be manifested. The failure of the liberal solution drives people to the Right, particularly when the Left alternative is unknown to these people except as it is caricatured in the media.

This is probably one of the most devastating problems of liberalism: the liberal analysis doesn't work. The liberals have been in power many times; at best, their measures make matters only slightly better, and sometimes they make things significantly worse. The liberal who adopts either the A or B position agrees that the war in Vietnam was a mistake and that we should get out. But he then finds himself incapable of explaining what the United States should do about Cuba or Bolivia or Chile except to have another Vietnam-style war within this hemisphere (after all, here "our" vital interests are at stake).[1] The liberal will tell us that blacks need better jobs, but what can he recommend if black people rebel after Congress passes antidiscrimination legislation? He can send in the troops as did liberal Governor "Pat" Brown of California and liberal Governor Hughes of New Jersey.

If Governor Brown was correct in 1964 when he said of the Berkeley Free Speech Movement, the prototypical student rebellion, that the students only legitimate demands had already been met and the continued unrest was caused by outside agitators, why not deal with them more forcefully? Why not, indeed? A voting population that accepts this analysis will also accept the need for a stricter disciplinarian to act on it. If the society really is making significant strides in dealing with racism, and blacks nevertheless burn down their own communities, what alternative do we have but to use more force? Liberal John F. Kennedy gave us the war in Vietnam as the only reasonable way to deal with people who would not accept our piecemeal solutions to economic and political domination.

Very few Americans are pacifists; if the war is justified, why not fight it to victory? Would we have made a compromise with Hitler? If the war

[1] John F. Kennedy, for instance, while running for the presidency, argued against involvement in the Quemoy-Matsu issue in Asia and instead focused on Cuba, only 90 miles off our shore.

in Vietnam represents an effort on the part of foreign forces to subvert the democratic government of South Vietnam,[2] and if communism really is evil, why not use all the force at our disposal to show the enemy that the friends of freedom will share any burden in its defense? The fact is that the conservative position is a reasonable and practical extension of many of the liberals' assumptions. In effect, the liberals encourage the growth of the Right by refusing to follow through on many of their own assumptions. This is especially true of the most visible type of liberal, the one who generally holds office—liberal A.

Liberal B, personified by the liberal college professor and a *very few* political figures, will criticize A on these grounds and call into question more fundamental aspects of the working of the society. But neither liberal B—nor his further Left associate, liberal C—is likely ever to hold a position of real power. B is likely to argue that the Democratic party can be reformed if people will only try harder, get started earlier, are more serious, use less rhetoric, and find more convincing candidates. Since liberal B wants to attain power and not merely to sloganize, he has to be practical. His plan is to infiltrate the system, slowly making it to the top; and once he gets power, to institute changes. Almost every area of contemporary life is filled with people who started out with this kind of strategy—whether they were going to infiltrate the university or the Congress or Madison Avenue or the medical profession or the judiciary or some large corporation. But in order to make it, they had to accept many aspects of the system. They had to master some trivia for a degree, or ignore students' needs as a teacher, or show little sympathy to radicals as an aspiring politician. They had, in other words, to win support inside the institution, and this they could do only by showing how good they were at what the institution demanded of them. For, if the people above them suspected they were not really committed to the institution, they would never advance. So, although they were surrounded by obvious injustices, they had to keep quiet. Otherwise they would never achieve real power. Moreover, they had to justify their choices—to themselves and to friends who may have been taking risks, and perhaps getting crushed. Says liberal B: "Can't these people see that it's more rational to do it my way instead of taking so many personal risks? What are they trying to prove? Only utopians try to achieve everything. I have a chance of achieving real power in the long run, and then I'll do the right things. After all, politics is the art of the possible,

---

[2] As George McGovern implied on May 7, 1972, when he told the press that he condemned "the invasion" of South Vietnam by the North.

and if I'm practical I'll try to get what's possible done." But slowly the mask becomes the face, and a life of justifying petty changes in one's attitudes and behavior for the sake of some future power ultimately ends up as a life in which the power achieved is used in ways that are fundamentally similar to those of the people liberal B originally wanted to replace. Liberal B rarely comes to grips with the reason why so many people who started out with his strategy and worked slowly through the system ended up as liberal A, or as outright conservatives.

Moreover, in a system built on stratified power, very few will ever make it to the top. And that leaves millions of despairing liberals whose lives will be spent in a lie—trying to get power through the system by making themselves into salable commodities, and then finding out that no one will buy.

The good 1930s liberals who did not achieve political power play an important role in determining the tone of the current American political scene. Many of them have achieved middle-class status—as professionals, businessmen, or union bureaucrats—and have acquired a considerable number of material rewards. Because imperialism has worked for them, they are less likely to be bitter about the system that kept them from positions of real power than bitter about the young people whose actions remind them of their own idealism during the New Deal period. The New Left seems to be telling them that they wasted their lives, that they sold out when they should have struggled harder. To people in their forties or fifties, the notion of leading an entirely different life no longer seems a viable option and the New Left's notions make them feel that their identity is at stake. If the system as a whole could have been changed when they were young and they did not change it, then—they reason to themselves— they must be corrupt. Not wanting to accept that judgment, they rebel against the whole analysis, turning on the New Left and attacking it as a movement of "wild dreamers and idealists."

Some 1930s liberals—especially on the campuses—have gone even further and have tried to ensure the failure of the New Left by fighting it and by trying to sabotage younger people in their personal or academic life, to *show* them that reality is tough and to prove it by making things as tough for the young people as they were for them. Threatened in their identity, these people become the most vicious antagonists of the movement, the most determined to show that a radical vision can never work, and that the only rational and moral thing is to accommodate oneself to minimal changes and living within the system.

The very few liberals who start to climb the rungs of power often feel much more seriously threatened by the Left than by the Right. For one thing, they feel they must clearly dissociate themselves from the Left if they are to be effective at all. Sometimes they will refuse to take any stands on controversial issues unless they are absolutely forced to (that's why senators so disliked Senator Wayne Morse of Oregon—he forced them to speak up about issues, on which they wanted to remain anonymous). Or they will make loud public attacks on the Left in order to dissociate themselves from it. But the effects of this kind of politics are self-defeating. When liberals with power want to adopt a position that the Left pioneered and made respectable, they have to combat the feeling that the position is un-American, since it is advocated by the Left.

More important, the very few liberals who do achieve positions of power soon discover that their positions do not give them the power they need. They must seek higher positions. The congressman runs for senator, the senator tries to become a committee chairman or runs for the presidency. And this requires staying in line and not antagonizing anyone. So the vicious circle continues.

Finally, there is liberal D. Assume for the sake of argument that he is elected president, and that people with views similar to his are elected to a majority of congressional seats. Suddenly, liberal D reveals himself, Clark Kent-style: here I am, a full-scale radical (he cannot have done this during his campaign) who sees that the problems we face cannot be dealt with except by eliminating the capitalist system. As soon as that happens, the stock market crashes, people are thrown out of work, and the Right organizes around the position that the president is causing economic havoc because the business community has lost faith in the economic climate. Where would such a person turn for help? To the people who elected him? But they did not know what he stood for when they voted for him, and have never even heard a good argument for the elimination of capitalism. So it is ludicrous to believe that he could mobilize enough people to his position to deal with attempts by right-wingers in the corporations and the armed forces to remove him by force. A civil war would not even get off the ground; even people who were sympathetic to some of the radical president's positions would feel that his opponents were justified in their outrage at his deception. Liberal D's strategy, in short, is simply a fantasy. The 1970s may well have their liberal glamour boys seeking political power, maybe even blacks or women or people who smoke dope and dress in psychedelic fashion. But such a person will not challenge the basic capitalist arrangements of society, and still achieve power within the present framework.

But suppose liberal D clearly announced his radical views and tried to work through the system to get votes? Here we have good empirical models to study. Both the Socialist Workers' party and the Peace and Freedom party tried this method. And both met the typical problems of working within the framework of bourgeois politics. The ruling class and its allies own the means of communication and prevent the radicals from getting access to it. The only way the Left can get a hearing from the media is to do something unusual—sponsor a demonstration or a strike or some other struggle—and even then, the Left's position is not likely to be heard because the media focus on the action, rather than the reasons for it. But this strategy of combining electoral with nonelectoral work has much to recommend it, and is a radical strategy, not a liberal one. I shall discuss it more fully in a later chapter.

Liberal C seems to be the position held by the most intellectually honest of the liberals, and it is very often a transitional step to radicalism. For even though C does not yet have a radical analysis, he has come to the conclusion that the normal political processes do not work well enough to respond to his message. And in considering *why* the established procedures do not work, he is likely to stumble on the existence of a ruling class and to become conscious of the connection between its power and the various social ills he recognizes. If, however, he does not become aware of this connection, his actions may well strengthen the hold of the system as a whole even as they may force modification of one small part of it. It is entirely possible that after the war in Vietnam finally ends, we will find some of the most vocal liberal C antiwar leaders, including those who have taken considerable risks—members of the Resistance, for example— either defending the system or trying to stop young people from moving to the Left by telling them that the system will respond to change ("See, we stopped the war"). To the extent that liberals C actually put themselves in opposition to the system, even on a single policy, they should be honored. But their position is incomplete, and can lead people right back into strengthening the oppressive system. Union organizers took many risks in the 1930s and 40s, but the trade unions they created are inadequate, to say the least. Indeed, the union struggle and its cooptation is a classic example of the problems produced by liberal C. Union organizers often saw their struggle as requiring structural changes in the relationship between workers and owners, and they achieved some such changes—for example, the establishment of collective bargaining, certainly an expansion of workers' power. But that achievement was enough to blunt the edge of militancy of the workers' movement, and the bosses accommodated themselves to it by increasing their exploitation abroad and by changing the form of the domestic workers.

Moral arrogance is almost always a necessary correlate of liberal positions A, B, and C. Since all of them start from the assumption that the ills of the system have nothing to do with its essence, the fault must be with the individuals who have gained power. This assumption may not always be spoken, but it necessarily underlies the belief that electing THE GOOD GUYS to office will make everything fine. Liberals who accuse radicals of being power hungry and self-righteous are overlooking the fact that they are the ones who talk about a small group of people getting power. It is precisely because radicals do not pretend to be any more intelligent and any more ethical than those who preceded them that they do not want to use the same techniques that deformed so many good people in the past. The radical does not seek to get the right person elected, to substitute "us" for "them." Rather, he seeks to break down the system of power and redistribute power to all people. The liberal calls for a new ruling elite; the radical calls for the elimination of ruling elites.

Indeed, the liberal position strengthens unnecessarily the whole foundation of rule by elites. Since the liberal strategy is most frequently based on permeation of existing institutions, which means taking the logic of those institutions seriously, the liberal is forced to lie about his own politics and to miseducate the people. The ethics of dishonesty, once adopted, force him to respect his opponents' dishonesty. No one dares blow anyone else's cover for fear that *his* cover will be blown in turn. Men learn much of this in their normal socialization into male chauvinist society: keeping one's cool is the highest virtue, and appearances count for everything. Those who gain most from this sort of procedure are those with the most to hide.

Closely connected with this is the logic of secrecy: because it is not acceptable to expose anyone or make anyone look bad, the key political decisions of our country are taken in secret. The liberal tells us that if we send him as our representative behind those closed doors, he will get us a better deal. But if people are to have any real power over their lives, they must do much more than have faith in their representatives. They must themselves be part of the decision-making process. The liberals continue to weaken the people's ability to make those decisions by agreeing to conduct political affairs in private. This is part of the reason liberals have never tried to organize a coherent, unified political force, with its own institutions, such as the underground papers (and the liberals' money would make the papers much more polished) or the Left's meetings in collectives or mass organizations. The moment the liberals put political issues to people in any coherent form, the people would want to comment and give advice, and perhaps force the liberals to define their position, and this would undercut their maneuverability behind closed doors. So the liberals, like the elites of wealth and power, depend on the quiescence of the masses —it is the logical correlate of the politics of compromise.

This is another reason why liberals almost always end up compromising away the most important parts of their program when they are in positions of power. They are afraid of mobilizing any kind of popular base lest that base get out of hand and go too far to the Left. They know they have achieved their position by compromise, and they cannot be sure that if they become uncompromising on a particular issue they will be able to maintain their support. Precisely because they eschew building an organization around an explicit commitment to their politics, they have no assurance anyone will approve if they now take a stand on principle. Their very dependence on an uninformed electorate is a source of their continued weakness.

The liberals of whom we have been speaking now are ordinary people, not members of the ruling class. But the ruling class has its "liberal wing," made up of those who view political questions in terms of the long-term interests of the ruling class as a whole, rather than short-term profits (although whenever possible they try to have their cake and eat it). The positions of this liberal wing should not be confused with positions that members of the ruling class take on particular questions. For example, insurance companies with investments in the cities may be opposed to the war in Vietnam and hence on the liberal side of that question, while still completely unable to accept even the most minor changes in social legislation for fear these changes might impinge on their profits.

If the liberals do not offer any real hope of changing the system in fundamental ways, they do offer the system an invaluable stabilizer against radical winds. Espousing the doctrine of realism, liberals have been able to channel many dedicated and sincere young people into a system that ended up affecting them far more than they affected it. The continued appeal of liberalism to young people cannot be accounted for by the achievements of American liberals; their record in power under FDR, JFK, and LBJ certainly makes one shudder. But what is the alternative? To be a radical is to pay a very high price. One may lose one's job, one's political future, one's freedom. The conspiracy trials are real—and it is not necessary to indict everyone in Seattle or Chicago to make clear the message that dissent is unsafe. If they indict a Catholic priest, who won't they go after? Besides, the public spokesmen the media have chosen for the radical movement seem so irrational at times. At least, the liberals tell us, we can deliver something real—immediate material benefits—because we can get power in the short run. The attraction of immediate power has turned the eyes of many a young idealist. But the power is always limited to ends sanctioned by the system in which it is achieved.

Of course, as long as people believe that the things radicals are talking about are far off, far off is where they will remain. But fewer and fewer people believe that: we are living today in an age that certainly seemed far off to the New Dealers, and we have inherited the mess the New Dealers made. The problems of capitalism have been blowing up one after another in our faces, and it becomes increasingly difficult to take seriously the notion that piecemeal reforms will do the trick.

Increasingly, the liberals appear to be like doctors who have chosen to treat a few hurting splinters on the body of a person who is dying from cancer. When confronted, the doctors defend their procedure on the grounds that these splinters hurt too, and how can they be criticized for relieving suffering in a sick body? But the radicals point out that in light of the progressing deterioration of the body, it is irrational to work on anything but eliminating the cancerous tumor itself, even if some of the splinters are temporarily ignored. If the analogy seems extreme, consider the deterioration of the environment and the crisis in the ecology. This is just one area in which the liberals are busily engaged in treating the splinters and praising themselves for their progress. Reputable ecologists tell us that there are at least a dozen different ways in which the ecology is permanently threatened, any one of which might be sufficient to destroy the necessary conditions for human life as we know it. The liberals inadequately focus on one or two of these, while the others continue to develop. This is what the liberals mean by being practical, and it is the height of irrationality.

In ecology, in domestic policy, in foreign policy, it is now becoming completely irrational to be "practical" in the sense defined by our system. We can no longer simply talk about "the long range" in abstract terms: the long range is almost upon us. That is why socialist revolution has to become the major topic on the agenda. It emerges from any rational look at reality. The liberals, with their unreasonable faith in the system, their faulty analysis of the way it works, and their arrogant belief in their own superiority, play a major role in confusing and obfuscating reality. When they are in power their actions give the illusion of change without its substance and when they are out of power their actions channel dissent back into the system, where it can easily be managed and controlled. The tragedy of the McCarthy campaign of 1968 was that it succeeded in taking so many people out of the streets, and into the dead end of reforming the Democratic party. Perhaps the next equally unfortunate step will be to take these same people into some third capitalist party that again refuses to challenge *the basic structures* of a class-dominated society.

Precisely because liberals speak to people who are conscious of problems in American society, they come into conflict with radicals who are attempt-

125

ing to show people the relationship among those problems. It is inevitable that liberals and radicals will battle each other on the question of whose interpretation better fits the facts, though the liberals have increasingly stopped arguing and are relying less on logic than on inertia and fear to do their recruiting for them. At most universities liberal professors have simply refused to engage in debates with radicals on any serious questions of political analysis, usually being content to keep on presenting their liberal framework in the classroom where they have total control, and refraining from any discussion in arenas where their assumptions might be called into question. In the 1960s this had the effect of abdicating the struggle for students' loyalties to the radicals, since even cursory examination persuaded most students that the radical position explains more of our current problems than does any of the material they read in their sociology or political science courses. The effect of this on the Left was mixed: on the one hand was the advantage of numbers; with a large community of people seriously questioning American society, any given student did not need to feel that he or she was taking a great personal risk in beginning to examine the Left's analysis of American society. The existence of a protective cover, a kind of Left milieu on campuses, was sufficient to deepen revolutionary consciousness there. And the absense of such a milieu in the usual factory or office is a crucial barrier. On the other hand, the liberal's abdication of any kind of serious intellectual debate meant that most of the recruits to the Left had never heard the best exponents of liberal thought and had never grappled with it. This is a problem not merely because the students are missing something important, but because this way of coming into the Left leaves them unprepared to engage in ideological struggle with those who have accepted the liberal ideology.

The result was the emergence of the gut radicals in the New Left, people who had no familiarity with any of the arguments for their own position. When asked why they felt as they did, these people would point to what was right in front of them: the television that every night showed the murders in Vietnam, the police whom they had personally seen beating up demonstrators, the binding and gagging of Bobby Seale in the court of "justice," etc. But things that seemed obvious to them were not always obvious to everyone else: Nixon would talk about ending the war while escalating it. The media would talk of Nixon's "bravery" for defying public sentiment and common sense. As demonstrations began to seem too risky and futile, fewer people would have the experience of seeing repression directly, and New Leftists would find it impossible to explain to others what was really happening. The inability and refusal of liberals to take part in the debate hurt the New Left, because it freed it of the need to develop in its adherents an adequate respect for intellectual argument.

It is important to distinguish between such professional liberals as political leaders, trade-union bureaucrats, and college professors and the many young people who grew up as liberals but who are open enough to change their views in light of their experience. Most radicals were themselves once liberals, and it would be a mistake to think that all liberals are unchangeable. But the hypocrisy of professional liberals can make radicals angry. They are always willing to support a cause once it is safe, but they are never willing to fight when they are alone. By 1971, when over 73 percent of the American public was against the war, it was quite popular to oppose it. But back in 1965 and 1966 and 1967 the liberals were no place to be seen. Probably the most distinguishing incident had its beginning in 1968, when Eugene McCarthy put himself forward as a man of courage, and urged students to stop demonstrating, cut their hair, and help elect him president. But the minute McCarthy failed to get the nomination, he disappeared from public life. Instead of using the movement he had organized, he completely abandoned it, providing no leadership for antiwar elements throughout the next few years. He did not even run for the Senate, and by abdicating that fight, opened up a seat for former hawk Humphrey. And then, four years later, he came around again, trying to build support for himself. Nor were McGovern or Kennedy any better: they both make pious antiwar pronouncements, but neither ever tried to build any sustained campaign among the people. Indeed, when they felt it opportune, they denounced antiwar activists as "too militant." Where, except in election years, do you find the liberals' antiwar movement?

The resentment that young people felt toward liberals threatens to spread to the entire range of liberal ideology itself, and this would be directly counter to the best insights of the Marxist tradition. It is easy to see that the liberal interpretation of American society distorts the picture and relies on ignorance and misinformation. It is equally easy to discount the liberals' various strategies for change. But it would be a mistake to generalize this attack to the underlying values that liberals espouse. Bourgeois civil liberties such as free speech, free assembly, and free press, along with bourgeois values of justice, equality, and freedom—all these elements of liberal thought must be preserved. In fact, the radical critique of American capitalism is precisely that freedom and equality and justice cannot be attained in a class society, in which institutions are constructed to preserve the economic and political power of one small class of owners over the rest of the population. Many liberals like to mishear what the radicals are saying, and to believe that radicals consider civil liberties unimportant. In

127

fact, what radicals are saying is that the liberties available today are illusory, that they are available only to people who are in basic agreement with, or at least do not seriously challenge, the class distribution of wealth and power. It is precisely because radicals take liberal ideals seriously that they see the need for a revolution in which these ideals could be more fully developed, so that they are no longer merely formal principles, but are part of the actual content of people's lives. The liberal strategy cannot do otherwise than strengthen a society that is the living falsification and negation of liberal values.

This contradiction between liberal ideals and the reality of life in the society liberals defend is the foundation on which radical ideas arise. Liberals must be criticized for not taking their own ideals seriously enough. But at the same time, it is important to appreciate the role that liberal ideals play.

Because liberals espouse certain ideals, it is possible, at certain historical moments, for radicals to make alliances with them around the defense of these ideals. Civil liberties may not mean much in a class-structured society, but they do mean *something*. There is a difference between a fascist society in which all opposition has been systematically silenced and a bourgeois democracy in which people are allowed to organize in opposition to the system within certain limitations. Marcuse and others are right when they point out that the freedoms in bourgeois society usually turn out to be illusory when they are used by a social force intent on challenging any of the basic dimensions of capitalist irrationality. But it does not follow that the limited space available for political work is not important. On the contrary, it is crucial—it is precisely the space that people won for themselves in previous battles that now provides them with room to push new battles forward. At some moments, the illusion of free speech may itself play a cooptive role in the struggle to change society. But the rulers of this country are almost always open to the possibility of pushing back the gains of the past and limiting freedom even more. The Left's position is therefore complex whenever a civil liberties battle emerges. On the one hand, it must point out the tremendous limitations already placed on free speech, which make it evaporate whenever a movement becomes serious and potentially powerful. On the other hand, it must battle to retain that level of free speech already achieved. Free speech is not the only value that we hold (imagine what we would say if a keeper in an insane asylum told us that the inmates could have no reasonable complaints, because after all they were allowed to say whatever they wanted to themselves or others in their padded cells). Free speech was fought for in the past because it could be used in the struggle to achieve a decent society. The last few years have shown that free speech is still extremely important because large numbers of people can be organized, and the conditioning of this society can be overcome. It is precisely for that reason that the government has stepped up its level of repression against the Left.

It is in this kind of struggle—to defend civil liberties from the onslaught of the rulers and their agents—that an alliance between professional liberals and radicals makes sense. The importance of such an alliance can only be underscored by the events of the past few years—for as the contradictions in the capitalist system become more explicit and more visible, the state relies increasingly on repression. Liberals often point to the failure of the Communists in Germany to recognize the danger of the Nazis sufficiently to make a joint front with the Social Democrats. This reading of history is misleading: at least half the problem was that the Social Democrats thought the Communists were a greater danger than the Nazis. The record is much clearer with regard to recent events in this country. In July 1969 the Black Panther party called a National Conference to Combat Fascism, urging all elements who opposed the growth of repressive political measures to attend. Professional liberals managed to keep silent or publicly refuse support when radicals called upon them to join in a common struggle against the use of the courts as an instrument of repression. Who spoke up when the Berrigans went on trial, or Angela Davis, or when Judge Hoffman went berserk in Chicago, or for us in Seattle? Not the liberals. Because this is a matter of life and death for the Left, it will undoubtedly continue to make overtures to the liberals. But there is ample reason for cynicism: despite all the liberals' pious incantations for freedom of speech, they have been remarkably silent when radicals have been dragged off to jail and when Black Panthers have been shot in raids on Panther offices and homes.

And when the pat phrase "law and order" is used as a justification for further escalations of repression, very few of the established liberal figures are willing to risk their positions or popularity in order to organize any kind of movement around civil liberties. The pattern of the early 1950s was repeated in the late 1960s and early 1970s: when the going gets rough, the liberals are nowhere to be seen. It was his battle with the U.S. Army that stopped Senator Joe McCarthy, not some organized offensive of liberals. Indeed, many of the leading liberals in the A and B categories have been willing to adopt the rhetoric of law and order when they thought it necessary to their political survival—with the obvious consequence that they reinforced this trend and made their own survival even more difficult without even further steps to the Right. Whether or not liberals have spoken up has usually been dependent on their positions; and those with less power and fewer aspirations to upward mobility have been more courageous. But, all in all, the liberals' record has been rather disgraceful.

Alliances with liberals to fight the growth of the Right and repression by the state are very important—but they must be based on certain governing principles. The Left should not, simply because it perceives itself as having less power than the liberals, agree to soft-pedal its politics as a condition for such an alliance. The Left should not expect liberals to praise radical politics, but neither should the liberals expect the Left to tone down its criticisms of the liberal strategies for changes. Insofar as the Left sees liberals as having contributed to the conditions that caused the growth of the Right, and defending a social order that depends upon the exploitation and oppression of millions of people around the world, it would be both a political and a moral mistake for the Left to abandon its anticapitalist organizing as a condition for a united front. The Left's alliance with liberals must be around the issue of civil liberties only, not around the entire range of political issues, tactics, and strategies.

The seriousness of this point becomes clear when we see the disastrous path followed by the American Communist party. During the New Deal, the Second World War, and the Joseph McCarthy period, the Communist party attempted to make broad, antifascist alliances by soft-pedaling the ideas of class struggle and revolution, supporting its position by arguing that professional liberals, and particularly the liberal elements in the ruling class, could not be expected to align themselves with any group that advocated the overthrow of the system. The Communist party believed that it was necessary to show them there was no threat to their power in order to persuade the ruling class to align itself with Russia against Nazi Germany, or with civil libertarians against McCarthy. So, after many years of fighting against the bosses in the early 1930s, in which Communist party cadres played a crucial role and earned much respect from rank-and-filers in the trade unions, after tirelessly working to build the CIO, the Communist party used the respect it had won to soften and play-down working-class militancy. Instead of counterposing itself to the right-wing leadership in the trade-union movement, or supporting other leftist tendencies, it abdicated the field to the Right, and then supported the right-wing leadership. It even went so far, in the name of "trade union unity," as to support a resolution at the CIO convention in 1939 that explicitly condemned "fascism and communism" in one breath. During the Second World War, the Communist party leadership in the trade-union movement tried to enforce a no-strike pledge, asking the workers to make sacrifices for the fight against fascism. But they never dreamed of tying this to a demand that the bosses should also make some sacrifices: the capitalists were allowed to profit without end from the war and without challenge from the Left. And, finally, in a supreme act of self-abnegation, the Communist party actually formally dissolved itself in 1943 to show how little of a threat it was. When it was reconstituted after the war, it followed policies designated more to serve the interests of the Soviet Union than to promote class struggle on behalf of the American proletariat. Needless to say, the result was a disaster. The Communist party managed to discredit itself among those it had been organizing: its changes in policies were not dictated by the needs of the American proletariat but by some accommodationist strategy aimed at convincing the ruling class that the Communist party was neither bad nor dangerous.[3] Ironically, all of these fluctuations had only the most minor role in influencing the liberal sections of the ruling class, whose policies toward the fascists and later toward Joseph McCarthy were dictated by self-interest and not by any abstract commitment to liberal principles. The Communist party succeeded only in strengthening people's illusions about the importance of liberal ideology, and in discrediting itself as a reliable source for militant leadership. Its history is the best example of why the Left must never try to soften its message of class struggle when it seeks alliances with professional liberals on the free-speech issue. It is precisely because the Left has a correct analysis of contemporary society that it is able to build a self-defensive movement when it is attacked by the forces of repression. If it sacrifices that message and plays it down for the sake of building a civil liberties coalition, it will find itself alone.

Normal levels of repression can be administered by almost any govern-

---

[3] Earl Browder, the leader of the Communist party, made the following incredible remarks at a rally at Madison Square Garden in New York on January 10, 1944: "Humanity has risen to a new level of intelligence. Capitalism and communism have already begun to march hand in hand toward the peaceful collaboration of tomorrow. This broad policy pursued in the interests of all, also imposes an obligation on all of us to reduce to a minimum, and if possible, to eliminate altogether, every form of violence in the life of every country. . . . I have long reflected on this matter and have come to the conclusion that the people of the United States are subjectively unprepared for a socialist transformation of society. In proclaiming such an objective, far from uniting the nation, we merely foster divisions that can only profit the most reactionary forces. So as to sow confusion in the democratic camp, the reactionaries are fighting the election campaign [the presidential elections of November 1944] under the banner of free enterprise; we Marxists must not fall into their trap by proclaiming the opposite message. . . . We declare quite openly that we are ready to contribute to the effective running of free-enterprise capitalism, lest the marvelous development of our economy be slowed down after the war."
Is it any wonder that working people felt betrayed and duped by this kind of dishonest Left?

ment, but when the state wants to heighten its repressions dramatically, it usually seeks to build mass support for this tactic. The standard procedure is for the state (or, as in Germany, sections of the ruling class that were not satisfied with the state's operations) to foster a movement among the population that offers the following kinds of analysis and programs: "All the problems you are now experiencing are due to the activities of group X (Communists, Jews, Negroes, students, hippies, young radicals, or some other minority). If we can only jail or otherwise repress and eliminate X, everything will be all right." Obviously, the Left has a much more compelling and rational explanation of the things that are bothering people. In times of political quiescence it is often difficult for the Left to get its analysis widely known. The means of communication are not available to the Left and in times of political quiet people are not interested in attending large political meetings or rallies. But when the people are aware that there is a political crisis, it becomes possible to get the Left's analysis fairly widely circulated—if there is an organizational mechanism designed for this goal and if there is leadership for militant struggle. But it was precisely at moments of this sort that the Communist party bound its own hands by refusing to engage in class struggle and anticapitalist education— for fear of antagonizing its liberal "allies." Such a strategy is self-defeating: the one thing that can undercut a strong move to the Right is a movement that shows people that moving to the Right is only strengthening the source of their oppression, and that what they need is a revolution, *not a scapegoat*.

Then wouldn't it be more practical to fight the tendency to move toward the Right by organizing people around civil liberties? Would not mass movement around this issue, with liberals in the leadership and radicals giving political and moral support, have wide appeal? The answer, based on the empirical evidence of forty years, is "no." Civil liberties in the abstract enthuses no one but the liberals, and they are almost always ready to modify their positions when the going gets rough. Most people will fight for civil liberties only when they feel that these liberties can and will be used to fight for other things they really need. If people believe that the Left is putting forward something worth fighting for, then people will fight for civil liberties as part of the means to obtain that something.

If, on the other hand, people believe that free speech is being used for no purpose at all, or if they believe it is being used to harm them (the news media have, for example, represented students and blacks as enemies of the workers), they will not oppose the undermining or elimination of many civil liberties.

The best way for the Left to win support for its defense of civil liberties and its opposition to state repression is to insist on its political analysis. But sticking by one's politics is not enough. The Left must also make an active attempt to reach masses of people with its analysis. In the past few years the Left has been wide open for repression not only because liberals refused to make any alliances with it, but also because it refused to take seriously the task of reaching large numbers of people with its analysis of society. The phenomenal growth of the Left in the past few years owes much more to the depth of the structural crisis of capitalism than it does to the organizing strategies of New Lefters. In fact, the Left has made no real massive attempt to counter the media portrayal of it as a group of bombers and trashers intent on destruction for its own sake (a portrayal, incidentally, often explicitly put forward by liberal antiwar spokesmen).

In a period of severe crisis in capitalism, the last thing the Left should do is become too closely identified in the public mind with the liberals. This is true not only because it would be dishonest to cover over our differences with liberals, but also because there is no group more discredited in American political life than the liberals. The liberals have had power for the past forty years, more or less, and their legacy is the war in Vietnam, the collapse of our cities, etc. George Wallace may well have played on racist sympathies among some of his supporters, but the bulk of his popularity has come precisely by criticizing the liberal clique that has dominated American politics. So powerful is the hold of the ruling class over all these liberals that George McGovern, once having won the Democratic nomination by identifying with the forces of dissent and even attempting to pick up on Wallace's populism in the primaries, was forced to repudiate the radical thrust of his constituency and seek respectability by identifying with the latter day New Deal democrats and their program —easily the most discredited group in American political life.

The liberal strategy is bound to fail, no matter how well-intentioned. The idea that you can deal with one or two serious problems in isolation from the general context of capitalist society is always bound to come to grief, since the proposed solutions never really get to the heart of the problem. Take the question of busing. The liberals have tried to solve the problem of decent education for black students by forced integration. The capitalist system is oppressing blacks in every way; and poor housing, poor health care, inadequate jobs, and police brutality remain constant in the life of the black child being bused from his or her ghetto. Naturally, tensions develop, clashes in life style and expressions of hostility by the black children against the children of their oppressors. So the white children face an unpleasant situation, discipline problems emerge, whites feel threatened, and education does not benefit very much. The more rational

133

white parents can understand that this situation is created by the racist structure of the society. But they do not see, quite correctly, how this one change in education is going to change the whole society, and they therefore do not see why their own children should have to suffer. Sometimes, this sentiment is colored by an extreme racism, and we do not want to apologize or cover up for the racists who oppose forced busing. But we can see the white parents' point of view. Little will be solved simply by changing this one variable. Yet that is the only variable that liberals are willing to tackle seriously. The Left must not follow the racist path of opposing this one change. But against the liberals it must demand that all the changes be taken together by a complete transformation of every aspect of society. Only a total transformation of the capitalist society will solve the problems, and any attempt to do less will cause resentments and sometimes actually make matters worse.

Disillusionment with the liberals has caused many people to move to the Right, out of a belief that it provides the only serious alternative. Part of this misconception is fostered by the media and by the liberals themselves, who often portray liberalism as a more moderate and rational version of the Left. Most people think the Left position is nothing more than a greatly extended and escalated program of liberalism—more welfare statism, more central control, more coercive legislation to deal with social problems—because they have never heard a simple and rational presentation of the Left's position. And since they see the liberal program failing to deal with their problems and even causing more problems, they see no reason to move to the Left. All the more reason to dissociate the Left from liberals' politics to show that what we are for is not just *more* of what the liberals are for.

Part of the reason for keeping the Left's political identity clear and distinct is that it would be dishonest to do otherwise. But since when, you might ask, does honesty play a role in politics? For the Left, honesty is its most important weapon. Liberals who have power can afford to be less than frank, and liberals who are aspiring to power have to be dishonest as the imperative of their political strategy. But the radical has no hope of quietly slipping into power: you cannot dupe people into joining a revolution, which, after all, requires of them great risks and commitment and many years of hard struggle. All the radical has to offer is his analysis, his vision, and his willingness to lead militant struggles and take risks in accord with that analysis and vision. The radical analysis will ultimately win out because it is the best one—not because it has acquired some momentary advantage by skillful manipulation and dissembling. Being courageous in putting forward one's ideas and leading struggles in accordance with those ideas may lead to the short-range problem of offending someone, but in the long run people remember and appreciate integrity. And as more and more of people's normal experience begins to corroborate what radicals have been saying, they are drawn to the Left. Much of the Left's most fruitful political work is in education: planting ideas and ways of looking at things which people will develop and apply to their own experience. This education would be drastically undercut if the Left had to govern what it said by a fear of not alienating its liberal allies in the fight against repression. Hence, the supreme rule of radical politics: ALWAYS SPEAK THE TRUTH. This does not mean being abrasive: indeed a corollary of this rule is: Speak in such a manner that people can hear you and come to grips with what you are saying and not in a manner that makes serious communication impossible. Many of today's young liberals will be tomorrow's radicals. There is a vast difference between liberal workers and college students on the one hand and, on the other, college professors, trade-union bureaucrats, and the young Democratic party politicians who spring up every four years.

Probably the greatest of the liberals' political illusions is the notion that with just a little bit more dedication the "good guys" can take over the Democratic party and, thereafter, the government. Since even these starry-eyed dreamers realize that the Congressional Democratic Party is largely dominated by an alliance of Southern racists and big-city bosses, they focus their attention on Presidential campaigns. And they are occasionally encouraged because, in years that the President is running to succeed himself, the opposition party has been known to nominate more "extreme" elements (e.g., Goldwater in 1964, McGovern in 1972), hoping thereby to guarantee the loyalty of these elements at some future time when the party's chance to win is greater and its candidate more centrist. The big financial powers, the political leaders, the public-opinion makers, and the normally loyal allies of the party then sit by neutrally or even actively support the opposition candidate, thus leaving nothing but the party's title to the faction that has "captured" it. Then, after the debacle, the party tells that wing, "We gave you your chance. Now be realistic and work us next time for a *real* victory. Better accept half a pie than none at all."

Left liberals must be completely deluded if they think they will ever again get the Democrats to nominate anyone as consistently Left liberal and untied to bosses as McGovern. And yet, the moment McGovern came close to power, the old liberal dynamic reappeared. The dynamic of a protest movement that had brought him from obscurity to victory in a few short months threatened to be getting out of hand. The logic of the

135

dynamic that was building could have led McGovern to victory through the building of a firm anticapitalist coalition, playing on antiwar sentiment, the tax revolt, the resentment of many working people against the wage freeze and rising food prices, the fear of pollution, concern about rising health care costs, and the residual populism on which Wallace had so successfully played. It was the only plausible road to electoral victory in a year when Nixon would get centrist votes anyway, and when voters had consistently rejected Democrats with a wishy-washy appeal. Not because it was expedient, then, but because he was being honest to his real commitments, McGovern backed away from the seeming "radicalism" of the movement building around him, surrounded himself with Pentagon and administration figures from the LBJ years, and (as it appears at this writing in summer, 1972) is determined to prove that if elected he would provide basic continuity with the politics of the past. Even at the expense of losing his most precious political possession, his image of integrity, McGovern repudiates his former programs for tax reform, fair welfare, and dramatic military cutbacks. Raised in the politics of conciliation, and torn between a genuine commitment to reform and an even stronger commitment to preserve and strengthen the capitalist system as a whole, McGovern (or any liberal likely to come close to power) is constitutionally incapable of rallying social forces into a real confrontation with capitalist power. In the clinch, the liberals' greatest loyalty is to the system they believe in, and not to the people they profess to lead.

Throughout the 1960s, the Left forced a nationwide debate on Vietnam, racism, and women's liberation—but this was not done by permeating our way through the institutions of power or by proving to the Democrats that we were responsible and willing to work with them. On the contrary, we forced the Democratic party to deal with the issues through demonstrations, sit-ins, marches, draft evasions, and confrontations, and the absence of such demonstrations in mid-1972 helped create a climate in which Nixon's claims that the war was winding down could seem plausible. Attempts by the Left to "use" the Democratic party are thus inevitably self-defeating: its message would be better heard if not translated through the voice of a McGovern, and it would have more of an impact on the entire political scene if it was building a serious electoral party that challenged the assumptions of both capitalist parties. Even liberals should realize that their own bargaining power within the Democratic party would be greatly enhanced if such a leftist party was being built.

One argument that liberals always make is that if you don't support the Democrat you will get a greater evil. For one thing, it's not always clear that one can know in advance who really is the lesser evil. Goldwater, had he been elected at a time when Democrats had control of the Congress in 1964, might have been prevented from escalating the war; Johnson, considered the peace candidate, was given a freer hand. The fallacy of "lesser evilism" is that we will always face terrible choices as long as the Democrats can blackmail us into supporting their strongly pro-capitalist lesser evils. It's only when the Left is willing to run that risk for a long enough period to build its own independent alternative that we have any chance of altering the cycle of two bad candidates, one of whom is much better on a relative scale, but both of whom really do not challenge a system that oppresses people. Of course, when the Left is not engaged in such an effort, it becomes reasonable to vote for a McGovern or other mild reformers. Better McGovern than Nixon. But better still—neither.

The impetus for reaching out to liberal Democrats is a good one: most of them are not professional liberals; they accepted liberalism because they never heard a coherent, nonrhetorical presentation of the Left's analysis together with a reasoned strategy for how the Left could proceed in a struggle for real power. But since this is the reason for entering such a venture, it is crucial that the Left not soften its critique out of fear it will offend people. The professional liberals, to be sure, have not attempted any moderation of their attacks on the Left even when they built their own political careers by trying to attach themselves to movements that the Left built (e.g., the antiwar movement). Senator George McGovern made a biting attack on the Left just before the Hatfield-McGovern amendment came up for a vote in the Senate, in a cynical effort to show how "responsible" he was. Muskie, Kennedy, and Lindsay have all attacked the Left when they could make political hay out of it. And liberal professors on every campus use their classrooms to put forward their politics, well aware that they are consciously ignoring the radical interpretation of the phenomena they are discussing. I remember one liberal history professor at the University of California at Berkeley who, having portrayed himself for years as someone who would fight the administration on behalf of the students, turned around and told radicals, "The blood of the Vietnamese will be on your hands if you don't support the candidacy of Eugene McCarthy!" That was in 1968, and if anything prolonged the war it was the illusions created by the liberals in 1967 and early 1968 that it was through the Democratic party that the war would be stopped that year. These are allies we should not fear to confront and even offend. If anything, our job is to expose the inadequacy of their nonalternative. But we must do so in such a way as to respect the intelligence and integrity of many young people who have accepted liberalism because all they have heard from the Left has been meaningless yippie-isms and frightening glorification of bombings and irrationality. Any approach to liberal young people must include an honest critique of the practices of the Left, particularly of those whom the media has chosen as "our" spokesmen.

Liberals will never provide a way for dealing with the basic problems of American society. Even those who are sincere in their desire to deal with the problems have an incorrect analysis of what the problems are, how they are caused, and how they can be dealt with. Their net effect is to lead people into channels of activity that sustain and strengthen the system of domination as a whole, even if they do yield minimal changes in particular parts. Often they have the temerity to talk about the success of their strategy in the past, ignoring the fact that the war in Vietnam reveals that the cost of their strategy in human terms as absolutely staggering and unreasonable. Their hopes for the future are based on elitism and manipulation: "Trust in me," a liberal tells you, "and, if and when I make it, I'll straighten things out. But don't rock the boat before that, or you'll just ruin my chances of making it." Meanwhile, the U.S. Senate, which must approve every war appropriation, could have been bogged down for the past several years if all the liberals had decided to use the power already available to them. Despite all the attempts to make political hay off the war, liberal senators refused to turn off their colleagues by using a tool that could have stopped the war without violating any laws—a filibuster to prevent any business-as-usual until the war ended. Meanwhile, we are sent to jail, shot in the streets, lose our jobs, see our friends made into fugitives—while the liberals patiently sniff the political winds to see which way they are blowing. The ecological crisis deepens, and racism and sexism continue to take their human tolls. And we are supposed to be patient, to wait for the time when another liberal will take office—who doesn't understand the problems, who could not act decisively even if he did, and who generally supports the class system and the structure of capitalism, and is often one of its chief beneficiaries. No wonder the appeal of liberalism has lost its charm for so many people.

5
Who Will Make the Revolution?

ONE OF THE most important questions remains to be answered: Who can make the changes necessary to reconstruct this society from one based on exploitation that benefits a ruling class to one based on maximizing human creativity, love, and the realization of human potentialities?

This chapter examines some of the candidates who have been proposed in recent years as possible agents of revolutionary change, and discusses some of the problems that have emerged in the development of each group. There must, necessarily, be an air of tentativeness. Many important questions about each group are yet to be answered: How will it develop? What strategies will it adopt? How will it grow? But one thing is clear beyond a doubt. Not only has American capitalism created problems, but it has also set the conditions for the emergence of a solution: the millions of people in this country who increasingly realize that their only hope lies in socialist revolution.

STUDENTS

Many political observers saw the emergence of a student movement in the mid-1960s as the first crack in the structure of capitalist political and ideological hegemony. As late as 1965, Herbert Marcuse could write of the success of American affluence in closing the universe of discourse and making serious change a utopian fantasy. Such an interpretation can now be seen to have entirely missed the dynamics of American imperialism and racism. The student movement did not emerge as some miraculous transformation of consciousness, but as an understandable response to the struggles of blacks and Vietnamese, the repercussions of which were be-

139

ginning to be felt on the college campuses. For example, although many students felt oppressed by the nature and functioning of the multiversity before the Free Speech Movement in Berkeley in 1964, the actual events of the FSM struggle were touched off by the refusal of the Regents to allow on-campus student advocacy of off-campus action in support of the civil rights movement. Free speech would never have been challenged by the Regents so long as that speech was not being used to challenge the Regents' interests. But the Regents had a vital stake in a racist society and it was racism against which the civil rights movement was moving, however ineffectively and even without a full understanding of what it was up against.

Similarly, the Vietnamese people's challenge to America's imperialist adventures helped the dramatic growth of an antiwar movement among college students. Students were being asked to fight in a war whose explicit aim was to prevent the falling of a precious domino which might upset America's worldwide economic and political domination.

At the same time, a variety of factors indigenous to the situation of students helped sustain a student radical movement once it emerged. Precisely because the student years are supposed to be devoted to asking serious questions and reflecting on the world, students have an opportunity to see the obvious contradictions between liberal ideology and capitalist reality. In their political science classes they are taught that the United States is a democracy in which the people have real power. But, in fact, they find that they cannot tell the difference between the major candidates' positions on the basic questions facing them. They hear constant praise of the progress that has been made in American society and then talk to the black person sitting beside them who is about to return home to the ghetto's poverty and despair. They listen to history and anthropology lectures in which the information is always presented from the standpoint of the ruling class, and in which women are relegated to positions of little importance.

Nor do the contradictions always affect *other* people: not only are students powerless in the society they are being trained to enter, but they are also powerless within the university. The teachers they respect are fired for being too interested in teaching or too concerned with the real problems of society. They cannot get courses that address the issues they want to hear about: instead, almost everything is geared to training them for some position in the larger society. But increasingly they are unsure if they want to enter that society on its own terms. And yet, they have little time to think about what they really do want, for they are loaded down by course work and short semesters or quarters.

In many ways the university is simply a microcosm of the larger society —one in which many of the contradictions are much more readily apparent. To many Americans, the war in Vietnam must seem far away: it impinges little on their lives except in the form of taxes and on TV. But a student finds that in the very next classroom are ROTC people who will next year be leading a battalion. Or that his professor has been working on a sociology project designed to study possible insurgent groups. Or that the chemistry or physics department is under contract to the Atomic Energy Commission or the Defense Department. Or that a classmate from two years ago has been wounded or killed in Vietnam. The contradictions in society are brought into sharper focus on the campus, and clarity increases the moment the students become involved in trying to change things. Students quickly discover that the alleged normal channels for change are never really open, that they exist simply to confuse and to stall, never to allow students any power. The illusion of responsiveness quickly gives way to the reality of inflexibility on major questions. As long as student demands are limited to changes in dormitory rules or similar trivia, a liberal administration can bend; but except for a handful of privately owned and well-endowed universities, very few liberal administrators are permitted much leeway on substantive demands. Very quickly the students learn that those who seemed to have power do not really have power; that the dean's or the president's power is only the power to do what serves the interests of a small group of men, the regents or board of governors or overseers, most of whom are prominent members of the ruling class. These men have interests that are served by keeping the university as a service station to society, a society over which they have economic and political hegemony.

The beginning of political wisdom is to understand that the main problem is *not* communication. The student movement learned this very early. It did everything in its power to communicate with the regents, the administrators, and the press. At first, it was astounded when it found its positions misinterpreted in the press and misrepresented by the administration. But after numerous face-to-face discussions with the regents, boards of governors, trustees, and administrators, the problem began to emerge: it was not a communication gap but a conflict of interests.

The emergence of the student movement was greatly facilitated by a variety of structural features of students' lives. For one thing, students have more time on their hands than working people: even though the universities and colleges have tried to pile busywork and speedups on them, the only real check is exams, which occur only once every five or six weeks. This gives students time to drift out of the academic routine and on to the more serious questions that often lead them to politics. Moreover, students are in a community with high density and hence are more likely to come into contact with· the few people who have begun to think in a nonconventional way than if they were living in suburbia. Students have access to a great deal of information, and campuses are an ideal setting for visiting lecturers or speakers who have had experiences that are not reported in the newspapers. Universities and colleges have areas for political activity—a variety of large lecture halls and outdoor rally places that have already been defined as socially acceptable sites for large numbers of people to gather to hear controversial ideas. For all these reasons, people interested in political activity have often spent much of their energies in campus communities, usually because they thought they would receive a higher yield on their time. This choice in itself has tended to reinforce the campus's more rapid move to the Left.

Students, then, have become radical more quickly than other groups not because they have some special virtue, but because features of their oppression and the oppression of others have been easier for them to see and to organize around, in part because of the special privileges they have received as students. Capitalist ideologists sometimes argue that students are the only Americans who will join in radical struggle because they are the only ones so far to have done so in large numbers. Such an approach ignores the unique historical circumstances that led to the growth of a student movement. In the 1950s students were considered the least likely group to move politically: they were "the lost generation" or "the silent generation," and in those days the same empiricists argued that all controversy in America was over, that we had reached "the end of ideology" and that all disputes would now be easily and happily resolved. In addition, it rests on the false assumptions that the events which moved students into struggle would not have serious impacts on the rest of society, and that students would abandon the insights they had gained about the nature of their society the moment they left the reinforcing atmosphere of the campus community.

The power of a student movement can be seen in the events of May 1968 in France. There, a group of students began a series of demonstrations around demands related to their training at the university. The example of their courage in fighting in the streets against the police inspired young workers who, over the objections of union bureaucrats and the French Communist party, organized a general strike which soon paralyzed the entire economy and brought France to the verge of a socialist revolution.

French students were powerful because they were able to break through

142

the apathy and sense of powerlessness many people felt and to show by example that courageous fighting was not simply a myth from the past. Because their militant confrontations ruptured the consciousness of domination the institutions of capitalist society has so carefully developed, they became a source of inspiration for young people around the world.

Then why cannot the students, alone, make the revolution in America? Herbert Marcuse has argued that a small minority of people who could see through the one-dimensional society, and could see its vast destructiveness, would be perfectly justified in taking state power for the benefit of the majority, even if that majority did not realize that such a move would be to its benefit. Marcuse is correct on the moral level: any way in which this society could be stopped from carrying out its murder and plunder of people and its destruction of the ecology would certainly be justified unless that way caused even more suffering and destructiveness. The majority of the people of the world (who are directly affected by American imperialism and hence should have some say) would certainly welcome a revolution in this country that alleviated their own oppression. But, in cold fact, a minority revolution is impossible. Any coup d'état would quickly be crushed by the well-organized forces of the ruling class together with their loyal friends in the armed services and the police. Only if millions of people were willing to fight for the revolution, and tens of millions of people actively supported it in a variety of ways, could it possibly survive. But this does not mean that the revolution must be based on some strict numerical calculation. Indeed, it was the French Communist party's very narrow understanding of what a "majority" meant that kept it from struggling for power when it had almost half of the population not only supporting revolutionary change but almost ready to fight for it.

It is precisely because the universities play an important role for the ruling class, both by training key sectors of the workforce and by perpetuating the myths of capitalist ideology, that the struggle for power in the universities is neither irrelevant or secondary. In addition to the impact that such struggles have on the students, who get a vision of the class nature of the society they will enter as workers, any power to effect the structure of the university is important in and of itself. All too often, student radicals have focused away from the university, thinking that the "real" people were someplace else. This view of the university as an "ivory tower" in which nothing important happens has been decisively refuted by the struggle of the 1960s: the rulers of this society have been just as anxious to keep control over their campuses as over any other piece of their property. The university is an important factory: it produces human cogs that can fit into an inhuman machine. To the degree that student

143

power demands are aimed at giving students real influence over what is taught at the university, what kind of research is done, and who will be allowed to teach, they will be met with determined opposition by the owners of the university.

But student power can become a cooptive device that leads nowhere. If all it means is student participation on committees that are stacked against them, or student control over trivial decisions, it can provide a convenient way for the administration to hide the real nature of the society the universities and colleges serve. But no general rule in this regard can be formulated. Each case requires its own careful assessment of the circumstances and likely consequences of student power struggles. For instance, demands for control over a student union building might be very useful at a community college, where the experience of having control over an area of one's life will raise expectations in students' minds that cannot be fulfilled in the work world they are about to enter and hence lead them to become receptive to the message of the revolutionary movement. The same struggle at Harvard or Stanford might simply remove a thorn from the side of students and make them happier during these years of apprenticeship for positions in the ruling class. On the other hand, a demand for power over hiring at an elite school might be used to hire radical professors who open young people to radical ideas and convince some ruling-class students that their humanity requires them to identify with the revolution. A struggle that was appropriate at one historical moment might be completely out of place later, when the students' consciousness had reached a higher point. The criterion must always be: Does this particular struggle help more people to develop class consciousness and to see the need for revolutionary transformation, and/or does it bring about a change in the university which in turn will help the development of revolutionary consciousness?

The student movement must always avoid the pitfall of relying too heavily on the advice or support of the faculty. Although faculty members do not have the same set of interests as trustees or administrators, they are usually faithful servants of the system as a whole. It is difficult for them to criticize a system that pays them more than $10,000 a year to do what they like best: talk about their ideas. There is a built-in tendency among students to think of the faculty as committed to reason, and hence to respect the faculty's opinion on questions of how the university should be constructed, what a good society would be like, and what steps are likely to lead to such a society. Students must remember how people became faculty members: for years they pushed all important questions to the side so that they could focus on the narrow questions

144

that would give them their Ph.D. thesis and a few articles for publication in some scholarly journal; then they spent more years proving to administrators and colleagues that they were no threat to anyone else's ego or political structure. The whole process of tenure is designed to root out the most creative and controversial and to ensure the dominance of mediocrity. In most cases the administration does not have to intervene directly in denying tenure to a controversial person: the faculty of the department has been so selected that it can usually be relied upon to do the administration's dirty work for it under the guise of "academic competence." Nor is the faculty acting in bad faith. In fact, many faculty members really believe that the teacher with interdepartmental concerns, the teacher who asks real questions about society as a whole, is utterly incompetent. This discrimination does not operate only against people on the Left: the very few creative thinkers on the Right find themselves similarly in trouble in finding positions in the university for the same reason, and often get their positions only because of intervention by the administration or trustees.

The point is that the faculty of most major universities or colleges is made up of a preponderance of narrow and silly people who, although they who have little understanding of their world, feel basically secure in it and threatened by anyone who proposes serious changes. They are no more competent to give advice on what life could or should be than a group of bankers or accountants. Indeed, they are often less competent, since they get paid to sell certain ideas and if they sell the wrong ones they usually don't keep their jobs.

Unfortunately, this same syndrome is often true for young college teachers as well. The young professor starting out in the early 1970s was in the university during the Vietnam war, the invasion of Cambodia, the Panther murders, the suppression of the antiwar movement, the rise of the women's liberation movement, the invasion of Laos, the rise of the ecology movement, and the flourishing of the hip culture. Through all this he managed to pass endless qualifying exams and language exams, and to write a thesis—and to do this without antagonizing the administration or professors in the department: with the job market in academia simply filled with qualified candidates, this young professor had to have really active support from several key professors in order even to be considered. In a period in which the most intelligent of his friends in the university were either forced out or dropped out, he managed to show a kind of single-mindedness and obliviousness to his world that has now been well rewarded. There are exceptions, of course: every once in a while a university will hire someone because he or she is unusual and creative and

145

controversial and can therefore be rolled out on ceremonial occasions to silence the critics. But by and large the young people who get teaching jobs today do not differ in significant respects from the hacks who preceded them. They may wear psychedelic clothes or ride motorcycles or smoke grass and be part of the hip milieu. But they have also managed to prove to administrators and colleagues that the substance of what they are doing is perfectly consistent with the normal functioning of the university.

The university system, like the system as a whole, is flexible enough so that some changes will undoubtedly be won from it, and some even given by the trustees in order to avoid an anticipated struggle. For instance, black studies and women's studies will be given in some places without a fight; in others, after student demonstrations and strikes, as long as the trustees and administration are assured that these fields will be as trivial and depoliticized as the sociology and political science departments. That is why, in all these struggles, the key question is control: who runs the program and for what ends. A black studies center run by black students from the ghetto is more likely to address itself to the question of racism and how to deal with it today than one run by black faculty who have been chosen by the university. Recently, special colleges in idyllic circumstances have been set up for a small elite who can there study and reflect on philosophy, literature, and psychology away from the strife of the city or large impersonal campuses. University of California, Santa Cruz, is a beautiful model of what to do with the students of the future who refuse simply to be trained for a job in society: give them an isolated and beautiful setting with teachers who like to think about "the profound" but not about the political crisis of modern capitalism. Students in these settings often find it hard to understand the very notion of oppression. They run their colleges, make their own rules, set up experimental classes on the lawn. What else could anyone want? This strategy may be used to deal with a small percentage of middle-class students, but the society's pressing needs for well-trained technicians at every level preclude the possibility that it will be adopted on a broad basis. But even on the small scale, these institutions can contribute people to the revolutionary struggle: although they temporarily deflect student radicalism, they also make it harder for people to adjust to life in America once they graduate, and hence provide a source of potential recruits to the movement.

Struggles on the campus often lead to situations in which faculty and administrators warn the students that they will "destroy the university." Students are threatened with tougher presidents or chancellors, with loss of the best faculty, who will go elsewhere to find quieter surroundings;

146

with loss of funds from the legislature; or with the closing of the campus by the governor or some other state official. The movement has usually been unimpressed with these threats. The faculty who will leave are likely to be teaching material that confuses students or is irrelevant: what kind of intellectual would leave a scene because of ferment and unrest at a period when his students had begun to act on their beliefs? A new president, though *possibly* more repressive (was Charles Hitch really so much worse than Clark Kerr at the University of California?), will still be trying to enforce the same status quo as the earlier one espoused.

Nor is the state likely to shut down its universities for any sustained period of time. By now students realize that the state is not educating them because it wants to reward them for being good in high school or because it would like its citizens to be knowledgeable and acquainted with the great traditions of thought and culture in Western civilization. The state takes the taxpayers' money to sponsor schools so that it can train people to fill the many jobs and services necessary for the efficient functioning of the society. Much of this training would otherwise have to be done by private industry. In the past, the universities did not train engineers and technicians. Private industry did. But now that industry has set up training programs in the universities, and the "community college," it does not want these institutions shut. The state, therefore, is as reluctant to shut down a campus as it would be to shut down a factory producing vital goods. It may do so in institutions where it feels it has lost control, but it will attempt to reopen the facilities as soon as possible.

If some state and junior colleges were shut down for a long period, it would indeed present a serious problem to those students bent on getting through as quickly as possible in order to get a job and achieve economic security. And their economic needs should not be dismissed as irrelevant. But what would happen if an *elite* university were shut down? Since students learn very little about their world, those who were looking for a real education would be missing very little. On the contrary, if the elite universities were shut down as the result of a student struggle, students would learn more in that struggle than they would normally learn during the entire school year. For instance, students learned more about America during their student strike in the weeks following the invasion of Cambodia than most of them had ever learned in political science and sociology classes. Reality cut through the liberal ideology and forced them to see America as it really is. There is no substitute for involvement in a real political struggle for finding out how things really work.

This is one reason why even allegedly "socialist" or Marxist intellectuals who refuse to engage in concrete struggle so often misunderstand the

American reality. I do not mean to suggest that study of theory and empirical facts is unimportant and that the only "real" education comes through experience. Both theoretical and empirical study are crucial to the development of a revolutionary. But the university does not teach anything about the most important questions, or, if it does, it teaches things that obfuscate and mislead. The university does not provide students with categories to understand their society or their own experience. The student movement must create its own institutions for research and theoretical inquiry into the nature of American society. It must provide a real education, but it is greatly hampered in doing so by lack of finances and facilities.

The problems of the student movement are greatly complicated by the fact that the university creates widespread anti-intellectualism amongst its students. Young people first approach the university with great anticipation that the "Mickey Mouse" level of high school is over and that real knowledge lies ahead of them. The shock of finding that the university treats them like so many pieces of raw material to be processed for societal consumption and that their professors seem to have no knowledge of, or concern about, what is happening in the world, brings wide-scale disillusionment. The response most typical in the early 1950s was cynicism and resignation: most students just decided to join the rat race and see if they could make it. In the 1960s a more common response was simply to drop out of the university and repudiate what it was about.

Unfortunately, many students generalize from the university to theoretical enterprises in general. If this is what intellectuals do, they reason, then why take intellectual study seriously? Having never been exposed to anyone who understood Marx or Lenin or Gramsci or Lukacs, they come to feel that intellectual pursuits must always miss the point and confuse people. Nor is this feeling altered when they run into those few academic Marxists and leftist socialist sect groups that spend their time debating about how many Trotskyist angels can fit on the head of a Stalinist pin or what is the correct analysis of Albanian communism.

The university and the intellectual establishment are the source of anti-intellectualism among students, and the reason for which so many young people have come to ridicule serious scholarship and theory are understandable. But the movement must fight this tendency, particularly among those who have become involved in political activity. All too often the underground newspapers that have grown up around universities and youth ghettos have tended to reflect this same anti-intellectualism, with disastrous results. Outsiders trying to discover what the movement is about often find nothing more intelligible than a few catchy slogans; they

148

must be really persistent until they are directed to the few decent books that have been written explaining the leftist perspective in America. Serious intellectuals who want to use their talents to advance the cause of human liberation often find themselves the subject of ridicule and rarely find ways to relate to the student movement. The most anti-intellectual ex-students often drop out of the movement within a year or two, having found ways of being mindless that require fewer personal risks. The student movement betrays itself and its own possibilities to the extent that it allows these tendencies to predominate.

Fighting anti-intellectualism is not always easy, particularly when intellectuals in the movement cling to forms of elitism and bourgeois individualism, mistaking them for the essence of intellectual life. Young intellectuals have come to consciousness in a society that considers their ideas a marketable commodity and in which job competition creates an atmosphere where intellectual work is done in isolation and used as a club in the struggle for self-validation. It is difficult for them to renounce their previous conditioning. But it is a must. The movement must show its followers that intellectual work can be used collectively and noncompetitively as a key tool in the struggle to overthrow capitalism. Only if we understand in detail how the system works can we know where it will be weak at any given moment and how to intensify its contradictions and bring people to an awareness of their potential strength. To do this we must also reject any constraints on intellectual inquiry. Our job is not to prove the slogans of the past, but to discover the truth about the world, no matter how complex.

Ultimately, the movement must strive to create alternative educational institutions that prepare people for the struggle ahead at the same time they offer an analysis of the past and present. Such institutions will address themselves to the question of human liberation and see intellectual questions from that perspective. At the same time, the colleges and institutes of the movement will have to eschew the failures of the "free universities" already flourishing around many campuses which promote anti-intellectual fads, from astrology and witchcraft to hip Christianity. Our institutes will study American society in detail, and provide the kind of information that can be used to transform that society. Moreover, they will study the past development of society and culture not from the standpoint of the rulers, but from the standpoint of ordinary human beings. The lack of financial resources is primarily responsible for the small number of such institutes currently in operation.

In the future, as more people become interested in such projects, institutes will be set up in working-class communities so that intellectual

149

life becomes a part of ordinary life and is not relegated only to the years of training for work. Precisely because the revolution depends on people taking power over their own lives, it is crucial to the revolutionary struggle. to disseminate knowledge and a love for truth to enable people to feel the confidence in their own judgments they must have in order to take power.

Another source of anti-intellectualism in the student movement derives from the hostility that various leftist sect groups have earned by attempting to force their own ideological framework on an uncomplying reality. The best of the Marxist tradition emphasizes the need to make concrete empirical studies of each situation, and to avoid imposing static categories on an ever-changing reality. Marx himself spent years engaged in painstaking research on the current trends in capitalism, noting that only by scientific study could one understand one's world. All the great revolutionary leaders, from Lenin to Mao to Castro, made careful studies of their own unique circumstances rather than relying on general Marxist formulas or even previous revolutionaries' experiences. They were all inspired by Marx because they all stressed what David Horowitz calls "the recognition of the class pivot of history and the class basis of social oppression, coupled with a clear commitment to one side of the social struggle: the side of the oppressed against their oppressors." [1] But they all eschewed any mechanical reliance on insights and strategies that derived from somewhat different circumstances.

The New Left, on the other hand, was confronted with the remnants of the Old Left from its start: people who refused to look at the way the world was because their organizations did their thinking for them. The first response of the New Left was to eschew ideology altogether, and instead to derive ideas solely from the individual's experience. But this was inadequate; our own experience did not provide categories that could explain imperialism. So naive empiricism yielded in a new search for theory. Many sections of the New Left began to adopt some variant of "hand-me-down Marxism," Maoism, or "Third Worldism." If the Old Left overstressed the role of the workers, various New Left groups had a mystical faith in the Third World and its power. This reached a height within the now-defunct Students for a Democratic Society. In its attempt to counter the emerging Progressive Labor party faction, the Weatherman faction adopted a version of Third Worldism that had little to do with the realities of politics and economics. While these two groups battled with each other, the Weatherman attempting to put its ideology into practice in a disastrous fashion, most young people became less and less interested

[1] David Horowitz, *The Fate of Midas* (Berkeley, Calif.: Ramparts Press, 1973).

in radical politics. This reaction was understandable: they realized that any sentence which started out "X is the key to the revolution" would probably be mistaken in some important regard. But it was also disastrous; for the Left needs thinking and research on these questions, guided by tentative hypotheses and a willingness to experiment, not a wholesale rejection of serious thought just because so much thinking in the past has been only high-level sloganeering. The emergence of the New American Movement in 1971 as an attempt to rectify these problems was a hopeful sign that many ex-members of the student movement have come to recognize this point.

The impact of the student movement in the 1960s was tremendous, and that impact will grow as more and more students take jobs in various sectors of the society. Ironically, having played a large role in reopening the political arena to fundamental questions, the student movement has recently been in a period of marked decline. The absence of any national organization has been particularly harmful: each campus has felt isolated from the others in the face of the repression their administrators were clearly unafraid to use. (After all, when student unrest emerged as a major political development in 1964, no one dreamed that only a few years later, students would actually be shot and killed on campuses around the country.) Additional harm has been done by those sections of the movement that appeared to be glorifying every irrational fad and suggested that it was time to pick up a gun and become armed revolutionaries. Campus struggles often seemed to come to a dead end because no other sectors of the society could relate to them. As a result, many student activists turned their attentions outward. But it would be a great mistake if in doing so they ignored the continuing importance of a student movement.

YOUTH

The development of youth ghettos and a "youth culture" in America over the past six years has had the most startling political consequences. Young people from all classes have increasingly come to identify with one another and against the established political and economic order. In part, this was fostered by the glorification of youth that has been part of the ideology of American society. The mass media glorified the youthfulness of the Kennedy presidency, always stressing its vitality, just as it sells consumer products by suggesting that they are the key to required youth: all of us are urged to join the Pepsi generation. In a society which makes old age a terror, and in which most of adult life is spent in useless labor,

151

it is natural to stress the glories of youth. Moreover, people who had little hope of living a decent life for themselves could, they thought, at least make things relatively pleasant for their children, sparing them the worst aspects of the struggles that the depression and the Second World War had inflicted on them.

In every way possible, youth was extolled and institutional arrangements for perpetuating youth, like the university, were extended and supported generously. This served an economic purpose as well: the job market simply could not accommodate the millions of new job seekers who would flood it if young people became part of the work force at eighteen. At the same time, the need for university-trained specialists and the need for men to serve in the imperialist adventure in Vietnam dovetailed well with this general trend to postpone the transition from "youth" to "adult."

The war in Vietnam helped to concretize the sense of solidarity among young people. It was an old man's war, it appeared, and young people were being sent to die for it. As increasing numbers of young people sought to evade the draft by flight or by refusing induction, their sense of aloneness began to dissolve. At the huge antiwar demonstration in 1966 one saw tens of thousands of young people coming together, and despite the scores of adult peace groups, labor and pacifist organizations allegedly bringing out their supporters to these demonstrations, when young people looked around they saw mainly other people like themselves.

As young people came to know each other in this new context, they began to see a common root in their experience. They were the generation for which everyone had sacrificed, the generation that was to inherit the material wealth that their parents had worked so hard to create. But, having passed through affluence, they found it empty. America might have many goods, but those goods were produced to make profit rather than to fulfill real human needs. Who wanted the car that would fall apart, or the plastic housing, or the computerized identity, or the ugly freeways, or the food with no food value, or the poisoned air and the gray-flannel-suit mentalities that were being offered to them as the great flowering of American civilization? And, to boot, all this ugly affluence was founded upon the exploitation of the peoples of the world, the murder of the Vietnamese, the oppression of blacks and women. In the end, affluence could be attained and enjoyed only if one was willing to sacrifice integrity and humanity—and to the young, that seemed too high a price to pay.

This shared experience was articulated in the music and dance of the 1960s. Underlying them was the feeling that it was now possible to have a new kind of life. The relations of production had become a fetter on the material possibilities available in advanced industrial society: that is, it no

152

longer seemed to make sense to defer satisfactions when it meant only a life of humanly meaningless labor, whose sole purpose was to create wealth for the already rich and powerful. In raising these perspectives the youth culture went far beyond the original directions of the student movement, which had been rooted in questions of foreign policy and civil rights. The youth culture was now directly confronting the essense of capitalist production.

But "confronting" is perhaps too strong a characterization: for the youth culture quickly identified itself not with a Marxist critique of American society, but with the cult of good vibes and experiences. The answer to capitalist production was to tune in, turn on, and drop out. Replace work with immediate gratification: heavy music, good dope, and sex. The effort to understand and to organize against the system was too goal-directed, too much like the world of Puritan ethics and hard work that people were concerned to escape. Verbal communication was too linear, and political analysis was part of the old world that had been rejected. Unless thought could be cast in a form that could be easily ingested with one's new food, new clothes, dope, and sex, it was irrelevant and outdated. Ingestion became the key. In short, the youth culture rebelled against the ethic of production, but did not advance to the point of rejecting the other side of modern capitalism—the ethic of consumption. True, it had markedly different tastes than "straight" society. But psychedelic clothes and electric music and leathers and wood instead of plastic are not, in and of themselves, really subversive of the system.

Nor is a culture that makes sex and marijuana freely available necessarily subversive. Although the dominant capitalist ethos still looks down on pleasure, there is little reason to believe that I cannot accommodate to pleasure in moderation. Aldous Huxley anticipated this aspect of the youth culture in *Brave New World,* which describes the new totalitarianism as secured by its willingness to distribute adequate supplies of sex and drugs. Pot may be a much better way of accommodating workers to their labor than color television. It is well known that soldiers in Vietnam, including those who support the war and who fight hard, frequently relax between heavy combat assignments with pot and sex. The key is moderation. And some people argue that once pleasure becomes generally distributed many people will find it hard to relate to the restrictive modes of society. But, in fact, some of these restrictions can be relaxed by an enlightened capitalism! The system went through an analogous phase in the Prohibition period, during which many people were made outlaws in order to get what they wanted; and during Prohibition many of those people may have come to see that there was something more fundamentally wrong with the system than its refusal to give them alcohol. But, when alcohol was legalized, capitalism did not fall apart. The legalization of pot will induce the development of a new industry of consumption, and make popular certain styles that are now current only in the youth subculture. Far from shaking capitalism, it will strengthen it.

The boom in the music business is another offspring of the new youth culture. The record business and the large pop concerts and rock festivals are ways for clever entrepreneurs to make money. The new youth ghettos have produced a resurgence of small businessmen, the "hip capitalists," who specialize in products for the hip community. Sometimes these capitalists are more community-minded than ordinary merchants, but often they are not. Those stores which support communes of people who are living and working collectively are the new family businesses—beautiful for the people within them, but not very helpful in dealing with the basic questions of distribution of wealth and power.

But does not the very fact of communality make things different? Yes. To the extent that young people learn to overcome their bourgeois individualist backgrounds and become concerned about others, they will be better able to participate in building a new society. But, unfortunately, communes can create a new individualism: the commune can still function as an individualistic entity with regard to the rest of the community.

If tuning in and turning on are not in themselves subversive of this society, what about dropping out? If everyone dropped out, certainly the society would face a massive crisis. But what percentage of the young people who identify with the youth culture actually do drop out? To date, every indication is that the numbers are not very great relative to the workforce as a whole, and that the distribution varies with class background. Many more upper-middle-class and ruling-class youth drop out than working-class youth. Moreover, unemployment is a serious problem in this society, and even if large numbers of young people dropped out, it would be quite a while before there was a shortage of workers, except in a few highly specialized fields. In fact, by voluntarily dropping out of the workforce and providing an ideology that allows many young people to live on a much lower income, the youth culture may be giving capitalism a boost. What if, instead of dropping out, tens of thousands of young people are organizing demonstrations demanding jobs—not just ordinary jobs but jobs that provide meaningful labor and workers' control? Capitalism might have a much harder time accommodating that demand than it has in allowing people to "drop out."

Dropping out seems to have certain basic limitations built into it: if everyone dropped out, who would make the wealth off which the dropout must live? The dropout is correct in saying that most of the wealth the worker creates does not go to him, but to the capitalist for whom he works, and that much of what he produces is not worth buying. But some goods are worth having, including food, clothing, and shelter, and right now these are not coming like manna from heaven. They are being produced by the workers. Working people have good cause to be angry at the dropout, since the dropout is living off the wealth they create. On the other hand, the dropout is right to respond that the anger should not be directed against him, but against the system, since it is not the dropout who forces the workers to continue working. Still, this response misses the workers' correct sense that in a decent society some work will still be necessary, and that the dropouts are in fact freeloaders. Nor does it help things any that dropouts are usually the children of the middle and upper classes and that they usually have an extremely strong elitism and hostility to working people. What's so different? the worker asks: these classes have always lived off our backs, and they are still doing it.

The class nature of the dropout community can be seen in a variety of ways. Consider the current interest in buying land in the country. Who has money for that? One might argue that anyone can do it if he gets together with a group of others and starts selling things in the city. This seems much like the argument that anyone can succeed under capitalism if he really tries—it misses the problems of maldistribution of wealth, education, etc. A few people may manage to move from one class to another, but most people stay basically where they are.

The fact is that the system *forces* many people to drop out, to live on welfare and food stamps, and to live together because they cannot afford apartments of their own. If the hip culture provides people who are forced out with a way of getting together without losing their dignity and self-respect, that is fine. But if it simultaneously makes poverty a virtue, it is hardly likely to cause any serious problems for the ruling class, which does not want to redistribute its wealth—a necessary prerequisite to solving the problem of poverty.

But we should not simply dismiss certain social demands because they are potentially cooptable. Marijuana may well be legalized in the near future, but as long as it is illegal, many young people are forced into conflict with the law. That conflict allows them to understand in part what it must be like for the black man in America, who is constantly in conflict with the law, and that identification often leads to support for the black liberation movement. And the very spirit of rebelliousness that comes

155

from breaking the society's sexual mores and drug laws often seeps into other aspects of the individual's life and makes it easier to participate in general rebellion against the society.

To the shame of Tom Hayden, his Berkeley Liberation Program of 1969 included the statement "We recognize the right of people to use those drugs which are known from experience to be harmful." But except for Hayden, virtually every other significant force in the New Left has unambiguously opposed the use of heroin, speed, and other hard drugs. The movement has always sensed that local and national police forces have been tolerant of these kinds of drugs, especially in youth and black ghettos, because they provide an easy mechanism for controlling people, turning them away from the political sphere and toward more conventional forms of crime.

But while attacking hard drugs, the youth culture has glorified beyond all reality the importance of psychedelics in the formation of revolutionary consciousness. To the best of my knowledge, marijuana heightens the individual's sensual awareness but not necessarily his understanding of the world. To a large extent this is also true of LSD and mescaline, though these drugs may have more content, since they seem always to accentuate the individual's awareness of the beauty in other people and in nature. Although that insight, in and of itself, does not lead one to political consciousness or activity, it helps. The day-to-day workings of capitalism desensitize us to other human beings and to the beauty of the world, leading us to view people and things simply in terms of expediency and getting ahead. To the extent that LSD makes such a view difficult, it is a progressive drug.

Obviously, LSD does not automatically awaken in people an understanding of capitalism, the ruling class, or repressive economic and political structures. Such understanding requires education and/or analysis. But it does present very forcefully a raw datum about how very beautiful and deserving of love are the world and its people. Then it is up to the individual to draw the appropriate conclusions. Good LSD is revolutionary in the same sense that good art or good music is: it gives us a glimpse of human freedom and human possibilities, and hence implicitly raises the question of why these possibilities are not being realized in our own lives. Needless to say, acid can be taken in excess and can be used as an escape from the concrete realities facing us in trying to change America.

The youth rebellion is infectious, and the ideas of the student movement have spread from the first student dropouts to reach young workers. The legitimization first of antiwar sentiment and then of antiestablishment sentiment was communicated through the youth culture to the young workers who would never have been reached by the too often elitist and isolationist elements in the student movement. The spread of wildcat strikes—like the one by General Motors workers at Lordstown, Ohio, in 1972—and the challenges that have recently been issued to union bureaucracies are examples of this rebellious spirit.

The youth culture is often not supportive of the movement and its struggles. "Laying back" and "letting it be" often undercuts the possibility of organizing any serious struggles. It was this passivity that made it impossible for the flourishing hip community in Haight-Ashbury to organize against the influx of Mafia and police that finally destroyed it. Large rock festivals and concerts have become spectator sports—and the "stars" of the rock scene often differ little from those of Hollywood. Despite all the talk about getting together and sharing a new community, most people at rock concerts are very alone and, except for their own immediate group, do not really feel themselves a part of something larger.

Despite the rhetoric of mutual respect and self-fulfillment, women in the youth culture are still very often treated as the playthings of men, unliberated and "a drag" if they will not sleep with whatever man wants them. They are expected to fulfill all the traditional womanly roles from cook (natural and health foods, to be sure) to ego supporter, child rearer and sex object. Especially in the world of rock music, with its male superstars, women are portrayed as mindless sex objects to exploit and degrade both in song lyrics and in the life style of musicians with their groupies.

The youth culture frequently gives the impression that its highest value is self-indulgence. Timothy Leary, the culture's self-described high priest, told a crowd of admirers in February 1969 that the key to the present was the "hedonistic revolution." According to the *Berkeley Barb* (February 15, 1969) Leary scorned all political activity: "Activist youth is tragic youth, alienated from the hedonistic future. It's just bad kharma. . . . The real activists are the dope dealers and the rock musicians. They're relevant because they're blowing minds and they're making people feel good and they're bringing neurological changes which create a new generation." But when people took Leary's message seriously, the very community they sought to build fell apart. Pleasure seeking as a step toward building an alternative community sounds like Adam Smith's justification for capitalism, according to which every individual should pursue his private good, and through the working of the capitalist marketplace all this private good will add up to the general public good. The mysterious workings of this "invisible hand" will make all selfishness and self-centeredness yield benefits for the whole community. This ideology worked no better for the

157

counterculture than it did for the bourgeois economy. Instead of creating harmony, it created the collapse of Haight-Ashbury, and then the slaying at the Altamont rock concert.

If the goal of life is simply good vibes and pleasant experiences, serious struggle will inevitably be avoided. Why become involved in hassles? Struggle, we are told, is a bummer. It is true that as long as the rulers have the immense power of the police and military at their disposal, those who struggle will face unpleasant consequences. Grooving on trees and flowers is less likely to lead one into trouble than demonstrating against the murder of Black Panthers Fred Hampton and Mark Clark. Why not let everyone "do their own thing"? "Different strokes for different folks." This position very often leads to a political quietism that is hard to disturb. While Vietnamese are being napalmed, some adherents of the youth culture are moving to the country to avoid the difficulties of city life. The rulers can always make it easy for young people to follow the alternative life styles that cause the least trouble for the ruling class. Or can they?

The answer is not yet clear. Perhaps the rulers can provide enough space for the hippie community to flourish; some elements in the ruling class may see this as the best way to coopt the new youth culture and defuse it of its subversive potential. But if the ideas of the youth culture become major elements in the consciousness of working-class youth they may have to be ruthlessly suppressed. After all, capitalism does not have unlimited power and its structural crises are real and have to be dealt with. If the rulers want to keep the empire, they will need young people ready to fight for it and the youth culture has made that less likely. We must never underestimate capitalism's flexibility and possible cooptive powers; at the same time, we must see that the crisis facing the empire has in many ways weakened the system, reduced the number of alternatives available to it and reduced the liberals' confidence in their ability to reform it.

But if there are real ambiguities in the youth culture, why has the Left so often lauded it, and described it as "our culture"? Why have some leftist theoreticians identified it with the revolution? Because the youth culture emerged at a time in history when the political universe of discourse seemed to be closed and when it seemed impossible that whites would show any fundamental opposition to American society. In the early days of the civil rights movement and even of the antiwar movement most whites found themselves very uncomfortable with the idea of a revolution. Those who did not fear it as an extension of Soviet totalitarianism to America, thought of it as a utopian fantasy. This pessimism was rooted in the experience of the past twenty years: the success of American imperialism coupled with domestic McCarthyism created a situation in which the vast majority of

Americans were essentially satisfied with their lives and unwilling to consider any basic changes. True, there was a "Negro problem" and a "poverty problem," but as long as the vast majority of white Americans were satisfied with the status quo, talk about revolution seemed to be a fantasy, believed in only by a very few holdovers from the old Left. The war in Vietnam, the notion of black power, the student movement—all played parts in weakening the self-confidence of the status quo. But the emergence of a youth culture that challenged the basic relations of production and the entire psychic structure that had been created to assist capitalism was certainly a qualitative leap toward a new political era. The youth culture portended the destruction of the media-manipulated consciousness in which white Americans had been living, and an awareness that personal problems were really societal problems. Moreover, this breakthrough was affecting the children of the vast majority of Americans, who themselves would eventually be a new majority.

Equally important, the emergence of the youth culture as a phenomenon independent of the formal Left movement, was a living critique of that movement. Many of the creators of the youth culture were dropouts from the movement as well as from school. They saw that the movement had not yet taken seriously enough the vastness of revolutionary change: it seemed not to realize that the new world would have to develop qualitatively different social conditions and relationships as well as a new political policy. Marcuse talked about the development of "a new sensibility . . . which rebels against the dictates of repressive reason, and, in doing so, invokes the sensuous power of the imagination." For Marcuse, the causes of past human domination are economic-political, "but since they have shaped the very instincts and needs of men, no economic and political changes will bring this historical continuum to a stop unless they are carried through by men who are physiologically and psychologically able to experience things, and each other, outside the context of violence and exploitation." [2] This insight—that the revolution had to do with transforming ourselves, not just transforming something out there in the world —added a crucial dimension to the revolutionary struggle and provided an opening into which the women's liberation movement would step with a more complete analysis of desirable changes.

Without a good grounding in radical history and economics, another tendency is apt to arise: totalism or utopianism, which always leads to inwardness and then to despair. The dynamic is already prevalent in many sections of the youth culture. Failing to understand the coercive power of

[2] Herbert Marcuse, *Essay on Liberation* (Boston: Beacon Press, 1969), p. 25.

social institutions and capitalist arrangements, people begin to believe that they can make themselves into fully human and loving people and create a new society right under the nose of the old order. Their main focus of attention becomes themselves or their collective, or their small community of collectives. All their energy is then devoted inward: "The rest of society can take care of itself. We'll just work on ourselves. Once we are fully developed new human beings, we will be strong enough to talk to others. In the meantime, who are *we* to be talking to anyone, since we're just as messed up as everybody else." But these negative character traits are formed and nourished by the political structure of capitalism, and after a few years these people begin to wonder why they are not really changing and why certain pervasive character traits continually reassert themselves. Equally important, in isolating themselves from the rest of the society, they seem to be ignoring other people's problems, precisely at a time when other people do not want to be ignored. The dynamic of social change passes them by as they become increasingly involved in their own lives.

Getting one's own head straight is not a new phenomenon. In every age there have been people who thought *that* the rock on which they'd build their church; and they never have. Socialist utopians built many communes in the nineteenth century. In the early twentieth century Eugene Debs led a group of several thousand socialist communitarians into founding such a community in the state of Washington. The most impressive such experiment was in Israel where the kibbutz movement created really beautiful socialist communes. But these communes, far from transforming the rest of Israeli society, have in fact become absorbed in a national chauvinist culture. Once they gave up a serious commitment to political and economic revolution, Israeli socialists soon discovered that the larger capitalist society would ultimately have more impact on their utopian socialist communes than these communes would on capitalism.

In fact, the dynamic inside many collectives is far more inward-oriented than any previous collective movement would have dreamed possible. Much of the Israeli kibbutz movement still is associated with a political party, Mapam, that at least puts forward a general program for socialism at election times. But American collectives sometimes act as if there was no outside world. Discussions often focus on the personalities of the people involved, their own interaction, their music and their grass. This inwardness is sometimes justified by the idea that no revolution will be possible until *after* we have transformed ourselves.

Such a notion ignores the concrete circumstances in which people live and are formed. The social and economic structures of capitalism continue

160

to function even when people decide that they are coercive and unjust, and they severely delimit the possibilities of human transcendence. People still have to sell their labor power in order to eat, or at least most people do. The police and prisons do not disappear simply because people no longer see them as relevant; neither does capitalist control over resources and productive facilities terminate when some people see that they should be operated in the interests of all, rather than for the profit of a few.

If everyone's consciousness were suddenly transformed, and if everyone saw the need for a new social order, it would be much easier to take over control of the factories and the instruments of government. But such transformations are not likely in the present order. After all, people develop self-centered and competitive attitudes because they are necessary for survival in this society. To recognize this is to overcome the elitism which characterizes so much of the youth culture and to begin to pose the really relevant question: how do we create the conditions under which those economic and social barriers can be transformed?

At the opposite extreme of this position is the one that proclaims transformations of consciousness to be irrelevant: all the necessary changes will occur after we take state power. This argument has a certain force: if we eliminate private profit and produce goods to serve human needs, eliminate power from above and give people power to control their own lives; the transformations in people are likely to be greatly accelerated. The first generation after the seizure of power may be made up of people who have been marred by capitalism. But if the institutions no longer exist to transmit that marred nature it will certainly die out in a generation or two. Psychoanalysis can be of only limited use in a society in which people's psychic problems are sustained by the distribution of power and the economic and political organization. But in a society in which these problems are merely hangovers from an earlier form of social organization, they will disappear just as quickly as miserliness gave way to mass consumption when capitalism passed from its accumulation stage to its advanced industrial stage, and psychological help will be very useful in this transition.

But this position does not deal with the most difficult step: taking and holding state power. We have argued that this will require a majority or something close to it, and getting such a majority is precisely the problem. Marcuse and others have argued that it is a problem because the society rules not just through direct force but also through a high degree of thought control and manipulation of desires. Counterculture theorists stress the need to break through that manipulated consciousness and create people whose needs are fundamentally antagonistic to and unmanipulatable

161

by the established order of corporate capitalism. This will make it possible to take and hold state power, to destroy the mechanisms of domination and redistribute power to the people.

Needed, then, is some middle path that combines changes in consciousness with the struggle to take power. In fact, this is precisely how the youth culture developed: through a series of political struggles that led to new changes in consciousness, which led to new political struggles, which led to new changes in consciousness. The struggle of the blacks and the Vietnamese was perceived by white youth as opening new possibilities for them. With this changed consciousness they began a struggle of their own, and what they learned in battling at the universities gave them a new consciousness which in turn led them to try to create living space for a new way of being. It is this dialectical relationship which must be kept in mind: our self-understanding changes as we change our own situation and this changed self-understanding then guides future changes in our situation. At each step we meet resistance from the guardians of the old order. If that resistance is not defeated or at least weakened, we are forced to limit our own development and self-transformation.

Concretely, we are arguing that a revolution of consciousness can never occur unless there is a simultaneous battle to expand people's political and economic power. To the extent that this is done, we will get institutions which in themselves have a profound effect on the collective consciousness.

No better proof is needed that changes in consciousness, by themselves, do not constitute a revolution than many of the major trends in the emerging youth culture. We have talked about some of them: the tendency to consume; the tendency toward passivity; the striking male chauvinism that permeates the music, rock concerts, and life style; the ability to forget about the Vietnamese and black struggles.

Alongside Marx there is Hare Krishna, and for every current that stresses the need for a more humane and rational society there is a strain in youth culture that encourages irrationality and self-indulgence. Let us remember the historical period in which we live: the development of a youth culture occurs as the bombs are falling on Vietnamese and Laotians and Cambodians, as blacks are shot in the streets, as political trials become a commonplace. Youth culture has tendencies within it that allow people to escape from this world, to accommodate themselves by drowning in the gratification of the senses or in the abdication of the intellect. When the concepts of love and humanity impinge on people, it becomes difficult for them to go on with their normal lives in the face of their knowledge that their government is waging an imperialistic war. But the concepts of love and humanity can be transformed into the substance of an ideology

162

that urges people to do their own thing or advocates acceptance of the new cult of Jesus (which is not much different from the old cult of Jesus). There are many tendencies within the youth culture and those that predominate will be in part determined by the extent that radical political activity becomes an integral part of that culture.

Another pervasive tendency is a new irrationalism, which seeks to deal with the problems of the alienated social relations of this world through escape into another. Hence the flourishing of astrology, Hare Krishna, Jesus freaks, and the like. There is nothing new in all this—economic systems of domination have always thrown forth ideologies of mysticism and esoterica to turn people's attention away from the real source of their problems in the social structure. Originally, Jesus became popular as an alternative to the real struggle for liberation the Jews were waging against their Roman oppressors. The rise of Christianity was the first revolution in consciousness: we do not need a second one like it. Concentration camps with paisley-colored barracks and psychedelic music and plenty of sex are concentration camps nevertheless. It is one thing to talk about transformation and consciousness; it is another to think that anything that is illogical and blows people's minds is automatically part of the revolution to make America fundamentally humane and beautiful.

Some of the currents in youth culture are relatively harmless. Consider astrology. The view that your personal characteristics and your fate are somehow determined by the position of the stars and moon when you were born offers relief from the anxiety of personal responsibility in a world increasingly difficult to deal with. "What's your sign?" is a frequent greeting in the counterculture; it provides a quick way to find something to talk about and a way of putting people into explanatory boxes without ever bothering to get to know them. Then there are the happy Hare Krishna fans, dancing around in their colorful gowns and singing their constant refrain. Based on the same Hinduism that helped keep hundreds of millions of Indians mystified and enslaved for thousands of years, the religion of Hare Krishna offers a way of lulling the mind to sleep that is almost as effective, but not as expensive or physically dangerous, as heroin.

Not all of the occult sects are equally innocuous. Satanism or devil worship encourages its participants to engage in evil. The Manson family may be the best known of the satanic sects but there are many others like it. Mystical notions of purifying oneself through the blood of the innocent are not new, but they have gained particular popularity among those who have been victimized by one guru after another in the youth culture. The life of least resistance makes many youth-culture participants easy followers of whomever they happen to run into. Nothing is too silly or too weird not to find its devotees. People are hungry for salvation, and if the youth culture cannot provide it through its institutions, many will buy whatever they can get.

The suspension of the intellect required by all these cults fits in well with the attitudes that the counterculture sponsored. Anti-intellectualism was a dominant theme of the youth culture from its inception. In part, this was a response to the anti-intellectualism that flourishes at the universities (whence many of the initial youth culture converts came) and it mirrored the general anti-intellectualism in American life. The intellect must be abandoned, many believed, so that spontaneity could reemerge to its rightful place in determining conduct. Underneath our corrupted mind, the culture seemed to hold, was a pure and untarnished self that could find expression only in emotional life. Real communication, then, would be only possible on the level of this kind of spontaneous expression. No wonder that Hermann Hesse, himself the guru of a previous cultural revolution that had failed in the Weimar Germany of the 1920s, became a popular culture hero in the 1960s. Nobody seemed to imagine that emotional life, too, was conditioned by social factors and not a pure "given." And once the intellect was ruled out, anything was permitted. The counterculture did not create a new flowering of aesthetic culture—for that would have required a discipline and rigorousness inconsistent with the path of least resistance that people sought.

It is crucial for the youth culture to begin to relate to people who are different from it and to begin to speak to them about their common sources of oppression. People in the hip communities must give up their arrogance and start talking to others in a language that others can understand. They must stop talking as if their way of living and dressing is the only one that makes sense. This does not mean give up their own culture or their exports to convince people to join it. But it does mean giving up the sense that "We are the future" and that those who do not agree with every detail of one's own program are in the dustbin of history. And it does mean emphasizing what one has in common with other people rather than one's differences. The Weathermen sent an underground communiqué once that said "Freaks are revolutionaries and revolutionaries are freaks." As a piece of rhetoric designed to win sympathy from the peace-love generation that so scorned their bombing tactics, this was quite clever. But it was wrong politically. The Left identifies itself as "freaks" on the basis of a logic that says: "if the people who drop napalm on babies are normal, then we are freaks." But the fact is that the real freaks are the people who run this country at the expense of everyone else in the world, and people

164

in the hip community have got to start showing others how there can be a community of interests between people with very different life styles.

In his book *The Trial*,[3] Tom Hayden emphasizes the necessity to build liberated territory. But this places the stress in exactly the wrong direction. It is important to build counterinstitutions to the degree that it is possible, but it is equally important to realize that the possibilities are extremely limited as long as the rulers have control of the state and as long as the majority of people are not yet on the side of dramatic change. While Hayden was busily working on his Berkeley liberation program events were unfolding that should have shown him how limited a strategy the "liberated territory" concept is. At that very moment, people were in the streets fighting for People's Park, a single block of land that had been left vacant by the university and which we in the hip community wanted to keep as a community park. The existence of the park did not challenge any immediate needs of the university, but it did challenge the Regents' right to absolute control over their private property. To reclaim their land they sent in thousands of National Guard, hundreds of sheriffs and police, helicopters, machine guns, tons of tear gas, and shotguns that succeeded in murdering one person and blinding another. They made their point loud and clear: no dual authority in Berkeley. And yet, Hayden still suggests that the movement concentrate on building liberated territory, which will become a center of revolutionary activity for the rest of the country. This strategy tends to reinforce the greatest weaknesses of the student movement and the hip communities: their isolationism. It is a strategy designed to create confrontations with the police over issues that appeal only to the members of the isolated communities.

This is not to condemn the struggle to create dual authority and to challenge the ruling-class's "right" to private property. But such struggles should be waged around issues that link up the interests of the hip community with those of the communities surrounding it. People's Park was a beautiful struggle in its time, but it proved a dead end as a strategy. What we need are strategies that allow most working people to link their interests with those of students and the hip community. Anything else will only perpetuate our isolation. Haydenism is isolationism, the kind of "liberated consciousness in one community" that everyone thought went out with Stalin.

In part, Hayden and others like him place little emphasis on talking to people in surrounding communities (Berkeley, for instance, is only about

[3] New York: Holt, Rinehart & Winston, 1970.

three miles from the heart of Oakland's white working-class area) because they believe that "We are the wave of the future." This notion to which Hayden often obliquely refers when he talks about the "dinosaurs" of the ruling class, has also been made popular by Jerry Rubin and by Charles Reich. Basically the argument is as follows: we are young and we are against American society as presently constructed, so when we take over— as we inevitably will, since the old do die off—we will remake society according to our norms and in accord with our transformed consciousness. But not all, or even most, young people in America consciously identify with the youth culture. To be sure, they have been influenced by it in part, just as the whole generation of the 1930s was influenced by the thriving leftist movement. But the engineering schools are still packed to the gills, and for all our impact, the universities continue to turn out their smartly packaged products. That these products will want to legalize marijuana is certain, and that by and large they oppose the war in Vietnam is also true, though to date very few have been willing to take any serious risks for their opposition. But it is less clear whether these people really agree that capitalism should be abandoned.

Even among the "we"—those who have dropped out of bourgeois society—there is hardly any kind of agreement on the need to overthrow private ownership of the means of production. The "we," according to Hayden, are "all those people with a stake in the future." [4] Pretty rhetoric, but who exactly are "we"? Does the young son of the ruling class have a stake in the future if he loves pot and good music and good sex and also thinks it's fine to live off the labor of the workers in his father's factory? Any serious study of young people today makes clear that many of them would be willing to fill the seats of power currently held by older men, and many more would be unwilling to struggle for anything.

We must remember that this society does not run on the basis of majority consent: a small group of people are able to keep nearly everyone else in line by their control over the means of production and the stacked political arena. The generational thesis makes sense only if one assumes that all who favor capitalism disappeared spontaneously and that hence there will be no opposition to the people with *our* values simply stepping in, taking power, and then redistributing power to the people. But power does not flow from the bottom up; it flows from the top down. And so the rulers manage to pick those hip young capitalists who share their values (though these youth may at times affront their senses of style) to be the new managers of the corporate state. Undoubtedly, the rulers of the

4 *The Trial*, p. 153.

country will have to make some changes to accord with the widespread influence of the youth culture, even as in the 1930s they were forced to make accommodations for the even more widespread feeling that working people should be allowed to organize into unions and be ensured an above-subsistence wage. But besides legalizing marijuana and adopting a hip rhetoric, what substance will these changes have?

Revolution by consciousness is very appealing to those who have given up on the possibility of reaching large numbers of people who are different from us, or to those who, like Charles Reich, counsel the Left that they can never expect to win a fight on the battlefield of power. As Charles Reich tells us,[5] and as Tom Hayden has argued on campuses around the country, it will all be very easy. The dinosaurs who hold power will die off and we will take over. Reich tells us that a political revolution is not possible in the United States right now, but that's OK because no revolution is necessary. Hayden is less comfortable with the notion that there will be no struggles, but he sees the struggles primarily in terms of maintaining liberated territory and fighting our "permeation of white, male, middle-class attitudes." [6] If we can change ourselves, and support Third World and black struggles to boot, we have nothing more to fear. Hayden and Reich will be culture heroes for a long time, because they tell people what they want to hear: what you're doing is right and will inevitably lead to revolution, and all you have to worry about is in your own head. It is the quintessence of elitism and self-centeredness, parading under the name of revolution.

Still, there is something very important in what they are pointing to. For there *is* a qualitative change in the consciousness of many people in the youth culture, and that change makes it possible to raise the question of revolutionary struggle among sections of the population that were previously more difficult to reach. To say this, to talk tentatively in terms of possibilities that have now been opened, allows us to raise seriously the tasks in front of us: how to fight the isolationist, self-indulgent, individualist, and chauvinist attitudes that have so limited the youth culture's actual transcendence of capitalist society. Once we reject both the mindless glorification of the youth culture and the blanket dismissal by such Old Left groups as the Progressive Labor party, we can begin to examine more systematically and scientifically the precise impact it has had on trends in employment, local political struggles, and interaction

[5] In *The Greening of America* (New York: Bantam Books, 1971).

[6] I focus on Hayden because of the enormous prestige and power he held in the 1960s, most of which was used to advance a weird combination of liberal ideas and superrevolutionary tactics.

among youth of various classes. Such a study, yet to be done, would begin to distinguish between distinct and sometimes counterposed trends in the youth culture—it would replace sloganeering with the kind of empirical study so necessary for revolutionaries to understand their society.

The idea of a "youth culture" and an emerging youth force (Woodstock Nation) was popularized by Jerry Rubin and Abbie Hoffman of the Yippies. At first, its sponsors recognized it as a myth, but the kind of myth that could itself affect and transform reality. As more and more young people became enthralled with rock music and dope, they increasingly sought some explanation of who they were and why they were the way they were. The myth of the Yippies and the youth nation, led by conscious revolutionaries, exposed tens of thousands of young people to a more fundamental critique of their society than had ever come through in the music itself. Through this exposure, many of them became convinced that more thoroughgoing revolutionary change was necessary. So the myth became self-fulfilling for literally tens of thousands of young people. As such, it played an extremely positive role in the development of antiestablishment consciousness among people who might never have been reached in any other way.

But then, along came the theorists and ideologists who attempted to use the myth as a fundamental political fact upon which to build an analysis of political change. Tom Hayden and the Weathermen substituted their own impressionistic responses to college campuses and youth ghettos for any serious empirical study of the current functionings of the economic and political structure. The results were often disastrous. Weathermen thought they saw vast transformations of consciousness among working-class youth but quickly became disillusioned and withdrew to acts of terrorism when no one followed them. More recently they have reverted to a Rubinesque glorification of youth culture, freaks, good vibes and dope. In the process they succeeded in doing what no army of police could ever do: they destroyed the 80,000-member Students for a Democratic Society. All this could have been avoided if people had been willing to investigate seriously what was actually going on in America. But one looks in vain for such information in the underground press or in virtually any movement publications.

A plea for rationality in assessment of the youth culture should by no means be equated with an endorsement of the unrealistic positions of Young Socialist Alliance or the Progressive Labor party. These groups go to the opposite extreme of refusing to see any revolutionary potential in the youth culture. Their members cut their hair, refrain from smoking

168

dope, and act straight so that "the workers aren't turned off." This position is ridiculous from two standpoints. First, it denies the legitimacy of the youth culture as a means of self-expression for young people. Instead of requiring its members to struggle with certain key problems (e.g., isolationism and chauvinism) it demands that they renounce their own identity as a precondition for being active parts of a socialist movement. Second, it rests on the false assumption that "the working class" simply cannot relate to changes in life style. But, in fact, sections of the working class, particularly young workers, are intrigued by the new life style and its meaning. That the hip community has not had a more dramatic impact on workers is more a result of its own conviction (reinforced both by the mass media and by the YSA and PL) that there could be no communication, than of the failure of any sustained attempt.

If I have stressed some of the limitations of youth culture, it is mainly to offset the excessive glorification with which it has been treated both within the movement and by the media. But I should mention some of its more important contributions. The notion that the community should be supportive of its members and their needs has not only fostered the development of free clinics, crash pads, drug centers and self-defense classes, but has also provided a base for the belief that these needs should be cared for by any decent society. Food coops have helped to alleviate the pinch of high prices for some, and have also helped stimulate the buying of health foods. The collectives provide a form for experiments in living that will be important in building a new society. The collectives are also important in providing people with a way of surviving in the period ahead and in breaking down the sense of aloneness that is such an important element in people's feelings of powerlessness.

The development of a youth culture has helped raise a number of important themes, with which any revolutionary movement must deal. Revolutionaries are not simply interested in a change of people in power; we are interested in a full-scale social revolution, which will involve transformations in the way people relate in every area of their lives. Much of the appeal of the youth culture stems from its ability to raise to consciousness the possibilities that are available to people: possibilities for relationships built on nonexploitative modes, possibilities for overcoming individualism and aloneness, possibilities to end the struggle for survival and to begin the phase of human history in which people do what they want to do. In putting all these questions on the agenda, the youth culture has gone a long way toward undermining the one-dimensionality of previous revolutionary movements. It has changed the very meaning of

169

"revolutionary," from the narrow activist concerned primarily with wage problems, to a broader conception in which the revolutionary must be seen as a builder of a whole new age in human history.

The great failure has been to confuse putting these questions on the agenda with the notion that the counterculture has already provided an answer. The impetus in this direction is understandable. Here we are, a few generations away from the time when human life will be radically transformed. We can see what the possibilities are, and yet we cannot ourselves be part of that transformed reality. So people grab at the most attractive solution: let's skip the intermediate steps, and pretend that whatever is possible then, is actual now, and becomes actual just because we will it so. The result has been disastrous: many people find the actual counterculture so unsatisfying that they despair of the ideal and become cynics and disillusioned liberals. I can hear it now, the talk that their children will be hearing in the 1980s: "Oh, you think you're so smart. Well, I tried that when I was in college, I mean, acid, communes, demonstrations, the works . . . and it didn't make me one bit happy, and in fact, it ruined a lot of people's lives. Those ideals are just an unrealistic phase that young people go through. But listen to me because I've had the experience." Because these people did not understand experience at the time, they will not understand it later. The ideals cannot be actualized in the context of capitalist society, because everything in the society forces people to make compromises whose effect is the negation of the best ideals of the counterculture. So what emerges is some inverted reflection of the capitalist order, and then people say, "Well, it's just human nature!"

But the effort to build a new culture ought not be dismissed as worthless or irrelevant. Rather, it must be combined and integrated with a self-conscious movement that evaluates how far one can go in the direction of self-transcendence and then pushes for the achievement of those realistic possibilities. A counterculture clearly integrated with a political movement and not counterposed to it can be invaluable in breaking down people's respect for illegitimate authority and authoritarian social relations in every area of life. And it can add a dimension of humor and creativity that is indispensable to the success of any liberating political movement. But it cannot substitute itself for the political movement, or underemphasize the crucial role that taking state power by the people will have in making a fuller counterculture possible.

In retrospect, the ruling class may have perceived the counterculture as more of a threat than it turned out to be. But the rulers had good grounds for concern. The counterculture struck at something very basic in the lives

170

of all Americans: a sense that their lives were basically inadequate. Many people have a moment in their lives when suddenly they look at themselves honestly and see with horror the compromises and petty corruptions they have been compelled to adopt to survive in this society. Suddenly, if only for a moment, everything is called into question—their jobs, their home life, their future plans, their previous accomplishments. But it is a piercing moment of honesty that people cannot bear to live with for long. They look around and see that everyone else has defined the world in a certain way that seems impossible to change. They feel alone. There seems to be nobody else who sees reality and is willing to do anything about it. And what's the point of trying to act alone—all you'll do is hurt yourself, your parents, your friends, your husband or wife, your kids. They won't understand, and you love them and don't want to risk their welfare or their feelings for some ideal. Idealists only hurt themselves. So get that idea out of your head, before it becomes too real for you and you can no longer deal with it. Suppress it, forget it, pretend it's just your personal problem, your youthful immaturity perhaps, or middle-age despair, or a psychic peculiarity. So the idea goes away, or is pushed away, and you may even resent people or circumstances that remind you that your life is built on lies and compromises and a continued acceptance of less than you could be or could have.

What if everyone came to that kind of realization at the same time and each person saw that other people were at the same psychic place? What if everyone said, "Hey, let's get together and change things?" If that is a pot dream of the counterculture, it is a paranoid nightmare for the ruling class, whose power depends on keeping everyone apart and afraid to share with others these kinds of deep hopes and perceptions. Suddenly there was a group shouting out in public where everyone could hear: "We are alienated because this society makes a meaningful and decent life impossible." No wonder it was so important for the rulers to distort that message.

The crucial point is that the counterculture emerges in response to the experiences of alienation and suffocation that are part of capitalist society. The counterculture is more an expression of that alienation than a solution to it, but since it raises the problem to consciousness it provides an important opening for a socialist revolutionary movement to show people that only the destruction of the capitalist system can provide the basis on which to build a humanly satisfying culture and way of life.

WORKERS

"Here we go again," a critic may say, "with the radicals' oldest myth: the myth of the working class. Why do you people always talk about the working class, making it seem as if workers are the crucial element in a revolutionary struggle? What about all the other groups you talk about as potential agents of revolutionary action?" But to a large extent these other groups can be seen as a part of the working class—those who do not own and control the means of production, and who consequently have to sell their labor power in order to survive. Part of the reason why radicals stress the working class is that working men and women constitute the overwhelming majority of people in this country, and we want a majoritarian revolution. "But there are other ways to slice the pie: women are also a majority." True. But workers, particularly those in basic industries of production, have a sense of their own collective power that is built into their work situation, in a way that women, highly atomized by the family structure, do not. What is more, the workers' sense of collective power is based on a reality that is crucial to any plan to take over the country (other than the military coups): the working class, particularly the industrial working class, has the power to shut down the society completely. Because they have their hands on the gears and levers that run the productive apparatus of America, workers could exert the only kind of social power that would effectively paralyze the ruling class: shutting down the economy and keeping it closed. Every strike—for example, the West Coast longshoremen's strike in 1971–72—gives the workers new proof of their potential power, though the ruling class can always deal with strikes as long as each is kept separate and uncoordinated from the others. But if the working class were to strike as a whole, in a unified and disciplined way, and were willing to stick out the struggle, the ruling class would be virtually powerless to stop it. Hence, it is crucial for the ruling class to prevent the workers from coming together, seeing their common needs, and fighting together in an uncompromising way. Every institution that the ruling class permits to flourish, every ideological current that it encourages, every political tendency it supports, and every struggle it conducts, is aimed at convincing the people that such solidarity is impossible ("It's against human nature to be anything but competitive with everyone around you") and undesirable ("All you will get is a new set of rulers who will be just as bad as we are—look at the gangsters who took over your unions—so why not settle for the present set of bad rulers?") and unnecessary ("Why, you're just on the verge of making great liberal

172

reforms within the system") and too risky ("We throw radicals out of jobs and into prisons, so you won't get anything for your trouble but a bloody head or worse. Why not go along with the present order, and get what you can for yourself?").

The job of the radical organizer, conversely, is to show people that a new society is desirable, necessary, and possible, and that leaving things in the hands of the ruling class is too risky for the entire future of humanity. The experience of the early 1970s, particularly Nixon's economic policies, has helped clarify to many workers some of the ways in which they are being victimized in the interests of the ruling class. An organizer must present some vision of how, both in the short and long run, it is possible to fight back without losing. A crucial part of the radical's task is to help people replace the cynicism their experiences have developed with a new hope and faith in themselves and in each other.

To talk about the "conservative" nature of the working class has been commonplace among political people. And that talk is a testimony to the success of bourgeois ideology. It makes it impossible to think seriously about ways to involve working people in revolutionary activity. It is quite true that for the working class as a whole, explicitly anticapitalist feeling today is lower than it was in the 1930s. But to leave the matter here is to obscure the historical reality rather than understand it, to fail to realize that it is a dynamic and changing reality, not a static one. To view that reality dialectically, in terms of its causes and the possible ways in which it may be overcome, is to reject the static analysis put forward by the media, which tries to convince both insurgent groups and the workers themselves that workers are essentially passive and conservative. It is a mistake to judge what the workers want from what the trade-union bureaucrats say they want, or to judge all workers in terms of the building trades, whose members' wages and politics have always made them the aristocracy of labor.

In the section on Powerlessness, we reviewed the major reasons why workers did not live up to their revolutionary promise of the 1930s, stressing three primary factors. First, there was the monumental failure of leadership, caused by the Communist party's refusal to take seriously the needs of the *American* proletariat, and its willingness to subordinate domestic strategy to the needs of the Soviet Union. In addition to defending the worst aspects of Stalinism, the CP also helped define the workers' problems in narrow economic terms, on the basis of its belief that the system could not meet the needs of a working class suffering from the effects of a major depression. Consequently, the CP did not prepare the working class for a period in which the expansion of America's imperialist empire brought about a rise in the standard of living of many workers. Second, there was the success of American imperialism (coupled with domestic racism and exploitation of women) in increasing the general wealth in American society, and hence providing more wealth to trickle down to working people. This is sometimes referred to as the "white skin privilege" of the American white working class, which benefits from the exploitation of domestic black and women workers at home. These "benefits" have played an important role in tying many workers to the system. Finally, we should mention the high levels of repression faced by those workers who were not content merely with higher wages, and who continued to raise fundamental critiques about the society. Such people were expelled from the union movement by the purges of the McCarthy era and were labeled dogmatists and adventurists by the CP. Moreover, they frequently faced loss of jobs and prison sentences at a moment when there was no movement to help them financially or give them moral support.

But all those factors came into being under a particular set of historical conditions that no longer apply. For example, the ascendency of imperialism and the military worked for a period, but this solution to the permanent economic crisis of capitalism is now being challenged. Imperialism is being weakened both by the successful struggles of people around the world, and by intraimperialist rivalry. In the next twenty years the American economic empire will probably shrink rather than expand. As a result, the wealth previously available for trickling down will decrease. Moreover, young working people are increasingly unwilling to fight imperialist wars in which they risk their lives to preserve the rulers' wealth. Increasing demands for social services and for the elimination of social evils caused by earlier neglect of human needs spur the development of widespread insistence that tax monies be spent domestically rather than for the war economy. Lastly, the imbalance that imperialism caused in internal economic development has finally caught up with the domestic economy, resulting in high levels of unemployment and inflation. It is difficult for those of us who came to political maturity during the period in which imperialism had temporarily stabilized capitalism to realize that things may not always be this way, and that, in fact, the stabilizing influence of imperialism has seriously declined since the onset of the Vietnam war. This change has already reflected itself in growing labor insurgencies, even among the section of the working class traditionally viewed as the most conservative.

Another factor that has changed is the kind of leadership available in the period ahead. The Communist party has been thoroughly discredited,

174

and many of its most obvious vices are not present in the New Left. Although publicly identifying oneself as a revolutionary is just as dangerous today—it may lead to losing one's job or to a conspiracy indictment—as it was in the past, the New Left does so publicly and proudly, proclaiming its politics and willing to argue them. This is a tremendous advance over the CP activists of the 1930s, who often achieved their positions by infiltration and by hiding their politics. While concealing one's politics may become necessary for some revolutionaries in special circumstances, as a general policy it is almost always bad except in circumstances of extreme repression. Further, the New Left is concerned about human problems, not just the financial problems of capitalism, and is therefore likely to be less cooptable. But the new leadership does have one important similarity to the CP: the New Left sometimes tends to deify the struggles of other countries, such as those of North Vietnam and Cuba, in the name of internationalism. In the late 1960s and early 1970s, most underground newspapers put their major focus on developments in the Third World. Although Third Worldism began as a reasonable response to American national chauvinism, it could become a serious liability if it were to give outsiders the impression that the movement is an agent of Third World people and is not really concerned about the American working class, and if it does not recognize the historical limitations on Third World societies.

To this last point one might respond that the movement is right to shun the American working class, since that class is racist and chauvinist to the core and has no chance of changing—it values its "white skin privilege." This position takes as an immutable fact what is really just a moment in the life of the working class, a tendency that becomes more or less significant depending on many other factors, including the conditions in the world and the alternatives the working class sees available. Ironically, those who would write workers off frequently belong to such groups—such as students or "upper middle class"—that were themselves viewed as immutably conservative a short time ago. The high-handed "writing off" of large groups like the American white working class in the name of our high moral standards is particularly preposterous in view of the fact that *every* white American has so much to overcome with regard to racism and chauvinism. What we should be asking is how and under what conditions workers can be radicalized. To assume this is impossible, and simultaneously holding that people from other classes have been radicalized at least to a limited extent, is to maintain an extreme version of the class chauvinism that capitalists have always taught.

The whole notion of "white skin privilege" has serious problems. White workers enjoy "privilege" only in relation to blacks and Third World

175

people; they are vastly underprivileged in terms of the material and social benefits that could be realized within the framework of advanced industrial societies. Weatherman, which popularized the idea of "white skin privilege" within the movement, performed a major service for the ruling class: its analysis focuses our attention (as this country's rulers have tried to do for so long) on the *relative* advantages of being a white worker under capitalism rather than on the absolute disadvantages. This is precisely the attitude that has kept the workers from making demands that seriously threaten the rulers' wealth and power and from engaging in militant struggle along class lines. Part of the white revolutionary's job is to show white workers that their privileges are, in fact, worth nothing: the privilege of selling one's labor in a dull and stupid and stultifying job that is dangerous and ruinous to one's mental and physical health in order to buy poisoned foods, shoddy goods, and cardboard houses in an environment being destroyed by capitalist avarice; the privilege of producing goods for someone else's personal profit; the privilege of raising children who will die in foreign wars to protect the investments of the bosses; the privilege of relating to other human beings as objects who will cheat you if you don't cheat them first; and the privilege of totally losing the love and respect of your children once they begin to see that the price you paid for the ranch style house and the second car was the acquiescence in the exploitation of blacks and Third Worlders and women—which the young repudiate.

It is true that under capitalism the U.S. high standard of living depends on exploiting Third World people. But the operative phrase is "under capitalism." If production were geared to human use instead of corporate profit, all white workers could enjoy a higher standard of living for less effort without exploiting the Third World. Although radicals should stress the dependence of capitalist societies on external exploitation (to prepare people for the time immediately after the revolution when internal production will have to be geared to rectifying the inequalities inflicted by capitalism throughout the world), international solidarity cannot be achieved by telling the white worker, as Weatherman did, that his goods already belong to the people of the Third World. This only reinforces the fears reactionaries are trying to instill: that the revolution will mean eliminating the goods the workers have acquired through hard work. After all, those goods are all they've managed to get out of selling their lives away for someone else's profit. And it would, in fact, be ridiculous to proceed as if a revolutionary program involved taking refrigerators away from white American workers to send them to Bolivians. The fact is that we can fill *all* people's key needs and solve the basic problems of scarcity, if we overthrow the capitalist system. In fact, when production is geared to human needs instead of private profits, many goods will last longer and there will be *more* for everyone.

To say that a person benefits from a system in some specific way is not the same as saying that he chose to have the system the way it is, particularly if some other possible system might benefit him even more. At least for the first twenty post-World War II years, working people went along with the system, in part because it took care of some of their material needs. But that does not mean they *chose* imperialism. People voted for Eisenhower because he said he would end the Korean adventure, for Johnson because he promised peace and accused Goldwater of being a warmonger. Moreover, the people have never had any opportunity to affect policy beyond the electoral arena. From the beginning, the working class has been more opposed to the Vietnam war than, for example, the upper middle class. For example, a 1964 Gallup poll reported that 53 percent of the college graduates wanted to escalate the war compared with 33⅓ percent of the people with only a grade school education. And in Campaign 72, Nixon was forced to portray himself as a peacemaker and to lie about his Vietnam policy in order to win popular support. The trips to China and Russia, seeming to portend a decline in international hostilities, made Nixon's lies about Vietnam de-escalation seem plausible. Nor can workers be blamed that nothing in their schooling or newspaper reading prepared them for the idea that their government systematically lies to them on every important issue.

One of the most serious difficulties in this discussion so far is the very term "the working class." In fact, the conditions of workers vary tremendously and so do their respective understandings of their situations. Some trade unionists in the building trades have incomes above $12,000 a year, while some farm workers make $1,500 a year. Even within the same factory and shop, different workers make different amounts and sometimes face qualitatively different working conditions. This is part of the reason it is more difficult to develop class consciousness now than it might have been in the mid-nineteenth century when Karl Marx was writing.

This is not the place to summarize all the strata of the working class. But we can at least mention some obvious examples of how stratification may affect the development of class consciousness.

1. *Managers.* In the upper levels of large corporations, managers are likely to be part of the ruling class, and in smaller firms they may be highly paid and identify their interests with those of the boss. Many managerial jobs on the lower levels are filled by people who began as part of the workforce, who fear that they could be thrown right back down again

177

if they do not behave. Although these people may have many common interests with the workers they supervise, they may be so preoccupied with their superior status that they suppress the common interests. Moreover, their task is to supervise and discipline the rest of the workforce. To the extent that they begin to identify with their job, and try to do it well, they develop patterns of thought that put the interests of their bosses first: this way of looking at a job inevitably weakens one's ability to develop class consciousness.

2. *Teachers*. Here the work situation creates conflicting demands; the one that wins depends in part on the person and, in part, on the social and political circumstances. A major aspect of the teacher's job is to socialize others to the capitalist social order ("Stick in your shirt." "Get to school on time." "Do the work I tell you to do." "Get my permission before you go to the bathroom." "Respect authority." And so on). To the extent that the teacher identifies with the established order, he sees himself as a professional, conveying Western values, and not to be challenged. On the other hand, teachers are supposed to be educators, bringing enlightenment to their students, and they can see that both the content of their courses and the way in which the school requires it to be taught squelch students and hurt their development. To the extent that this latter concern plays a role in teachers' minds they can begin to develop class consciousness and reject the notion of themselves as "professionals" somehow removed from the struggles of others. A first step in this direction may be to promote antiauthoritarian practices in the classroom.

3. *Teamsters*. The whole nature of a truck driver's work stands against the development of class consciousness. Behind the wheel he is isolated and alone, and he does not depend on collective effort, as do workers who put trucks together on an assembly line. On the other hand, as a member of a powerful union that can shut down important aspects of the economy by a strike, the teamster can also feel his social power as a worker, and so can come to see that it might be possible for workers really to change things. A janitor, for example, might not be able to sense this: he is likely to perceive his own work as peripheral and himself as replaceable. To date, the Teamsters Union has functioned independently of the rest of the labor movement, and has used its power to enhance its workers' earnings. But the emergence of a rank-and-file caucus within the Teamsters in the past year suggests that there may be a development toward using some of that feeling of power to address some of the more fundamental issues facing the workers.[7]

[7] In 1972 some Teamsters joined in a nationwide antiwar effort by labor unions, which held its first meeting in a Teamsters' headquarters in St. Louis.

4. *Industrial workers.* In industries such as auto and steel, where the workers can see both their own power and the collective effort required to build a society, we may expect that structural factors will work toward the development of class consciousness, although those factors may be offset by others (e.g., strong repression against radicals initiated by liberal-talking union bureaucrats, racism, threats by the company to shut down some operations permanently in light of competition, etc.).

All these examples represent tendencies, not firm predictions; when we get down to actual organizing we will have to look at the concrete situation as it develops. We can be encouraged by the high level of working-class militancy reflected in the large number of strike outbursts in the late 1960s and early 70s. But if this trend is somewhat reversed in the period ahead, we need not feel that we are entering a new period of quietude, just as growth in militancy in the immediate future does not necessarily mean that a revolutionary working class is just around the corner. To be serious is to have a long-term strategy, and the development of revolutionary consciousness may occur very quickly at a crucial moment if the correct kind of groundwork has been laid for years before.

5. *Government workers.* One area of particular interest is the rising militancy among government employees. The tremendous growth of city, state, and federal budgets has caused a serious fiscal crisis. The growth itself is caused in part by the need of big business to have many of its functions serviced by the public because it would be a serious financial drain for business to finance them itself (e.g., training personnel by technologizing the schools and universities; aid in transportation by building more airports, harbors, and roads; aid in developing new products by government subsidization of research and new production processes). But the growth is being paid for by working people, who bear the brunt of taxes. As the tax squeeze causes demands for tighter control of spending, government workers end by facing a gradual erosion of their own material standards. When normal businesses are faced with workers' demands, they can make some financial concessions by raising prices and increasing productivity. In a capitalist economy, the state has no option (except to raise taxes on working people) and is hence much less flexible. Since the state apparatus is controlled from the top down either directly by capitalists or by those who identify the interests of the capitalists with the interests of society as a whole, the state is not likely to pursue its other alternative: to demand that the capitalists pay for the special services they receive. So the state responds by arguing that public employees do not have a right to strike because they have a sacred trust to the public.

But the special obligation to the public can work both ways. And increasing numbers of government employees are beginning to see that the state does not place a very high priority on the public's needs, unless those needs neatly dovetail with the needs of some private corporate interest. Hence, the radical side of union struggles in this area expresses itself in terms of the need for better public services, or quality education, etc. As James O'Connor points out in "The Fiscal Crisis of the State," "Service workers quickly learn, precisely because they have been trained to think in terms of social relationships, that they are in fact in the service of the state administration and private capital and that their jobs really consist of establishing the pre-conditions for profitable business, training "human capital" rather than educating human beings, and exercising control over subject populations . . . when they take their normal function seriously they are at once faced with a gross shortage of resources—classroom space, buildings, hospital beds, land welfare funds, training funds, and so on—that is, their normal function requires far more resources than their real function." [8] Increasingly, these humanistic concerns for those whom they are supposed to serve has played a role in the struggle of state employees. Nor can this group be easily bought off by higher wages, since these wages will not be forthcoming as long as they must be paid for at the expense of the working class as a whole. Government employees have to raise such fundamental critiques of the operation of the state if they are to win alliances with other sections of the working class whose initial financial interests are opposed to giving higher pay to state employees.

The development of a strong student movement and the recent emergence of national welfare rights struggles points to another potential base for radical consciousness: those who are state dependents. For, even with all the success of imperialism during a certain historical period and even with the relative affluence of the American working class, poverty and various forms of financial dependency have by no means been eliminated. On the contrary, behind the myth of unlimited affluence stands the reality of near-starvation for millions, hunger for tens of millions, and inadequate health care and housing for tens of millions more. The poor are not usually considered a potential base for revolutionary action because it is widely believed that they are not willing to fight for anything more than simple material benefits for themselves, and that the system is flexible enough ultimately to absorb these people by meeting their demands. But these are improper assumptions. For one thing, the emergence of the National Welfare Rights Organization has demonstrated that many poor people are

[8] *Socialist Revolution*, no. 2 (March 1970): 34–94.

willing to fight for much more than simple material gain, and that they feel as alienated from society and disgusted by its imperialist adventures as any other group. For another, there is no reason to believe that the system is infinitely powerful in its ability to coopt material demands. If the society could have eliminated poverty, why has it not done so up to now? Recently it has been said that after the war in Vietnam is phased out, much money will go into dealing with poverty. But no real effort was made in this direction before the war, and there is no reason to believe that this will change. Until it becomes as profitable to fight poverty as it is to fight Communists, there will be no serious effort to deal with poverty. And even when it becomes profitable for some corporations, who will then finance liberal candidates who talk about "the crisis in our cities"? The corporations that benefit from military expenditures will put up a hard fight before they let go of the budget. In this context, even reformist demands for more money for the poor can cause serious problems for the capitalist society and can become a mechanism for further radicalization and struggle.

Any demand for better care for the dependents on the state, or for expanded social services in general, however, is likely to find opposition among large sections of the working class, who are asked to pay for most of these services through higher taxes. The mechanism for dividing the working class against itself is ingenious: the rulers simply explain to the workers that they will have to pay for cleaning up the social mess that capitalism has wrought. The huge expenditures for the military or for serving the special needs of the large corporations are never challenged, but are assumed as an inevitable part of the budget. Instead, the capitalist-controlled legislatures and Congress focus their attention on the small expenditures for welfare, medical care, and, more recently, pollution control, telling us that we can have these things only if *we* are prepared to pay for them.

In this context, many people end up resisting the expansion of governmental social services, thus providing a popular base for the most reactionary sections of the ruling class, who couldn't care less what happens to their workers when the workers can no longer be used to make a profit for them. At times, these alliances do succeed in curtailing social services, and this success gives some sections of the working class its only taste of political power. So the system manages to manipulate sections of the working class in such a way that its only experience of power occurs when that power is exercised against other sections of the working class.

An important part of the problem lies in the tax structure itself, which redistributes wealth from the workers to the owners by taxing the workers to pay for services that are needed by the large corporations. The tax system shows who has power in America. Corporate capital, except during rare moments of national crisis, completely escapes taxation. Corporate managers, as James O'Connor points out, "completely shift the corporate income tax to consumers—mainly wage and salary earners—in the form of higher prices." Further, "Property tax falls mainly on the working class, not on the business class. Within the core cities, residential properties assume the larger share, and commercial land and buildings the small share of the total property tax burden." [9]

Although the tax revolt has been used primarily by the Right to curb expenditures for welfare programs, it can become a major issue through which to unite working people around a leftist program. Struggles to shift the tax burden onto the wealthy can be an excellent mechanism for raising class consciousness. If such struggles have not as yet been waged, it is in part because the Left itself has not attempted to put forward a systematic critique of the tax structure coupled with a program for action.

Of course, we should not underestimate the power of the bourgeois media to confuse people about the issues, particularly by stressing the self-serving argument that unless the big capitalists are given special benefits, the investment climate will be affected and jobs will be cut back. This is typically garnished by threats that the corporations affected will move out of the state to some place where they will get better deals. The argument should not be written off as totally spurious: as long as the capitalists have all the power, they can punish the people for any serious infringement on their rights by throwing the economy into temporary havoc. But this threat must be exposed and dealt with by raising the antitax struggle to an explicitly anticapitalist level, and by organizing a national movement to confront the tax structure in every state and on the federal level.

The term "the working class" usually conjures up visions of the industrial working class: seldom does it suggest the other sectors of the working class. In fact, as Herbert Gintis points out in his article "The New Working Class," new sectors of the working class are becoming increasingly important. Says Gintis, "Today 'business organization' is paramount; the enterprise has been transformed into a massive bureaucracy, 'efficiently' organized, through a hierarchy of control and authority, towards the maximization of output, insofar as this is compatible with the maintenance of capitalist class relations. Processing, transmitting and coordination of information, not the transformation of raw materials through the application of energy, are increasingly central." [10] In the first fifty years of this

9 *Ibid.,* p. 68.
10 In *Socialist Revolution* 1, no. 3 (May–June 1970): 13–43.

century, Gintis tells us, the percentage of educated white-collar workers in the workforce more than doubled: in 1900 it was 17.6 percent; in 1950, 36.6 percent. During that same time, the percentage of professional and technical workers doubled and the percentage of clerical workers more than quadrupled. In the five-year period between 1965 and 1970 the number of professional and technical workers increased by 25 percent, clerical and kindred workers by 18 percent, and service workers (including teachers) by another 18 percent. During the same five years, skilled and semiskilled workers increased by only 6 percent, and unskilled workers decreased by 4 percent.

Educated laborers quickly realize that they are still "human capital" to the capitalists. Technicians, engineers, and researchers "discover that they are wage earners like everyone else, paid for a piece of work which is 'good' only to the degree that it is profitable in the short run. They discover that long-range research, creative work on original problems, and the love of workmanship are incompatible with the criteria of capitalist profitability —and this is not because they lack economic profitability in the long run, but because there is less risk and more profit in manufacturing saucepans." [11]

One striking example is the huge number of layoffs from Boeing in the 1968–71 period because of a decrease in orders for airplanes. More than 100,000 technicians and scientists and engineers were laid off in this period; all of them had talents that could have been used to make other kinds of products, and to help solve the mass transportation problem facing Seattle, Boeing's home town. But the owners of Boeing continually rejected proposals for any projects that would not yield a sure profit within a year, and instead proceeded to dismiss their educated labor by the thousands.

For this new working class, as for the old, a central problem is the impossibility of putting creative abilities to work. And this problem grows

[11] Andre Gorz, *Strategy for Labor* (Boston: Beacon Press, 1970), p. 104. The growth of the "new working class" does not represent a decline in numbers or importance of the "old working class." Between 1900 and 1970 the percentage of male workers in blue-collar jobs increased from 45.5 percent to 46.8 percent. The growth of both blue-collar and white-collar jobs as a percentage of the total workforce has been made possible because Marx's prediction about proletarianization has in fact come true: an increasing percentage of the workforce are those who do not own their own tools of production but must sell their own labor power to someone else who can afford to buy it. As Albert Szymanski puts it in "Trends in the American Working Class," *Socialist Revolution* 2, no. 4 (July–August, 1972): 113: "The significant trends of the last seventy years have been the decrease in independent urban proprietors and the rapid decrease of both agricultural laborers and independent farmers on the one hand, and the rapid increase in the "new working class" on the other.

directly out of the essence of capitalist production, which thus creates the great potential for radicalization that exists amongst these sectors of the population. This will be especially true for those younger workers who enter these fields not because they need to overcome poverty by getting a good job, but because they have been led to believe that in some way their work might be fulfilling.

In this respect, the struggles in the university are a crucial prelude to major successes in the offices and factories of educated labor. For the multiversity is a factory precisely in the sense that it attempts "to adapt the worker to his task in the shortest possible time, and gives him the capacity for a minimum of independent activity. Out of fear of creating men who, by virtue of the too 'rich' development of their abilities, would refuse to submit to the discipline of a too narrow task and to the industrial hierarchy, the effort that has been made to stunt them from the beginning: they were designed to be competent, but limited; active but docile; intelligent but ignorant of anything outside their function; incapable of having a horizon beyond that of their task. In short, they were designed to be specialists." [12] But this means that revolts against the stifling tendencies of the system occur earlier in the life of individuals, when they are still young enough that they do not stand to lose everything by fighting. The student movement, insofar as it produces a radical critique of the university, is simultaneously planting the seeds for a future rebellion of educated labor. Anyone who writes off "the working class" has simply not thought seriously about the revolutionary dynamic we are discussing here. Unless, of course, capitalism can deal with the problem by providing increasingly strong diversions from the monotony of work—by accepting and developing, for example, those aspects of the youth culture that accentuate sensual gratification and making them more generally available (e.g., legalizing pot, creating massive rock concerts and light shows, making sex more readily available, etc.—in short, following the model outlined by Huxley's *Brave New World*).

Educated labor is the section of the working class that is most often nonunionized, and this presents both an advantage and a difficulty. The difficulty is that many of these workers have accepted the bourgeois notion that they are above the "workers," and hence do not need organizations to defend their rights as workers. On the other hand, once the reality of their work situation hits them, they do not have to channel their outrage into a union structure that has already proved itself stifling to militant action. It may therefore be possible that "educated labor" will develop for itself new

12 *Ibid.*, p. 107.

forms that allow it to carry on the class struggle without duplicating the pitfalls of the trade-union structure.

In its present form the AFL–CIO is often a greater help to the rulers than to the workers. First, it has completely failed to develop any vision for basic social change relevant to the workers' needs. Instead, its sole political strategy is to rely on the Democratic party, within which it sides with such candidates as Hubert Humphrey, who have long been identified with the wishy-washy liberalism that has dominated American politics for the past forty years and solved none of America's social problems. No wonder that workers who feel real discontent are attracted by the seeming radicalism of Governor George Wallace's populist anticapitalist, pro-"little man" rhetoric. Since trade-union bureaucrats helped to construct the present social reality and have little in the way of program to change it, even their own rank and file often sees them as part of the establishment rather than as a force for serious change. Second, the trade-union leadership often attempts to hold back the militancy of the rank and file, fearful that it will jeopardize the pleasant arrangements that have been worked out between themselves and the industrial management. Often the labor bureaucrats really believe that they have done the best they could for the workers, because they know better than their membership how tough the bosses really are. After all, they reason, they were once militants themselves (twenty or thirty years ago), but now they need to be "responsible." And being responsible means framing issues for struggle that can be won, while leaving the wider societal issues (like the war in Vietnam or decent social health care or housing or jobs for the unemployed) to "the politicians" (i.e., the Democratic party). Each union struggles only for those of its members' needs that are peculiar to the industry involved, while the needs that workers have in common are ruled out as irrelevant. This policy, in turn, furthers the isolation of each union from the others: each is accustomed to think only in terms of its own needs, and therefore it is difficult to generate support for another union when it is striking for *its* needs. So the labor movement becomes weaker, and the bureaucrats use this weakness as further proof that the union is too weak to take on larger issues. It's a vicious circle: the unions define their politics along narrow self-interest grounds, every union afraid to be the first to stick out its neck on social issues, and this very narrowness becomes the cause of rank-and-file apathy. Moreover, not all trade-union bureaucrats are misguided liberals who remember the good old days when the union movement was alive, but who are too afraid to help revive it. Some union leaders are gangsters pure and simple. It was not only in the old days that labor insurgents got beaten up or killed, as the murder of Joseph Yablonski

185

in the United Mine Workers recently demonstrated. Many workers reason that it is simply too risky to challenge the mobsters and their friends in public office who have made a sham of union democracy. Third, the structure and tradition of the unions has been so completely geared to accommodation with the system that even when insurgents and reformers manage to win an election, they find their mandate narrowly constrained. They are able to win by urging greater militancy on the traditional issues, but it is precisely the narrowness of these issues that is the problem. But what concerns the alienated worker is his total powerlessness, and it is on this front that even the insurgents have no program for struggle. The whole idea of workers' control is seen as too visionary. So instead of building the groundwork for a long-term struggle, both within the union and among other union forces, instead of developing a political strategy, even the insurgents quickly yield to the pressure to produce immediate contractural material gains. The irony is that the insurgents achieved power on the vaguely articulated hope that they would really make some basic changes, and they soon find that once they have decided to limit themselves to being practical, even their more militant stances on the old issues fail to generate much grass-roots support. Then, not understanding what has happened, they blame the rank and file for being "apathetic." One need only look at the growth of rank-and-file caucuses and wildcat strikes of the early 1970s and to the popular support George Wallace has managed to tap to dispel this notion of apathy. The union movement itself has generated the apathy it uses as its excuse.

Entirely new kinds of unions and union organizations may be needed. One need not write off the entire labor movement (certainly there are decent labor leaders in some unions, and every union is filled with younger members who decidedly favor a move toward the Left). But neither should organized labor unions be approached as something that can be gradually reformed from within. A new orientation to working-class struggles is necessary, one that focuses on the worker as a full human being and not merely an accumulator of capital.

A new union movement, possibly in the form of workers' councils, is necessary to focus on the issue of power, including the power to determine every aspect of the work situation and the wage scale. Unions, or workers' councils, should fight for control of the training schools to ensure that they begin to train full human beings capable of exercising their intelligence to make real choices for themselves, and not merely narrow specialists with stunted capacities. The union, or workers' council, must struggle for control of the work situation to ensure that work is assigned so as to maximize the worker's creativity and individual development, and not just the profit of the corporation. It must struggle for the workers both as producers and as consumers: it must fight for societal changes and it must fight for a say in the kinds of things produced. The orientation must be toward structural reforms—reforms that redistribute power from the capitalists to the workers. Such a new union movement, precisely because its tasks were explicitly anticapitalist, would find itself strengthened in its struggle to the extent that workers overcame their chauvinism and racism and could align with other sectors of the population—particularly women, blacks, and Chicanos—who were also engaged in explicitly anticapitalist struggles.

If this last thought seems too utopian, we must remember the remarkable transformations of consciousness that have begun to occur among various sections of the population as they begin to struggle. The black movement, seemingly centered on narrow civil rights demands in the early part of the 1960s, was moved by the dynamic of its struggle increasingly to identify itself with internationalist concerns. The white student movement, rooted in its own special privileges, was moved by the dynamic of its struggle increasingly to identify with the black liberation struggle and the women's liberation struggle. There is every reason to believe that this dynamic will repeat itself when the workers begin to struggle for workers' power and not just for wage benefits. And this tendency will be strengthened by the fact that educated labor will be much affected by the student movement which already places a high emphasis on fighting racism and chauvinism.

What we have been arguing is that certain objective conditions exist which make possible the development of radical consciousness among a large section of working people over the next fifteen years. This radicalization is not inevitable, and the ruling class will use every trick at its disposal, including the massive repressive power of the state, to make sure that it does not occur and that those who seem to be having any success in moving people in this direction are isolated and crushed. A great deal depends on the Left, its sophistication and willingness to take risks and to experiment, its openness and its ability to work hard and long, and its ability to show people that their interests as human beings can only be served by revolutionary struggle.

In discussing "the working class" we have referred to the Left organizing workers. But the organizers should not be conceived of as outsiders, from some other group. Most of them will undoubtedly be people who are affected by the same problems as are workers, and who realize that their own liberation depends on the development of a revolutionary movement. The entire proletariat has many similar problems, and organizing must be done around those issues that unite the proletariat in struggle against the bosses.

There has been some criticism of people from the student movement who decide to become factory organizers. This criticism often displays a misunderstanding of the ambiguous position of "student." Unlike the members of other social categories, the student can remain a student for only a limited period of time. Students are workers-in-training. Many of them are from working-class homes. What's more, there is nothing illegitimate in young people from middle-class origins identifying with the workers and becoming organizers. In part, this is just a natural extension of their coming to self-consciousness as part of the greatly expanded new proletariat. After all, they too will have to sell their labor power or starve, although they can sell it at a higher price than unskilled workers. This will even be true of some young members of the ruling class, who come to realize the destructiveness of the system, and who decide to identify with the struggle against capitalism. More and more people from every class will come to realize that their own humanity and their own liberation requires the destruction of capitalism. Such people should not be crucified on the cross of their class background, but should be welcomed into the new American revolutionary community.

One hesitation sometimes expressed of "organizers" is that they become involved in politics not out of a gut reaction to their own oppression, but out of a sense of "liberal guilt." This distinction may explain the behavior of liberals who do not opt for the revolution: they simply do not feel personally oppressed and their liberal politics are nothing more than a penance for an otherwise enjoyable life. But some forms of guilt are rational and even liberating. When a person has decided to dedicate his life to overthrowing capitalism, what difference does it make if part of the motivation is an unwillingness to live off the exploitation of *other* people? One way that some people are oppressed by capitalism is that even the good things they could have are available to them only as the products of an exploitative system. If living in capitalist society does violence to one's very nature, that constitutes an oppression as real as the oppression of not having enough to eat. To deny this is to be thrown back into some form of vulgar Marxism in which human needs are not on a par with material needs: a complete distortion of Marx made possible for the Old Left only by virtue of the fact that Marx's Early Philosophic Manuscripts were not available in translation in the 1930s. It is far from wrong for people to feel a little upset at being part of a system whose normal operations involve the exploitation of hundreds of millions of people around the world.

Another objection to the notion of "organizer" is that it sounds elitist; it suggests that the organizer is ahead of the people. The nonelitist way, presumably, would be the spontaneous development of consciousness. Unless conditions are ripe, no organizer can appear on the scene and after a few months (or a few years) make a significant impact on people's consciousness. But even under optimum conditions, consciousness does not always develop spontaneously, and there is nothing wrong with the active role of a catalyst. Nor should we hold the view that all people's political consciousness develops at the same rate: special circumstances of background and situation will make some people come to a socialist consciousness more quickly than others. It *would* be elitist if these people, content in their special understanding, were to refuse to attempt to reach others. In fact, this has been precisely the mistake of the radical sections of the student movement: they believe they have an understanding that would clarify the perceptions of others, but they disdain bringing it to others on the grounds that the people aren't "ready" yet.

Needless to say, the manner in which one organizes must not make it impossible for people to hear and respond. Organizers cannot approach people with the assumption that they are better than the people they are going to organize, or that they are selfless. But while the organizer must always avoid feeling—or even appearing to feel—superior to those he is organizing, he is correct in feeling that he has a *better* understanding of the world than those who do not yet share a class analysis of American society. Nevertheless, people who do not yet have a socialist consciousness can have much to teach those who do, particularly about the ways the concrete workings of capitalism make the abstraction "oppression" a daily reality for millions of people.

The "organizer" or "revolutionary cadre" is not someone without a set of needs of his own. He (or, of course, she) is someone who comes to understand that his own liberation depends on the revolution, and that to have a revolution, many millions of people will have to share his desire for it. It then becomes one of the organizer's needs that other people develop an understanding of the ways this society oppresses them and the ways it oppresses others, because only when other people share this awareness can we together create a society in which everyone's needs will be fulfilled. This is especially true when we realize that to some extent the oppression of other people *is* our own oppression, because it is impossible to be a full human being in a world in which others are downtrodden.

In the period of its decline in the early 1970s, the New Left often accepted the argument that because most of its members were not personally

189

oppressed by Vietnam, busing, the rise of Wallace, the wage-price freeze, industrial health and safety pensions or taxes, it was not quite honest for the movement to concern itself with these issues.

This position was best summed up by James Weinstein: "Radicalism is based on an awareness of one's own oppression." [13] There is nothing wrong with the thought as stated—but there was considerable wrong with the way that people acted upon it. True, radicalism is based on our own oppression —but we cannot accept the underlying assumption that we are isolated individuals whose primary concern is ourselves. To some extent, of course, the vision of isolated selves having fates independent of one another is an inevitable product of capitalist society. But a revolutionary movement must combat that conditioning and help people to develop new needs for themselves, rather than merely fill the needs that have been formed by the capitalist structure. Probably one of the most important needs that a revolutionary movement must help foster is the need for the self-fulfillment of everyone. We must come to develop as *our* need, a prerequisite for *our* fulfillment as human beings, that other human beings be able to fulfill *their* needs and realize *their* potentialities. To the extent that one develops a sense of human solidarity, to the extent that one overcomes the isolationism and individualism that are the hallmarks of bourgeois ideology, one begins to feel the oppression of other human beings as one's own. In fact, it is only by developing this sense of solidarity that it will ever be possible to unite a working class that has so many diverse and sometimes, in the short-run, even contradictory sets of material interests.

Throughout this discussion I have been tempered and moderate in my claims about the sources and likely consequences of working-class radicalization. I have focused primarily on those aspects of working-class life that increasingly are producing radicalization, even when the material wealth of working people is growing. I have expressed this caution because I do not believe that the American economy is on the verge of an economic cataclysm analogous in its impact on the consciousness of working people to the great depression of the 1930s. On the other hand, as I mentioned in earlier sections, the period of seemingly unlimited possibilities for the ruling class is over. In the past seven years, the U.S. ability to set the terms of trade and investment throughout much of the Third World, and even in the large industrial countries devastated by the Second World War, has been seriously curtailed. And that tendency is likely to become more important in the 1970s. As a result, the ruling class will increasingly be forced to choose between cutting into its own profits or into the wages

[13] In *Socialist Revolution*, no. 10 (July 1972).

and benefits of the workers. Nixon's economic policies represent the thinking of one powerful section of the ruling class that has made the decision without room for ambiguity: Let the Workers Pay.

Whether we have an explicitly conservative administration or one that pretends to liberalism, the general pattern is going to be the same: the material wealth of working people will be challenged and curtailed. The demand that increases in pay be tied to increases in productivity is part of this pattern: owners of factories are saying that workers will get more only if the owners' profits go up. As the crisis in the economy deepens, we are certain to see more pressure on the workers' material standards, and a consequent increase in working-class militancy. But, as did *not* happen in the 1930s, this militancy will emerge in a historical period in which the questions of material wealth have been linked by radicals to the more fundamental question of control. The one value of past mistakes is that you can learn from them, and it is highly unlikely that the revolutionary leadership in the coming period will allow an emergent militancy to remain focused simply on material issues.

The working-class movement of the coming period is not likely to be dealt with in a fashion similar to that of the 30s. In that period, it was always possible for U.S. capitalism to try its ace in the hole: military expenditures and expansion to control foreign markets. But that strategy was tried, successfully for a time, in the 40s and 50s and is now breaking down. So what exactly will the program of the ruling class be? The alternatives are not unlimited, and more and more it will seem clear to growing numbers of people that a fundamental irrationality exists in the capitalist system. Still, the capitalists may be able to pull it out of the bag once again, if they can direct the workers' resentment over their lost material prosperity to some other group. This strategy has worked against blacks and welfare recipients in the present period, but is unlikely to continue to be successful unless some more logical target appears.

Dare we suggest that such a target might once again be our economic rivals in Europe and Japan? If so, we could imagine how, in order to deflect attention from their own programs of forced austerity for the working class, the rulers of this country would blame all our difficulties on rival imperialist powers and attempt to restir the sentiments of nationalism against our former cold-war allies. Perhaps that strategy will have greater success than their campaign to make Americans believe they were really threatened by tiny North Vietnam. To what extent the working class will buy this new nationalism would be hard to predict: a great deal will depend on the effectiveness of the Left in countering this strategy with one that helps people see their real enemies. The period ahead is filled with many possibilities for the working class; its political direction is very fluid. Different sections may move in different directions, and if there is to be a socialist revolution, important sections of the working class will have to be, and can (given the likely conditions of the next decade) be, in the lead.

BLACKS

The black community has a higher degree of revolutionary consciousness and willingness to sacrifice for basic change than any other constituency group in the revolution at this time. The data speak very clearly: Watts and Newark and Detroit and Birmingham and dozens of other cities have convulsed in antioppression riots not as a result of the work of skilled outside agitators, but because black people have increasingly perceived the impossible conditions under which they live. The present consciousness is the culmination of many years of struggle, and it is likely to increase. Ironically, it was Martin Luther King, the darling of white liberals, who helped build the current dynamic by leading thousands of people into struggle and raising the hopes of millions more. The failure of the civil rights movement to begin even to touch on the basic problems of the urban blacks coupled with the great resistance that ensured its ultimate failure to integrate blacks with whites, was a major factor in producing the Black Power movement and its revolutionary consequences.

Revolutionary consciousness in the black community, however, is motivated less by "rising expectations" than by a growing sense that struggle is the only option. As James Boggs puts it in *Racism and the Class Struggle*,[14]

> Today 35% to 50% of black young people are unemployed and roaming the streets, their only future a prison cell or a rice paddy in Southeast Asia. Automation and cybernation have made the unskilled, undeveloped labor of our young men and women increasingly expendable. Displaced from the land, concentrated in the slums of the nation's cities, we are no longer needed as producers. Yet we are constantly urged by the mass media to become consumers in order to keep the mass production lines of America operating at full capacity, even if we can only get the wherewithal for such consumption by one or another form of hustling. Hence

14 New York: Monthly Review Press, 1969, p. 169.

at the end of the road for millions of our people looms only a prison cell.

The black community's high degree of consciousness about oppression has not led to a unified response. While blacks have fewer illusions than whites about the liberals and about gradual reform, they also have a very high degree of cynicism about changing the situation. As a result, many blacks opt for individual approaches, trying to make it on their own. An amazing number of young blacks articulate a completely revolutionary analysis of their situation, but act only as individuals and shun organized political activity. These people will sporadically direct their justified hatred of the system toward a particular act of violence against police or some other symbol of authority, but their cynicism prevents them from joining any organized force.

Despite the high degree of consciousness, then, the black community has produced very few organizations for radical political action. The contrast between the high degree of sympathy for the Black Panthers in the black community and the low percentage of blacks who are actually willing to join the Panthers is instructive. Of course, joining a black revolutionary organization is more dangerous than joining a white one, because there is much less restraint on police violence in the ghetto than on violence against whites. To join the Panthers in the late 1960s was literally to risk death— quite different from the amount of courage it took to join Students for a Democratic Society (SDS).

And there are conservatizing tendencies in the black community as well. There are still class divisions among blacks, and the strategy of the rulers is to intensify them. Increasingly, the white rulers will use black administrators and black henchmen to keep control of the black community. "Safe" blacks will become mayors, congressmen, college administrators, and store managers in black areas. The cities that have been destroyed by white capitalism will become the inherited territory of blacks, although the whites who now live in the suburbs but still run the major industries and banks of the city will make sure that their remaining economic power and their control of the media are used to back "responsible" black candidates (i.e., those who do not challenge the basic distribution of wealth and power). The black bourgeoisie finds that its rise to power is carefully guided by the white power structure.

In the section on racism I discussed the economic reasons why black capitalism is not a real alternative for the ghetto. Some blacks will make it, undoubtedly; but most will not. Equally important, the dynamics of a racist society continually forces black people from every class to be cognizant of their blackness, and hence to be aware that their fate is intertwined with that of every other black person. When the troops opened fire in Newark or at Jackson State they made no distinction between those who were upwardly mobile and those who were not.

The increasing reliance on "law and order" as a way of dealing with the "black problem" by the white rulers forces all blacks into increasing solidarity and antiestablishment sentiments. As the oppression of blacks begins to resemble that of any other colonial people, the phenomena of Vietnam are repeated within the United States: the colonialist attempting to make war against the rebels ends up making war against the entire people. Even moderate blacks are forced to come to the defense of the more revolutionary elements, if only for fear that failure to do so would discredit them totally in the black community.

The failure of integration and the increasing fears of genocide have produced, particularly among young blacks, a readiness for a much higher stage of political struggle. These youth have already been engaged in a variety of confrontations with the police, the school system, construction unions, housing authorities, health and welfare administrators, etc. They are often explicitly anticapitalist and anti-imperialist, identifying with those forces that fight against the U.S. exploitation of the colored peoples of Africa, Asia, and Latin America. And, as James Boggs puts it, they recognize that their struggle is against "a whole power structure comprising a complex network of politicians, university and school administrators, landlords, merchants, usurers, realtors, insurance personnel, contractors, union leaders, licensing and inspection bureaucrats, racketeers, lawyers, and especially policemen—the overwhelming majority of whom are both white and absentee, and who exploit the black ghetto in much the same way that Western powers exploit the colonies and neo-colonies in Africa, Asia and Latin America." [15] Further, these young people have learned enough from the failure of the civil rights movement; the violent deaths of Martin Luther King and Malcolm X; and the repression of the Black Panther party to have lost any liberal illusions they may have had about how to change this society. This group does not represent the entire black community, but it *does* represent a rising tendency.

It is true that the economic structure of capitalism requires a series of underdogs, and that black people are singled out for this role in American history. But racism is not simply an economic phenomenon to be dealt with solely on an economic level. Although racism is sustained by

[15] *Ibid.*, p. 181.

capitalism and serves the interests of the rulers, it has taken on a life of its own, totally independent of the interests it serves and the economic arrangements it facilitates. Many whites, having been socialized into a racist society, will retain their racist practices, even if those practices are not in their economic interests. Once ingrained in large numbers of people, it requires special attention and special struggle over and above the general struggle to overthrow capitalism.

For the black revolutionary movement this situation poses some special problems: How does one relate the struggle against class oppression to the struggle against race oppression? How does one relate to whites who want change if the whites themselves embody, to some extent, the racism that the class society has fostered? Can blacks make a revolution without the aid of the whites?

One set of answers has been provided by the nonrevolutionary part of the black nationalist movement, including the Black Muslims. The Muslims hold that all whites are automatically evil and cannot be trusted or dealt with, that blacks should build their own institutions with an orientation toward eventually controlling their own land. This approach rests on an incorrect analysis of the ways that racism is sustained. White people are not born evil, though conditioning in American capitalist society may well make them act in evil ways, especially toward blacks. But the capitalist system exists for blacks as well. They too suffer from it and are deformed by it, and hence it is on that system that attention must be focused if either blacks or whites are going to build a new society.

The belief that black people can solve their problem by simply moving to a certain area of the country and setting up their own society or, as Marcus Garvey once thought, by returning en masse to Africa, simply does not come to grips with the real issue. If blacks attempted to do anything of this sort, they would find it economically impossible and politically forbidden, and ultimately they would have to confront the military might of the capitalists' repressive powers. Similarly, although some counterinstitutions can successfully be built within the capitalist framework, at the moment these institutions threaten seriously to weaken the hold of the capitalists over one of their important sources for imperialist exploitation, the rulers will move with all the powers at their disposal to crush them. A political strategy that does not prepare black people for sustained struggle aimed at overthrowing the state is doomed to failure.

Any emphasis on national identity, then, must deal with the political and economic situation of blacks as it exists concretely in racist America. Nationalism is important in the black community because black people share a certain fate *as blacks*. But that fate is linked to the economic and political order, and it can be altered only by overthrowing that order. In this respect, cultural (or, what Bobby Seale used to call "pork chop") nationalism can lead people in a wrong direction by focusing their attention on their blackness instead of on their situation. Quoting black writer James Boggs once again, the struggle for Black Power "has nothing to do with any special moral virtue in being black, as some black nationalists seem to think. Nor does it have to do with the special cultural virtues of the African heritage. Identification with the African past is useful insofar as it enables black Americans to develop a sense of identity independent of the Western civilization which has robbed them of their humanity by robbing them of any history." [16]

Black people in America *do* have a history, but it has largely been a history of exploitation and resistance to that exploitation with varying degrees of intensity. After all, racism is a white problem, or better, a problem with whites. But it is a real problem, with real consequences, that have to be dealt with, and while ideally it should be dealt with by whites without bothering blacks at all, that is not likely to happen. Racism is not going to go away (as some members of the black bourgeoisie who favor black cultural nationalism like to think) when blacks act proud of their heritage and sure of their personal identity. Racism is not simply an aberration curable with a little integration, a little love, a little study of black history, etc.

At the same time, cultural nationalism may have value as a transitional step in the development of a black revolutionary movement. Racism does have severe psychological effects on both blacks and whites. A sense of one's own worth and identity may be an important precondition for revolutionary struggle, and emphasis on one's cultural heritage may play a part in developing that sense. There is nothing intrinsically more valuable in black than there is in red or in white, but the notion that "Black is beautiful" plays a very important role in the development of self-esteem. But if people are not willing to move beyond this stage to ask "How do we free black people from the economic and political circumstances that oppress and degrade them?" the problem will not be solved. To get to this point we have to understand that not everything black is good, that some blacks exploit other blacks, and that black life will not achieve its potential for beauty as long as it is held down in racist and capitalist America.

In colonies such as Vietnam or Algeria or other Third World countries, nationalism is good precisely because it necessarily leads to revolutionary

[16] *Ibid.*

struggle. Nationalism plays a positive role in Vietnam because the imperialists' need to exploit the country makes them put its national interests second and hence the nationalists always oppose them. Even those Vietnamese who want to remain neutral for personal reasons are pushed farther to the Left by the logic of the situation. "So pork-chop nationalism is good," it might be argued. "It is not merely a therapeutic step but a position that will inevitably lead to struggle." This argument presents two problems:

1. Even in the Third World there are nationalist figures who have made accommodations with the imperialists, in part because they think it to the advantage of their own and their people's welfare. The arguments in favor of these accommodations sound convincing to sections of the American black bourgeoisie who are overly impressed with America's power and still believe that its bad points can be reformed away. No matter how bad things get for the rest of the black community, these bourgeois will find ways to avoid any serious struggles as long as there is still room for them and as long as their culture does not become illegal.

2. The black colony in the United States is not analogous to the colonies of imperialism elsewhere. When the Vietnamese organize around their national solidarity, they have the potential of including almost the entire populace. This provides an excellent base from which to build a struggle against the imperialist. But in the United States, people of color are in the minority, and a struggle based solely on their special position, a struggle that did not also orient itself toward the oppression of millions of whites, would be doomed to failure.

An overemphasis on cultural nationalism makes these ties and bridges very difficult to build. For these reasons, increasing numbers of blacks have moved beyond cultural nationalism to revolutionary nationalism—to the kind of nationalism that underscores the beauty and value of blackness and simultaneously talks in terms of the class structure that oppresses both blacks and whites and of the need to overthrow that structure.

Weathermen, and other sections of the Left that have given up the hope of making any majoritarian revolution, at this point usually interject the notion that blacks, together with people of the Third World, can make the revolution on their own—hence, any concern for a black movement that reaches out to whites and provides a language that enables blacks and whites to see their struggles as similar simply reveals national and racial chauvinism. This position presents several problems.

1. It is racist in its consequences. No amount of moral exhortation will suffice to offset the incredible burden this position places on blacks and the irresponsibility and adventurism it allows to whites.

2. There is no reason to believe it is true. The notion that "the spirit of the people is greater than the Man's technology" makes sense in a colonial situation where the vast majority of the people sympathize with and support the guerrilla movement. But in America, the likely result of this position is mass annihilation of the black minority, with most whites standing by, "deploring the violence on both sides."

Blacks could, it is true, exert a high price in such a race war by engaging in a disciplined guerrilla struggle, and the fabric of American society would crumble. But it would crumble toward some kind of fascist dictatorship, not toward socialism. The proposal that blacks do it alone is rarely advanced by blacks, but often suggested by whites interested in showing how well they have "dealt with their racism." It conjures up a vision of a dictatorship of Third Worlders and blacks over a reluctant population—a kind of nightmare when one considers the resistance such an idea would raise in the minds of so many whites. Nor would whites be wrong to resist: if the revolution were to bring about a further loss of liberty for them they would have good grounds to oppose it. So the very putting forward of this idea encourages people to be willing to go to any lengths to resist the revolution. Once again, the Weatherman ideology comes to the rescue of the ruling class!

On the other hand, if it was possible to overthrow American capitalism and racism through a dictatorship of blacks and Third Worlders, and impossible to do it in any other way, such a dictatorship would be appropriate. However, any serious reckoning with the technological power of this society would have to conclude that as long as whites are fairly solidly behind the government or willing to tolerate the use of its military might, there is no way for the government to be overthrown from outside, short of a completely devastating nuclear war.

But if race war did not bring liberation at least it might bring a certain dignity to those blacks whose only other alternative is degradation and continued repression. If it really were impossible to move anyone into the revolutionary struggle, and if America were to continue on its path of escalating repression, Huey Newton would be right in telling people that blacks have only two choices: reactionary suicide or revolutionary suicide. No human being could possibly want to see the consequences of a race war in this country. But at the same time it should be remembered that large sections of the black community have explicitly decided that they will not walk like prayerful Jews into a new fascism's concentration camps. Blacks will resist, and the race war, while ultimately leading to the destruction of black people in this country, could tear the country apart and seriously weaken its power to enforce imperialism elsewhere. Some black militants have been too quick to use the threat of race war when they did not get what they demanded, and then found that they could not deliver it on demand. But that does not vitiate the possibility that a dynamic is being built which will lead in that direction.

If race war is a possibility, it is one we wish to avoid if that is humanly possible. And so will any black who is not willing to lead himself and others to their destruction. A preferable alternative would be to build a struggle that can overthrow capitalism without simultaneously destroying most of the American people. Such a struggle can be facilitated by the development of revolutionary black nationalism oriented toward the overthrow of capitalism rather than a final war of desperation. Such a nationalism would be characterized by the understanding that the capitalist system is the source of the problem and that in order to overthrow capitalism it will be necessary at some point to work with revolutionary whites.

"At some point" is the operative phrase. There is no reason black revolutionaries should have to work with whites now, or at the first available moment, and there are many reasons they shouldn't. For one thing, whites have always had a tendency, based in part on their racism, to want to run the show for blacks. This has had the effect of stifling the development of black leadership in the past, and should be avoided. Second, the problems of the black community are quite different than those of the white, and mixed organizations might underemphasize the needs of the one in the interests of the needs of the other. This would be particularly true in questions of style and language: the communities are sufficiently disparate to require completely different forms of organization and action. Further, their past experiences have given good reason to distrust the commitment and seriousness of whites who consider themselves revolutionary. This distrust will be overcome only by years of serious work by a white revolutionary organization which can begin to move whites away from racist attitudes and toward serious and prolonged struggle. Blacks have good reason to say "Show me, first"; even the blacks closest to collaboration with the rulers have often been driven to this position by the failures of whites to take their professed ideals seriously. At the same time, this separation of blacks from whites may have a salutory effect on white organizations if it reduces the white liberals' tendency to follow blacks' advice on issues just because they are black, even when there is no reason to believe that blackness adds any special competence. But when serious progress has been made among whites, a united revolutionary organization will have the highest priority.

Within the black community itself, different forms of organization are likely to develop for different sectors. For instance, the Black Panther party developed out of an interest in organizing those the Panthers called "the lumpen"—people who could not get jobs because of the increasing mechanization of capitalism and its practice of hiring blacks last and firing them first. The Congress of Black Workers was formed in response to a different kind of goal—to provide a way for black workers to deal with common problems that could not be handled through a racist union structure. Other forms will undoubtedly develop in the course of the struggle.

For blacks to be oriented toward working with whites in the future as equals in a revolutionary struggle in no way implies that in the meantime it is inappropriate to support struggles that seem to have an antiwhite perspective. On the contrary, black revolutionary organizations are both right and wise to confront white racism at every possible opportunity, even among sectors of the population who will eventually be sought as allies against the ruling class. Ideally such struggles would attempt to educate people about why it is in their long-term interest both to oppose racism and to transform themselves. Good examples of such struggles are the demands for more jobs for blacks and for open enrollment in the universities. At first, both demands are likely to be opposed by sections of the white working class on the grounds that they will take away jobs or university places from whites. It is this fear that allows the rulers to manipulate white workers and set them in conflict with blacks. But blacks cannot be expected to accept their economically inferior position because to do otherwise would antagonize whites. On the contrary, it is up to whites to begin to realize that the appropriate response to black demands is to join them and to add to the blacks' demands the demand for more jobs and university places for all.

Some whites object here: "Sure, that's good to ask for, but in the short run we won't get those jobs or university places, and so it will mean turning over what is ours to blacks." But, in light of the history of the union movement over the past thirty years, such an argument can only be made in bad faith. For the union movement has not made any serious struggle to expand the job market or the universities so as to accommodate those on the outside. On the contrary, union leaders have made striking accommodations with political leaders and have never demanded an end to unemployment as a precondition for their support. White workers have used their unions to ensure their own employment. More often than not, the unions have themselves kept blacks out or placed them in subordinate positions within the union. Consequently, most unions have rightfully lost all their credibility with blacks. If jobs are given to blacks, if unions are opened up to them, and if university places are assigned to them, perhaps that will

200

force white workers to stop focusing on how to divide their piece of the pie and start asking how to get more pie from the capitalists.

"But won't this cause a backlash?" Certainly the media have done their best to create a reaction among whites. And it is sickening to see the government, which itself sustains racist practices (from its treatment of blacks in the army to its indifference to the black poverty that is a direct result of capitalist exploitation), step into these conflicts as the morally pure arbitrator, cooling down whites whose racism has run away with itself. The fact is that racism in this country has acquired an independent life, and that life is greatly strengthened whenever it appears that blacks are going to get economic benefits that would otherwise go to whites. Of course, this reaction has always been the virtue of the racist system for the rulers: when white workers fight black workers, women fight men, and American workers fight Vietnamese, no one ever focuses on the ruling class itself. So the backlash will come, in the short run. It can only be avoided if blacks, women, Vietnamese, and everyone else who is exploited accept their exploitation quietly. It is perfectly clear from the history of the liberals and reformists of the past forty years that no quiet reform, slipped through while white workers are not watching, is going to equalize the situation between blacks and whites. Nor will any quiet reform, slipped through while the ruling class is not watching, significantly expand the percentage of overall wealth that white and black workers are fighting about. If anything is to change it will have to be through open struggle.

To the degree that it takes seriously the job of educating whites about the real role of racism a white revolutionary movement can play an important role. The struggle between black and white workers makes sense only in the context of a society with a finite and relatively small amount of wealth, which has to be divided between the two. But in this society both blacks and whites could be infinitely better off if wealth were taken away from the ruling class and redistributed to everyone. Even more important than taking away the rulers' wealth is redistributing their power, so that production can be geared to human needs instead of the rulers' profit. Most of the things that money is used for in this society could be adequately provided for everybody (housing, food, medical care, transportation) if production were arranged with that goal in mind. Equality between blacks and whites does not have to mean downgrading the standard of living; on the contrary, it would make it possible for everyone to be far better off. "But wait," says the white worker, "isn't socialism far away? In the meantime I've got to eat and take care of my family." Three responses: (1) Socialism is far away only as long as you and most other people like you think it is. It could be around the corner if you decided to make it your priority. (2) Black people have to take care of their families *too*! (3) There are intermediary struggles, which could be won in the immediate future, that would guarantee that you did not lose much by giving blacks equality in jobs, housing, and education. Those fights could take more away from the rulers in the short run even though they did not come close to socialism. But those fights will not be fought as long as you think that an equally good option is to exploit blacks. Aren't we all tired of being pawns in the rulers' games?

Unfortunately, the white Left has made no serious attempt in the past ten years to do this kind of education and to lead fights that would bring together the interests of blacks and whites against the rulers. It has been content to join liberals in shaking a morally reproachful finger at the white working class instead of attempting any sustained organizing. It has described as "organizing" such ventures as the one that occurred when a group of people in Hayward, California, moved into a white working-class neighborhood and, not finding instant transformation, gave up after six months and joined the Weathermen! Or the events that transpired when a small group of white revolutionaries in Cleveland took jobs in factories: they became so completely proletarianized that they were too tired and discouraged after work to become the center of any serious organization of working people. Or the efforts of some of the more obvious sect groups, which go to a factory to work and try to shove the whole of their revolutionary politics down everyone's throat the minute they arrive. Or the kind of Saul Alinsky organizing that actually fosters racism: get people to demand more things for their own neighborhood by applying pressure on the system, which the system deals with by taking something from somebody else who is also a part of the working class.

Despite numerous pleas from the Black Panther party and other revolutionary forces in the black community that whites could be of great help if they started to organize in the white community against racism, the white movement has failed to make a serious effort in this direction. Instead it has contented itself with conducting demonstrations, primarily demonstrations *against* repression of the black movement rather than demonstrations *for* demands that would alleviate some of the worst aspects of economic oppression. While it is certainly true that police occupation of the ghetto should end, it is also true that the focus on repression has provided a convenient way for whites to direct all their organized activity against the state and very little against the capitalists, who ultimately run it. Probably the silliest approach the white movement has made to the problem of repression against blacks has been the sponsoring of demonstrations, as occurred in the late 1960s, in which small groups of people run through the streets trashing random cars and store windows. This merely gives further license to the police to use their repressive power. It does not change anyone's opinion on how to assess the black struggles these demonstrations are allegedly aimed at supporting.

The impetus for participating in trashing demonstrations to support black liberation is understandable. It is easy to see why some New Leftists wanted to scream, yell and trash after Fred Hampton was murdered in his bed in Chicago and there was no reaction from people around the country. Or when George Jackson was murdered. The murder or jailing of black leaders is certainly worth getting upset about, and the apparent indifference of even allegedly sympathetic young people can be extremely frustrating. It is not too hard to understand why at such moments one feels like saying to blacks, "If you're going to die, I'm with you and I'll show you that I'm willing to die too. And I'm willing to share your fate by going to jail. And if that turns people off, who cares? They managed to sit back and show how morally obtuse they were when you were suffering." It is an attitude whose force I understand, but ultimately it is the height of self-indulgence and bourgeois individualism. In the end, it will be of no service to the black community if we participate in acts that strengthen the possibilities of a race war and then prove our own courage and moral fortitude by fighting and dying on the side of the blacks. *We do not need martyrs, we need revolutionaries.* And revolutionaries will find that the hard work of reaching whites is both less glamorous and more time-consuming than an afternoon trashing spree. Militant demonstrations may sometimes be appropriate tools in organizing whites, but the criterion must always be: Does this help us or hinder us in organizing whites who can align with blacks in revolutionary struggle? *not,* Does this action prove to me my moral courage and integrity?

The backlash argument, on the other hand, should be used with caution: it can be turned against anyone who tries to organize in any serious way against capitalist society. It should not be acceded to by blacks struggling for their liberation, or by whites attempting to organize in the white community. It may well be that many older working-class whites (not to mention lower-middle-, middle-, and upper-middle-class whites) will reject strategies that lead them into conflict with the ruling class.

In the long run it may be in the interests of these people not to be racists, but if they refuse to see that and continue to act in their racist fashion, they must be treated as racists. But this assessment of others is often too quickly accepted by many people in the white movement who have never really tried any extended campaign to reach these racists. It is all too easy to forget where we came from, and that we ourselves shared racist attitudes not all of which have we managed to purge from ourselves. It is even easier to turn our morally righteous condemnation against those who have not yet changed and write them off as lost forever. But it can be appropriate at times to be angry. When whites in a union vote to continue policies that de facto exclude blacks, or a neighborhood keeps blacks from moving in, or a police unit agrees to enforce a racist order, the people involved should be held accountable for their actions. To the extent that these whites knowingly choose the side of the ruling class, they will have to be treated as opponents in the short run.

The backlash argument is often put forward by the worst racists. "Look," they say, "you're offending me by what you're doing." The fact of the matter is that such people want the status quo to remain, and anything one does to alter that status quo seriously will offend them. It does not offend them if you channel your protest into electoral activity for a liberal who tells you he's against racism, because they know this channel is highly unlikely to lead to change. But when a candidate comes along who is really serious about fighting racist institutions, these people dislike him because he is "irresponsible." There is no way to win once one begins to take the backlash argument too seriously.

Moreover, many people who warn that certain actions will offend them are actually impressed and inspired by them, despite their momentary anger. This happened all through the building of the antiwar movement. People would warn us not to engage in activities that caused confrontation and disturbed their lives. But many of these same people eventually changed their minds about the war and about society through these confrontations, and began to move to the Left. They hated us for doing it, and still denounce us, but they now see things somewhat differently. Each situation requires an examination of the probable short- and long-range consequences of a given activity. One cannot act out of knee-jerk moralisms, but neither should one let the rulers and their media set the terms for political action. What is needed is a careful and sophisticated understanding of the people one is trying to work with.

Holding people accountable for their actions even when it antagonizes them may be an extremely useful approach. I once organized a picket of Rosh Hashanah (Jewish New Year) services at an Oakland synagogue attended by the judge who railroaded Huey Newton to prison. We demanded that the Jewish community itself take some action to dissociate itself from the racist who was praying with them. Although no official action was taken, many members of the synagogue were visibly shaken and explicitly committed themselves to dissociating themselves not just in word but in deeds from the judge's action. Making people feel that they cannot escape their political and economic life by retiring quietly into the suburbs may push some people farther to the Right, but it makes others take their role more seriously and attempt to change it.

Another example is calling policemen "pigs." Many people criticized this tactic but in fact it has had very good results. Among those policemen who had some desire to relate to the community, the designation "pig" has caused a serious personal crisis: many of them either left the force or faced emotional breakdowns. More importantly, it compelled many young people who might otherwise have joined the force to reconsider, because they started to think about what it was that caused people to call the police "pigs." Moreover, the use of the term "pig" for those who enforce the law has had the effect of demystifying the law for many people, helping them see that it is not some abstraction that is being enforced, but a particular kind of law that derives from a particular kind of legal system, both of which themselves can be challenged and called into question. The designation "pigs" did not turn policemen—until then nice guys enforcing a classless and nonracist system of justice—into bad guys. It did not bring about any appreciable rise in police violence, although there was a rise in people reporting and complaining about the *continued* violence of the police. The designation helped to clarify reality, both for the police and for many people, and this clarification helped to remake reality.

Police are an extreme example; it is almost impossible not to see their role in maintaining a repressive order. In most cases, attacks on people who are not in the ruling class but who are acting in a racist manner, must be sufficiently tempered to leave them room to change. Almost never should ordinary people be written off as "racist pigs" or told that they have no part to play in the movement for social change. To respect a person's humanity means to recognize that he can change, and the movement must always provide openings for people to do just that. But we must reject the notion that conflict with people always makes it impossible for them to hear what we are saying. Sometimes it does just the opposite. Wherever possible, that conflict must be connected with a struggle to move people into conflict with the system—for they must understand that the capitalist system, not *they,* is the problem.

Part of the reason I have spoken a great deal about the role of a white movement in support of black liberation is that I am not qualified to give detailed advice to the black community on how it can best organize its struggles. But we must reject those who say that whites have no business discussing black struggles and that whites should simply follow black leadership. There was a time in the white movement when a group of otherwise intelligent whites could be psychologically coerced into giving credibility to any hypothesis, no matter how wrongheaded, if it was advanced passionately by a black person and accompanied by denunciations of those whites in the room who did not automatically agree with it. The dynamic reached its height in 1964, when assorted local black community leaders in California and New York explicitly denounced as "racist" those who refused to support Lyndon Johnson's reelection and opted for building an independent movement outside the sphere of electoral politics. But it was pervasive throughout the period 1960–67, was used in support of a variety of positions (sometimes mutually contradictory), and it subsided somewhat only with the emergence of the Panthers, who said that people could disagree with some blacks (though not with the Panthers) without being incurable racists themselves.

The injunction to "Follow black leadership" is meaningless until one specifies *which* black leadership. Even among the revolutionaries, there are several different forces, and whites must use their own judgment about which ones are most likely to lead in a revolutionary direction and then seek to support those forces. Even then, the best way for whites to support black revolutionaries is to build a white revolutionary movement, and it may be that the best leaders of the black movement are no more qualified to suggest how to work in the white community than are a variety of whites who have been organizing there.

The mystique of following black leadership is a response to the previous mistake of quashing black leadership. Some people think they have to prove they've "dealt with their racism" by subordinating their own judgment to that of the leaders of the black liberation struggle. This may help them work off their guilt complexes, but most blacks find them a bit ridiculous. They are also less than helpful—for when they see something they might criticize or offer advice about, they tell themselves they have no right to say anything. They end up hanging around the black movement doing odd jobs and trivial tasks instead of organizing in their own community according to its needs.

Of course, it is always easier to abdicate one's responsibility for leadership and for devising programs by finding some group which can be endowed with all wisdom. Then it becomes a great heresy to question the authority or good sense of anything the appointed group does. For the Old Left that group was the Communist Party of Russia, while for the New Left it switches every year. Former *Ramparts* editor Bob Scheer once told a group of whites who were waiting for the start of a Washington conference called by the Panthers that they shouldn't ask any questions about what the Panthers were up to: "If Bobby Seale told me to stand on this corner for ten years," Scheer told the crowd, "I'd do it without asking any questions." A few months later, Scheer was telling people that it was women's leadership that had to be accepted unquestioningly. Then it was the Chinese, the North Koreans, and who knows which will be the next group that has the corner on all virtue, truth, and wisdom?

The notion of following black leadership is often tied to the following argument: because blacks have suffered most from capitalism, they are the most revolutionary force and hence the people most likely to provide good leadership for everyone. What a series of non sequiturs! True, black people have suffered more from capitalism than most other groups. True, they are one of the most revolutionary forces in America, not merely because they have suffered, but also because many blacks have come to realize that their suffering is not inevitable and can be fought (other oppressed groups, e.g., Appalachian whites, or nineteenth-century Mormons, did not always respond to oppression by struggling against it— oppression can also lead to defeatism). But why is it inevitable that those who have suffered most know best how to deal with the causes of that suffering? Certainly an oppressed person is best qualified to describe what that oppression is like, and is best qualified to state when that oppression has ended. Here the victim is the authority. But the way the Puritans, Catholics, Mormons, Serbs, Greeks, Lithuanians, or other oppressed groups have dealt with their oppression offers no evidence that they had any special understanding of it. History shows that the most oppressed people are often so deformed by their oppression that they cannot think clearly about how to deal with their situation. This does not mean that black people are less likely than others to know what is best to do; whites have been at least as deformed as blacks by capitalism. Rather it is to suggest that the criterion for leadership should be the intelligence and relevance of the leadership, not the force of oppression of the person who suffers it.

The emergence and subsequent decline of the Black Panther party as a major force in the black community illustrate some of the problems we have been discussing. First, white radicals such as Tom Hayden told people that they must look to the Black Panther party for leadership, and that, if they did not, they were racists. The Panthers were deified and proclaimed as "The Vanguard of the Revolution" and anyone who criticized them "must be an objective pig." This approach simply stifled political discussion in the white movement. Moreover, while glorifying the Panthers, the white radicals refused to do what the Panthers urged them to: to organize the white community into a political force capable of alliance with the Panthers, giving them political support and defense from repression. Whites were willing on occasion to organize a support demonstration from their predominantly student base, or to run through the streets trashing windows,

207

but they were not willing to do the hard work of developing a political strategy that explained to whites why racism was not in their own interests. Meanwhile, the Panthers tried desperately to build alliances with whites, only to find that every group they reached out to disappeared before an alliance could mean anything. The Peace and Freedom party disappeared almost the moment the Panthers began to deal with it, the Yippies turned out to be a media-created mirage, and SDS dissolved just as the Panthers made an attempt to contact them. Finally, drowning in repression and isolation, the Panthers attempted to set up a United Front Against Fascism in 1969, only to find that the only white group to take the conference seriously was the Communist party (which, at least, contained some lawyers who could represent the Panthers in court and raise money for them). The ease with which white revolutionaries latched on to the most romantic aspects of the Panthers, particularly their ideas about armed struggle, was balanced by their refusal to look seriously at the rest of the Panthers' ten-point program or to show whites how that program was relevant to their own needs.

At the same time, some of the responsibility for this isolation must fall on the Panthers themselves. They oriented toward the "lumpen," the "brothers off the block." But they refused to ally with the League of Revolutionary Black Workers (which later became the Congress of Black Workers) when the League leaders came to the Panthers seeking to work together. The Panthers never developed a program that spoke to the needs of black workers in the workplace, yet any serious analysis of modern capitalism would have forced them to see that it was precisely in the workplace that blacks had their greatest potential for social power. The Panthers responded to this argument by pointing to the large numbers of blacks who were unemployed and for whom survival was the key. But here again they could have developed a political strategy that would have aligned them with potential allies among the white unemployed and white poor. Demonstrations, initiative campaigns, and electoral work could have been organized around the demand for more jobs for blacks and whites, more aid to the poor, an end to military expenditures and rechanneling of that money into the inner city, etc.

While the Panthers spent a great deal of time talking about armed struggle, they continually refused to lead or call for demonstrations around any political issue except their own survival. They would sponsor an initiative for community control of the police, or a demonstration around freeing political prisoners, but these struggles were not likely to make them new friends. If you did not already see why you should be in favor of black liberation, the Panthers did very little to help you see it. There is no question that if the Panthers had called for a major demonstration demanding jobs, peace, and an end to repression they would have gotten much more support from both blacks and whites than they got by focusing only on defense of the Panthers.

On moral ground it is difficult to fault the Panthers. The repression that they suffer cannot even be imagined by most of us: the entire police power of the American capitalist state (including the FBI, army intelligence units, and state and local police) had singled them out as the number-one target to be destroyed. Faced with infiltrators of every variety, and with constant physical assaults by the police, it became increasingly difficult for them to conduct the kind of open discussion of politics and political struggle within the party necessary for the development of a sound cadre and a rational investigation of political alternatives. Given the pressure, the Panthers fell back into increased reliance on glorification of the gun, self-defense through armed struggle, and a mouthing of Maoist clichés, all of which made it even easier for the white power structure to portray them as madmen and hence to escalate repression with public consent.

Nor could these problems be dealt with by the development of a breakfast-for-children program or a shoe factory to distribute free shoes. Such activities helped the Panthers win support among the poor in the black community, but they do not constitute a convincing strategy around which to mobilize people. Self-help and charity are somewhat different from, though not necessarily counterposed to, revolutionary politics. Until the Panthers can develop a strategy that involves people in concrete *struggles* for their basic needs, there will be an irresistible tendency to polarize into a revolutionary romantic strategy ("Pick up the gun now") or into simple reformism, the kind of nonconfrontational strategy that may create temporary popularity in the black community but never leads to dealing with the basic problems. Survival programs are not unimportant; they are extremely significant to those without adequate food, clothing, shelter. But in and of themselves they do not constitute a political program. A much more promising development in the past few years has been the organizing done by the Congress of Black Workers, which has attempted to develop rank-and-file caucuses at the workplace and has used its strength in that arena to build community programs as well.

Whatever the critical weaknesses that led to the decline of the Panthers, their contribution to the development of a revolutionary movement should not be underestimated. The Black Panthers emerged at a time when most blacks were still oriented primarily toward cultural nationalism and heavily influenced by the Black Muslims. The Panthers combated that influence: they distinguished between whites who supported racist policies and those who did not. This position was much more threatening to the white establishment than any Muslim position: the ruling class does not care if blacks don't love them, as long as they don't attempt to take political power away or to undermine the basic structure of capitalism. The Panthers taught people to see the striking similarity between the situation of foreign imperialized colonies and the domestic black colony. In teaching us to see that the black struggle was the struggle of an oppressed nation, fighting not for some kind of homogenized equality with plastic America, but rather for its own national liberation and full self-determination, the Panthers made a major contribution to our theoretical understanding. It was precisely this understanding that now makes it possible for us to see why even black separatists may, for brief historical periods, advance the development of a movement that will have to become anticapitalist if it is ever to reach fruition.

And the Panthers taught us that almost all prisoners in America are political prisoners who would never be in jail under a less exploitative social system, a system that was not based on competition and setting people against each other. More specifically, they showed us that it was impossible for a black to get a fair trial within a legal system set up to protect a racist political and economic order unless that trial itself was converted into a public show, thus requiring the rulers to demonstrate how fair they are.[17] The Panthers completely demystified the legal arena; they taught us that in a war of liberation the key question is not "Who fired the first shot?" but rather, "Who is the oppressor and who the oppressed?"

Racism is not going to disappear spontaneously. Neither are the various responses to it in the black community, from black capitalism to cultural nationalism to revolutionary struggle. Whichever tendencies may predominate in the future, the facts of life in the black community will ultimately push more and more people into a revolutionary direction. And revolutionary black groups will arise to provide leadership for that force, which will itself at some point be ready to link up with other revo-

[17] It is ironic that after jailing black leaders such as Angela Davis or Bobby Seale, on charges that were clearly dreamed up for political reasons, the rulers of the country should congratulate themselves on their fairness when juries refused to convict. The acquittals are not a vindication of the system, but only a proof that if the people had not won previous revolutionary struggles which gained them the safeguard of trial by jury, the rulers would have even *more* arbitrary power. As it is, Seale and Davis spent precious years of their lives in jail waiting for a chance to acquit themselves. And the Supreme Court has recently moved to limit the protection the jury system offers—by ruling that convictions in noncapital cases no longer require a unanimous verdict.

lutionary forces within American society to build a successful revolution.

One of the great failures of this book is that I do not have enough space to dedicate equal attention to the movements of Chicanos, Puerto Ricans, American Indians, Asian-Americans, and other oppressed national groups within America. To a large extent, the analyses of the reasons for their oppression and the strategies for dealing with it would be similar to those mentioned in discussing the black struggle. For all these groups, no national liberation is possible in the context of capitalist society, and only by uniting with other oppressed groups and anticapitalist forces will these struggles have any chance of ultimate success. At the same time, just as is the case for the black liberation struggle, each oppressed national group may find it desirable at particular moments to organize independently and to place primacy on the development of national consciousness, which in turn may then move in a revolutionary direction. It is crucial for white Americans to keep in mind that all of these groups have good reason to distrust us, that our struggles will never be won unless that distrust can be overcome and we can learn to struggle together against the common source of oppression, and that ultimately we want to unite with the elements in these national liberation struggles which have an anticapitalist consciousness.

WOMEN

Ignoring the frequency of women's struggles throughout history, many people have viewed the recent emergence of the women's movement as a unique historical event. The fact is, even within the United States, the struggle for the liberation of women has a long history, marked by important victories and stinging defeats. Probably the most significant victory was gaining the right to vote. But focusing attention exclusively in that direction had severe limitations. In order to win the vote, many sections of the women's movement played down any political vision, thereby attempting to show that voting women would not be a subversive force. People were united around a least-common-denominator politics, and once the battle was won the women's forces had no clear direction in which to move. Entering a period of history in which American imperialism and domestic repression were on the upsurge, and strikes were brutally put down, the suffrage movement temporarily lost its motion and internal coherency. The coalition that had been formed around the vote had no unity on how the vote should be used. The demand for the vote was pushed by a women's movement that had a bourgeois character and, in feminist Kate Millet's words, was never "sufficiently involved with working women, the most exploited group among its numbers." Nevertheless, the gains made during that struggle were not insignificant—women today would probably be even more oppressed if they did not have the right to vote. The bourgeois struggle for civil liberties is always important—but always vastly inadequate. But it does decisively put on the agenda the next stage of revolutionary struggle.

To many women looking back at the collapse of earlier phases of their movement, it is obvious that the analyses put forward then were vastly inadequate. They never dealt fully with the psychological oppression of women and their oppression within the entire economic structure of the society. On the contrary, even during the struggle for political equality the old stereotypes about women's weaknesses were still present. The concept of legislation to protect women and children never included the question of protecting men, too, from abominable conditions.

The women's movement that emerged in the last decade has taken several organizational forms and political foci, not all of which have been mutually compatible. The National Organization for Women fights primarily for equality within the capitalist system. Equality looks much more attractive to upper- and upper-middle-class women than to working-class women, so it is almost exclusively the former who come into NOW. Taking the narrowest possible reformist approach, this organization attracts women who want to advance only themselves, but have little awareness or concern for the class and racial divisions in a society that makes so many of their black, Chicano, and working-class sisters victims of extreme oppression. Slightly to the left of NOW is the National Women's Political Caucus, a reform element in the Democratic party. The more radical feminists share with NOW the focus on women's oppression as the sole area of their concern and believe that all other problems are merely outgrowths and reflections of this basic problem. But unlike NOW the more radical feminists sometimes maintain that a complete social transformation is needed, to be made by women, in which every form of oppressive sexual structure will be eliminated. As distinct from the "feminists" who place the oppression of women at the center of their explanatory framework, there are a number of variants of women's liberationists. The liberationists recognize the integral connection between the oppression of women and the economic structure of capitalism, and hence see the women's struggle as a central but nonexclusive part of the struggle to build socialism. Women's liberationists do not believe that the women's liberation struggle should be subordinated to any other struggle, but at the same time they recognize the crucial nature of other struggles and attempt to link the women's struggles to other anticapitalist struggles. Complicating the picture

212

are coalitions of women around single concerns, like the pro-abortion coalition, sponsored largely by the Young Socialist Alliance women. These coalitions often attract women from a variety of political perspectives. But their own internal dynamic is complicated by the role of the Young Socialist Alliance, which tries to retard the development of socialist politics in these coalitions, so that they can recruit women with the most advanced consciousness into YSA itself.

Even demands for simple equality can cause a crisis in the functioning of capitalism if they are seriously pressed. Equal pay for equal work, meaningful labor, and compensation for socially necessary domestic housework cannot be met by the capitalist system as presently constituted. Capitalism *can* handle these demands as long as they are addressed only to a small group of upper- and middle-class women. But if they became the basis for a serious movement of working-class women, they simply could not be met. The rulers would probably try to raise workers' taxes to pay for these increased social expenditures, and would do what they could to foster resentment between men and women. But although this tactic would find acceptance among men highly committed to male chauvinism, it would be less likely to work than when the same tactic is used to pit whites against blacks. The reason is obvious. Men and women live together, and financial benefits accruing to women would be seen by many working white men as benefits to their family as a whole. Hence, rather than accepting increased taxes, or vastly increased prices, it is likely that a movement would develop to shift the tax burden and the social costs of employing women back onto the corporations. Faced with any kind of serious threat to their profits, the corporations would fight with all their considerable power to undercut these demands.

One tactic we are likely to see in the near future is the acceptance, with a great deal of fanfare, of the notion of equal pay for equal work and more jobs for women, as a principle by many large corporations and by government. This will be coupled with genuine breakthroughs for middle-class women in some professions, and professional schools may actually recruit women, just as they recruited blacks a few years ago. But this will not be accompanied by any substantial change in the conditions of *most* women. On the contrary, these advances, coupled with such social services as free child-care centers in university towns and suburban areas, and with frequent pious statements about the urgency of this concern as a new national priority, will be used to cover up and deflect attention away from the continued picture of economic and social exploitation for the vast majority of women. Hence the need for a women's movement based on, and fighting for, the needs of women from working-class families.

MEN—THE ENEMY?

Just as a split has emerged among blacks between those who think the main enemy is capitalism and those who think it is whites, so the women's movement has different strains that place their focus variously on fighting capitalism and on fighting men, or on some combination. Some striking analogies can be drawn between the arguments that apply here and those that apply with regard to the oppression of blacks. Although it is true that the system benefits the ruling class most, men have become its agents in the oppression of women. After all, it is not some abstraction that comes home from work every day expecting to be waited on, have his ego soothed and served, have his sex on demand, have his woman bringing up children and not seeking any fulfillment outside the sex role defined for her. It is not some abstraction that refuses to hire women, or hires them at low pay, and uses their bodies to sell their products, and keeps them from having legal control over their own bodies, and rapes them in the streets at night, and objectifies them whenever they walk down the street. It is not some abstraction that does all this. It is men. What's more, these are not merely irrational acts, which can be dismissed as trivial. Added up, they constitute a very impressive system of power and privilege which nearly all men have over women. Even as whites get concrete benefits from racism, so men get concrete benefits from sexism, and that is part of the reason that chauvinist attitudes toward women persist after women point them out and confront men with them.

At the same time, most men do not have real power over their own lives and could not change the sexist structure of American society if they decided to without engaging in revolutionary struggle. The class structure makes most men totally powerless over every area of their lives, except their relations with their women. To understand the situation of most men, to understand why they are willing to exercise power over women in the ways they do, this fact of powerlessness must be taken into account. Men are not born chauvinists. It takes a certain kind of society to instill male chauvinism in them. Anyone familiar with North Vietnam or China (where sexist institutions are being challenged and eliminated, and where male chauvinism has been seriously combated by changing societal structures) can see that it is not the genes of men but the characteristics certain societies foster that promote chauvinism.

"But even if men are not intrinsically bad, but only conditioned to be so, given that conditioning, they will never overcome it until women organize and take power away from men, who can never be expected on their own

214

to give up their societal privileges." There is something very compelling in this argument, and any man who has taken the issue seriously knows that it is easier to renounce our privileges when the women around us are organized and diligent in keeping us in line. From the standpoint of men who want to change themselves, the development of an independent women's movement is welcome. It worked the same way with racism: whites did not deal with their racism in any serious way until they were forced to by blacks.

At the same time, just as the white-skin-privilege argument misses the way in which racism keeps whites in line for capitalist exploitation, so this "male privilege" argument misses the way in which sexism ends up not being a privilege at all. Men have the "privilege" of seeing women used as a reserve force of cheap labor which then becomes a threat to union militancy. Men have the "privilege" of assuming the financial responsibility for supporting a family which exercises a moderating effect on any militant union activity. A man has the "privilege" of dominating a wife and children, of being "king of his castle" while he is denied fundamental control over any other significant aspect of his life. And even at home he must conform to the exploitative patterns that society prescribes, having been taught nothing else. Men have the "privilege" of conforming to masculine stereotypes that often deny them any expression of human emotion or frailty. Men have the "privilege" of being alienated from other men: looking upon other males as competition for jobs, women, and status. And men have the "privilege" of being alienated from women: fearing, degrading, abusing, mystifying, worshiping, but never coming to understand or respect in their own right, half the human species.

The oppression of men may be much less stifling than the oppression of women, but both roles are bad enough to enable many men to realize that the alleged benefits do not outweigh the detriments. Add to this the fact that capitalist society uses sexism as a way of keeping both men and women from focusing on the benefits they could have if they were to struggle against the capitalist social structure as a whole, and we see that there are good reasons for men to join the struggle against sexism.

At this point some people leap to the following position: Since sexism is sustained by capitalism, there should be no independent struggle for women's issues, but only the one struggle for socialism. Once we have socialism there will be no more sexism. The same argument is made about black demands, by a group called the Progressive Labor party. Let me try to separate what is right in this position from what is obviously wrong.

It is right that sexism cannot be defeated as long as capitalism exists,

215

and that the overthrow of capitalism will eliminate the economic motivation for the exploitation of one group by another. But this approach neglects the fact that sexism has other than economic determinants. An idea can be originated or sustained for a certain amount of time for one reason, and then continue for a quite different reason. Ideas take on a life of their own, independent of the economic forces that first caused them to be widely accepted. And the more basic the idea to one's thought patterns, the more likely it is to sustain itself, even when it no longer plays a useful function. Thus, for instance, the idea that one should be thrifty, which was a product of the early stages of capitalist accumulation, did not die as soon as capitalism entered the stage of needing expanded consumer markets. On the contrary, it took several generations' worth of conditioning to make common the idea that one must spend in order to be fulfilled as a human being. Once the revolution eliminates institutions that benefit from sexism or racism, the struggle to eliminate these phenomena from consciousness will accelerate and will achieve success in a short while. But the overthrow of capitalism will not in and of itself overthrow all vestiges of racism and sexism. Then why struggle for the overthrow of capitalism if you're a woman or a black? Because that overthrow is the *necessary precondition* for the final destruction of racism and sexism.

"Sure," many women say, "but if the overthrow of capitalism isn't sufficient for the overthrow of sexism, how do we know that we are not being asked to join a revolution that will simply give us new oppressors? After all, men *do* benefit from sexism. Perhaps they will set up a new social order that exploits women in new and unique ways? Why should we subordinate our struggle to the needs of that struggle?" The objection is well taken. One might answer by saying that once people no longer spend their days involved in meaningless labor for the sake of someone else's profit, and once people's lives are no longer structured in such a way that their own success depends on the failure of others, and once the primary ways in which people spend their time are no longer dependent on mutual exploitation and on robbing the peoples of the world, then the appearance of exploitative modes with regard to women or blacks will be seen to be a hangover from the past and will die out in a few generations. But this misses much of the force of the women's objection. It makes it sound as if, for women, the revolution will be simply another accomplishment on the level of getting the vote—another step that will make it easier for them to launch a further struggle. But women do not want a further struggle; they want to struggle *now* for their liberation and they want any revolution in which they participate to be in part directly a struggle for their liberation. They do not want to have to struggle against sexism in the men who made the revolution—a revolution these women have made possible by their sacrifices.

The time to begin the battle against sexism is *now*, and that includes fighting against the male chauvinism in the movement. The movement that makes the socialist revolution must be one that has already made serious strides toward fighting its own chauvinism and racism and takes those issues to be priority issues within itself.

Further, it is ludicrous to say that there are no women's issues. There are obvious ways in which women are oppressed and men are not. These struggles should not be subordinated to any others, for the escalation of struggles against sexist institutions itself advances the whole revolutionary struggle and hurts capitalism.

The rulers will always attempt to use these kinds of struggles to divide the potentially revolutionary forces. Capitalism is ingenious. It gives almost everyone some stake in the system, and almost everyone can find some way in which she (or he) is better off than someone else and benefits from someone else's oppression. But people can also learn how much better off they and everyone else could be if the whole system were changed. At this point some people say, "Well, then, let's not antagonize men by confronting them with their chauvinism or asking them to join in struggles against sexist institutions from which they benefit." That is ridiculous. Women have a right to struggle against sexist institutions and chauvinism without being told that they are antagonizing some other important group—after all, that other group has been antagonizing women. But at the same time, just as blacks should not write all whites off, so women should not write men off. Instead they should provide them with psychic space to change. And just as whites organizing against racism in the white community must attempt to show whites the ways in which the black liberation struggle is ultimately in white people's own interests, so men organizing against sexism will attempt to show other men that it is in their interests to support that struggle. Certainly, some men will refuse to listen to any of these arguments and will identify their interests with those of the entire sexist structure. In the short run they will have to be treated as if they were no different from the sexist pigs who most benefit from capitalist exploitation —the men of the ruling class. But it would be incorrect to treat as the enemy those men who have come to see that their chauvinism must be fought, but have *not yet* fully succeeded in changing themselves.

Sexism, like racism, is deeply ingrained in the psychic structure. It cannot be wished away and it will not simply disappear the second people decide to change themselves. And as long as we live in a society whose

217

dominant institutions support and, in many subtle ways, continue to inculcate these attitudes, we cannot expect a new man, completely free from them, to emerge. Neither can those of us who are men excuse those evidences of chauvinism we find in ourselves on the ground that society makes it very difficult for us to transform ourselves totally in a short period of time.

One of the best ways for men to come to understand their own chauvinism and the operations of sexism in society as a whole is involvement in struggles against sexist institutions. Just as antiracist consciousness among young people was furthered by their participation in activities in support of black studies programs and in defense of the Black Panther party, so antisexism struggles can have a massive impact in changing the way men view themselves and their world. These struggles are particularly valuable for overcoming the "Oh, I'm so terrible, I can't stand myself" attitude many men have adopted in order to avoid seriously dealing with their own chauvinism. We do not need self-haters, we need revolutionaries: men who are willing to struggle alongside women for the full liberation of women.

There is one crucial difference between the black struggle and the women's struggle. When blacks began to work with whites in the civil rights movement they were creating a kind of integration that did not exist in the rest of society. So when the experiment did not work and blacks decided to have all-black organizations and to build their movement around consciousness of black identity, they did not have to alter some basic feature of black or white life. Most whites have none but the most cursory contact with blacks and vice versa, so that complete organizational separation did not create any new problems. The covert white racism among those who had worked in the civil rights movement could now be dealt with by whites in their own way without interfering in the lives of blacks who were developing their own consciousness in their own way. Since most blacks felt oppression from whites primarily in terms of the white system (represented by white cops, white bosses, white store owners, and white welfare workers), and not through deep personal relationships with whites, it was no great problem to tell whites to go their own way, and perhaps in ten or twenty years it would be appropriate to form joint organizations or have much closer coordination between movements.

Women have no such luck with their oppressors. In a male-dominated society the social structures require women to depend on men. Almost every social arrangement is built around the monogamous family, and women have a difficult time escaping that arrangement. Women's communes may work for a small percentage of women, particularly for students and those from upper- and middle-class backgrounds, but they are highly unlikely to be a solution for the tens of millions of women who are the potential base for a mass revolutionary women's movement. And even when women live in these communes, they often feel a natural sexual attraction to men that they are not willing to suppress. So the problem becomes: how do you deal with the oppressor when you have a close personal relationship with him? The tactics will have to be somewhat different from those employed by the black movement, because personal struggle must become a more intense focus. The women's movement had to develop a tactic that could support women in these personal struggles.

SMALL GROUPS

The solution that has met with widespread acceptance is the formation of small groups of women who meet with each other at least once a week. In these groups women come to see that problems they used to consider personal are in fact societal, that they are shared by many others, and that they are a product of the social arrangements of a sexist society. The emphasis has been on developing the ability of every woman to understand her own experience, and on the formulation, by women acting together, of a systematic analysis of their own oppression. These consciousness-raising sessions have played a crucial role in developing both the political understanding and the self-confidence necessary to deal with the men in a woman's life who constantly objectify her and chauvinize her.

More recently, the same approach has been tried by men attempting to deal with their own chauvinism. Men in small groups begin to examine themselves and their patterns of behavior to see how they function as the oppressors even of those they love. These groups have the danger of degenerating into "bull sessions" because men often do not feel the urgency of the problem as do women. But when they are taken seriously these meetings can help men take the first steps towards self-transformation. More recently, some mixed groups have been tried with varying degrees of success, often depending on the men's willingness not to attempt to dominate and control. All these groups are designed to solve the most immediate problem facing women: the need to deal with chauvinism on a daily basis in their own lives.

At the same time, it is becoming increasingly clear to the women in these small groups that there is a limit to how far men and women can transform themselves and to the amount of change women can get in sexist institutions as long as there are no basic changes in the American economic, political, and social system. This limit has produced two different responses among women: Some have simply given up on men

219

altogether and have decided that only with other women will they ever find fulfillment. The experience of the small group helped these women reject both societal sex roles and the kinds of games that set women one against another. They were now prepared to develop deep and lasting relationships with other women, and this stimulated the growth of the lesbian movement. But most women have decided that their only alternative is to struggle even harder for revolutionary transformation of the society as a whole. And this requires coordination and mass struggle, which the small groups did not provide. In fact, many small groups fell apart over this issue, because some of the women felt that political activity itself was a "man's ego game" and that the important thing was to continue to develop the "sisterliness" that the small groups promoted. Anselma del'Olio, writing in a women's underground newspaper,[18] described another key problem: the tendency toward back-biting and destructiveness against anyone who attempted to provide political leadership or put forward a political vision: "Productivity seems to be the major crime, but if you have the misfortune of being outspoken and articulate, you are accused of being power-mad, elitist, racist, and finally, the worst epithet of all, a male identifier." Many sensitive women could not adjust to such an atmosphere and abandoned the small-group effort.

Recognizing some of the problems, many small groups have now begun action projects designed to have community impact. There are numerous health collectives working on free clinics, women's centers, media collectives, and women's caucuses in some areas of the professions and the trade-union movement. But as long as these groups remain isolated from one another, or meet only for an exchange of information and not for the development of mutually binding strategy, they are likely to play no more than a peripheral role in the struggle to confront real power in capitalist society. This will leave the public and political face of the women's movement to the upper-middle-class-oriented National Organization for Women, the National Women's Caucus, and the single-issue pro-abortion coalition, none of which represents the militant and nonreformist women's liberation consciousness that developed among so many women in the late 60s and early 70s. But that consciousness is not likely to have great political significance unless new forms can be developed which give the women's liberation movement more political and organizational coherence.

Without abandoning the independent form of the women's movement, it may be possible for it to work within a larger arena that includes men as well. A national leftist party would have to provide adequate space for

[18] *Liberated Guardian,* March 1971.

the participation of women in an independent women's movement and in small groups, just as it would have to provide space for men to give serious attention to their own chauvinism. But there is no a priori reason why men and women could not work within the same general political framework if there was adequate sensitivity to the problems and adequate room for independent development and political activity. Such a party would be viable to the extent that it gave serious attention to sexism and did not simply tag "women's demands" onto a general program whose emphasis was elsewhere.

Just as we saw that not every black group that is independent of whites is automatically revolutionary, so not every women's organization will automatically be revolutionary. Even women's groups that are not explicitly anticapitalist, however, can serve an important transitional role in the development of revolutionary consciousness. But in the final analysis, a revolutionary women's movement will distinguish itself from the form of women's struggle analogous to the black's "pork-chop nationalism," both by leading women into explicitly anticapitalist struggles and by showing them the ways in which men's attitudes are a product of specific circumstances and can be changed.

Thierrie Cook [19] suggests that a *revolutionary* women's movement would develop a strategy that combines struggles on the social, political and economic level. The struggle by women to control their own bodies will require a political assault against abortion laws, against laws that penalize the unmarried, and against laws that prohibit homosexuality. At the same time, this struggle will involve rejection of the many sexual myths and stereotypes that lead women to believe their role is to give their bodies and their whole lives to a particular man. The struggle for equality will include the political struggle to end discriminatory laws and to force equal opportunity, but it must include the struggle for equal pay for equal work, the elimination of tracking in education and employment categories, and full compensation for all socially necessary labor performed by women, including childbearing and rearing and housework. The struggle for independence will include challenges to monogamous family arrangements as the only legally sanctioned form (cf. the U.S. government's outmoded restrictions on food stamps to "nonrelated households") and will attempt to develop ways in which women can develop themselves independently of their assigned role as child-raisers and educators. The struggle for dignity will include an attack on all role-playing in sex, and attacks on the institutions that reinforce the stereotypes, from the media and advertising to the

[19] One of the women who went to Hanoi in 1970, to negotiate the "People's Peace Treaty," which declared peace between the people of the United States and Vietnam.

medical profession and the schools. Crucial to all of these concerns is a strategy that recognizes the needs of black and Third World women and the pivotal role of working-class women in the struggle for liberation. To date, the women's movement has had ideas in all these areas, but like the male-dominated movement, has failed to develop and promote a coherent and unified public strategy that can really speak to the issues involved.

A strategy must recognize the critical importance of the family in maintaining the capitalist system. Within the family, women are the primary producers, sustaining a critical institution which in turn allows men to return to the outside world where they act as producers of materials and services. Production within the family is unpaid and hence, in a capitalist system, not considered valuable—but it is nevertheless a pillar upon which the system rests. Within the family, women are exploited, do not have control over their own bodies, and are in almost every way forced to be subservient to the needs of their husbands. The primary significance of the family, aside from its critical task of producing more workers for the capitalists, is in providing an ideology that makes capitalist society bearable. Central to this is the notion of the split between the public and private realms. The family is the private realm (and thus the capitalists do not have any responsibility for supporting the critical functions in society that the family provides, particularly child rearing) into which the worker can escape after a day of exploitative labor. Here, in his private realm, the worker is king: his home is his castle. As long as he has this social refuge, he is taught that the rest of the world can be accepted. The ideology of the private/public dichotomy also helps to weaken workers' militancy: a worker dare not engage in struggles that would endanger his home and family, the only worthwhile fact in his life. And yet, this very split, what New American Movement activists Peggy Somers and Kathryn Johnson have called the "sexual division of production," is self-undermining, because home life in itself can never live up to the tremendous expectations put upon it, particularly when women have been forced to abandon so much of their potential in order to fit themselves into their primary role of "homemakers." But while particular families fall apart or remain together in misery, the basic distinction of public vs. private is maintained, and one dreams of something better in the future ("the man of my dreams" or a "nonmonogamous marriage"). A program built around the family cannot call for the abolition of the family at a time when there is nothing that could conceivably replace it. The family still provides the only acceptable form of human expressions of warmth and love, and this cannot be dismissed as expendable in the interest of future revolutionary aspirations. Particularly for lower-income people who have not yet enjoyed the limited gratifications a stable family life can sometimes provide, a program for the abolition of the family would be seen as absurd (a fact that white women's liberationists were taught by their black sisters quite sharply in the late 1960s). But programs can be developed which demand an end to the sexual division of labor (focusing on demands for payment of women's work in the home and for unionizing domestic laborers), a socialization of work in the family (including community-controlled child-care centers, communal kitchens and laundries, and employee demands for half-time jobs, maternity/paternity leaves, and other mechanisms through which business can take responsibility for the support—but not control—of family life), and a reintegration of the public and private realms (particularly through struggles that attack the ideology of the split, and institutions that promote the notion that individual experiences are "personal" and can be worked out only by personal effort and not by political changes in the society).

TRANSFORMATION BEGINS NOW

The development of the women's movement has become one of the most significant aspects of the revolution, both because of its contributions to human relations and its theoretical insights. In some ways, the women's movement is probably the most radical of all the constituencies that will join in making the new American revolution, because the oppression of women is the oldest form of the exploitation of one group of humans by another, and its elimination will therefore require the most fundamental transformations of society.

The women's movement has always insisted on the continuity between the people who make the revolution and the society they will create. It is true that new societal arrangements will greatly accelerate human self-transformation, but these new arrangements will never be created unless people begin now to change themselves and to develop needs that these new arrangements will satisfy. Men have sometimes given lip service to the need to transform themselves in the course of revolutionary struggle. But it was the women's movement that began to put the idea into practice. The women's movement has shown us the need to eliminate the ego games that flow from the competitive structure of capitalist society. So much time has been wasted over meaningless arguments conducted by men in the movement to show their relative intellectual virility. Deep human relationships cannot be viewed as a sidelight, to be squeezed in only if possible; rather, they are an important part of the revolution. People must no longer be afraid to express emotions in their political work. Competition, posses-

223

siveness, domination are modes of behavior that must be fought against not *just* after the revolution but right now while we are making it.

Abolition of monogamy and elimination of sex roles, the freeing of children from the limitations put on them by parents who feel the need to possess them as property, the reeroticization of the body, the elimination of sex taboos—all these goals have been removed from the sphere of utopian fantasy and have become the object of concrete political activity as a result of the women's movement. The women's movement has shown us how present sexual practices are not the result of a timeless "natural" way of being, but rather are produced by concrete historical circumstances. The limitations on human sexuality necessary when human life was constantly confronted with scarcity will no longer be necessary when human life has abolished scarcity. By freeing human life from the need to center attention on the struggle for survival, the revolution opens up the possibility of a sex that exists mainly for the purpose of giving happiness and not solely for the purpose of reproduction and preservation of the species.

Already we have a taste of this in the development of Gay Liberation movements, whose members refuse to see their sexual relationships as serving reproductive functions. Gays have come to see the beauty in members of their own sex and they feel no need to subordinate their feelings of love to any societal goals. The feelings of love and human solidarity that have been stamped out by this society will be part of life after the revolution, and it will seem perfectly natural for people to express them in physical ways and not just verbally. In the meantime, it is critical to support the Gay Liberation movement and protect it from those who would attempt to impose their sexual mores on others.

UTOPIANISM

We must not fall into the trap of pretending that the revolution has already occurred. That is just the other side of pretending that there are no concrete steps other than political organizing that can be taken toward creating the new humanity today. We must avoid the utopianism that suddenly wishes away the legacy of millennia of exploitation and the subordination of women. Social and psychological structures are real; the fact that they can be changed somewhat now and significantly in the course of the revolutionary struggle does not mean that they have been defeated the moment we recognize them and begin to struggle against them. Two examples of this mistake come to mind immediately.

First, there is "the sexual revolution." Many people welcomed the liberalization of sexual attitudes that accompanied the development of birth control and the "hip" culture. But many women discovered that all it meant was a new pattern of exploitation. Now they were supposed to be ready game for many men instead of one. Nor had the attitude of these men changed significantly—women were still meant to be consumed. This is not to suggest that sexual liberalization is bad; only that it is not a panacea. The reeroticization of the body and the development of non-exploitative human relationships will never be completed until capitalism is overthrown. In the meantime, however, it will be necessary to experiment with new ways of living together that attempt to overcome the exploitative modes of the past. Nonmonogamous marriages, groups of people living together in nonmonogamous communes, communes that are monogamous but provide an extended family for child rearing, extended families that do not live together but eat together and provide mutual child care—all these experiments are already being tried, and others will certainly develop. It is likely that these new forms will to varying degrees overcome some of the worst aspects of previous forms of exploitation, while they will to some degree incorporate those previous forms in new ways that are themselves unsatisfactory.

On the basis of what is learned in these experiments, others will be possible, so that when the revolution takes place there will be some experience upon which people can rely in deciding for themselves what their next step will be. In the meantime, even those with full self-consciousness and real dedication to escaping the mistakes of the past will inevitably incorporate in themselves some of the possessiveness, self-centeredness, and desire to dominate that is the legacy of the society in which they grew up and in which they must continue to function. In this last thought is the real tragedy of being born before the revolution, and it is a recognition that people try to fight through two classic avenues of escape. The first is the one that is taken by all those who talk about "the human condition": to take what human life has been through the course of human history, when that history was dominated by the struggle for survival, and to say that that is all that human life can ever be. Acceptance of this line makes the basic failures of human relationships inevitable and inescapable. The second is to say that, if only we were serious and tried harder, if we had better therapists and more Esalen-type institutes, we could fundamentally alter human relationships now. This approach usually ends up serving a small group of people who have managed to ignore the web of exploitative relationships in which they are involved by the very fact that they live under capitalism. The hardest position to hold, because it is so frustrating, is to realize that human life changes in significant ways, and that you can be a part of making those changes and even benefit from the effort, but that it is impossible for anyone who was born into capitalist America not to be marred and deformed in important ways.

Some people say at this point, "Who are we to be trying to change things if we're still unstable as human beings?" But people are never going to be totally sane as long as capitalist social relations and relations of production remain, and the only way those relations are going to disappear is if people overthrow them. It is true that in the course of that struggle we can make serious advances toward transforming ourselves, but it is not true that "new human beings" will emerge as long as people have to sell their labor power to those who have capital. If we could become fully realized, loving, and humane human beings before the revolution we would not need it. Jesus tried that strategy once—leave the state to Caesar, leave him the economic realm, and just work on yourself. The idea of loving one's neighbor as oneself is as old as Leviticus, and many people have tried to do it. But except for a few rare individuals, usually living in exceptional circumstances, human beings cannot make these ideals real as long as their survival depends upon living in accord with economic, political, and social structures that belie and undermine them in a thousand ways each day. The people who overthrow capitalism, then, will still have some defects of the old society; to ask them to wait till these defects are eliminated is to ask them not to make a revolution at all. Most women in the movement have come to realize, however, that not only men have been marred by capitalism, but that women, too, through their oppression, have been deformed by the system, and that they too could be written off as imperfect, if one were to apply righteous criteria.

This last point needs further elaboration. As we said on the section on the black movement, the fact that a group has been oppressed does not give it a corner on virtue or wisdom. On the contrary, if one way in which it has been oppressed is by being denied the opportunity to develop certain skills of self-analysis, simple recognition of that oppression does not automatically abolish its effects. Some women in the movement, however, accepting the mistaken notion that the oppressed should be glorified, have held that whatever is feminine is good and whatever is masculine is bad. As therapy this may be temporarily helpful; as a guide to action it is not. One particularly destructive application of this principle is the claim that careful thinking and analysis is a masculine trait that has been used to keep women enslaved; men think in abstract terms and avoid the concrete and the emotional, and therefore these skills are themselves to be despised as useless and masculine. But although men have indeed used reason and abstraction in destructive fashions, it does not follow that they are bad in themselves. Rather, they should be used differently: to serve the cause of liberation instead of the cause of oppression. What is needed is a new synthesis of the abstract and the concrete, the rational and the emotional, that which was best in men and that which was best in women, rather than a vindication of one at the expense of the other.

Our caution about utopianism comes from the lessons we have learned from the failures of the Old Left, whose members spoke constantly of the emergence of a new, socialist humanity "after the revolution" while living lives whose style and values seemed completely oriented toward individualism and away from building an open community of fellowship. This played an important role in allowing members of the Old Left to become completely assimilated into American life once they changed their views on one or two topics. Of them it was really meaningful to ask, "What makes you think that after the revolution things will miraculously be different? Certainly nothing in your life indicates any significant new directions." The New Left has attempted to avoid this error by beginning the struggle of self-transformation *now*. On the one hand we should understand why that struggle is bound to have only limited success in the context of a capitalist society. On the other hand, the style of life that develops around this kind of personal struggle provides us with some grounds to believe that once the impediments to its success are removed there will indeed be significant transformations among people.

We see the revolution itself as a process, whose cataclysmic event (taking state power) is the logical step after a series of struggles with oneself and with the economic, political and social structure. There are many reasons why a new Stalinism could never arise after a revolution in advanced industrial society. One of the most important is that we could learn from the old Stalinism, and could take concrete steps to avoid it. The women's movement and the dynamic it introduces guarantees that no one need take the revolution totally on faith—for the kinds of changes we want to see are part of the very process of making the revolution.

The woman's movement makes explicit what was implicit in the struggles of other sectors of the revolutionary movement—that the new American Revolution is not simply a revolution to destroy imperialism, though that would be a sufficient reason for a revolution; not simply to destroy racism, though that would be a sufficient reason; not simply to destroy sexism, though that would be a sufficient reason; not simply to end the exploitative relations that exist in production, though that would be a sufficient reason; not simply to save the world from ecological disaster, though that would be a sufficient reason; but also to begin to build an entirely new humanity. It is, in the real sense, the beginning of human history: the time when women and men decide what they want to be and begin to construct themselves accordingly. We are at the very beginning of that revolution now and will probably not live to see its full culmination in the flowering of a new humanity. But we can be part of the generation that sweeps into the dustbin of history those last impediments to this new era: the American ruling class and those ruling classes around the world that will fall along with it as the capitalist world is overturned through revolution.

CONCLUSION

A number of forces in America have revolutionary potential, and to some degree that potential is now being actualized. Even if only a part of it were actualized, it would easily constitute a majority of the population. These forces are already in varying degrees of political motion, and there is every reason to believe that the objective conditions which gave rise to that motion will continue to produce and sustain them.

I do not mean to suggest, of course, that all these forces are of equal potential significance. If all people who are now living as hippies decided to sit the revolution out while a significant percentage of working people decided to join it, the revolution would not be dramatically weakened. Indeed, any combination of groups that did not include a significant representation of the working class would find itself, in the final analysis, incapable of taking and holding state power long enough to redistribute power to the people. But, it should be added, that is in the *final* analysis, not in the beginning of the struggle. And it would be wrong to decide that radical struggle has no point unless it is a struggle by the working class. On the contrary, it may be precisely these earlier struggles that provide the context in which radical elements in the labor movement will begin to believe that struggle *is* possible and will begin to channel the workers' discontent into the political arena. This is what happened in the 1960s, and the 1970s have already begun to produce a serious reawakening of class consciousness and struggle among sections of the working class.

At the same time, I have carefully eschewed the conclusion that revolution is inevitable. It is possible that the militance we now see developing among workers may remain in isolated pockets and may never lead to the formation of a unified radical political force. Or, if such a force emerges, it may make mistakes that set it back seriously. But, given the economic structural problems outlined in the first section of this book and given the growing awareness of these problems and their connection with the political structure, it *does* seem almost inevitable that the next twenty-five years will see some kind of cataclysmic breakdown in American society.

What happens at this point, however, will depend in part on what *we*—you and I—are doing in the meantime. If we have spent the next several years preparing people for that breakdown, explaining what the alternatives are, transforming ourselves as we come to understand our situation better, and building a revolutionary force that can move decisively at the appropriate moment, the revolution will occur. But history is made up of human decisions, which exist in a certain context. Although that context is not set by us alone, it does permit us to make choices that can create a new society. The rest is up to us. And to circumstances that are still indeterminate.

It is up to us, because it is possible to move in each area and to actualize its revolutionary potential. It is quite possible that this will not occur, that in each of these possible sources for a revolutionary movement, or in most of them, accommodationist tendencies will prevail. Or it is possible that although each group wants to smash the state, each will be unable to overcome the tendencies that make cooperation difficult, so that black will not work with white, women with men, student with worker. Or that one group will attempt to overthrow the state before the potential support for that action among other groups has been mobilized. What actually happens will depend in good part on what you do.

On the other hand, circumstances may arise that make the revolution impossible. The ecological crisis may fast approach the point of no return. Or the United States, in an attempt to defend its imperialist holdings, may trigger a nuclear war that would leave such devastation in its wake that it would be impossible to talk about the elimination of scarcity again for hundreds of years. These possibilities are real and may point up both the urgency of the revolution and the foolishness of becoming involved in reformist adventures that permit twenty problems to worsen while solving one.

The great weakness of capitalism is that it depends upon human beings, while creating the conditions in which these human beings come to realize capitalism's inadequacies and destructiveness. Capitalism is producing social forces that can no longer be counted on to remain passive and to acquiesce in their own exploitation and the exploitation of people around the world. Without those people, neither the industrial nor the military machine can continue to function—so it will literally be possible to stop the whole capitalist operation. In this sense, the spirit of the people *is* greater than technology.

229

But I stress again that I have been speaking about tendencies and possibilities. Those tendencies and possibilities show that it is naive to dismiss Socialist Revolution as impossible or as a fantasy of idealistic youth. It would be equally naive to think that all these possibilities were now being actualized and that revolutionary change is around the corner. The movement of forces that began to develop in the 1960s is in relative disarray in 1972. The combination of external repression and internal mistakes have caused confusion and despair. The workers' movement is the only force that is moving into a period of relative upsurge, and that upsurge is still limited and narrowly defined. Those limitations may quickly disappear and the labor upsurge may restimulate the development of every other section of the developing revolutionary movement. But even if that does not happen immediately, and even if there is a period of relative decline, the basic structural analysis presented here is in no way invalidated. We are not about to make the mistakes of the 1950s, when a temporary lull was interpreted to mean that people's basic problems had been settled and that gradual liberal reform was all that was needed to tie everything together. In the long run, the forces that capitalism produces cannot be adequately dealt with inside capitalist society; our job is to make the long run short enough so that the world is not destroyed in the meantime.

One of the greatest errors that befell the New Left in the 1960s was to belittle its own successes. Of course, the rulers tried to encourage disillusionment and despair. This is an old labor-relations trick that management learned quite early: Never admit that anything you gave the workers was a result of their successful strike. No. It is because of the bosses' generosity. Similarly in politics. When Johnson was restrained in invading North Vietnam and then forced to drop out of the 1968 election, when Nixon was restrained from using tactical nuclear weapons, was forced to withdraw speedily from Cambodia, and finally was forced to withdraw many American troops from Vietnam before the election, it was due to the pressure the antiwar movement had created. Yet, instead of building on its partial victories, that movement despaired of having failed to stop the war completely, and most of its adherents simply gave up. Only then, with the movement in collapse, was Nixon free to mine the harbors and bomb freely. By having utopian criteria for evaluating its own success, the movement undermined its own sense of worth, just at the moment when its impact was beginning to be felt in sections of the population that had previously been quiescent. Failing to sense its own importance, the Left indulged in inwardness and sectarianism and finally fell apart. It must take itself more seriously as it rebuilds itself in the 1970s.

6
Strategy and Tactics

THE FIRST STEP

THE strength of capitalist society has been its ability to convince those it has exploited, and whose human potentialities it has suppressed, that it was acting rationally, in everyone's self-interest. This is sometimes called "bourgeois hegemony"—the ability of the ruling class to portray its particular interests as the interests of all human beings. In the international arena, the United States represents itself as interested only in peace, domestically only in prosperity. Who can be opposed to these aims?

The first task of the revolutionary movement, its most important task within the next few years, is to destroy bourgeois hegemony and develop a radical consciousness among each of the potential constituencies for revolutionary action. It will do this by showing people what international peace meant for the U.S. bourgeoisie: the right to exploit the peoples of the world peacefully, without interference, and that this is no longer possible, as the Vietnamese have shown. It will show people that domestic prosperity meant prosperity for the rulers, with wealth trickling down through a class-stratified society and never quite reaching tens of millions, even in periods of boom; that capitalist prosperity is linked to racism, sexism, the destruction of the environment, inadequate health care, unfair distribution of wealth, and the suppression of the human potentialities of a large part of the workforce. It will show people that they and their children and their children's children will increasingly be deformed by a system whose exploitation is re-created in every set of human relationships and every economic, political, and social arrangement it creates. The first strategic goal of the revolutionary movement, then, is to create a new

231

understanding and a new self-consciousness so that people become aware of their situation, understand their oppression and the contours of capitalism's irrationality, and begin to counterpose themselves and their needs to the system.

Accomplishing this goal requires a new understanding of what it is to be human, and a new emphasis on beauty, love, creativity, self-expression, and human solidarity. These are the values that the revolutionary movement must seek to perpetuate in every area of human experience. We must always be cognizant of the tremendous cooptive powers of the capitalist order, particularly when struggles are simply for more material benefits. At the same time, we must eschew those who seek love and creativity for themselves at the expense of creating it for others: human solidarity requires that we do not pretend that material goods are unimportant for the poor and for those who have previously been colonized or otherwise exploited. The revolutionary movement must show people that there is no contradiction between meeting people's material needs and being fulfilled as human beings, and living in a nonexploitative society.

This new understanding is already developing throughout the world and in various sectors of the American population. Bourgeois hegemony is already cracking on the campuses, among women, young workers, the hip communities, and the black community. More and more the questions being asked are "How do we bring this system down?" and "What will a new society be like?" On the other hand, we should not exaggerate the current radical consciousness. In many areas it has just begun to flourish and it certainly is not yet reflective of any widespread understanding of the really monstrous nature of the American capitalist system. The very fact that some people think the only thing needed to overthrow American society is to come to consciousness of its exploitative nature shows that these people have not really come to an adequate consciousness—they have moved part of the way, but do not yet have a full understanding of how the system works to perpetuate itself, absorbing many who thought they were in the process of changing it. The new "consciousness theories" of Charles Reich and others are simply sophisticated expansions of the "generation gap" theory; both misunderstood the class nature of American capitalism, and both, by helping to obscure the real issues of the distribution of power and wealth, end by strengthening the hands of the exploiters.

We are not interested in promoting the illusion that the new generation is morally more pure or more beautiful or more sensitive than the old, or that it has miraculously experienced a change of consciousness that will permit it to transform the society radically as it begins to infiltrate positions of power. The new generation is just as likely to become corrupted by the experience of trying to succeed in capitalist society as did the old. All it took was unemployment in the late 1960s and early 1970s to destroy the illusion that everyone was going to drop out of this society. Once the surplus started to dry up, even the most freaked-out hippies began to reconsider the question of work. And the failure of the Left to build any counterinstitution to the Democratic party has ensured that many who have the "new consciousness" will be working inside the Democratic party. But once one looks for work and power through the established capitalist institutions, the process of corruption begins to take hold in the best-intentioned people, whether or not they belong to the hip-love generation.

Destroying bourgeois hegemony is not simply a question of showing people that the present system does not serve their needs as well as would some alternative; it also involves showing them that the alternative is worth the risks involved in attaining it. After all, not too far behind the rhetoric of American democracy and civil liberties stands the reality of American power. The cumulative effect on people's consciousness of generations in which those who struggled ended up without jobs, or in jail, or with bloody heads or napalmed bodies, cannot be overestimated. Many people are reluctant even to consider new ways of seeing themselves and their world if they sense that such a view is likely to lead them to actions that would bring on their own downfall. Hence, part of the task of destroying capitalism's world view is to show people that it *is* possible to struggle without being defeated. The contribution of the Viet Cong to the American movement is, in this sense, incomparable: the Viet Cong showed that a purely rational assessment of arms, munitions, tanks, airplanes, and technological power was not a good basis on which to decide whether a struggle could be won—the human factor is also crucial. The Viet Cong, together with the domestic black movement, made the American movement possible, and the defeat of the Vietnamese in any explicit way would set back the American revolutionary movement for many years by giving people a sense of futility and powerlessness that would be hard to overcome.

The government's reliance on repression is crucial in sustaining a feeling of powerlessness. It does not have to put everyone in jail to get the message across ("If they'll go after a priest, like Berrigan, they'll surely go after me if I get out of line"). This fear is not recognized even by many who experience it; instead it is translated into an unwillingness to listen to or consider arguments from political radicals whose programs can be seen as impossible in the *given* social order, and hence "impractical."

The revolutionary movement must show people that the revolution does

233

not mean self-destruction. It *will* involve many risks and there is no way to guarantee that people will not be jailed or killed—that is already happening to people in the struggle. But at the same time, we must avoid turning a necessity into virtue, and pretending that those risks are what the revolution is about. I remember a history professor at Berkeley, Reginald Zelnik, who used to accuse radicals of not being serious because they weren't taking enough crazy risks. Some radicals were impressed with this *macho* theme and actually identified the revolution with showing how little they cared for their own lives or safety. But most people are not willing to change their self-understanding and their acceptance of bourgeois society if the alternative is only heroic antics.

Nor does the revolution mean chaos. When used by the rulers, the phrase "law and order" means the law necessary to preserve their exploitative order. And many people who have responded to the phrase use it as a synonym for their racism, or their respect for the present capitalist order. But its mass appeal goes beyond, to include millions of people who have good reason to want order: they have experienced disorder—in the depression and in war—and they know that disorder is frightening and not particularly conducive to self-realization. Many of these people might be willing to give up their attachment to the capitalist system, but they fear the unknown and they see the revolution (as the media try to portray it and as some revolutionaries confirm) as an endless series of bombings, with nothing being built. These fears must be spoken to, both to develop in the people who have a recognition that the political struggles ahead involve building a new order while tearing down the old and to show them that the disorder of the present world flows inevitably from the capitalist system. Disorder is inherent in the capitalist world: nothing that frightened people can do is going to stop the peoples of the world and the oppressed people in this country from struggling. The quickest way to re-create order is to destroy the present unjust order and create one that does not force people into situations where they must challenge the established order for the sake of their own physical and mental survival.

Given the representative of the Left on whom the media tend to focus, it is understandable that many Americans should perceive it as being primarily interested in destruction. Abbie Hoffman popularized the juvenile strategy of petty theft as a way of expressing resentment against the system and providing a way for middle-class dropouts to live comfortably. The Left has never adequately understood why working people want to hold onto those few goods they have managed to buy through the sweat of their labor. Some elements in the New Left consistently confuse the desire to eliminate private ownership of the means of production with a totally non-

Marxist idea: taking away from everyone their personal possessions. Given that confusion, the New Left has never adequately understood the good reasons for people's upset about rising crime in their communities. It is true that this problem will largely be solved in a socialist society, but a crucial part of a leftist strategy is to explain why that is so. It is not bourgeois to be concerned about being mugged when walking down the street, and the Left must speak to that concern and explain that most crime will disappear only when people do not face extreme material deprivation and an alienated life.

A related error of the New Left was the glorification of terrorism as an instrument of revolutionary politics. In fact, terrorism is a variant of liberalism. The terrorist thinks that a mass movement is impossible, so he decides to substitute himself for the movement. The tactic usually reflects the same kind of contempt for the mass of people as is found among elitist liberals: since the people are incapable of coming to see the truth through political activity and education, the terrorist must act without them, and often in opposition to what they would have chosen to do. The usual consequence is to strengthen the established order in two ways. First, terrorism threatens most people and makes them feel that the crazy revolutionaries have put their own lives in danger. Hence, they are willing to tolerate an even higher level of repression and cutbacks in civil liberties as the only way to preserve their safety. Since we are fighting a system, and not a particular individual or a particular building, no terrorist act is likely to cause sufficient damage to the rulers to undercut the even stronger negative effect it is likely to produce among many people that we want to win over to the revolution. Second, terrorism creates passivity in those sections of the population that favor the revolution. Radical politics becomes increasingly a spectator sport. But this is just the opposite of what we need. The key to building revolutionary consciousness is to give people a sense of their own potential agency, and this can be done only by getting people involved directly in struggle. But when it seems so much more romantic to blow up a Bank of America building than to organize block meetings or hand out leaflets at a factory or organize yet another demonstration, the majority of activists start to feel inadequate and give up active organizing.

"But if people really want order, won't it seem more reasonable for them to seek it through repression than through revolution? After all, the fascists make 'order' their slogan, and isn't it possible that as the revolution gets closer, people will become more and more nervous and hence support an American-style fascism?" Yes and no. It is true that when disorder grows, repression seems attractive to those who run America. But everyone has learned a lot about fascism, and no one welcomes it. Powerful sections of the American ruling class know that to give anyone the power that was given to Hitler would create a force that might endanger their own power in the not-too-long run. After all, the German ruling class faced serious problems even when Hitler was doing well. The American ruling class is not eager to surrender its current power to a powerful state apparatus, even if that apparatus is set up by one section of their class to forestall revolution. Moreover, it was not repression alone that quieted the German population—it was repression tied to a program of rebuilding the military and then expanding geographically, thus buoying up the economy and making possible economic recovery. Repression is an ideological tool—it works to fool the people for a limited period of time. After that, if they still do not have enough income, or if there are not enough jobs or if work is still alienating or if the air is still poisoned, they will not continue to be fooled. The German program of repression worked because it was tied to a viable economic program. But what will be the program of the fascists in this country? The economic program of the fascists in Germany in the 1930s has already been tried in the United States—by the liberals. It was the liberals who used militarism and imperialist expansion after the Second World War to avert a return to depression. That program is now in crisis. It will take a brand new economic program to deal with the crisis of the coming decades. And nothing short of socialism will succeed in dealing with the basic problems that cause the unrest which repression attempts to direct into channels not threatening to capitalism. So repression is to be greatly feared in the short run, but it is no answer for the capitalists in the long run.

PREPARING FOR POWER

Many people think of a revolution as if it were a coup d'état—a small group of men and women suddenly take over the government and do things differently. This is a mistake. The Socialist Revolution is not a coup. At a certain point some people may occupy government buildings and issue proclamations, but the essence of the revolution is in tearing down the power of the ruling class and remaking society through the power of the people. The process begins many years before the seizing of state power and continues for many years thereafter. The revolution involves the active participation of tens of millions of people on one level or another. The first step is to break down bourgeois hegemony and give people a sense that they can and should struggle for a new order. But the second and crucial stage is to prepare people for taking power in every area of their lives. This has two aims: (1) to progressively weaken the power of the bourgeoisie and undermine the functioning of its institutions, and (2) to develop in people the facility for making decisions and exercising power, an experience everywhere denied them under capitalist society.

One instrument in this process will be the establishment of people's councils in each area of life to develop plans for that area when the people have power and to lead struggles to get that power. For instance, workers' councils in factories must be established in which workers discuss how they would run their factory if they had power, including what they would produce and how they would run training facilities. Workers' councils could lead assaults on institutional arrangements, as well as provide a force for pushing unions into serious struggles with the bosses. Such struggles would not by themselves achieve socialism, but, as Andre Gorz points out,[1] there are intermediary goals worth fighting for that limit the power of the capitalist and provide steppingstones to the final transfer of power. Gorz calls these goals "non-reformist reforms" because although they do not overthrow capitalism, they *do* transfer some power. For instance, a struggle for workers' councils which will define work conditions, a struggle for workers to have facilities at work where, at a certain period each day, they can participate in political debate; a struggle for free, community-controlled but federally financed day-care facilities; a struggle for students to be able to choose a set number of faculty members in each department, or to make campus rules governing political activity, or for the autonomy of a women's study program or a black study program at a university—all these seriously cut into the power of the rulers and provide people with leverage with which they can make further demands.

It is certainly true that any reform always contains the possibility of being cooptive in the sense that people struggling for it may stop fighting once the reform has been won. This is more likely to be the case in struggles around reformist reforms—those that give people some specific good, usually money, the cost of which can be quickly passed back to the consumer in the form of higher prices or to the people as a whole in the form of higher taxes. But nonreformist reforms give power to the people, even if it is not enough to enable them to control their own lives. Therefore they may whet people's appetites for more power, at the same time showing them they are competent to run things. A classic experiment of this sort occurred during the Berkeley Free Speech Movement's student strike. The administration had virtually ceased functioning, and the students ran

[1] In *Strategy for Labor* (Boston: Beacon Press, 1968).

237

the university for a short period, setting up classes and keeping order on the campus. Students who participated had a marvelous experience in power: they suddenly discovered that all the myths they had been fed by administrators—that students couldn't handle things for themselves and that a bureaucracy of experts was needed—were in fact mystifications.

Fighting for these kinds of reforms shows people that there is something concrete to fight for and the notion of "revolution" begins to have some meaning for them. Even when these struggles fail, they give people an idea of what the revolution would be all about, although of course in greatly modified form. This is important, because we should not fool ourselves into believing that the system will yield easily to these demands— it may fight ruthlessly to avoid any such concessions. But the struggle itself gives people a better idea of why they must fight for the entire revolution.

People's councils should be set up not only in the place of work, but also in other areas: in the neighborhood, to struggle, for example, for people's parks and rebeautification of the environment, for free public child care with trained supervision responsible to the community, and for collective bargaining for rents and mortgages; in the schools, for control over the curriculum and personnel; and citywide councils on questions of beautifying the city, fighting pollution, providing free health care, enforcing strict standards of industrial health and safety, etc. These councils could function in two ways: (1) to mobilize forces to win power from such existing institutions as the city council, state and local boards, etc., and (2) to act as an independent force that could begin to implement programs on its own.

At all points the councils would be encouraged to be visionary: to develop programs that would be ultimately desirable, and then to fight for them, rather than to limit their vision to what is currently conceivable. The task of these councils is to develop a new vision, and in the process to develop the forces that could implement it. In every area of life, people should be encouraged to answer concretely for themselves the question, What will life be like after the revolution? Since it is the people who will have to make the new society, it is the people who will have to start thinking about these questions, talking about them on the job and in their neighborhoods, and then struggling for the achievement of a new society or parts of it right now. A revolutionary movement would distinguish itself from the rest of the political arena precisely by its refusal to be governed by the criteria of being acceptable to the powers that be (which ultimately means, acceptable to the ruling class) and by its attempt to involve masses of people both in the formulation of and struggle to achieve concrete societal goals. The revolutionary, of course, would not play a neutral role

238

in all this: he would be pressing for his own vision of what struggles are important and how to win them. None of this involves the assumption that the people have a mystical wisdom; people are formed within definite historical circumstances, and can change themselves within certain limits. The establishment of these councils is part of our self-transformation. It is quite different from a strategy that says that we should elect the best person to office and then hope for the best. The more people begin to think about what is possible for them, given the present development of technology, the more they can experience capitalism and the ruling class as restraints that should be overthrown.

I have stressed struggles for nonreformist reforms because in the past, struggles for other reforms were easily assimilated. At the same time, we should not overestimate capitalism's ability to provide both a high standard of living for everyone and adequate social services. There are moments when even the most narrow demands for wage increases cannot be met by the system without causing crisis, and at these moments such demands can legitimately be advanced by a revolutionary movement. This will be increasingly true as imperialism loses more of the nations and territories it has exploited and faces an increasing number of intraimperialist rivalries. For instance, the demand for a guaranteed minimum income of $6,500 a year for a family of four does not institutionalize any transfer of power from the rulers to the rest of the population. Nevertheless, it is a demand that the rulers cannot meet at this moment without cutting back expenditures for defense of the imperialist empire. Hence the demand will not be met, and many people struggling for it will see the need for revolution.

Even if the demand for an adequate income could be met, we would still struggle for it: anything that eliminates human suffering is good and progressive. We do not hold the theory that people should be worse off so that they can become revolutionaries. But we do not believe that energy should be spent on reforms that can and will be easily met by the system if the achievement of those reforms strengthens the hold of the system and hence guarantees the preservation of other forms of exploitation and domination. On the other hand, these reforms should not be opposed: in the long run anything that betters the human condition frees people to strive for more fundamental changes.[2] But they have a low place among

2 We totally reject the idea that if things get worse, people will become more revolutionary, and hence that a radical movement should try to make things worse. Any movement that appears to be callous toward the needs of people, however material and unrevolutionary those needs, will never win the people's trust. We may not fight for small wage benefits when our time can be better used elsewhere, but we do not welcome defeat as a base for radicalization.

our priorities. It is good to put iodine on scratches, but iodine will not cure a malignant tumor. Obviously, a situation in which people are starving or suffering under intolerable conditions cannot be analogized to minor abrasions; hence the revolutionary movement takes on the struggle against poverty, for adequate food, free and adequate health care, and for welfare rights as high priorities. But the analogy might have some force when applied to the problem of raising the salaries of employed workers. In such struggles people are not likely to come to revolutionary consciousness; on the contrary, they are likely to be bound back more tightly to the system.

Still, no formula will work. At times even the lowest-priority struggle can be moved in a revolutionary direction or can help in the development of class and revolutionary consciousness if creative revolutionaries are participating in it. Even reforms that can be met by the system are sometimes worth fighting for, because they can encourage people to feel they have the strength to continue fighting for more important things. A great deal depends on *how* the reform is won. If it requires a struggle, it may help people develop a sense of agency, crucial to giving them the confidence to take power for themselves. On the other hand, even important reforms, given to the people as a gift from the capitalists or their representatives in the legislature and Congress, may tend to reinforce passivity and make people less willing to struggle on their own. What we need is not a reliance on cookbook recipes, but concrete studies of specific economic, political, and social circumstances. We may find that the most trivial wage struggles, rightly eschewed by the New Left in the 1960s, will have the potential for becoming revolutionary in a period in which the state steps in to freeze wages and run the economy directly in the interests of the rulers.

The fear of cooptation is legitimate: this system has time and again

---

The same concept underlies our attitude toward elections. Writing in mid-1972, I certainly hope that McGovern wins the Democratic nomination and the presidential election, not because he will be able to change things, but because even the few good things he might do would be extremely valuable for people, strengthening their ability, if more radical alternatives were available, to continue fighting for their needs even if McGovern were unwilling to take the next steps with them. Further, McGovern could end the most murderous and genocidal war in recent history, and he could lessen the climate of repression and violence. Finally, a liberal Democrat in power would help undermine the perennial myth that the liberals would make the fundamental changes necessary to save America *if only* they were in power. Although any New Deal that a liberal might bring would certainly be opposed by some sectors of the ruling class, it would in fact only streamline and make more effective the system of capitalist exploitation. But, in raising hopes and in ending a disastrous war, a liberal victory would help bring people back into politics and they would soon move further to the Left than any liberal had hoped or planned. On the other hand, while hoping for a victory of liberals in 1972, I also hope that the Left begins to build an alternative that will make it possible for us to escape the perennial choices between lesser evils that always face us in election years.

shown its great flexibility. But that flexibility derived from an expanding imperialism; there will be much less of it as the imperialist empire contracts. We will always have to be historically specific in deciding whether or not a particular struggle will lead in a revolutionary direction. The Weathermen once tried to settle this by applying a mechanical formula: the only struggles in which we should participate are those which are explicitly anti-imperialist. This formulation misses the point. Many struggles that have nothing explicitly to do with imperialism actually weaken the U.S. ability to exploit the Third World. The critical need is to weaken the system and to weaken people's attachment to it by changing their understanding of themselves and of the society, and these transformations of consciousness are not always the result of explicitly anti-imperialist or anti-capitalist struggles. For those who like to deal with certainties, who cannot stand the ambiguities and risks of a struggle that may not move as expected, a formula like the one Weatherman suggests—or even one based on "nonreformist reforms"—would give great comfort. But if we are to make a revolution in this country we will have to involve ourselves in struggles that might go the wrong way—but which contain the possibility of mobilizing tens of thousands, and may move in the correct way if the revolutionaries are intelligent and tough and willing to engage in political struggle with those with a different political understanding.

BRINGING PEOPLE TOGETHER

The two main points of strategy so far discussed have been the defeat of bourgeois hegemony and the development of struggles that prepare people for power and progressively weaken the power of the rulers—"nonreformist reforms" and the fight for people's material and spiritual needs. The third part of a revolutionary strategy would be devoted to accelerating the struggles of potentially revolutionary forces and bringing them together into common struggle. In part, this coming together will flow naturally out of the logic of those struggles, but in part it will have to be consciously fostered by a revolutionary movement, or by the revolutionary sections of each potential constituency. Uniting struggles is crucial if the ruling class is not to succeed in setting each group against the other.

A revolutionary movement will put forward plans and struggles that show the relationship between different groups and lead different groups to struggle in each other's interest. Let me give an example from the program that we developed in the Seattle Liberation Front. We formulated as an initiative to place on the ballot the following four-point proposal, centering on our opposition to the war and the exploitative tax structure which helped finance it:

WHEREAS the state and federal governments tax working people to support the needs of large corporations (from defending their foreign investments by wars like the current one in Southeast Asia to training their corporate managers and engineers at the university to directly suppressing workers when they try to strike for higher wages and control of working conditions), and Whereas the needs of the people are not being met by the current tax structure and the current distribution of goods, and Whereas the Legislature must be directed to do much more to fight the destruction of the environment, to fight institutionalized racism, and provide adequate jobs, housing, and medical care for all working people, black and white, Therefore the Legislature shall provide implementing legislation for the following, including constitutional amendments where necessary: 1. No citizen making less than $10,000 a year shall pay any state taxes on his income, nor any state sales tax on food, clothing, housing or household appliances or furniture, nor any property taxes on property worth less than $30,000. Any citizen making between $10,000 and $14,000 a year shall have his taxes on income reduced by one-half (including federal income tax as provided for in section no. 4). Each of these figures shall be raised $1,000 for each dependent. These figures are for the base year 1970 and shall be automatically adjusted to meet rises in the cost of living and inflation. The tax burden normally carried by these people shall be shifted to corporations and businesses whose property assets are $300,000 or more and to persons whose income is over $30,000. A control board, elected in statewide general elections, shall be empowered to use injunctive remedies and to impose prohibitive fines and jail terms for any corporations or businesses that attempt to pass the extra tax burden back to the consumer in the form of higher prices, rents, interest rates or other such mechanisms. 2. No citizen of the State of Washington shall be required to participate in or train for any foreign war. The state shall provide adequate protection for those who are so required by the federal government. 3. No firm, corporation, or business shall participate directly or indirectly or shall contract itself to any firm, agency, corporation or governmental institution that is participating directly or indirectly in the pursuance of foreign wars, declared or undeclared. 4. A state Commission, elected in statewide general elections every two years,

242

shall be empowered to receive all Federal income tax which residents of the State of Washington are required to send to the Federal government. That commission shall hold all such income tax and shall spend it in the interests of the people of the State of Washington until such time as the Federal government ends all foreign wars, stops spending more than 10% of its annual budget on military or military related projects, and eliminates all tax on people who would not be taxed under provision no. 1. Specifically, this money shall be spent to finance projects designed to rebuild and beautify the cities (starting with the specifically exploited black community), combat the pollution and destruction of the environment, provide adequate health care, jobs and housing for working people, provide for enrollment in the university for all racial minorities and working class children (anyone from families making less than $10,000 a year in 1970—adjusted for inflation and rises in the cost of living in future years), provide mechanisms for black community control of police, provide for child care centers and other mechanisms to free women from their special oppression, and provide for the retooling of factories in war-related industries so that talents of the workers may be used to produce goods to satisfy human needs and not to make war and serve corporate profit. All citizens who would be required to pay state taxes under provision No. 1 and all corporations shall be required to pay their federal income tax to the state commission, and provisions shall be made for their protection from any attempted reprisals by the federal government. No one making less than $10,000 a year shall be required to pay this or any other income tax. No one making between $10,000 and $14,000 a year shall pay more than 50% of his current rate on federal income tax.

This kind of program has several strengths. It relates the money spent on imperialist war to money that could be spent on needed social services. But it does not abandon the workers whose income depends on war operations: rather, the state is to retool those factories so that they can produce socially useful goods. The initiative contains things people understand immediately, such as taxes, and things about which they are initially suspicious or hostile, such as black community control of police, and hence provides the opportunity for an organizer to show the connections among them and to engage in serious political education in the process of getting signatures and building support for the initiative. Our experience showed us that people were willing to listen because they approved the

243

section on taxes. It is an explicitly class program: it emphasizes what working people have in common and consciously puts them in opposition to monied interests who would oppose this proposal. It raises antiracist and antisexist demands and replaces vague sentiment with concrete programs. It does not merely talk about what we are against, but includes hints of some of the things we are for. In order for it to be passed, working people would have to unite behind it. Unlike demands that could be raised in. for example, one particular factory, this kind of program emphasizes what workers have in common with all other workers.

This type of program does not represent a transfer of power in any structural sphere; it is just a series of reformist reforms. But they are reforms the society would never grant, because they interfere with its ability to carry on its imperialist adventures and to redistribute wealth from the poor to the rich. It is a good example of why we cannot rely on simple-minded criteria about which struggles are "reformist."

A critical weakness with this initiative was that we tried to put everything in it. Programmatically that makes sense, but as a tactic it didn't, because in trying to mention everything we guaranteed we would *win* nothing. We were so concerned about doing adequate education that we failed to use the initiative as a vehicle for people actually to take some kind of power. People liked the idea, but they also realized that as formulated the initiative could never pass, and if it passed it would not be implemented. It would have made more sense to use this as our background educational material and to put on the ballot a program that, while being explicitly anticapitalist and uniting working people, would not have tried in one fell swoop to include every issue under the sun.

Emphasizing the need to unite struggles leads to another key point: struggles in which people practice taking power for themselves could in fact occur in a racist or sexist context, and could reinforce that racism and sexism. This society is expert at taking from one oppressed group to give to another. People could begin to act on what they sense to be their own needs at the expense of other powerless groups. Saul Alinsky was famous for that: the white communities he organized in Chicago became heavily racist because he urged them to struggle for their most narrow interests and did not attempt to link them up in struggle with blacks for their common benefit. This wrongheaded approach has recently been endorsed by those who claim that the revolution will occur spontaneously as people begin to discover their own needs. But the fact is that the revolution is not just about discovering ourselves and what we are really like. It is also about changing ourselves and our needs. Metaphysicians sometimes explain that our "true needs" or our "real selves" are somewhat different from what we think

244

them to be. But these "true needs" and "real selves" are not previously existing entities which we discover with a bit of careful psychic research. Rather, the phrases are prescriptions: they tell us what we think we and others ought to be like, suggesting that this "ought" can be realized in the process of transforming the society. We ought to develop new needs. One of the new needs we must develop in the course of the revolution is the need for universal self-fulfillment. That is, a revolutionary begins to develop as his own need, and as a prerequisite for his own fulfillment as a human being, the need to have other human beings able to fulfill their own needs and realize their own potentialities. If we call this need "human solidarity," we can see that a key part of a revolutionary strategy is to increase human solidarity.

COMMUNITY AND POINT OF PRODUCTION ORGANIZING

One good reason a revolutionary strategy should place emphasis on electoral initiative in the period ahead is that the initiative form allows one to raise class questions in such a way as to stimulate class-wide solidarity, e.g., the shifting of the tax burden onto corporations, banks, and the rich. It would be nice if unions would raise these kinds of issues in strikes, but even the most militant rank-and-file caucuses have eschewed this sort of thing as too "impractical." In a way, this makes sense: why should one union on strike have to bear the entire burden of fighting for a social change that will benefit everyone? Even the argument of the union bureaucrats and the bosses seems to make some sense: how can you expect the industry in which you work to be the pioneer in a given area of social reform when no one else is doing the same thing? Moreover, in the case of such issues as taxation and free health care, it does make more sense to be striking directly against the government. And how can a single union do that? So even the most militant rank-and-filers usually direct their energy not at getting their union to address wider social issues, but at getting it not to sell out the interests of the workers on the particular issues that usually come up in contract negotiations. The city- or statewide initiative then appears as a plausible mechanism for fighting social issues, providing the initiatives are put forward in a manner that accentuates their class content, and not sneaked through in the hope they will win while nobody notices what they are really about. The initiative campaign has an additional possibility: it can bring together around a radical struggle trade-union militants who do not know each other, and give them a sense of

245

their potential strength. Initiatives, after all, can win at least some victories, and in the next few years winning some class victories in the larger community may be the most important thing that can happen to stimulate militant activity in the labor movement. Further, an initiative campaign may help to legitimate ideas that eventually will be taken back into specific unions and adopted as their own struggle. Consider the demand for 30 hours' work for 40 hours' pay, or the demand for workers' control of work conditions. Both may be considered remote today. Yet, it is quite conceivable that if these demands were placed on an initiative and a statewide campaign waged around them for a few years, they would be seen as sufficiently legitimate for some unions to raise seriously in strike demands.

City- and statewide initiatives, if drawn up carefully and well thought out, may be the most effective front to fight against the capitalists in the coming period. Highest priority should go to the following kinds of proposals: health care initiatives, on the statewide level providing for free medical care at the point of delivery for everyone in the state, on the city-wide level providing for community control of hospitals for medical facilities; tax initiatives, abolishing or limiting property and sales taxes and shifting the tax burden to the wealthy and the large corporations; industrial health and safety; rent control; ecology control; free child-care facilities with trained supervision under community control; 30 hours' work for 40 hours' pay; and statewide requirements for workers' power over work conditions in the factories and offices.

There are a variety of other struggles that must be fought, even if the initiative form is not immediately available. For instance, the development of new regional governments around large cities has been engineered precisely to undermine the possibility that people might, through gaining control of big-city government, actually establish democratic control of economic development. The new regional governments often rationalize the regional arrangements, sometimes in very progressive ways (e.g., providing funds from the suburbs to subsidize schools and social welfare projects in the inner cities). But at the same time they withdraw all control from the residents of the inner cities (usually blacks or other minority groups), hence ensuring that progressive steps will be carefully restrained and not conflict with the needs of corporate dominance. Struggles against the unprecedented power of banks to determine how the social surplus will be allocated is another important focus. Here, a critical weapon may be the unions' decision to fight for control of their own pension funds, which often supply vast amounts of money for bank trust funds to invest in capitalist ventures with no redeeming social worth. Programs designed to

246

give the elderly a meaningful opportunity to spend their later years can be another important area of struggle—and here the Left can also engage in building counterinstitutions by providing within the socialist movement itself a real place for the elderly (who can often teach us a lot about how the capitalist system exploits working people, and who are often articulate and smart enough to be top-notch organizers, given a framework in which to operate).

At the same time, a serious revolutionary strategy must focus on the unique importance of the point of production. Workers may be organized in their neighborhoods and as consumers and taxpayers, and these organizations are important. But it is in their position as workers, with their hands literally on the means of production, that they have their greatest potential strength. For here they can shut down the society if they so decide. So it will be crucial for revolutionaries to work in production, helping to develop an awareness of class consciousness, and playing leadership roles not only in the particular struggles that actually emerge but also in the struggle to redefine the issues that are appropriate for unions. An increasing number of young workers have radical leanings—but for the moment they can see no sensible national force with which to link up. This is part of the reason why, in the short run, statewide and community-wide struggles around class demands can be so important—because they will bring these young workers together. Feeling their collective strength, they may be much more prepared to engage in serious struggle in their respective unions when they believe that they are part of some kind of broad political movement. But a critical part of the orientation must be to return to the shop to organize—first around the initiative project, but also and most importantly around the whole gamut of issues that affect the lives of workers in the shop. No formula can be worked out a priori; and another advantage to bringing people together in community-wide struggles is that workers not yet ready to join a socialist party might still be prepared to come to this kind of meeting, and learn from each other about techniques for raising issues with fellow workers that have been tried by people in different shops and plants.

The development of rank-and-file caucuses in the unions has tremendous importance in the immediate period ahead. These caucuses can provide a way of bringing radical consciousness to the fore in the working class and giving people a sense that they can link up with the larger struggle to remake America. The danger I have already pointed to, however, must be kept constantly in mind: rank-and-file caucuses see themselves primarily as instruments to make the unions more militant fighters for the things unions traditionally fight for, or as means of eliminating corrupt leadership.

These fights are certainly important, but unless they are seen as part of a strategy that moves further and attempts to redefine the whole function of unions, they will end up having little lasting significance. The critical point about the unions is not that they are corrupt and do not fight hard enough for the issues they raise, but that they have become accomplices in a distribution of power that leaves the worker basically powerless. While it would be ridiculous to start organizing by telling people to abandon their unions completely, unless we begin with a broad critique of the way the unions have been completely integrated into the capitalist order, we are likely to build a rank-and-file movement that has no more impact on changing the basic structures than have reform movements in the past. This is why I suggest the formation of workers' councils at work and people's councils in the community, to begin to raise the larger issues now, including a critique of the labor movement and the function of unions as they have been defined in the past thirty years. We must reject the notion that the only goal of the revolutionary at this stage is to build rank-and-file caucuses even when they focus only on narrow issues. We do not have to repeat the mistakes of the reformers of the past just because we are a new generation of working-class activists.

A SOCIALIST PARTY

In talking about a strategy for revolution we have been implying the existence of an agent—a revolutionary movement. That movement exists, but it is at a very low level of self-awareness and unity. Obviously, a party or parties are needed that can unite and provide leadership. Unity between whites and blacks or men and women may not be in the cards for the immediate future, but parties that see this unity as a desirable goal and that can provide leadership in this direction are crucial and must and will be created. A party or parties must at once coordinate activity and help to spark new activity. The party must be structured in such a way that it maximizes creativity and the need for action, while operating in a completely democratic fashion that allows people within it to carry on serious debate. It must avoid the sectarianism that characterizes groups like the Progressive Labor party or the Revolutionary Union and the opportunism that characterizes groups like the Socialist Workers' party and the Young Socialist Alliance.

Only through a party mechanism can struggles in the factories and workplaces be translated into a more general political crisis for the capitalist state as a whole. No matter how many workers are upset about their specific conditions, unless a party can give coherent expression to the common aspects of various workers' demands, a party prepared to substitute a real political and economic alternative for the present order, there is no chance that people will be willing to opt for an overthrow of the established order. Many anarchists try to justify a "no party" position by pointing to the fact that the Communist party of France actually impeded the development of a revolutionary situation in France in May 1968. But in fact, other organized parties played an important role in advancing the struggle. It was not because it was a *party* that the CP went astray, but because the CP of France, like every other European CP, has been dominated by Moscow for the past forty years, and Moscow has tried to influence these parties to perpetuate the status quo, for fear that any drastic change might anger the Western capitalists and provoke a "protective reaction strike" against the Soviet Union as the supposed source of worldwide communism.

Classically, there are two kinds of socialist parties: the mass party composed of many millions of workers, such as existed in the Socialist party in America before World War I; and the vanguard revolutionary party, such as took state power in Russia in 1917. Probably the critical difference between the two revolves around the issue of decision making within the party. The mass party, typically, allows for much greater spontaneity at the bottom and more participation in decision making. There is no assumption of organizational discipline, so people with contending ideas remain in the party and often even speak as its representatives despite their differences with one another on specific matters. Typically, such parties have lacked sufficient organizational cohesion to mount any coordinated long-term programs of political action except for electoral campaigns. Moreover, as they become increasingly focused on electoral activity, they become subject to the dynamic of the capitalist-controlled arena, choosing their own leaders for their ability to win votes at the polls. But these choices themselves reflect the attitude of the bourgeois press toward socialist spokesmen—its willingness to play up certain leaders as "responsible opposition" and to denigrate, lie about, or ignore others.

The result can be seen from what happened in the New Left: leadership was chosen by the press, and not democratically from the bottom. Because in the mass party there is no structure of control from the bottom to the top, leadership is often unresponsive. Insistence on extreme democracy sometimes leads to endless debates; nothing gets officially decided, and a vacuum is created into which step the media-chosen representatives of the mass movement who begin to speak for it. This lack of structure permits the development of a top-heavy bureaucracy that cannot be checked on the national level, or to a general resentment of leadership and consequent leveling tendencies that accentuate the centrifugal nature of the party and eventually render it powerless as a national force. The reaction to all this among the cadre is either despair that leads to local organizing that links up to nothing, or to joining tightly-knit, disciplined cadre organizations that do not place enough emphasis on democracy.

Vanguard parties, on the other hand, see themselves as advanced in consciousness and strategy from the bulk of the people who eventually must side with the revolution. Their function is both to stimulate the consciousness of the majority, and to act on its behalf. Sometimes, as happened in Russia, the vanguard party actually makes the revolution for the majority. A vanguard party typically is governed by "democratic centralism." The concept of democratic centralism has two parts: (1) decisions within the party are arrived at democratically after vote by the membership; and (2) decisions once made are binding on all members. The members must reflect the party line in their mass work, even if they are permitted to organize factions within the party to change the line. What is more, the central leadership is generally given broad powers to interpret policies in-between meetings or votes, and although decisions made by the leadership can, theoretically, be challenged later, they are binding on members for the in-between periods.

Vanguard parties, then, have much greater organizational cohesion and have the power to mount nationwide programs of action not limited to the electoral arena. This is a great advantage if, as we argue, the ruling class refuses to allow socialists, even if elected to office, to dismantle the present apparatus of economic oppression without a severe military battle. Only through a unified and previously-thought-out campaign could the forces of counterrevolution be prevented from successfully pulling off some form of right-wing coup. On the other hand, vanguard parties have typically given excessive power to their central leadership, often with disastrous results. The leadership may attempt to use its power to ensure itself against any future challenge, thus making a mockery of formal democratic procedures. Or it may, as in the Communist parties of Western Europe and the United States, follow a nonrevolutionary line that completely thwarts the revolutionary impulses of the membership, brings out the worst in them, and turns the party into a sham. The membership is encouraged to develop qualities of submissiveness vis-à-vis constituted authority within the party that often carry over into submissiveness to all constituted authority, even that of the capitalist class. Those members who are seen as the best parrots of top leadership are advanced, while those who are talented are often stifled because they represent potential threats to the leadership. Learning a party line then becomes a substitute for original thinking and empirical work; initiative and creativity become thwarted, and party members begin to sound more like political engineers than like fully developed human beings. People on the outside, already indoctrinated by a profound fear of Soviet-style regimentation and repression, find their worst fears confirmed when they meet party functionaries who seem to have voluntarily imposed upon themselves those qualities of soul that people hate the capitalist order for imposing. The party, and through it the revolution, appear not as alternatives but as more of the same.

Obviously, then, what is needed is a party form that combines the emphasis on spontaneity, personal development, and participation in the decision making of the mass party with at least some of the organizational discipline, ideological harmony, and national nonelectoral focus of the vanguard party. Such a party would have the greatest concern for internal democracy, including the right to organize factions, but at the same time would ensure enough coherence so that once a decision was democratically arrived at, it would be carried out with dedication and recognition that the real enemy is the capitalists—not those in opposing factions, or even those in sect groups.

The need for democracy is critical if a socialist party is ever to become a mass form in American society. The American working class, after all, is literate, intelligent, and capable of leading its own revolution. Unlike parties developed to fit the needs of the peasantries of underdeveloped countries, an American party must be designed to recognize the special strengths of the American proletariat.

I believe that the most likely way such a party could emerge in the next few years would be for the most politically conscious people on the Left to begin immediately to build a mass party, aware of its critical problems and continually trying to educate people to understand why the mass party must be more disciplined and organizationally coherent than the mass parties of the past. It is only when a mass party is formed which begins to attract large numbers of working people that it would be possible to raise the question of a vanguard party without making that vanguard party simply a product of student, youth, and Old Left constituencies. Once a mass socialist party had been built, and possibly in the process of building it, it would be possible for those elements who recognized the deficiencies of this form to decide on two possible strategies: either to try to move the mass party toward greater organizational coherence and toward nonelectoral political focuses, or to build a separate vanguard party that saw the importance of the mass form but also its limitations.

Why not start out the other way, with the vanguard party building the

251

mass form? Because the mass form would be seen as a front, and hence would be unlikely to attract the creative elements that would make it real.

On the other hand, even a mass party cannot have organizational coherence unless its formation is preceded by the existence of a cadre group that at least shares a common vision of such a party and a common strategy for building it (which is still much less than a vanguard party shares: viz., a common strategy for going from here all the way to the revolution). I learned this the hard way, when I helped form the New American Movement as a kind of preparty formation without first establishing such a cadre group. I circulated a founding document and called for people who agreed with it to come together to begin work on programs. Unfortunately, many people who responded to the call did not really agree with the politics put forward. They responded to the fact that *something* was happening and that was better than nothing, but they came prepared to change the entire thrust of what we had wanted to do. In my naiveté, I thought that, since our founding document explicitly stated that people who did not agree with the politics should not try to become part of the organization, I had adequately dealt with the problem. In fact, a much more careful building process was needed, in which the initial founding group carefully recruited people who agreed with the politics. Once any organization is actively involved in mass political work, of course, there is no way to screen membership save by becoming a sect group. People usually come into a movement because they are attracted by what it *is doing;* if its programs address the needs of working people, they are likely to be recruitable. The problem is for the organization to get to the point where it actually *is* doing something public enough for working people to hear about. It's in that earlier phase—getting the organization off the ground—that more caution must be exercised in recruiting people who want to make the organization a viable political force. It is inevitable at this point in history that any leftist organization is going to attract many more people from "educated labor" and the student movement than from other sections of the working class. But this problem can be overcome if the organization attempts to develop programs that are public, dramatic, and that speak to the needs of *all* sections of the working class (e.g., some of the initiatives I suggested above). But, if the people who are first attracted ask themselves, "What are the problems and organizational forms that make *us* feel at home?" and develop activities that simply meet their *own* needs, the organization that emerges will never become a *mass* party capable of leading a mass struggle for socialism. Hence a limited cadre group is necessary with a shared vision of how to attract masses of Americans.

Of course, even sectoral organizations that appeal to only one part of the working class, if built around explicitly socialist politics—as the New American Movement *was*—are valuable, but they are less than what is needed, and less than what is possible.

One of the greatest weaknesses of the New Left was its antileadership tendencies. Any serious political party must reject the notion that leadership is illegitimate or elitist in itself. But, of course, it is critical to develop good leadership, characterized by (1) involving as many people as possible in political debate, decision making, and activity, rather than trying to hoard it for itself; (2) attempting to impart to as many people as possible the skills of leadership, so that no one becomes absolutely indispensable; (3) trying to make its assumptions and activities explicit so that others may learn from them; (4) trying to articulate the relationship between any particular program, action, idea, and the more general visions that we hold; (5) honesty; (6) ability to keep in touch with the language, needs, and problems, not only of the organization's membership, but also of those whom the organization ultimately hopes to attract or speak to; (7) a deep understanding of the American economic and political structure, constantly increased through new study and new insights. But just as it is incumbent on any leadership to take great care to develop leadership in others and to use its talents, not as a ticket to stardom, but as a means of strengthening others, so it is incumbent on any organization that hopes to succeed to give strong support to its leadership. Leadership must feel that it is able to experiment, to make mistakes, and to fail in particular struggles, or else it will never become truly creative and imaginative. It must be given a chance to develop its programs, and not be dismissed too quickly. At one point, during the days of the New Left, anyone who had been around for over a year was considered "old leadership" and had to be replaced by "new people." This is totally ridiculous. And it was part of the New Left's tendency toward anti-intellectualism and antileadership—the tendencies that eventually made the most creative people in the movement feel so stifled they had to quit and go elsewhere.

TACTICS

Let us now consider some of the tactics that will be necessary for such a revolutionary strategy as the one we have outlined, although these tactics will of course be subject to modification in light of scientific study of the social forces obtaining at any given moment. The first series of tactics center around the development of new information and new ways of self-understanding that will help defeat the bourgeois hegemony. In this connection it will be necessary to develop a revolutionary art and music and dance. Further, we must have new media, including liberated television and radio stations, and our own movies and magazines. Most importantly, we will need a national and several regional newspapers that can convey what is really happening in America and around the world. The underground media have seriously failed to provide real information about America. We need a newspaper that is honest, that tells the truth about the country and the truth about the movement, that encourages serious journalism and is not directed primarily toward convincing people of the correctness of a particular analysis but rather toward giving them adequate information from which such an analysis can be built. No understanding can possibly develop among masses of people until a certain amount of information is available to them, and no such information will ever be taken seriously if it is seen as part of an enterprise whose obvious and primary purpose is propaganda. There is, of course, no such thing as objective news coverage: selection of material always represents a point of view. But a newspaper that reflects the interests and needs of the Left need not sloganize and focus on developments in the movement to the exclusion of everything else in the world.

Probably the most effective tactics developed by the New Left have centered around confrontation of one sort or another. The purpose of confrontation politics is to unmask and reveal, to break through the illusions of bourgeois ideology and illuminate the true nature of a situation. Confrontations are most strikingly used against liberals, whose pretty rhetoric is often a cover for deeply conservative attitudes and actions. For instance, behind the façade of reasonableness of every campus administrator stands the naked force of police power. To reveal that, to bring it out in the open, is to show many students that they are not in a haven of rationality, but in an institution (like most others) controlled from the top down, and one which relies on force, not reason, to keep its procedures going. Students have sometimes been puzzled by the seeming unanimity among faculty members on political issues: all of them seem to think America is either all right as it is or in need only of reforms that can and eventually will be achieved through the system. Confrontations against departments that fire radicals, or refuse to hire blacks and women, can help to teach students that the university faculty feels as it does not because liberal arguments won out in impartial intellectual debate, but because those who hold other positions have been systematically discriminated against in hiring and tenure procedures. Confrontations around the war, the military, racism, sexism, and ecology have all helped to focus attention on these problems and at the same time have forced people with power to

254

define their positions more clearly than in the vague statements they offered in the newspapers.

Equally important, confrontations have broken down the general sense that things are all right, or will be soon. The kind of closed political universe that Herbert Marcuse describes in *One Dimensional Man* has been firmly broken; people no longer have confidence that everything will be solved through the system. This has given people much confidence in their right to raise their own grievances in a strong public way. The refusal of some people to play the game according to the rules of the ruling class has given many others the possibility of looking at the political, economic, and social world not as an inevitable "given," but as something that might be very different. Confrontations have done this precisely because they were not cool and intellectually detached, but because they were emotional and aimed at putting people up against the wall. Very strong and decisive acts were necessary to pierce through the ideological training we received growing up in America. We had to smash the manipulated consciousness to break on through to the other side. And confrontations, often involving police, did it: the politics of blowing people's minds was the politics of the Free Speech Movement, the Pentagon and Stop the Draft Week demonstrations, the confrontation at the Democratic National Convention, etc.

Another important aspect of confrontations is their effect on the people who participate in them. Confrontations help break down the civility and socially conditioned self-restraint that often hold people back from fighting for what they need. Confrontations give people a sense of their own potential agency—they find that they are able to act in the world instead of merely to view it. Suddenly one realizes that history is made by ordinary human beings like oneself, and not by supernatural creatures one can only read about in the newspapers and see on television. It is just this sense of potential agency that is crucial for building a revolutionary movement.

There are many kinds of confrontations, of course, and demonstrations have been only one form. Sit-ins, mill-ins, teach-ins, and individual confrontations have also played their part. Demonstrations have been particularly important to the extent that they have forced the media to acknowledge the existence of a movement. Media coverage rarely tells anything about the beliefs behind a demonstration, but the very fact that the demonstration has been made visible to the country shatters the world of harmony and preestablished order in which the military is in its heaven and all's right with the world.

Don't confrontations polarize and antagonize people? Yes, but they also force people to deal with certain things. They may resent the demonstrations—we are not running a popularity contest—but eventually, as people

255

change, they come to see the relevance of the tactic as well. One must judge these matters concretely in particular situations by looking at the likely consequences of action. First, one should ask whom one wants to move and how. For instance, since the demonstrations are usually not geared to winning support from the middle- and upper-middle-class parents of the young people who are demonstrating, to use those parents and their friends as a weathervane is to miss the point. They are the last people ever to join in the struggle to change society. At certain moments in the struggle their support may be needed and tactics may be geared accordingly. But one must carefully decide who are likely constituencies before attempting a given tactic. Every time a union strikes, the newspapers and television accuse it of not caring enough about "the public interest," but that doesn't stop the workers; they know that in this particular struggle the public doesn't count as much as winning specific demands, and that may require the application of a certain kind of power that turns people off. Unlike unions, students, young people, blacks, and women seldom have the kind of power it takes to win. But by taking a hard line they may plant the seeds for a future victory. For instance, by taking the "immediate withdrawal" line in 1965 vis-à-vis the Vietnam war we isolated ourselves from the vast majority of Americans. But our line was the only one that made sense, and hence we were able to win people to that position even though at first it offended them. A confrontation tactic must be judged in terms of whom one expects to influence in the short run, whom one expects to influence in the long run, and whether one's tactics are understandable by those groups. It will not always be possible to make totally accurate calculations, but one should do one's best. When in doubt, do the thing that is morally more correct; at least that is a good reason for acting in a particular way, and can be explained to others as a good reason.

The fear of antagonizing people is the essence of the Left-liberal politics —it reaches its height in the Young Socialist Alliance and its Student Mobilization Committee. YSA traditionally sets up single-issue front groups around one slogan ("Bring the troops home now" or "Free abortions for women") and then fights hard to keep those groups from moving beyond that slogan to any further understanding of politics that would require it to develop a more explicitly socialist or anticapitalist perspective. At the beginning of development of consciousness around the issues involved, this kind of approach is helpful in getting an idea understood. But later, when, according to the Harris poll, 73 percent of the American public favors withdrawal from Vietnam, as they did in spring 1971, the position becomes merely a reflection of the current state of thought. And the job of a leftist political organization is to move ahead, to try to give leadership to a movement, and not mere expression to its least common denominator. At that point, YSA or SMC (its front group) ends up holding back the development of political consciousness, and poses its traditional antiwar marches against any higher level of activity at a time when millions of people would respond to a united antiwar movement call for greater militancy. So YSA takes on the job of liberal Democrats, providing a socialist-sounding rationale for nonconfrontation with the system—at a time when confrontation would separate liberals from radicals, would force many liberals to reexamine their position, and would push them decidedly to the Left.

YSA's tactics may be a disaster for the antiwar movement as a whole. But they are useful in building YSA. When people in SMC or any of the other front organizations start to develop a broader political perspective, they are quickly recruited into YSA, where they can work on a fully-developed socialist perspective with the most narrowly sectarian politics. The idea is, "If you want to be a socialist, you have to join our vanguard revolutionary party." If the antiwar movement, for example, had been allowed to develop according to its natural tendency of increased political consciousness, people would be less inclined to join YSA. So these vanguarders try to retard the development of the mass movement in order to build their sectarian party! It makes sense from the standpoint of YSA-SWP (Socialist Workers party, its parent organization), because they believe that their sectarian party will be *the* vanguard revolutionary party, and that building it is the most important political work that can be done. But for the movements they attempt to control, the results are disastrous. Of course, none of this would have been possible in the antiwar movement, if such people as Tom Hayden and Rennie Davis had not pushed early SDS away from the antiwar struggle because it was too reformist—a position they later spent time repenting.

The style of leadership that YSA-SWP provides is the antithesis of what is necessary for a socialist organization. Socialists cannot attempt to gain leadership by hiding their politics, then quietly recruiting into their organizations the best people in the mass movements. This was the strategy of the CP in the 1930s, and it is usually disastrous. For one thing, it is dishonest to win leadership on some other basis than your politics when it is your politics you are trying to advance. Again, it is *bad* opportunism—you manage to win temporary power but you fail to educate people. And if you fail to educate people you will never be able to hold them when the going gets rough. If people do not agree with your politics, and you do not try to convince them by being up front, they will no longer support you when you try to take the next steps in the struggle. Good leadership is always a little bit ahead, helping people to take a few extra steps on the road to the development of consciousness.

This dishonest approach was also used by the Bay Area Revolutionary Union during the 1972 ILWU dockworkers' strike. When members of the New American Movement suggested linking the ILWU strike-support demonstration with a demonstration occurring on the same day in support of demands for an end to racist and sexist hiring and employment policies at Pacific Telephone, the Revolutionary Union feared that the issue of the dockworkers' strike would be "lost." It argued that the public would be antagonized by the effort to show the link between one working-class struggle and another. To top it off, the Revolutionary Union argued against the inclusion of a few paragraphs of political explanation of the strike in the leaflets announcing the demonstration, on the grounds that workers cannot be expected to read anything political! (These are the people who say that others have a "contempt for the workers"!)

The strategy of all these "revolutionary vanguards" is transparent: they hope to manipulate people into revolutionary struggle, and then the party suddenly appears, to lead that struggle and grab power for that vanguard party. But if people can be led into a "socialist" order through manipulation by a leadership that does not have enough faith in them to explain its programs to them, they can probably be led right back out again by another leadership. If people are ever going to be convinced to fight for socialism, they are going to have to know what it is and what the revolutionary analysis is and be willing to fight for it themselves.

There is an opposite extreme, of course: hit everyone over the head with your full political vision before you've even had a chance to begin a conversation ("Hello, I'm a revolutionary socialist. Who are you?"). To be honest does not mean to be aggressive and obnoxious. Here, as in so many other areas in politics, there is no single correct formula: practical wisdom is crucial.

ELECTORAL ACTIVITY

At some moments in the course of the struggle it may be appropriate to use electoral activity alongside militant confrontations and other forms of political struggle. There are several good reasons the New Left has tended to shy away from the electoral arena until now. For one thing, elections are oriented toward winning, and the pressures are strong to compromise beliefs in order to win (or at least to make a good showing). The news media play a large role in interpreting candidates, and discount those whom they consider "not serious" and "irresponsible." To the extent that a candidate puts forward programs that cannot be met without redistributing power and wealth, he will be discounted and ignored. Furthermore, participation in this arena seems to validate the system to many people: "After all, even you radicals have your chance at the polls. If you don't win, that just means the people don't like what you have to offer." But the cards are stacked against us; it would only add to the confusion to participate. Moreover, besides validating the electoral system, participating in it may also validate the governmental apparatuses connected thereto. For instance, someone who runs for city council presumably believes that the city council has some power. But very little real power lies in most elective offices. The more people in a revolutionary movement look to the electoral arena, the less they actually prepare themselves for the struggle with the state which will be inevitable if they are ever to come close to taking power. What is more, instead of moving decisively to undermine the capitalist order, people begin to think that perhaps they should wait until the next election, after which things will "surely be different." The stronger the socialist forces become, the more they feel they can wait for a new election, not realizing that events will not wait for them—and that the capitalists can manipulate circumstances in the intervening period to make it even more difficult to take power. Probably the supreme example of this was the Social Democratic party in Germany: feeling itself close to power, it decided not to earn itself the name of being unpatriotic by opposing the imperialist war (World War I) in which the Kaiser was about to engage. Or, consider the Communist party of France in 1968, which, in a situation of general strike and with half the population mobilized, told people to go back to business as usual and wait to win the battle through an election—which it then lost. The whole electoral arena suggests passivity on the part of most people— they are asked to do very little except cast a vote. But what is needed in this country is to activate people into political struggle, not just to tell them brand X is better than brand Y.

One of the important reasons we need to activate people into political struggle is the strong likelihood of counterrevolutionary violence. In the unlikely circumstances that a Chilean-type situation were to arise in the United States, there is every reason to believe that the Right would launch a military offensive to overthrow a socialist-leaning government. Even such mild liberals as the Kennedys and Martin Luther King have been assassinated—and in periods when there was no real threat to the capitalist order. If socialists ever took power through electoral means they would have to deal with a rebellious military bureaucracy that had much technology on its side (though the majority of troops would probably rally to the side of the revolution—particularly if the army becomes "volunteer" and hence composed of black people who join for a high pay they cannot get in ordinary jobs) and an uncooperative police force, as well as numerous quasi-military rightist groups. The only way such a government, once elected, could take power would be to assure the capitalists that it did not really mean business—otherwise the capitalists would start closing down their firms and trying to precipitate a major depression. Now, if people were not ready to defend the socialist government, if the entire focus had been on winning an election and not on the extraelectoral dimensions of politics, there would be no chance for the government to survive. Thus a socialist movement that focuses all its activity in the electoral arena and educates people to that strategy for making a revolution will certainly lose, even if it wins an election.

Nevertheless, a revolutionary movement that understands all these limitations and makes concrete plans to offset them by a full range of political activity and struggle outside the electoral arena can sometimes use that arena for good purpose. This will be particularly true in the period directly ahead, when most people still focus their attention in that direction. Many people do not take ideas seriously until they are put forward in the electoral arena. If one uses it imaginatively, the electoral arena gives an opportunity to speak to many people never reached before. It is crucial that a revolutionary movement be structured in such a way that people who are reached through electoral activity are given an opportunity to move into discussion groups and people's councils immediately—that the electoral arena be used as a place of recruitment, rather than as the main focus. But this does not mean being halfhearted about electoral activity. On the contrary, one should integrate this activity into the life of the movement, constantly discussing its limitations, but at the same time using creativity and imagination to maximize its usefulness.

The initiative process is often a better method than running candidates. Initiatives focus attention on issues rather than persons. As such, they give people a taste of what elections will be like after the revolution, when the people will decide directly on most important issues themselves, rather than electing candidates with whose views on some matters they agree and on others they disagree. Of course, at present candidates receive much attention, and so for some time in the future it will still be relevant to run them, particularly in federal elections where no initiative procedure yet exists. The danger is that the candidates are seen as the full embodiment of the movement, which shifts attention away from understanding that it is ordinary human beings and not superstars who make history. Still, a candidate who is sensitive to this concern can demystify the electoral arena and use it as a way of getting people together to take power for themselves.

The formation and building of a mass Socialist party that can combine all these different functions—from running candidates at the local and national levels and sponsoring initiatives to coordinating local organizing activities and sponsoring the formation of people's councils, to initiating rank-and-file caucuses and spearheading the development of a new labor movement, to organizing regional and national educational and media outlets, to promoting confrontations and demonstrations that help clarify for people the nature of the system and how to fight it—is one of the most pressing tasks on the agenda for anyone who believes in serious social change in America. If such a party could be organized within the next few years, it could in ten years put socialism on the agenda in America. By that, I do not mean that the socialist revolution would be fought and won in the next ten years, but rather that the question of socialism would be the major political issue in America and the major topic of debate, and people would constantly be in a position to support demonstrations, candidates, initiatives, and programs of action that they could clearly see as being part of the struggle to build socialism. Socialism could be as central in the American political consciousness of the late 1970s and early 1980s as the war in Vietnam, taxes, busing, and law and order are right now.

This can happen only if a clear national force exists that is organized, coherent, and explicitly oriented toward putting socialism on the agenda. Beyond all else, it must be a political force, contending for political power around its own program. *Power* is the key word—it is not sufficient for an organization to emerge that is for socialism; that organization must have a strategy for taking power and must contend for power. Some people think that much mass education must be done before the organization orients itself toward power. But the education cannot and will not happen first, because very few will be listening. Most working people do not want to be lectured, figuratively or literally. By the time they are willing to listen to the Left, they know that something is wrong in their lives. What they want to know, more than anything else, is how to move, what to do, what can be changed. Political education is certainly not unimportant—on the contrary, it is crucial. But a leftist organization must find a way to incorporate this education in a program for change that makes sense. Bourgeois hegemony will be broken only by a Left that offers a real alternative and helps people find ways to achieve power for themselves in the political and economic arenas.

In this sense, it must be understood that it is not stupid for working

261

people to work inside the Democratic party. Although the Democratic party will never provide a mechanism for serious change, it is better to have one-tenth of a pie than no pie at all. So until the Left can put at least some alternative into the field—a Socialist party that takes the struggle for political power seriously at every level—most working people are not going to take the Left very seriously either. One caution: I do not mean that the sole or even primary focus has to be electoral activity, though this *must* be included and taken very seriously. The word "party" is confusing because we have only two kinds of models: the Democratic and Republican parties on the one hand, and the Communist party on the other. We do not need a reduplication of either model. Rather, we need a party that combines a nonelectoral focus with electoral work, that really supports struggle in every arena, that is tough, honest, intelligent, *democratic,* and obviously and openly concerned for the needs of the people.

Everyone on the Left is willing to give lip service to the development of such a party, but few are willing to attempt to build it. Some people are waiting for a new Trotsky or Lenin to come around who will be universally recognized as having the leadership skills necessary for such an undertaking. The Left must stop hoping for some deus ex machina—it has only itself, and the new Lenins and Trotskys will be *formed* only in the process of building a real revolutionary struggle, rather than being clearly recognizable from the start. Other people believe that the party will emerge spontaneously from below—for people to try to form it consciously is "undemocratic." This is nonsense—the categories do not make sense, because there is only a "below" in the Left these days. The second a person has an idea and tries to organize around it, he or she becomes "top-down." Under these circumstances, the only nonelitist thing one can do is nothing. This is pure stupidity. Another scenario sees a party gradually emerging from local organizing projects. Unfortunately, precisely because there is no national Left force, many of these local organizing projects are quick to fall apart. Their members feel isolated and despairing. And, if they are addressing basic problems, the people they attempt to organize quickly come up with the question, "Well, you tell me that these problems are basic to the capitalist system and require structural change. But where is the political force on a national level that can bring about the necessary changes? Why shouldn't I align with the McGoverns and Humphreys and Kennedys—at least they have a plan for getting power that seems to make sense, whereas you are just a group of isolated agitators." The argument is so convincing that most of these projects have fallen apart and their organizers now support liberal Democrats. Those that have survived have often done so by narrowing their concerns in such a way that the issues they deal with can be solved on the local level, i.e., dealing only with issues that do not strike at anything critical to the capitalist system. Furthermore, waiting for these local projects to initiate a national party has another difficulty: very little in the organizers' experience prepares them to think in terms of national strategies. The kind of organization they would be likely to found would have the same decentralist and centrifugal tendencies that caused early SDS so many problems: it would be more of a communications network than a force that could develop a unified national strategy. Communication is good, but we need something broader, something that can not only communicate what is now happening, but can also generate much that is new and provide a place for people who are not organizers but working people who cannot spend their full time doing political work but who *do* want to build socialism in America. That kind of party will have to be consciously formed—it will never appear by itself.

One of the worst problems faced by the New Left was the ego-tripping and pettiness and personal attacks that made the Left a very unpleasant place to be. To some extent, this was inevitable in capitalist society, where everyone is socialized to think of himself first, and in a movement that came primarily out of the universities, where students are taught to compete and the whole object is to get oneself a high-paying job. But the special excesses of the New Left can only be understood in terms of another factor: most people did not believe they were doing anything important in their New Left organizations. To some extent, this was a misunderstanding of politics: the antiwar demonstrations did not end the war, but they *did* put very serious constraints on the war policies that could be pursued. It was only when internal dissension and cooptation into the McGovern campaign had so disorganized the antiwar movement that it could no longer organize massive and sustained demonstrations that President Nixon felt he had the political power to do something that was militarily possible ever since 1965: to mine the port of Haiphong and engage in "no-restraint" genocidal bombing of the North. But to some extent the New Left had a point: as long as its base was primarily students, and not the working class, everyone knew that the talk about "revolution" was so much metaphor.

The obvious way to deal with this problem was for the New Left to change its orientation and develop programs and styles of organizing that would speak to the interests and needs of working people. Ironically, it totally misunderstood its problem and adopted a solution that compounded it. It took the internal ego-tripping, bad "vibes," endless political debates on trivia, and lack of human solidarity in its organizations as the root of the problem instead of its symptom. And, rather than address the real

263

problems facing most working people in America today, it focused its attention on rooting out these symptoms. Small-group discussions, internal soul-searching, mutual recriminations for being too elitist, focus on its own organizational forms—all these replaced development of any serious program or struggle for power. In the name of antielitism and good social relations between people working together, the Left became even more elitist, refusing to address in any serious way the problems facing most working people in America.

A new party will avoid these problems only if it starts by implementing programs and struggles that are relevant to the needs of working people in America. In that way, a different kind of person will be recruited to the organization, one whose life experience makes him a bit more desperate for social change and hence a bit less self-indulgent and less inclined to think he has endless time to get his head straight. Further, those remnants of the New Left who will be recruited will understand the need to curb their tendencies toward mutual suspicion and recrimination if they see that the party is really doing something. That this is possible can be seen from the fact that so few New Leftists are willing to criticize Ralph Nader publicly, despite the elitist form of his operation, because they sense that he is confronting the corporations and educating people in a real way, and they are not. If we had a party that did all the things—and more—that Nader has begun to do, and at the same time was democratically structured instead of really top-down like Nader's operation, and if that party were really saying things that spoke to the needs of the American people, I believe it would be possible to recruit from among previous New Lefters without fear that they would simply re-create the climate of antileadership, antistructure, anti-intellectualism, and inwardness that has so destroyed everything in which they have been involved. Ralph Nader, of course, is not our model in terms of strategy—we do not want people to become accustomed to waiting on lawsuits and depending on the press to cover their press conferences. We want to mobilize working people so that they themselves are the leadership and their *struggles* are the means of obtaining power.

If all this seems visionary, it should not and cannot be. History does not stand still while the Left gets itself together. The New Left reached millions of people in the 1960s and then abandoned them, leaving them without any sense of direction. But shortly those people will be reabsorbed into the mainstream of capitalist life. Many people who work for McGovern in 1972 do so even though they would have preferred to work on a strategy designed by the Left, had there been one. These same people will be less and less open to the Left if no new political force emerges. The political crisis will deepen—it is bound to. But if there is no viable Left strategy, people will have to look elsewhere. And they will. The people who were temporarily exposed to radical ideas in the 1960s at the height of the antiwar movement will be lost to liberalism. And many working people, hearing the only serious criticism of this society coming from the Right, will be much attracted to the George Wallaces. "Hearing" here is critical: the Left may have the best analyses in the world, published in monthly journals and uttered by a few sect groups and isolated organizing projects and by remnants of a student movement. But it will not be *heard* by working people until there is a political presence, both in electoral form through candidates and initiatives, and in the form of a unified and developed alternative program for the unions at the rank-and-file caucus and workers' council levels. Even with a party, nationally organized and coherent in strategy, we will be facing the overwhelming problem of misrepresentation by the media, but without the national organization contending for power, there is not a chance that people will take any kind of leftist activity seriously.

THE POSITIVE APPROACH

Without in any way deemphasizing our outrage at the ways in which capitalist society oppresses blacks, Third Worlders, women, workers, and almost everyone else, we should be careful to devise strategies that accentuate the fact that our revolution is not simply negation. People have a right to feel that the political movement speaking to them does not negate everything about themselves and their past. Too often the movement of the 1960s seemed to be attacking the American people as a whole. This is stupid tactically and shows a wrong understanding of American society. Most people have never been called upon to ratify America's racist, sexist, imperialist, and exploitative structures, and cannot be held accountable for their existence. It is a difficult struggle to overcome the pervasive indoctrination all of us receive in this society, and those who have managed to do so should not treat those who have not as enemies or as worthless.

What's more, the history of the American working class is full of important struggles by men and women who at great personal risk resisted the capitalist order. The history of resistance and opposition is not taught in school, but it should play an important role in the development of a radical self-consciousness. The American people do not have to be ashamed of their past, but only of the past of their ruling class and those who controlled the government and manipulated the media. We can use

265

the bicentennial celebration of the American Declaration of Independence in 1976 to raise important questions about American history and to identify with its progressive side. But we must be careful to combat its reactionary side: the notions that America is an exception, that America is better than other countries, that America is "worth fighting for," etc. We have to demystify the concept of "America" by continually raising the difference between those who rule America and those who work in America and live here, but who would be much better off with a New American Revolution that overthrew the capitalist order. The attempt to use American symbols against the capitalists can be very creative and exciting, but it must eschew a terrible danger: legitimating the idea that there is one homogenous "America" with a common set of interests. We are certain to hear many liberal politicians running for office in 1976 on a platform of a "New American Revolution" and using the old Kennedy-style rhetoric about "getting this country moving again." But we are unlikely to hear many of them calling for ownership and control of the economy by the people and the replacement of the ruling class by a genuine democracy on the economic and political level. Even worse, the 1976 bicentennial is likely to be used to stir up "patriotic" feelings that can be manipulated to justify support for governmental policies that could not earn support on any other grounds. This is particularly dangerous in the period ahead because there will be a tendency for a section of the ruling class to move toward greater economic and political nationalism as a response to the growth of Germany and Japan. So any radical approach to the American tradition must clearly attack the kind of patriotism that has always been a cover for war and oppression.

CONCLUSION

There is a limit on the amount of serious discussion of tactics and strategy that can take place in abstraction from the real situation in which revolutionaries will find themselves. Most of what has been said in this chapter follows from our basic commitment to democracy. We want to build a society in which the people have power, and we know that can happen only in a democratic manner, with the people themselves creating the new society. Our strategy flows from this commitment and is geared to developing both a consciousness and the conditions that will make it possible for people to join in the struggle democratically to create a new socialist democracy.

Much of this discussion has centered on an isolated American move-

266

ment—yet there is reason to believe that the revolutionary struggle in America may reach a crescendo because the European or Japanese working class are in struggle. The struggle is worldwide, and one immediate task of the revolutionary movement in America is to establish organizational links with working-class movements in Europe and Japan so that a worldwide strategy can be devised in response to the growing tendency toward intracapitalist rivalry.

With all the yelping about internationalism that some people on the Left have done in the past few years, in practice all that it has amounted to has been passing resolutions in support of the PRG or carrying Viet Cong flags to demonstrations. A serious revolutionary movement would organize international conferences of the nonsectarian revolutionary movements in all the advanced industrial societies, coupled with an ongoing exchange of information about economic developments and organizing experiences, as an immediate and necessary prelude to the development of a worldwide strategy for struggle.

We do not pretend to be prophets; as social scientists our job is to study the social situation scientifically, understanding which forces created it and which are likely to change it, and then to advance those tendencies and take those actions most likely to produce a movement and objective situations from which socialism can emerge.

7
Violence

CAN THE American Revolution occur without violence? This is a crucial question, which worries most socialists. And for good reason. We detest violence. In fact, part of the reason for the revolution is to decrease the amount of violence in the world. More particularly, many of us who are currently deeply involved in revolutionary activity suspect that violence will claim our own lives and the lives of those we love. Any way that violence can be avoided and our mission still accomplished will be sought out and explored.

But when the question of violence is addressed to the Left, it is only to distort reality. The real question must be asked of the rulers of this country: will *they* allow their system of unequal power and wealth to be overthrown without violence? This is an empirical question, and part of the answer is already in: the rulers constantly use violence to maintain their social order, and that social order reeks with violence. Let us explore this question a bit more carefully.

The fact that American capitalism has promoted the use of one word— "violence"—to apply to such different phenomena as the torture of North Vietnamese prisoners by American soldiers and the throwing of a rock through the window of a branch of the Bank of America shows how contorted language can become. Only in a capitalist society could we have a language that can see no difference between human pain and the alleged right to property. The revolution rejects this identification: violence must be understood as the causing of unnecessary pain to human beings.[1] Be-

[1] We want to distinguish, however, between two types of "necessity." Some pain will be necessary to achieve people's goals for themselves, and they will voluntarily undergo the pain for that purpose. For example, if they allow doctors to cause pain to them in order to cure them of some malady, we would not say that the doctors

cause we view human suffering as a primary concern, we see pain inflicted on human beings and destruction of material objects that cannot suffer pain as entirely different. Of course, there can be a connection between the destruction of property and the creation of human pain, and it must have been this connection that originally provided the cover under which violence became redefined to include property. For instance, if you use herbicides against the crops of Vietnamese peasants and bomb their homes you have deprived them of their means of survival, and hence you are the cause of the physical pain they will soon suffer. It might then be reasonably argued that the meaning of "violence" should extend to include destruction of that property the absence of which will immediately lead to the creation of unnecessary human pain. It is with this kind of violence that I am concerned, and it is this kind of violence that the revolution aims to reduce or eliminate, by destroying the most violent social system ever known to man.

Capitalism is not just violent when it feels itself threatened, as in the war in Vietnam. It is violent in its *normal* operations. And this institutionalized violence is usually overlooked by people who ask revolutionaries why they introduce violence into politics. The fact is that violence of a greater magnitude than could ever be perpetrated by the revolutionary already exists as an integral part of American capitalism.

Consider the domestic violence perpetrated by the capitalist system. In the United States, close to 12 million people suffer from malnutrition and are on the verge of starvation. But the government pays people not to grow food so that there will not be a surplus that would adversely affect prices on the market. That is violence—and the people who participate in that decision have caused violence. The capitalist economic system creates classes of people whose members do not have enough money to provide themselves with adequate food, housing, and health care. In San Francisco recently it was reported that the infant mortality rate among blacks was three times that among whites. That is violence—and all who help to sustain American racism, from the government to the bosses to the unions, help to maintain that violence. When abortion is illegal and women are forced to seek help from unskilled practitioners, all of them suffer pain,

---

had committed violent acts. On the other hand, pain may be inflicted without the consent of the people involved, for the sake of achieving some social good that they may or may not accept. In this case, one might want to argue that pain was still "necessary" because there was no other way to achieve the desired and desirable goal. But it would add greater clarity if we agreed to call this "violence," and then simply added that there are going to be some cases in which we will want to say that violence is justified, rather than sophistically arguing that it is not violence at all.

many of them are permanently injured, and some of them die. That is violence. When auto manufacturers resist improvements that could make cars safer because it might decrease their profits, they cause violence. And when they use their considerable influence and money to oppose the funding of mass transportation that would cut pollution and make travel safer—again because it would cut into their profits—they are violent. When food manufacturers use chemicals whose long-term effects on human health have not yet been tested and which later turn out to be deleterious, they are violent. When state coverage of health programs is reduced and people are thrown out of hospitals or kept from seeking medical help because they do not have enough money, the people who supported these cuts are acting violently. When newspapers refuse to print statements by black radicals about the actual conditions of ghetto life, suggesting instead that there is something strange and deplorable about black people who follow revolutionary leadership, they help create a white backlash that often manifests itself in violence. Nor am I engaging here in debaters' tricks—these are all legitimate instances of the violence embedded in the normal functioning of American capitalism. And the fact that it is never talked about is a testimony to the complete success of the rulers in so mystifying their system that many people do not even perceive themselves as the victims of violence. The newspapers, the media, the schools, all make consideration of this sort of question impossible. Every newsman asks the Left, "But what about violence?" But no newsman has ever asked the President, "Do you believe it is right to use violence in pursuit of your foreign policy aims—as you have done in Vietnam— or in pursuit of your domestic aims—as you are doing in raising unemployment in order to deal with inflation, thereby ensuring that more people will be unable to afford adequate health care, housing, food, etc.?"

Although the internal violence of the system is tremendous, it does not compare with the violence that capitalism creates around the world. In the chapter on imperialism we discussed the ways this violence works: through preventing countries to industrialize, or forcing them to industrialize only in accord with the needs of American capitalism and extracting from them a great deal of wealth, particularly in the form of raw materials. But we have not adequately stressed the meaning of this whole system for the average peasant in India, Bolivia, or Ghana. The wealth extracted by General Electric, Standard Oil, the Bank of America, United Fruit, or any other imperialist venture is wealth that could have been used to feed, clothe, house, and give medical care to the hundreds of millions of people who live in those countries. Nor can this violence be measured

270

simply by the additional money the colonial people would have if the imperialists did not take it from them. Equally important is the social system the imperialists have to sustain in the exploited country in order to ensure a government that permits them to continue their exploitative relations at the same high level of profit. These social systems would be overturned very quickly if they were not sustained by American economic and military aid—and these social systems bring incredible suffering to the people who must live under them. Then, you may ask, why don't these people rebel? They do, all the time. American weapons and, as in Vietnam or the Dominican Republic, American troops put these rebellions down. Every day, tens of millions of people are hungry who need not be, get no medical care when it could have been available, have inadequate housing and clothing—all directly as a result of the American economic system. Nor should we abstract this system—for its operations are manned by human beings who every day make concrete choices which help to sustain it. The pleasant gentleman on the Long Island Railroad reading his *Wall Street Journal* or the quiet technician working in Palo Alto or on Route 128 in Massachusetts, the Wall Street banker or the assistant secretary of state or agriculture or defense, the professor of political science who runs the institute on Latin America or the liberal senator—all participate daily in making decisions that sustain the daily violence upon which this system rests. If it was right to try Eichmann and other officials of the Nazi regime for crimes against humanity, even though they did not personally kill anyone, then surely the violent men who surround us, with their gentle manners and sweet smiles and well-manicured lawns and all the rest of the petty concealments that hide a life of "honorable" crime, should be tried for their crimes by the peoples of the world. It is on practical, not moral, grounds that we think such trials should not take place.

Until now we have discussed only institutionalized violence—the violence that occurs when the system is working smoothly and no one is questioning it. But the system has an army and police forces to deal with the situation when people no longer accept their exploitation. The police use violence all the time against people who, having been deprived by the system of any way to achieve what they need, resort to stealing or other illegal means to get money. Violence is constantly used in defense of property, because the people who control the government and make the laws believe that property is more important than human life, or, more to the point, that *their* property and the property of the people they represent is more important than human life. Violence is constantly used to enforce the authority of the rulers—hence they will forcefully imprison people for marijuana use because these people have challenged the authority of the rulers by flaunting one of their irrational rules.

Politically, violence is the key to the system's ability to maintain itself. Violence is used against strikers to keep them in line, against political demonstrators to frighten them, and against revolutionaries to suppress them. This violence takes two forms: beatings and murder and jailings. Jailing people is a form of violence: it works because people know that if they resist arrest, guns and clubs will be used against them. Behind the majesty of the courts stands the violence of the police and the jails, and very few people would pay much attention to a legal system so obviously biased in favor of maintaining the established order if that legal system did not have guns and clubs to enforce its decisions. The jails are filled with people who, in a just political system, would be free—people who were faced with the choice of slowly being destroyed by the system or taking a risk and doing something that exposed them to the destruction imposed by the jails. The killings at Kent State, Jackson State, People's Park, and in countless ghetto uprisings, the systematic assassination of leaders of the Black Panther party, the jailing and beating of political protestors—all must be added to the calculus of the ways in which this society is violent.

The police force operates under certain restraints: it cannot bomb a campus, for fear it might also hit the professors and students from ruling-class families. But no such restrictions exist on the counterinsurgency operations engaged in worldwide by the military in order to suppress people who want to run their own country for their own benefit. So the military and the CIA can proudly display the remains of a Che Guevara or some other rebel leader—after all, that's what CIA and military business is all about. Consider the Vietnam war—it is already responsible for the death of over a million civilians, the wounding of millions more, and the forcible removal from their land of many millions more. Professor Samuel Huntington of Harvard University recommends the best way to win the war: force the Vietnamese into the large cities and bomb the countryside until the bomb craters are running with the blood of Southeast Asians. In 1972, President Nixon began full-scale bombings of the cities of North Vietnam, coupled with minings of harbors and bombings of dikes. Every power plant, every bridge, every factory was to be leveled. Special antipersonnel bombs were introduced with pellets that had been designed so that when they entered a human body they could not be traced by X ray. In 1972, mass murder and destruction was the public policy of the United States. And then, even the liberals would turn around and focus more attention on some outraged youth who had smashed a window in exasperated protest, rather than deal with the massive horror created by American capitalism. When the war ends people will say, "Oh, that was all in the past." But a system that causes that kind of suffering is not in the past until fundamental changes are made that make such behavior unnecessary in the future. The only effective change would be the elimination of the economic structure that requires the exploitation of the peoples of the world. Until the overthrow of capitalism the American capitalist system will use its military power to keep people from struggling for their independence. It will prefer, of course, to have armies from dependent countries fight the American battle for America, since this will cause fewer internal political tensions. But it will not cause a decrease in violence, only a change in the victims of that violence. The whole strategy of Vietnamization and the attempt to create a multinational army in Latin America are part of this clever device to get Third Worlders to fight Third Worlders, in support of local elites that could not on their own resist popular forces within their countries.

The question of violence is being answered for us every day by the ruling class. Will they allow us to revolutionize the world nonviolently? Absolutely not. On the contrary, they will fight to the last drop of *our* blood and the blood of every mercenary they can buy or coerce.

Revolutionary violence must be understood in this context. The aim of revolutionary violence is completely defensive: to defend people from the violence inherent in the capitalist system and the violence unleashed against those who attempt to change it. It is crucial to understand that when a revolutionary picks up a gun he is responding to the violence that already exists in the system. The aim of revolutionary violence is always to eliminate the total amount of violence that exists in the world by creating a social system that no longer depends on exploitation, underdevelopment, sexism, racism, and powerlessness.

But isn't there a paradox in this position? Is not the revolutionary introducing more violence into the world? The United States would be perfectly happy with a Pax Americana: if everyone quietly accepted American control over most of the world, there would be less violence. When the Viet Cong picked up their guns they were raising the level of violence. This argument holds true for the short run, but the revolutionary is, by definition, someone who stands back and looks at the long run, and realizes that he must be willing to sacrifice his life in the short run for the sake of a better world in the long run. Every year imperialism imposes, let us say, 13 units of violence on my country (or an American revolutionary might say that he sees his country imposing, say, 143 units of violence across the world) in the course of its normal functioning. Now, for the course of the next four years we will try to make a revolution, say, and we know that the imperialists can double the level of violence by adding overt violence to their covert violence. But when, after four years the revolution succeeds, the level of violence will decrease to two units of violence (what remains being the legacy of underdevelopment which will be eliminated after twenty more years of internal economic progress). So, in the long run revolutionary action will significantly decrease the total amount of violence. Obviously, if this were just a fantasy, it would not justify violence. But one need look only at China, where the total level of violence has dropped astoundingly over the past twenty years, and then at India, where wide-scale starvation is still accepted as a fact of life in a social system that cannot break its ties with imperialism.

Sometimes it is argued that the use of violence as a means will inevitably create a violent society, because once people get used to violence as part of their life, they start to re-create it. But there is no reason to believe this is true. Once the institutions that create violence have been undermined, the continuation of violence is highly unlikely. "Sure," one might argue, "but once people become involved in violence, they will never set up institutions that will undercut it. Look at the Soviet Union: it started out with all sorts of good intentions, but because of its violent start the men who formed its institutions merely prepared the way for violence in a different form." This argument, however, is both abstract and ahistorical. The Bolsheviks took power in a virtually bloodless coup, and their first act was to end the war and bring the troops home, thus significantly decreasing the level of violence. Violence became a significant factor again only after the civil war started, and in that case it was fostered by the invasion of troops from the United States, Britain, and France. During the civil war institutions emerged which did in fact create the possibility of later violence, but it was the concrete circumstances of the world, particularly the emergence of hostile forces committed to defeating the revolution, which were primarily responsible for pushing the Soviet Union in the bad direction it finally went. To generalize from that situation to all situations misses the point. Consider Cuba. Cuba's revolution was brought about by a violent struggle, but the general level of violence in Cuba has markedly decreased since the revolution and there is much less needless suffering in Cuba today than there was before the revolution. Perhaps this will change as the economic pressures become greater and the maneuvers of the U.S. capitalists to destroy Cuba become more ruthless. In dealing with this issue, the specific circumstances, not some abstract theory, are crucial, and in the case of the American revolution, at least one factor will be very different. The United States is the center of the imperialist system; its machinations have been responsible for increasing the level of violence in the revolutions that have occurred in other countries. When that center itself becomes the target, no outside forces will come in and raise the general level of violence. On the contrary, revolution in America would set up a series of events that would lead to revolution all around the world. The collapse of the American economy attendant on wide-scale struggle here would create international havoc and thus the conditions for significant struggle in all of the advanced industrial societies, where revolutionary forces would find it easy to seize the moment. At the same time, the lack of U.S. military support would cause many dictatorships and colonial regimes to topple. The international revolutionary ferment would undoubtedly spread to Eastern Europe, and the Soviet Union, far from being able to come to the aid of the ruling class in America, would ultimately be involved in internal revolutionary struggle as well. So a violent revolution in the United States might well lead to the elimination of violent social structures all over the world.

From the international perspective, then, we can see that the American revolution would be a great landmark for all humanity. Indeed, even if the revolution was not a success internally, it would be a great boon to mankind by causing the United States to withdraw its military from foreign countries in order to fight at home, and by causing economic chaos. Civil war and chaos might bring a much higher level of violence to the people of the United States. But they would reduce the total amount of violence in the world by eliminating the power of the major source of exploitation and by weakening the international capitalist system. The United States is not the only evil country in the world, and if an unsuccessful American revolution simply transferred the role of chief exploiter to Japan, Germany, or Russia, it would not be worth it. But such a hypothesis ignores the actual economic and political relationships that exist in the world, which make it almost inevitable that severe economic crises in the United States would be translated into severe economic and political crises elsewhere.

Nothing that American revolutionaries can do to create chaos and civil war would not simultaneously create the conditions for revolution. The reason is simple: this system runs because people want it to run. As long as most people are ideological prisoners of the system, no meaningful chaos could be created. Bombings and assassinations could cause great paranoia, and a black rebellion could cause bloody fighting—but the system could still manage to function, if most people remained loyal to it.

A much higher degree of repression in this country is possible without in any way abandoning the empire. The real danger to the system comes when it can no longer count on a majority of its people to give it active or passive support. At that time real chaos is a possibility—but so is revolutionary seizure of power. So why direct one's work toward something no one really wants—internal chaos—when the same amount of energy directed toward building a revolutionary movement could bring about something we *do* want? Furthermore, even though chaos is a possibility, once a majority of people are on the side of the revolution, it is a very abstract possibility. We are committed to building democratic revolutionary organizations that reflect the will of the membership; if a majority aligns itself with us, it will mean that they have chosen not chaos but revolutionary struggle.

. There is no guarantee that the rulers of this country will not opt for chaos sooner than for revolution, hoping that people will get so sick of the chaos they will forget what they were fighting for and accept any force that promises to reestablish order. But it is highly unlikely that any group of people who have moved as far as revolutionary struggle would then allow themselves to be deflected from their goal. We must have faith in the humanity and intelligence of people: before they engage in struggle they will think things through, they will understand the risks and why they should be taken. No one is going to trick or manipulate millions of people into revolutionary struggle, because people who have been manipulated will simply back out and leave their manipulative leaders without anyone to support them. Revolutions are not like getting on the wrong train— people can back out of a revolution whenever they become unsure of what they are doing and why. That is why opportunism is always wrong: it is, finally, self-defeating. No one will ever be manipulated into struggling for chaos if they really want a revolution.

But we are far from the day when a majority of the people will want a revolution. There is every good reason to think that a revolution will not occur in this country before fifteen or twenty years, and it may be as far as thirty years away. There is no way to predict these things in the abstract—much depends on the rate of success of other struggles around the world. Even more depends on how successful the revolutionary movement is in this country in providing intelligent and courageous leadership. In the immediate period ahead the primary job is to change people's consciousness, *not* to engage in armed struggle.

I contend that very few acts are right in themselves, and that it is always crucial to ask how a particular militant act advances revolutionary consciousness and for whom. The criteria for assessing any form of militant action must be whether it will be understandable to the relevant communities and whether it will make those who do not understand react in a way that seriously impedes the revolutionary development of those who do.

Underlying these criteria is the assumption that one always aims to increase the number of "relevant communities" wherever revolutionary consciousness is being advanced. Nor is it enough to argue that relevant communities could be made to understand a militant action; the action can be justified only when reasonable steps are taken to ensure that it will be understood. It will often be impossible to know in advance exactly how a particular action will be distorted by the media. This should never be used as an excuse for avoiding struggle, but reasonable assessments should be made, and one should always be sensitive to the understandability criterion. "Understandability" also provides a guide for terrorist activity. For instance, most Weatherman trashing activity (particularly trashing car windows parked along the street—something Weatherman did during its "Days of Rage") clearly should be avoided. On the other hand, one might well criticize those involved in People's Park for not taking more definitive action against the oppressors when the whole community saw itself as resisting an occupying army. "Understandability" does not mean comprehensibility to the press or the bourgeoisie. We must avoid the ruling-class notion of one undifferentiated community, with similar sets of needs and interests. But we must make our actions understandable to potential allies in the struggle to overthrow capitalism. The criteria proposed will require subtle and intelligent application, not mechanical formulas. We will have to study the period carefully, its potentialities and its problems, before deciding what kind of tactics will be appropriate. One can defend revolutionary violence in the abstract without feeling that it is appropriate at any particular moment in the struggle.

It is my assessment of the present period, that the revolutionary movement should rely primarily on a strategy of non-violence probably at least for the next ten years. Such a strategy will undercut the capitalists' ability to confuse people by pointing to a few broken windows or a few bomb explosions. Although it is quite true that the facts should speak for themselves—compare the destruction of some windows with the destruction caused in Vietnam by a single hour of bombing—it is nevertheless true that people are confused on this topic. Since violence in the period ahead cannot possibly be used effectively enough to stop the imperialists, it would be better to avoid it altogether. Or, when it is used, it should be made clear that it is used in self-defense, as, for example, in defense of the ghetto from invading police. Nonviolent action can help to pull the wool away from many people's eyes.

A focus on nonviolence in the movement would do much to overcome the rather sick tendency to glorify armed struggle and the gun that characterizes some factions. It is quite true that eventually we must resort to armed struggle and self-defensive violence, because it will be the only way to act in solidarity with our brothers and sisters around the world and to create a new American society. But this violence will be accompanied by great sadness. The revolutionary hates violence and hates to see innocent people killed. It is precisely out of this hatred of violence that the revolutionary is willing to take great personal risk so that violence can be permanently eliminated or vastly reduced. The revolutionary must always be infused with love and respect for human life, and, all other things being equal, should always opt for the path that causes the least amount of hurt to other human beings. It is this very love for human life that forces a revolutionary to resort to self-defensive (i.e., revolutionary) violence. A tactical use of nonviolence might help put these issues in perspective again.

But nonviolence does not mean passivity. Too often in the past few years the pacifists have been passivists as well. They have had a few militant spokesmen, like Dave Dellinger, but they rarely acted as a militant force. This has tended to discredit the whole notion of nonviolence. Nonviolence should be adopted by the movement for revolutionary change as a tactic. But that does not mean the revolutionary movement should take its political leadership from professional pacifists. Nonviolence must be used militarily, to clog up the operations of the war machine, to challenge the functioning of government, war factories, welfare bureaucracies, universities, polluters, etc. The focus must be on action, but with the clear announcement that it is intended as nonviolent action. Such action must also be distinguished from the moral witnessing in which principled pacifists have been involved. It is not my intention to suggest *individual* acts of heroism or submission to arrest as a proof of strong feelings. Politically, these tactics are often stupid: the risk of jail sentences is seldom worth the publicity the action may create. Rather, mass actions should be planned which involve mobile tactics and which aim both to disrupt nonviolently and also to avoid arrest if possible. It is not my intent to lay down a formula applicable to every situation, even for the immediate future, but to advance arguments for publicly stating our nonviolent position when we involve ourselves in demonstrations over the next few years.

It would be both dishonest and unwise to pretend that we are nonviolent in principle. On the contrary, at every possible moment the arguments about violence should be taken on and defeated. We must carefully explain to people the nature of this society and its violence, and why the rulers will probably make violence inevitable for us just as they have made it a necessity for peoples of the Third World. People must be prepared for the fact that the ruling class has it in its power to make the revolution in this country bloody and violent. And they must learn that we do not welcome violence and that the only way to avoid violence is for enough people to move decisively to the side of the revolution. The rulers must come to understand that if there is to be a sea of blood, it will be made of their blood as well. The one thing that can make the American revolution *less violent* is the clear and public determination of a majority of people to defend that revolution with violence.

We must carefully avoid any tendency to confuse tactical nonviolence with a new principle of nonviolence. We must expose the immorality of the nonviolence principle. In a world in which there was good reason to believe that nonviolence would move the oppressor to stop oppressing, there would be good reason for nonviolence. But in this world, nonviolence simply guarantees that the oppressor can continue to oppress without challenge, because when you seem to be effective in your challenge the oppressor can simply have you wiped out. And although it may be moral to choose personal destruction rather than cause violence to another, it is clearly immoral to make that choice for someone else. The American movement cannot turn the other cheek for the Vietnamese. An approach that allows violence to continue in order to preserve one's personal morality is immoral.

The evidence of our everyday experience and of recent history make it irrational to believe that the ruling class will give up its power without a fight. Right now, it is murdering tens of thousands of Southeast Asians every month, without the slightest concern. And it has never had much hesitancy in using guns against unarmed civilians. It will always be able to justify its use of force to at least that part of the population that still retains its racism and/or sexism and/or national chauvinism, and that will be all it needs to keep control. In fact, a movement which makes it clear that it will never rely on violence in self-defense will never become a mass movement unless it seems so clearly reformist that no one believes the state will ever feel threatened enough to use violence against it. When the majority of the people are on the side of the revolution, they will never agree to sit quietly while ruling-class guns fire on them. Revolutionary suicide is not a program through which one can build a mass movement.

Many people misunderstand the historical example of Gandhi. Gandhi did not win a social revolution; there was no social transformation in India that led to the abolition of a ruling class. The Indians won home rule, with a consequent strengthening of the Indian bourgeoisie. Nor was that primarily the result of Gandhi's actions; rather, it was the result of the devastation English capitalism suffered during the Second World War. England's empire was crumbling and the United States was stepping in to pick up the pieces, and to replace colonialism with a more sophisticated neocolonialism. Gandhi played an important role in accelerating the process in India, but he was dealing with a declining imperialist power and his program in no way expropriated the expropriators. The revolution is yet to occur in India, and Gandhi may have actually helped to sustain a system of domination by making the national question predominate over the class question.

The whole question of violence must be faced head-on, particularly because so many people who claim to be against violence make that statement only when they do not support its aims. I have met many Irish people who condemn movement tactics because of violence (by which they refer to breaking windows or blowing up a bathroom in the Capitol) but support Bernadette Devlin and the Irish fight for freedom in England; I have met many Jews who criticize the movement on similar grounds but who send money used to buy guns for the Israelis; I have met many workers ready to act violently against scabs when they are striking. The real issue is whether the people support the ends you propose—if they do, the violence issue begins to recede dramatically. Of course, insofar as movement people begin to talk as if their *end* is armed struggle, they are not likely to build much popular support. In and for itself, violence is abhorrent. The context makes it necessary—never desirable.

Am I suggesting that the end justifies the means? Yes, with some important qualifications. The end must itself be justified. The means must in fact be means to that end. The means must create the least possible amount of evil consistent with the achievement of the ends, and that evil must be in total less than the evil that would have existed if the end had not been achieved. "Does this mean that the revolutionary is committed to an objective ethics by which ends can be judged?" Absolutely yes. The revolutionary is firmly committed to the notion that it is better for human beings to be happy than to suffer, and better for them to realize their human potentialities than for them to be stunted and prevented from realizing themselves. The revolutionary is firmly committed to this idea, not merely as a subjective preference, but as an objective moral truth.

Let me reiterate. The means *must* be a means to the justified end. One could never justify lobotomy as a means to human self-realization. In fact, it leads to the opposite. So it is crucial to find out if a particular path does in fact lead to the desired end. This is an empirical question, usually, and not a philosophical one. Since we cannot always have perfect knowledge of causal relations in the social and political spheres, we will have to follow the course most likely, in light of what we know, to lead to human fulfillment. It is because a socialist revolution is the precondition for human self-realization that it is justified and that anything that is in fact a means to that revolution will be justified. "Now," one might object, "does that mean that one can go about randomly murdering people and oppressing one's followers in the name of the revolution?" No! None of this would lead to the socialist revolution. If in building the revolution people transformed themselves in ways which made them more hateful and less sensitive they would end up not building the socialist revolution at all, but something different. Why, then, does this not apply to violence as a whole? Because violence does not destroy the possibility of building a new order when people understand why they must engage in it; how objectively detestable it is; and what in the specific circumstances necessitates it. Violence can be used as a tool. It does not have to take over and use you. If there be any doubts on this question, one need only meet the North Vietnamese whose open espousal of and participation in violent struggle has in no way diminished their humanity but made it stronger and more definite by sensitizing them to the dilemma of the revolution.

We are in favor of the revolution neither because it is inevitable nor because it will bring a small group of us to power. Neither is the case. We are in favor of the revolution because we believe in human dignity and in the capacity of human beings for self-development and realization. We would therefore not be justified if we used means which had the effect of creating less rather than more human self-realization and development, less rather than more human dignity. But we must make this judgment in a historical context. We are not introducing evil means into an otherwise neutral world in order to achieve ends that we claim will be beneficial to humanity. Rather, the world is filled with injustice, debasement and destruction of human beings, human dignity, and human capacities. If we did not act at all, the world would be *worse* than if we acted to create a socialist revolution, even using means that in themselves are ugly.

It is not simply a question of adding up comforts or units of pleasure. We are talking about the most sacred thing of all—human life. We believe that human beings deserve a high degree of respect just by virtue of their being human. So we can never take this question lightly; every time we grapple with the question of violence it must be with a sense of awe and respect for each individual human being and his human potential. This means that there is a very strong prima facie presumption against violence, and while we are saying that it may sometimes be necessary and justified, we are also saying that a revolutionary movement should do everything in its power to avoid violence wherever that avoidance does not permit an even greater amount of violence to persist. While I believe it would be immoral and unwise to deny the forces of revolution the right to use violence, I do not believe that there is any circumstance foreseeable for the next ten or fifteen years in which the Left ought actually to use violence.

Won't people abuse the notion that a means is justified if it leads to the revolution? Not any more than they would abuse anything else. After all, "leading to the revolution" is not merely a vague concept. The revolution is not contentless. The revolution is about the abolition of the ruling class and the emancipation of human life from a period when it had to subordinate itself to the necessity of survival. The revolution is about giving people power over their lives so that they can determine for themselves the future course of history. The revolution is about ending the exploitation and fixed sexual roles, about making it possible for human beings to relate to each other in noncompetitive and loving ways. A means can be discredited to the extent that it can be seen not to be leading toward the building of such a society. But when one evaluates that question one must be careful to do it realistically—by understanding the functioning of institutions and what it will take to overthrow them. If you as an individual love everyone, that will not necessarily make it possible for human beings to love each other; even if many individuals loved everyone and the majority did not, the bombs would still fall on Vietnamese. There are economic and social institutions that operate in a coercive manner, and they will not be overthrown by individual acts of love. That does not mean they will be overthrown by hate—no, they will be overthrown by a mass movement that comes to understand the need to overthrow them, and this mass movement will be built in part by love and in part by hard thinking, political agitation, struggle, suffering, jailing, and self-defensive violence.

Doesn't the whole approach that relies on violence at any stage negate any previous claims to democracy? No. Because a majority of people cannot change the system through the system, and the violence will be used against you long before you come close to getting a majority, and then justified through the press and media. So self-defensive violence will be necessary at a stage prior to the building of a complete majority, although also after a much greater mass movement has been built than exists now. What right will we have to use violence when we are not even a majority? We are already a majority of the people of the world, and *that* is the relevant constituency. But even a minority has the right to defend itself from unjustified violence against it—and we have been concerned to show that it is precisely in response to that kind of violence, systematized in the operations of capitalism, that the revolutionary struggle is forced to confront the question of self-defense.

part 3
The New Society

8

Socialism: The Only Alternative

THROUGHOUT this book we have attempted to show why we regard social revolution as both desirable and possible. We have shown that the powerlessness people experience at work and in their homes is not a personal, psychological problem but rather a structural political problem. People feel powerless because in crucial respects they *are* powerless, and this powerlessness is not a product of the "human condition" but of the specific social and economic organization of society called capitalism. We have shown that capitalism leads to imperialism, and that it helps sustain racism and sexism. And we have shown that forces exist, themselves produced by capitalism, which could unite to overthrow it and create a new social order.

But what do we want? In a word, "socialism." Unfortunately, that word has been so misunderstood that it is often more confusing than illuminating to use it. We retain it because it is associated with a long history of human aspirations with which we essentially identify. But let us make clear what we mean by "socialism." Socialism is the ownership and control of the means of production, and, through that, the control of all areas of life, by the majority of people who work. So socialism is another way of saying "power to the people": power to control all the basic institutions that affect our lives. Socialism is radical democracy, democracy extended to every area of our collective lives. It is the intention of this and the next chapter to spell out what this means in more detail. In part this can be done by trying to distinguish our aims from populism and from what came to be called socialism in Eastern Europe.

287

WHY NOT POPULISM?

People have already come to see that the kinds of changes in consciousness predicted by *The Greening of America* will not be possible without changing the basic structures of American life. Because of this, the new group of neopopulists seem to be talking sense. The most famous of these populists is Ralph Nader, whose campaign on behalf of the American consumer has gained national acclaim. In 1972 Jack Neufield, a writer for the *Village Voice* and adviser to former Attorney General Robert Kennedy, published a "Populist Manifesto" which gives insight into the future of this revived political tendency.

Nader and Neufield are remarkably good at portraying the ways in which the large corporations have tricked, deceived, and robbed the American people, and in showing how the government is an active accomplice in this. Their work has often been more insightful than that of the New Left, because they have been willing to do much of the research and investigation that has been neglected so badly by aspiring revolutionaries. Their research has been invaluable in destroying the myths of a benevolent corporate elite that modifies its greed in order to produce goods to serve the people. And Nader's enthusiastic reception by large numbers of Americans shows that the latent anticapitalist sentiments in the country are not too hard to unpack, with a bit of cleverness, hard work, and a sense of drama and confrontation. The Left owes thanks to the work that Nader and his followers continue to do.

But, despite all the good research and confrontations sponsored by the new populists, their analysis of the problem and hence their proposed solutions are woefully inadequate. Nader condemns "the socialism of the rich"—a reference to the fact that through the tax structure and the control they exert over the government the rich are able to redistribute wealth away from the workers and to themselves. But hidden in this, and made explicit by Nader and some of his lieutenants, is an explicit hostility to socialism in any form. On the contrary, Nader wants to rejuvenate capitalism and make it work again by breaking up large concentrations of wealth. Neufield suggests that we break up the biggest corporations: the various divisions of General Motors, for instance, could be separated and sold to new owners with only minimal inconveniences. But how does this deal with the basic problems that capitalism causes? Consider who would benefit. If there were five GMs instead of one, would the worker at each have any more power? Or would most Americans? No. Who would own the new GMs? Precisely the same class of people who owned the single old one. Unless there is a complete redistribution of wealth, the average working person will not have sufficient money to buy stock in the newly created corporations. Control will once again go to the wealthy. Possibly, the breakup in concentrations will provide an opening for a few upper-middle-class people to buy stocks that were not previously on the market, and hence give them more wealth. But this will merely enlarge the class of capitalist owners. It will not change the basic framework. The new owners will have the same interests in maximizing their capital, and the corporations will continue to make all their decisions in accord with this criterion. The majority of working people will still have to sell their labor power to the highest bidder, will still have no control over the work situation, will still be used both at work and at home to maximize the profits of the rich. Unquestionably, the lawyers will benefit: they will have years of court work in dissolving old corporations and creating new ones—certainly a boon for Yale and Harvard lawyers, but of slight interest to the rest of the country.

Neufield suggests that workers seek participation in management. The unions, he says, should begin making membership on boards of directors a bargaining issue. But, far from changing things, such a direction merely helps to integrate the workers into the capitalist framework. Given that framework, it becomes rational for workers to demand things that are in the long run destructive to their own interests. (It becomes rational, for example, for the worker at a defense plant to pressure the government into spending more money on weapons production, even though this distorts the economy and heightens the likelihood of imperialist adventures.) The workers will still have no real control over what gets produced and how, nor will they get any significant share of profits, but they will now feel that they have a stake in the whole procedure. They will begin to see the world through the eyes of the capitalist. This is why de Gaulle, the reactionary leader of France in the 1960s, was so much in favor of workers' participation. Participation is a far cry from *control,* and it is only when people have control over the economy and over their work situation that they will be able to deal with their powerlessness in every area of life.

Nader and the populists shun any proposal for real democratization of the economy. Instead, they focus their solution on the creation of an expanded governmental bureaucracy that honestly attempts to regulate industry. We do not object to a plan that would get the regulatory agencies to do their job honestly. Or even to a plan that would expand their powers to force some of the corporations to stop poisoning our foods and our air, stop putting bad drugs on the market, etc. But the whole enterprise seems like a classic case of too little too late. If Nader himself were elected president in 1972 and if a sympathetic Congress were elected with him, it might seem plausible that he could institute some sort of regulation. But this misses the whole context which created the trouble in the first place. The concentration of wealth will still prevail in the period ahead, and candidates at every level will have to moderate their ideas to that reality.[1] If a few slip through, they will be isolated. It is more likely that someone will be elected who is less honest than Nader, but who sees the potential popularity of Nader's rhetoric. He will make some changes but not enough. And even those few changes will be combated fiercely by the press and the large corporations, and by their representatives in Congress. Moreover, because these new officials themselves will have attacked socialism and leftist ideas in order to show that they were responsible in their assent to power, they will now find they have no popular base to support a serious assault on the corporations. Hence, they will feel it necessary to move to the Right to show that they have not turned into Communists overnight. Some of the problems will be dealt with, but inadequately, and others will be left untouched because they are too hot (e.g., Neufield's suggestion that banks be more carefully regulated). The net effect of the populist crusade will be to strengthen the system as a whole by making people believe that the election of a populist will solve all problems, whereas, in fact, whatever New Deal emerges from the crusade will probably be just as inadequate and just as subservient to the long-term interests of wealth and power as was the last one. The business community will kick and scream just as it did during the era of Woodrow Wilson and the era of Franklin D. Roosevelt. But its interests are likely to be strengthened through the process.

The strategy of relying on the creation of a big governmental bureaucracy that will honestly police the corporations depends for its success on good will and the vicissitudes of politics. The conscientious bureaucrat will still be subject to his higher-ups, and if he starts pursuing a line that embarrasses his president he will be quickly kicked out. And what chance does one bureaucrat have of mobilizing popular support behind him, when his superiors in the bureaucracy say he is getting out of line, and the large corporations can use their economic power to buy time and influence

---

[1] One particularly cynical example of the way in which populist rhetoric can be used by politicians without any expectation that the populist program would be passed is the 1972 McGovern campaign. While campaigning on the issue of tax reform, McGovern bought a full-page ad in the *Wall Street Journal* to reassure the rich that he really wasn't a threat. He reminded the rich that his tax program could not pass without the approval of Congress—intending to imply that a conservative Congress would quickly bury his proposals. Meanwhile, he was telling his youthful supporters he was the embodiment of integrity and the new politics.

through the media to challenge his judgments? The construction of a large bureaucracy does nothing to give people direct control over their lives—the bureaucrats are neither elected nor directly responsible to the people. And the corporations can only be controlled by going through this national bureaucracy.

Neufield is ready to raise the question of public ownership—but only for the large utilities, and only as mediated through a national control board similar to those that now govern other "public" ventures, like the New York Port Authority. While these ventures will eliminate profiteering on vital necessities, they still leave basic policies in the hands of the capitalist class. An example is the board set up to manage the communications satellite. It is supposed to be controlled jointly by the government, private business, and the public. But the people appointed to represent the public are all from the class of owners, and so are most of the government appointees. The result, as has been shown in the "partial socializations" of the economy that occurred in England and France, is that the "public" corporations operate no differently from private ones. The workers are still exploited, and the interests of the community as a whole are never adequately weighed. That is why socialism does not mean only formal public ownership but ownership and *control*. Until the basic decisions facing an industry are put directly to the people affected by them, there is no public control and hence no socialism. On the contrary, this pseudo-socialist form of public ownership is precisely what deters people from accepting the idea of socialism. Because they have found that their lives are not substantially improved when a particular industry is nationalized in the context of a general capitalist economy, they wrongly conclude that the problem was taking ownership in the first place. For all these reasons we are likely in the next decade to find intelligent capitalists supporting parts of the populist program, including nationalization of some industry, though it will most likely be those industries that do not seem to be making much profit on their own. It does not harm the capitalists very much if, with adequate compensation, the government takes over the Penn Central system (once the railroad has gone bankrupt in the capitalist market). Such nationalizations serve two purposes: to free capital from unprofitable enterprises so that the capitalist can reinvest it in a better money-making field, and to make socialism unpopular, by showing people how little difference nationalization makes to their lives.

The worst thing about the populist approach is that it miseducates people about the nature of the problem, and hence its failure is likely to lead to disillusion. Many people, particularly young liberal lawyers and professionals, would like to believe that the basic problems of America can be solved within the framework of the present system. They have been impressed with the fact that the populists talk in detail about the many areas of corporate control: they are not superficial, as are many politicians. But because the populists' account misses the basic ways in which the central dynamic of capitalist competition affects every area of life, they end up with a series of recommendations that only treat symptoms. The lack of analysis is particularly startling when one looks at Neufield's account of crime: he is quick to suggest prison reform, fighting corruption in the courts, and the inefficiency and stifling of initiative in the police force, but he completely misses the fact that most crimes committed in America are rooted in the present economic order, and will only intensify unless that order is altered. Naturally, a radical is in favor of prison reform, etc. But why do people steal and what is there in people's lives that drives them to heroin? Unless one grasps the essentials, the programs for reform often seem to miss the point. And then one is tempted to lean toward some conservative explanation: "Well, human beings are just bad by nature." Neufield himself almost says as much when he comments on racial disputes: "We do not argue that these disputes can be eradicated; racial and cultural hostilities are a fact of life." [2] In the end, the populist seems all too willing to leave intact most of what we find deplorable in capitalist America.

DOES THE SOVIET UNION HAVE SOCIALISM?

Our criticisms of partial nationalizations should show part of the reason we do not believe that socialism now exists in any country in the world. Socialism means ownership and *control* of the means of production, democratically by the people, rather than by a governmental bureaucracy. The critical element in our understanding of socialism is the democratization of the economy and of all areas of political and social life. In the Soviet Union, this does not exist. The Communist party runs everything, and the Party is not a democratic institution, but is dominated by a group of bureaucrats who in most respects fit the notion of a "new ruling class." The people are unable to organize any effective opposition elements, either inside or outside the Party, and hence have no effective way of making their will known, short of armed rebellion. Powerless to affect the decisions

2 "Populist Manifesto," cited from the unpublished manuscript.

that affect their lives, the people in the Soviet Union are far from having socialism.

The Soviet Union does, however, have a high degree of welfare statism. And in this respect it is similar, though somewhat in advance of, Sweden and other countries that supply the minimum social welfare benefits all humans deserve. This feature should not be minimized. People in these countries are not deprived of medical attention because of the expense, people can get work to support themselves, their minds and bodies do not decay because they have too little money to buy food. These basic needs matter very much to those who cannot satisfy them, and in these respects the people in the Soviet Union are far better off than many people in America. But while it is a contingent fact that when socialism is established, all these basic human needs will be met, meeting these needs is not the defining essence of socialism. It is a necessary condition for people to be free and self-determining, but it is not a sufficient one. Slaves may be materially satisfied, but they are slaves nevertheless. Socialism is about power over one's life and circumstances; it is about freedom and self-determination, and these do not obtain in the Soviet Union. Nor is there any indication that the USSR is moving in that direction; the ruling class seems to have strengthened itself in the past decades sufficiently and to have retreated far enough from the ideals of socialism that it would be hard to envision anything short of a revolution establishing socialism in the Soviet Union. And, to the extent that other "socialist" countries are under the military or economic control of the Soviet Union, the same is true for them.

"But doesn't this show that revolution is no alternative, because a ruling class will always reemerge no matter what the original ideals of those who make the revolution?" No. This argument misses the historical context in which the revolutions in Russia, China, North Vietnam, Cuba, etc., developed. Marx predicted, accurately, that socialism would only be possible in an industrial society whose material base—the technology and factories and skilled workforce—was sufficiently advanced to make possible the elimination of scarcity. As Marx correctly saw, the advanced industrial societies had all the prerequisites necessary for abolishing forever the domination of man by irrational forces. But the countries that are now called socialist were all backward peasant countries, often prevented from developing by the capitalist countries that influenced their economic life. The main task of their "socialist" revolutions was to build up the industrial bases to the point where it was possible to talk about the elimination of scarcity. But in trying to industrialize, these countries faced a hostile capitalist world which would attempt to isolate and destroy them. In 1919, for example, the last remnants of the economic infrastructure of Russia were destroyed by the crippling civil war that was spurred by the United States, Britain, and France. The United States actually invaded Russia that year, but the American working class was so opposed to this invasion (refusing to load cargo for the "American Expeditionary Force") and the Russian working class was so determined, that the United States, Britain, and France were forced to retreat and allow the Soviet Union to live. Lenin himself realized that socialism could never be built in one country, and expected that a European revolution would soon occur which would enable the working classes of the advanced industrial societies to aid in Russia's economic development. The revolutions did not succeed, and the Soviet Union was forced to industrialize alone. The tremendous hardships this imposed on the Russian people, coupled with the extra burdens of Stalin's ruthless and paranoid dictatorship, almost rival the sufferings faced by the people of England, France, Germany and Italy over the several-hundred-year period of their capitalist development. It seemed worse in the Soviet Union, both because of the concentration into a few decades of what had taken several centuries in the West, and because of Stalin's obvious and unnecessary evils. I omit comparisons with the United States, since it is difficult to find any analogy to the hardships suffered by tens of millions of slaves in the course of America's history of capitalist accumulation.

The great disservice done by the Communist parties around the world was to describe the Soviet Union, developing under extremely difficult circumstances that put industrialization, not socialism, on the agenda, as "socialist." This discredited socialism with people everywhere, especially in the Soviet Union and Eastern Europe. In taking the real for the ideal, in making a virtue out of necessity, the Communist parties helped undermine people's confidence in the ideal. Add to that the continued apologies for a regime whose paranoid excesses were inexcusable and you have all the ingredients for the widespread disillusionment experienced by so many good idealistic people of the 1930s. The same thing will happen again if the American Left tries to identify its aspirations with any existing state, whether China, North Vietnam, or Cuba. These states have much to recommend them: They have begun to deal with many of people's basic material needs, and unlike the Western nations during their period of capitalist industrialization, they have a real concern for the welfare of working people and a real interest in promoting liberation for women within the limits imposed by continued material scarcity. The rulers of these countries, unlike the ruling class of the Soviet Union, are not interested simply in self-aggrandizement and stabilization but are committed to building a socialist world eventually. Nevertheless, these countries do have "rulers," and these rulers are not elected representatives of the people. The people do not control the economy and are rarely directly consulted on crucial issues. These countries may be moving toward socialism, but it would be a critical mistake to say that they have achieved it. There is no socialism until there are substantial procedures through which the workers decide the basic questions facing them.

One objection to this account, often offered by people who associate themselves with the Left, is that, although all the limitations on these countries flow from the decision to industrialize, that decision itself was incorrect. The Soviet Union, according to the argument, should have dedicated its resources toward the establishment of democracy within its own party and within the country as a whole, and toward a revolutionary foreign policy aimed at stimulating the development of revolutionary movements around the world. Had this occurred, the Soviet Union might have been able to produce the conditions for revolution in other countries. And once that happened, industrialization would have been a much less painful process. Some proponents of this view argue that such a path might well have led to the overthrow internally of the Communist regime by reactionary elements, taking advantage of this new-found democracy to stir up strong residual nationalist feelings against the internationalists in power. But the risk was worth running, they argued, since the alternative was to preserve in power a regime that actually stymied the development of revolutionary activity around the world, and discredited the workers' revolutionary movement in the process. But this is a thoroughly "iffy" argument, abstracted from the actual historical situation in which intelligent and dedicated people had to make their decisions. It is less important for us to be Monday-morning quarterbacks than to realize that these countries cannot now be considered in any sense models for what we mean by socialism.

To the extent that these self-described "socialist" countries removed themselves from the sphere of capitalist exploitation by prohibiting capitalist investment and trade, they play an important role in the worldwide struggle against U.S. imperialism. Capitalism's internal contradictions increase as its room for expansion declines, so when we urge international solidarity it is not simply on some abstract moral grounds but also because in a real sense our struggle and the struggle of the Vietnamese, for example, are the same. We do not need to say that China, Cuba, etc., are "socialist" in order to see that they play a progressive role in the long-term struggle for human liberation. Nor do we want to be unduly harsh in our criticisms:

many of these countries are doing the best they possibly can, given the conditions of underdevelopment, material scarcity, and military threat under which they have to operate. We should not impose on these societies evaluative criteria derived from the possibilities extant in an advanced industrial society.

It is precisely because we recognize the limitations imposed by the objective conditions in which these societies emerged that we warn against the overglorification of the Third World that occurred in the late 1960s in the New Left. All these countries, faced with conditions of scarcity, under-development, and military threat, are likely to follow paths designed to ensure their survival in the short run, and those paths will not necessarily be consistent with building the international revolution or socialism in the long run. We may condemn the Soviet Union's aid to North Vietnam or to Cuba as woefully inadequate and see how that limited aid may tie these countries to improper policies. We may understand that the massing of 800,000 Russian troops on China's northern border, together with the rapid growth of her traditional enemy, Japan, might drive China to seek accommodations with the United States even at the expense of tolerating U.S. involvement in Southeast Asia. National interests may force China to ally with the dictatorship in Pakistan against Bangladesh or to support other conservative developments, and the absence of structures for or-ganized opposition within China may make these policies widely accepted by the Chinese people. These historical tragedies are the product of unique and unfortunate historical developments; they are neither to be explained away or justified. International solidarity requires us to support these regimes when they are threatened by the United States, Japan, or other imperialist forces, but it does not require us to become apologists for every turn in their domestic or foreign policies. But our criticisms must be made with a sensitivity to the material circumstances of these countries. These countries have helped advance our struggle, and our struggle will greatly help them and make possible for them the development of a real socialism. Not because Americans are special in any way, but because material condi-tions exist in America to create socialism and at the same time avoid some of the problems these countries inevitably had to face.

Further, we should not excuse away things we deplore. Nothing could be more disgusting than the sights of the Russians welcoming Nixon to Moscow, the Chinese bringing Nixon to meet with Chairman Mao, at the very time when the United States is escalating its murder in Vietnam. No matter what accommodations must be made with the capitalists, nothing warrants treating this war criminal as an honored guest. To do this re-quired, both in Russia and China, the active suppression of those few remaining Communists who remembered the old ideals of socialist internationalism. The welcomes that President Nixon received in Moscow and Peking were the necessary conditions for his becoming even more reckless and destructive with human life in Vietnam. The ruling classes of these so-called socialist states acted disgracefully in the spring of 1972, and became accomplices in America's international banditry.

WHAT WILL THE TRANSITION TO SOCIALISM BE LIKE IN THE UNITED STATES?

The situation in which socialism will come to the United States is totally different from that in which it emerged in Eastern Europe and in Asia. The United States is an advanced industrial society whose material base is adequate to meet all the material needs of its citizens and those of people around the world. Furthermore, the agent of revolutionary change in this country will be a highly diversified working class, literate and intelligent, that is capable of running things for itself and deciding on seemingly complex issues.

Immediately the socialists take control of the U.S. economy a high level of material prosperity will be possible in the United States and much of the rest of the world. Because we are so highly industrialized, it will be possible to decrease dramatically the amount of time the worker spends in work, at the same time producing adequate material goods for ourselves and helping to advance the underdeveloped parts of the world. The revolution will be experienced not as a new but goodhearted taskmaster, but as a liberation and freeing from much that is unpleasant in life. In this situation, it will be impossible for a new ruling class to emerge that encourages people to delay gratification, while itself benefiting from the labor of the majority. Since the United States is the strongest military power in the world, with atomic weapons sufficient to destroy everyone else and hence sufficient to defend itself, no group will be able to argue that people must surrender their liberties or make other sacrifices in order to defend socialism from any "external threat."

The working class that will be part of the American revolution will have a high degree of intelligence and competence in running things. American workers have been heavily indoctrinated in anticommunism and hence are particularly sensitive to the mistakes created by a Stalinist direction. Moreover, one of their main motivating forces for making the revolution will be the desire to reclaim power over their lives; for many American workers, simple material scarcity is not a problem. Having fought for power in a

297

real sense, having seen through strategies for "participation" and other cooptive schemes, such a working class will have developed the acuity not to be duped by a group of persuasive charlatans. To think otherwise is to believe that Americans are specially unintelligent—and I see no evidence of that. We must have enough faith in each other and our collective intelligence to believe that we can learn from the mistakes of the past and can transcend them.

Given the extreme difficulties of bringing off a real revolutionary struggle in this century and given the tremendous psychological and media advantages that the ruling-class and bourgeois ideology has, it is entirely possible to argue that no revolution will ever take place, that people will be tricked out of it. I do not think this is true, but I do think that the events of the future are not inevitable, but depend on many contingent circumstances. Not the least of these is what you, the reader, decide to do with your life. But if a revolution is actually accomplished, if people *can* learn to see through all of society's sophisticated cooptions and can organize themselves as a successful political force, it does not seem plausible to argue that they can then be duped into giving up the benefits for which they fought so hard.

Precisely because a capacity to transcend capitalist ideology and a high degree of political involvement and sophistication are prerequisites for making a revolution, there is every reason to believe that the tens of millions of people who must be involved in the revolution will know how to keep power once it is taken. The struggle itself is the guarantee, because that struggle will require the people themselves to become involved in constructing democratic institutions and plans for every area of their lives. Here is the importance of mass struggle: unlike a coup d'état, the struggle is self-justifying because it prepares people to take control over their lives and to make critical decisions. If tens of millions of people consciously engage in a struggle for socialism, that in itself ensures that the decisions made after the revolution will be relatively sane. Many elitist college students argue against socialism this way: "What makes you think that if you give people power, they will make any better decisions than are made now by the current rulers? After all, working people are racist and sexist, and support bad policies." The answer, at least in part, is that no one is *giving* people anything: the revolution is not a coup d'état by the few on behalf of the many, but a struggle of the many to gain power over their own lives. In order for people to win that struggle, we will have to overcome our own sexism and racism, otherwise we simply will not be able to put together the forces that could make a revolution. We transform ourselves in the course of that struggle, and to the extent that we fail to do so, we will also fail to win the struggle. Not every decision that the people make will be the best possible decision, but the process of making decisions will make us all better and more fulfilled in the not-too-long run.

Revolutionaries are not magicians; they do not expect to pull out of a hat some mysterious and undreamed-of entity. The struggle to change society will embody some of the characteristics of the new society itself. Thus it will involve the attempt to democratize every area of social life, and to involve everyone in the process of deciding what they want to see in a new society. The struggle will insist on the greatest amount of civil liberties possible consistent with actually waging the struggle (the qualification means that, e.g., we do not respect the right of an FBI informer to join our groups and lie about us, and then defend this as an instance of free speech). Most important, we will insist on the right of those within the revolutionary struggle to disagree with the majority, and to organize around its oppositional viewpoint with full access to the means of communication and media available to the majority. We will through these and similar procedures ensure that we have a high degree of familiarity with and belief in basic democratic procedures which will then be a natural part of our activity after the revolution as well.

Anyone with even the slightest degree of familiarity with the New Left knows how little chance there is that these commitments will ever change. If anything, the fear of repeating the mistakes of Stalinism have led to an overemphasis on procedure with only minimal concern about the importance of procedure to the accomplishment of a goal. Lest power be too concentrated in the hands of a single individual and group, the New Left has often gone to the opposite extreme of repudiating all interest in power and destroying any leadership that came forward. Reacting to these "ultra-democracy" tendencies, a variety of leftist sectarian groups have emerged that have gone to the opposite pole and have thereby ensured only a minimal following. But a working class spurred into revolutionary activity at least in part in response to its antiauthoritarian sentiments is not likely to fight to the death for a new order and then quietly yield to new tyrants.

Nor will democracy be eroded by apathy. Current apathy and non-participation in elections is not a reflection of people's failure to care about what happens to them. Rather, it reflects their correct perceptions that the present political arena gives them little opportunity to affect their own lives. Increasingly, this has become true in the unions, where key decisions are made at the top and the membership has no real chance to play a decisive role in the formulation of policy alternatives. Ironically, the same kind of apathy set into the New Left, but for the opposite reason: in its overemphasis on process, meetings dragged on so long and questions were considered and reconsidered so endlessly, that the meetings began to take the place of political activity and themselves became the central activity. In that context, people correctly saw that nothing important would be decided and left the meetings to those who were really seeking to turn them into group therapy sessions. But when an organization has real issues to decide, real power to decide them, and a reality factor that limits endless debates, the apathy rapidly disappears. Meetings of the boards of directors of corporations rarely have attendance problems.

SUGGESTED READINGS

Boorstlen, Edward. *The Economic Transformation of Cuba.* New York: Monthly Review Press, 1968.

Deutscher, Isaac. *The Prophet Unarmed.* New York: Vintage Books, 1963.

Horowitz, David. *Empire and Revolution.* New York: Random House, 1969.

Marx, Karl. *Early Writings.* Edited by T. B. Bottomore. New York: McGraw-Hill, 1963.

9

After the Revolution

THOSE WHO are committed to the revolution have written almost nothing about what things will look like thereafter. And for a good reason. Socialism is the beginning of the epoch of human freedom and the end of the time when some men control all others. But once human beings are genuinely free, how can we know what they will choose to do? We can have some idea based on past behavior, but we cannot have a fixed blueprint. To the challenge, "What is your new society going to look like?" the first answer must be, "This is not *my* new society, but *our* new society, so what it will look like will in part depend on what you want it to look like." A liberal running for office may give a more satisfying answer; he will be able to make authoritative statements, since he is trying to put himself in a position where he will have power that others will not. But for the socialist revolutionary, the task is to build a society in which everyone together decides what it will be like.

Still, people have a good reason for asking the question. After all, if you are going to make sacrifices to build a new social order, you want to have some idea of what the order will be like. To say "We will all be free" is poetic, but contentless; people want to know *why* this freedom will produce desirable results for humanity. I cannot answer this question for everyone, but I can answer for myself, and I can tell you what I as one individual with one vote will argue for, and what kind of society I believe will be possible. I shall try to outline what will be possible after a fairly substantial period of control by the people, not what it will be like one or two years after the people have taken power, when the transition is still going on. So let me put forward one vision, among many, of what socialism could be like and would be like if others agree with me when we all get together to construct our new society.

POLITICAL AND ECONOMIC ORGANIZATION

Every important political question would be put directly to the people for their consideration and decision. We already have the technology to do this easily. Every home would have a very simple voting device, possibly attached to the phone or television receiver, which would send a message to a central computer in the city or area recording the vote. Prior to the vote, issues would be debated in newspapers and on television and in mass meetings in the community, with every major side given equal opportunity to present its position. At the local, regional, and national level there would be an elected body of delegates (each recallable to his district any time 10 percent of the voters signed a petition for a new election) whose responsibility would be to decide which issues would be put to the people and how to formulate them in the clearest possible way in order to maximize understanding and to bring out the potentially controversial aspects of the proposal under consideration. Any group that felt some key question was not being put to the electorate or that some key viewpoint was not being represented publicly on television, at mass meetings, or in newspapers, would circulate a petition stating its viewpoint. Signatures of 1 percent of the voting population in the relevant area would give the group the right to (1) write its own proposal to be put directly to the people, and (2) air its views on the media (it would be given more time than any single position normally is, on the grounds that its view had not previously been given exposure in the usual debates on relevant issues). The government would have an executive branch, most of the key positions of which would be filled by elections. But the executive would have little originating power, since the key decisions on policy would always be put to the people. Because of human fallibilities and weaknesses, important decisions, which should have been presented to the people, might occasionally be made under the guise of simple bureaucratic or administrative decisions. But rarely would such decisions have severe consequences, because they could always be challenged by those who were affected by them and brought directly to the people, and the official could simultaneously (if his fault was judged malicious) be recalled.

Civil liberties would be guarded and extended. For one thing, people would be more interested in them, since the decision-making power would now be in their hands. One of the great problems in capitalist America is getting people to take civil liberties seriously when they see how little power those liberties actually give them. What does freedom of the press mean to a striker when he knows that the press is owned and controlled by the bosses? How important is free speech if the only people who use it are the privileged kids at the elite universities? But when real democracy exists, as it will under socialism, civil liberties become vital. One way in which civil liberties can be made more real is by making the means of communication available to a much larger number of people. Every community will be given several television stations and many radio channels to develop its own programming. The only national programming will be around political issues that must be decided nationally. Similarly, funds will be made available for the creation of a variety of newspapers in each community, instead of one or two big ones. After the establishment of the first few communications outlets, the franchises for the next will be given to those who can show that their programming and political content would be substantially different from that already available, so as to avoid homogeneity in development. Any interested community group would be allowed to develop its own program for at least one station, and if there were more groups than time, there would be rotation each year or six months. Considerable time would also be allocated for artists and dramatists, for poets and moviemakers, so that their work could reach many people. Resources would also be made available to publicize political rallies or political programs, particularly from oppositional groups.

For the first hundred years, at least, the key decisions would probably remain in the area of production. Many economists argue that it would be possible to decentralize the economy without in the slightest decreasing its efficiency. But we would be in favor of decentralization even if it meant an additional cost. A decentralized economy would be easier to control and ecologically more sound. Regions of between 15 to 20 million people would be established to replace the present states, and those regions would themselves be composed of a variety of autonomous municipalities. In order to maximize the fulfillment of human needs and eliminate needless production, the economic area would be governed by a rational long-term plan developed every few years and approved by vote of the electorate. The plan would be developed from the bottom: each work unit and each consumer entity would submit its ideas and desires to a community board which would try to adjust them into a coherent whole, then resubmit the adjustments back to the populace for approval. Thereafter, they would be submitted to a regional board that took all the ideas and tried to develop a regional plan, which itself would be sent to a national board, which would try to adjust the regional plans. The last step would be to send that

303

plan back to everyone for approval. Equally complex planning now takes place in the Department of Defense and other areas of the government, with one crucial difference: the people consulted are members of the boards of directors of large corporations instead of the people as a whole. Because the process would be complex, we would want two key qualifications on the procedure:

1. The plan would be voted on not only as a whole, but also with separable components (much as is the present budget before Congress) so that people who liked most of it could vote "yes" on the question of making the plan as a whole the basis of discussion, and could also vote against any section of which they disapproved.

2. Any plan would have to allocate a great deal of the social surplus to each locality, so that a significant part of the wealth created by each community was in its hands to use, hence avoiding a situation in which people from far away tell people who have worked to create wealth that they cannot use even part of it in ways in which they desire.

Every community must have enough resources to experiment with education, housing, creativity, etc. The regional and national plans should deal with the minimum necessary number of issues: e.g., where to build new cities, how to solve general ecological problems, how to arrange transportation between localities, foreign trade, taxation, and long-term financing. The regional and national plans would have as one key task the allocation and redistribution of resources in such a way as to guarantee that no one area suffers because it does not have adequate natural resources or because a main source of its economic strength (e.g., car manufacturing or mining) is shut down for reasons of preserving the ecology. But since the idea of giving each community a large sum initially for discretionary planning is key to this conception, the national plan is likely to be less complicated than the present federal budget in an unplanned economy, because so much that is now decided nationally will be decided at the local level.

The key unit in the plan is the local community, whose power and resources would be greatly expanded. The emphasis for each community will be on experimentation, and funds will be made available so that minorities and individuals within each community who do not like the drift of the majority can experiment on their own. Within each community, the key centers of power will be the workplaces. Each factory or office will be democratically controlled by those who work there. All decisions that primarily affect the workers (e.g., work conditions) will be totally under their control. On the other hand, we do not envision a society such as

304

that developed in Yugoslavia, where workers' control of each factory was not balanced by community, regional, or national control of the economy. There, without central community planning, the workers in each factory and each area began to develop specialized interests and began to relate to other groups of workers as competitors. If an economy composed of factories, each run by the workers, is governed only by the free marketplace, it becomes nothing but a rerun of capitalism on a higher level. It would be unlikely, for example, that one group of workers would agree to shut down its factory because it was producing an unnecessary commodity; instead, the workers would try to convince people the commodity was necessary and even, perhaps, to conceal its harmful effects, if it had any. Only a larger regional and national framework can assure people that their talents will be used creatively and that they will never have to suffer want and hence will enable them to accept the closing of their workplace for the common good. So it is crucial that the productive life of a community be decided by a balance between the claims of the worker in the workplace, which are to be given much weight, and the interests of the community as a whole.

It should be noted that community control has quite different effects under socialism than under capitalism. In a capitalist society, the "community" is class-stratified, giving people a series of conflicting interests revolving around their relative wealth, and giving to the wealthy a disproportionate opportunity to influence the opinions of the rest of the population. But in a community in which the means of production are owned collectively and controlled jointly by the workers who work in them and the community as a whole, and in which the means of communication are equally accessible to all, community control becomes at once more possible and more desirable.

In building a democratic socialist society there will be some conflicting claims that all of us will have to weigh carefully. We want to maximize democratic control and initiative and we want to minimize work. We want to maximize efficiency and we want to minimize waste. Sometimes we are going to make mistakes. Other times, we will be faced with complicated decisions that require us to weigh several different factors at the same time, and there is likely to be disagreement. For instance, in deciding how large the decentralized units are going to be, we will have to realize that while in a smaller group each individual's opinion has more power, a larger group is better able to carry out its decisions in the real world (this is not true under capitalism, where a small group has most of the power, but it will be true in a socialist democracy). So we will want to build various-size units with different responsibilities, depending on the tasks we are seeking to accomplish. Robert Dahl, in his book *After the Revolution,*[1] shows some of the complications that we will face. But his antiradical argument, never made explicit because its foolishness would then be too obvious, seems to go: (1) problems are complicated, and (2) revolution is a simple solution, so (3) making a revolution must be irrelevant. From this it follows that we should leave all these complicated questions up to sophisticated liberals like Dahl, who know how to deal with them. We might be less skeptical of Dahl, former president of the American Political Science Association, if he had not been one of the chief apologists for the capitalist system, a proponent of pluralism, and a firm believer that people already have democracy in their localities. We recognize that there will be many difficult problems to work out after the revolution, but we have no intention of leaving the most important of them to crews of elite experts who supposedly know what is best for us. We'll let the engineers build the bridge, but we'll decide how and if we want it built.

WORK

The conditions of work will be decided collectively, and workplaces will be governed by those who work in them. Given the present level of technology, much less the probable advances of the period ahead, it will be possible immediately after the people take control of the economy to reduce substantially the number of work hours for the individual without in any way reducing real wages. One way in which this will be done is to employ the unemployed in the production of necessary goods. But the most important way will be to eliminate all wasteful production. Production will be geared to goods that last instead of goods that fall apart to satisfy the need for new markets. When the economy is no longer geared to the trash can, the same amount of labor will produce more lasting social goods, so the total amount of work hours required to fill social needs will be less. Advertising will be seriously curtailed, duplication of production reduced, and consequently needs for new kinds of goods will be seriously reduced. Once production is geared to human needs, and needs are not artificially created, there will be much less production time necessary. For instance, vast rapid transit systems, built on ecologically sound models, can replace the production of automobiles. Sales jobs, insurance jobs, promotion and advertising jobs, and many governmental jobs will be seen as socially useless labor, and billions of hours of office work and secretarial work will

[1] New Haven: Yale University Press, 1970.

be eliminated. The elimination of this kind of work in a capitalist framework would be frightening—because the people involved would simply be put on the job market to compete with everyone else. But the elimination of all this useless work in a socialist society would be coordinated as part of a plan for reemploying everyone, and reducing the total number of hours that all people had to work. Add to this the increase in automated work, which at this point would be welcomed rather than opposed by the workers (since automation would mean less work but not unemployment and economic insecurity), and it can be safely predicted that within a very short period of time, probably not more than twenty to thirty years, the average workday would be five hours and the workweek four days. And both would decrease progressively in the next period.

No one will be allowed to live off the work of others: everyone must work. Some college students seem to think America is a giant cookie bowl into which you reach whenever you want a goodie. The fact is that the wealth of this society is created by the people who work, and no one has a right to devise for himself schemes to get out of doing his share. In a capitalist society, where many cannot find work at all and where work is completely alienating, it is no wonder people try to escape it. But in a socialist society, while the total amount of work will be greatly reduced, the work that remains will have to be shared by all. To a large extent work will seem much more meaningful because the work conditions are under the worker's control and he is working to serve his fellow human beings' needs, but some work will still be drudgery and some will be unpleasant. A just distribution of work will permit inequalities if, and only if, they improve the position of those who are worst off, and the offices and positions to which the inequalities attach are open to all.[2] In general, this will mean that unpleasant labor and drudgery will be done by everyone in the community on a rotating basis. We do not, of course, want to call a doctor away from the operating table to collect garbage, but we do want to create enough medical schools and training programs so that, were a particular doctor unavailable, someone else would be able to take his place.

Not only the worst work, but also work in general, will be rotated to the greatest degree possible consistent with the wishes of the people doing it. This will involve two key societal changes:

1. Job categories will have to be much changed from the present, and many tasks that are now combined in the hands of a "professional" will be distributed to a number of trained personnel. For example, paramedical

[2] Cf. John Rawls, *A Theory of Justice* (Cambridge, Mass.: Harvard University Press, 1971).

training could be given to a very large percentage of the population so that most of the work of the average medical doctor could be competently handled by people with a more limited but still proficient training. Or, to put it another way, people whose present jobs require only menial work and limited use of their intelligence would be given broader training and jobs would be more broadly defined to give them opportunity to use their intelligence. So, for example, we might find that the design of a building was discussed and decided not merely by a group of architects, but also by the people who were involved in constructing it and the people who were going to use it. In some limited areas, special expertise and long training would still be called for. But every attempt would be made to share expertise, develop it widely, and to have the expert in a given area use at least part of his time to teach his talents to as many people as wanted to learn.

2. Job assignments would be rotated at given intervals, separated by vacation periods and periods to learn new skills and techniques. Rotation would allow people to experience several kinds of work in their lifetime, and the training periods would guarantee that they learned how to do different jobs well. Rotation would also ensure that new perspectives were brought to most assignments, to provide additional creativity in the work situation. Rotation would not operate merely in relation to similar kinds of of jobs, but also to different ones: people would shift among managerial, labor, clerical, skilled, farm, and other work so that each person had a full variety of experiences.

To the greatest extent possible, consistent with getting all the necessary jobs filled, job allocation would be voluntary. People would choose the job they wanted to be rotated to, with the proviso that jobs with power over others (managerial, for instance) and jobs that were unpleasant could be held only for a limited number of years. In the case of the least pleasant jobs, there would have to be accompanying compensation so that people who did them even for a limited time had additional benefits, such as significantly short workweeks or longer vacation periods.

The whole context of work will have a totally different significance, because increasingly as basic human needs are met work will become a form of experimentation and creativity. And the fact that a person has to work only a few hours a day will represent a qualitative change for those forms of work that involve drudgery or unpleasantness, since it will then be possible to go home, rest a little, and afterward engage in other activities. This is crucial, because it enables us to replace a leisure class with a structured period of leisure for everyone, so that everyone actually has the time and energy to develop his potentialities. But we should not

308

underestimate the development that will take place in the work situation itself. One of the most important products produced by factories under workers' control is the self-development of the workers themselves. It will not be unusual, for instance, for workers to invite lecturers, concert artists, etc., to their factories or workplaces. Nor will it be unusual for there to be daily discussions in the workplaces of the political issues that face the workers in the factories and in the community. And these activities will be seen as integral parts of being a worker in this society.

One reason that a serious reduction in work hours will take twenty to thirty years to accomplish (though a 32-hour workweek could certainly be instituted immediately) is that people will want to involve themselves in a crash program of reconstruction for Vietnam and other Third World countries harmed by U.S. imperialism. It would be possible both to assist these countries and to eliminate all poverty within the United States in a very short period of time, if that became the national goal. Unlike long-term loans that currently put the Third World deeper and deeper in debt to the United States, these operations would be given to help redress the capitalist exploitation of the past and to create a world market which could begin to develop trade on a relatively equal footing between countries.

THE SOCIALIST COMMUNITY

When I was growing up in the 1950s I remember reading all kinds of good ideas about what society could be like. For a long time I puzzled over why, given these ideas and modern technology, the reality was getting worse and worse. I did not realize that the people who were making money from the present reality had the power to stop, sabotage, or undermine any proposals for sweeping change put forward in the political sphere. But if these people no longer have power, it will be possible to construct truly rational living arrangements. In this important sense, the socialist revolution is the effort to give rationality some efficacy in human affairs.

Most American cities will have to be rebuilt, some almost from scratch. When rebuilt, they will have to be remodeled so that they are aesthetically pleasing to the occupants. Here is one area where a great deal of experimentation will take place, not just in city planning but also in the architecture of individual buildings. The basic task will be to decentralize the cities, and in many cases to split them up physically, relocating parts of them in different sections of the region. One of the tasks of the regional and national plans is to develop locations for the new cities in accord with the strictest ecological safety concerns. A great deal of time and creativity

309

will be directed toward ensuring that the living and working units that make up a city do not destroy the ecological foundation of the area, but instead enhance it.

Decentralization of the city will involve, among other things, bringing the workplace and living quarters into close proximity, so that as much as possible there is no need for transportation to work. That idea would sound horrible in the present American city; factories and office buildings are almost always monstrosities. But when the people own everything and it is up to them to decide what kinds of buildings they want in their neighborhoods, factories, offices, and stores will be made to beautify the neighborhood, rigorous concern will be given to ensuring that pollution is controlled, and the final product will be a pleasing environment. The rebuilding of our cities will not be completed overnight, but will go on at least for the next sixty or seventy years. But the very fact that we have begun to move in that direction will have an exhilarating effect on people, who will see all around them in quite literal ways how they are beginning to construct a new world. Although the socialist revolution does not automatically solve the problem, it does create the necessary preconditions for its solution.

Decentralization and bringing work close to the home should also make it possible to reduce the transportation facilities needed inside the city. Underground mass transit, much extended beyond the limits of some of today's subway systems, can fill most of the remaining needs. It is technologically possible to build subways that are virtually noiseless, and relatively pleasing inside, as well as to provide good live entertainment on some cars and total quiet for reading or contemplation on others. Above ground, most city streets will be planted over with grass, shrubs, and trees, with walkways, moving sidewalks for the infirm, and even play facilities. There will still be some streets for bringing needed goods to central distribution points, but much of the city will look like a park. On the periphery of the cities will be some of the forms of transportation we know about today, e.g., air travel in vehicles that have been greatly improved with regard to their pollution problems; electric automobiles, for private groups of people to go off into the country to enjoy themselves. All automobiles will be made without locks or keys, so that anyone can take one when it is needed, but no one can own one. Transportation within the city would be free, and for longer distances the fare would be considerably reduced; under socialism it should cost no more to go across the country than it does to go a very short distance today.

Probably one of the first actions of a socialist government would be to make free such essential services as health care, transportation, utilities, and housing. All forms of cultural activity would be free, and one of the main tasks of local government or administration would be to provide plans for making cultural experimentation possible for everyone. As a beginning, of course, we want every neighborhood to be equipped with adequate musical supplies, sports supplies, painting supplies, sculpture supplies, knitting, embroidery, macrame, etc. Each neighborhood should have facilities for the development of film, and facilities for the presentation of concerts and plays, as well as printing presses for leaflets, poetry, books and community newspapers. One of the highest ideals of the socialist revolution is to liberate and actualize human creativity. That is why we can adopt the slogan that workers and students used in the 1968 French rebellions: All Power to the Imagination.

Education will be radically transformed in our socialist community. For one thing, schools for youngsters will no longer be prisons. While basic skills will be taught, the greatest energies will be placed on allowing students to develop their talents by exposing them to the greatest possible range of creative activities. There will be no grading, but comprehensive reports on each youngster's development. A key element will be helping young people learn how to work and act together, at the same time respecting each person's individuality and uniqueness. Particularly in the elementary school, there will be no pressure on people to learn isolated facts about the world: the main emphasis will be on learning how to play, how to create, how to be an individual, and how to live and work collectively. The course content in high school is likely to resemble that of today's best liberal arts colleges: an introduction to the full variety of human thought, science, art, music, literature, and history of the past, taught not as isolated subjects but from a point of view that integrates all these fields. It is only when this kind of basic appreciation of the achievements and disabilities of the past are fully assimilated that the student can begin to specialize. There is no reason that most of what is today taught in college cannot be learned as thoroughly and perceptively at an earlier age, providing the student has not gone through the systematically moronizing experience that now goes under the name of elementary and high school education. The next level is learning some series of skills, for one's first set of jobs, and this learning will be repeated periodically as jobs are rotated. Every time one learns a new skill, however, time will be allowed to pursue in-depth education in some other area of intellectual and artistic interest, so that one can use one's leisure more intelligently.

So far we have been talking about the structured periods in which education is the primary activity. But, after the socialist revolution, education will have a much broader role. Every community will begin to develop facilities for extensive educational opportunities in all areas of human intellectual life. Given that at least half of our day will be free, many of us will avail ourselves of this kind of opportunity, and education will become a permanent feature of life, not limited to the youthful period, or rotation intervals. But, unlike some of the "free universities" that developed in the 1960s, education will be serious and rigorous. Our most gifted intellects will be encouraged to give their time to this kind of activity rather than to writing esoteric articles in journals primarily to prove themselves deserving of promotion. It is sometimes asked whether this educational system will be consistent with community control, since it seems contradictory to give students or those who do not know a subject democratic control over what is taught in that subject matter. But there is no real contradiction: within a field the person who knows what should be taught about it must be the person who knows the field. The community and the students will decide, together with the educators, what fields they want to learn about and what kinds of material they want stressed in presentation. You do not have to know the answer to the question, What is the relationship between the work of D. H. Lawrence and the historic period in which he wrote? to know that you would prefer to focus on that question than on the question of what twentieth-century critics said of him, though both may have some intrinsic interest. In general, education becomes an ingredient in every area of one's life, and the perverse separation between action and understanding so characteristic of life in presocialist societies is ended.

Democratic control over the means of production requires democratic ownership, for all the reasons that we have tried to make clear throughout the book. A rough equality in general wealth and income is a necessary condition for equality of political power. Ownership of property that allows one to employ other people for one's own profit, or the benefit from the labor of others without doing corresponding work (e.g., by receiving rent from a house or apartment building) must be eliminated in a socialist society. Many people have misunderstood Marx on this point, though he takes great pains to make it clear in the *Communist Manifesto*. Elimination of private property means elimination of all property that the individual does not need for personal survival and happiness, but which can be used to exploit others. Personal property, on the other hand, is not eliminated. To spell this out: the revolution does not mean that you have to give up your home (unless it is a mansion that could easily house five families) or your stereo or your television set or your clothes or anything of the sort. Some members of the hip community have emphasized that possessions in America are plastic and unsatisfying—and they may be

312

right for themselves—but the revolution is not renouncing material goods —that is the Christian philosophy, not a socialist one. While it is likely that under socialism people will no longer equate fulfillment with the ability to acquire objects, and while many of the goods produced today will no longer have much of a market, many material possessions will be made more widely available.

Many socialists have failed to understand the great appeal of the slogan "law and order" and have simply equated it with a sophisticated racism. It is certainly true that it is used to excuse racist practices and as a general distraction from real problems. But legitimate order need not be stifling to creativity and spontaneity. It is quite sensible to want to know that the things one works for are secure and the people one loves are safe. A socialist society could ensure this kind of order and make it real, while minimizing the role of law in daily life. Most of the crimes that we know today would simply disappear under a socialist society: why steal when there is an abundance for all? And when a society has been constructed in which every person has a stake, and in which each is allowed to develop those parts of himself that seek fuller realization, antisocial behavior becomes minimal. One need only look at such experiments in decentralized socialism as the kibbutz to see that even in a capitalist context the units that have moved in the direction of socialism have also seriously reduced or even eliminated crime. Still, particularly in the transition period, it is not unlikely that capitalist ideas will continue to influence some people to try to take advantage of others. In these cases, a law aimed not at punishment but at changing people, by helping them to realize what is best in them, is needed. Courts will not be run by professionals, but by real juries of peers. Trial by peers had much revolutionary potential when it was originally fought for by the bourgeoisie, but like so many bourgeois ideas, it was meant to benefit only themselves. Judges, lawyers, and a whole professional mystique have made the law almost completely impenetrable to the ordinary citizen. Our courts will be run with one simple principle in mind: how to make the defendant most capable of becoming fully human. Procedures will be relatively informal, and the juries will be given the widest powers to make decisions about how the trial should proceed, consistent with a wide range of safeguards for the accused. Wherever possible, sentences meted out to the guilty will be directly relevant to the crime and to the person involved, helping that person to change. If it is reasonable to believe that the accused is a real danger to society and must be isolated from the rest of the population, he will be sent to penal institutions quite unlike our present facilities. Penal institutions will be in large areas, like big islands in the oceans, where the convicted can bring his family and have visits from his friends. The institution will be largely self-governing, with all work devoted to making the island or penal area self-sustaining economically. The only guards necessary will be those involved in keeping the prisoners in the area, but none will be employed for internal operations, since the prisoners can do this for themselves. And there will be ample psychiatric and educational facilities so that people can really remake and expand themselves while in prison. The whole idea is largely a transitional one, since it is highly unlikely that there will be much crime in a new society, particularly as it begins to move out of the period of history in which a sizable portion of a person's day has to be spent in production.

Many people mistakenly interpret the idea that socialism does away with the bourgeoisie as a class to mean that they are brought together and collectively shot. No! It means very much the same thing as we now mean when we talk about eliminating a certain kind of work, such as running elevators. You eliminate a social role, and help people learn to fit into a new one. Periods of transition are always difficult, but they are not always bloody, and the transition in this country will be no more bloody than the armed forces of counterrevolution force it to be. But once the people are *firmly* in control of power, it is more sensible to err on the side of gradualism than to make intolerable the lives of the remaining sections of the wealthy. In Cuba, for instance, people who had abnormally high wages before the revolution are generally allowed to keep them. Even huge estates remain in the hands of the previously wealthy until they die off—at which time they are inherited by the people. It is impossible to give a blueprint for transition, but we should try to maximize humanity even if that means slowing down some immediately obtainable goods. If the means of production and the state apparatus are firmly in the hands of the people and the capitalist class is *decisively* derailed from its position of power and influence, we can afford to be gentle.

HUMAN RELATIONS

It should be clear that in our socialist community we place as one of our highest goals the full development of each person. And we understand that this is achieved only through the full development and liberation of all. Indeed, the one is inconceivable without the other, for one of the chief needs of each person will be that every other person be fulfilled and their potentialities developed to the greatest extent possible. People will be spurred to creativity and to invention, to the development of

314

beauty and love, both because it is self-fulfilling and because it is a positive contribution to society. We hold here a view of collectivity far from the reduction theories that have lately emerged in sections of the New Left. We do not believe that collectivity should ever mean the sacrifice of one's talents or skills or the abandonment of one's individuality and uniqueness. It is precisely these things that make each human being precious and which a socialist society seeks to maximize. Collective sharing, collective living, collective activity, and collective loving must develop out of an appreciation and love for each individual member of the collective, and not out of the sense that the collective itself has a transcendent worth unrelated and far superior to the sum of the worth of individuals that compose it. It may be inevitable that experimentation with collective enterprises in an otherwise capitalist society will lead to despair and disillusionment, because as long as the capitalist world still has so much real power all around us, we have good reason to feel that people may continually be falling back into its frame of exploitative and competitive mind sets. But the result has been an overly paranoid preoccupation with "bourgeois attitudes" and "individualism" that has led to the actual negation of individuality, uniqueness, and creativity in people who are attempting to make the revolution. The result, so far, has been to drive away the most creative and talented and sensitive people, who are unwilling to sacrifice their sense of themselves and their correct perception that they have valuable qualities which ought to be developed. This is just one of a dozen different areas in which the attempt to realize a socialist life in a capitalist context turns into the worst form of utopian idealism and quickly yields disillusion with the very ideals we are fighting for. It is astonishing that so many people who should know better seem to fall under the sway of this romanticism, believing that they can create real socialist social relations right now, even though they think of themselves as socialist revolutionaries. But if that were feasible, why have a revolution at all? Why not, following the strategy that first Jesus and then his followers have unsuccessfully tried for the last two-thousand years, simply urge people to change and to realize how beautiful things would be if everyone voluntarily decided to be different? Absurd. And yet many revolutionaries buy this idea and become disillusioned when they find that people in collectives or in the revolutionary movement are still unhappy. Instead of seeing that this is precisely a confirmation of the theory that it will take substantial revision of the society to change the character of life, they despair of their ability to make basic social change.

But while today we can take only very limited steps in the direction of creating a collective life that respects the individual's uniqueness and creativity, once society is in the hands of the people, much will become possible. It is quite likely that a variety of new forms of living and working together will emerge that are unthinkable or unworkable today. For one thing, it is highly unlikely that the monogamous family will attract many people. Even today monogamy has so completely broken down that divorce rates in many states have reached 50 percent or higher. But divorce only accentuates the problem rather than solving it: the problem is built into the very idea that one other person can forever fulfill all the individual's needs for love and intimacy. The monogamous family today is kept together primarily by the fact that husbands and wives see each other as private property. But when property relations break down generally, and when people begin to treat one another as ends and not just as means to their own purposes, the whole syndrome of possessiveness that today appears to be part of "human nature" will largely disappear. As a result, most people are likely to have a variety of relationships of varying intensity, and to live in extended family units in which many people together share a living facility and some aspects of child rearing. There is likely to be some variety in the kinds of arrangements to which this will lead. Some will be large houses in which individuals each have their own room; there are no permanent couples and everyone shares the housework and the child rearing. Another possibility is the same arrangement composed of nonmonogamous couples who have a primary commitment to each other but also relate to others in the house. A third arrangement is monogamous couples who share the housework and child rearing with other couples or individuals in the house. A fourth arrangement, similar to many kibbutzim, is for couples to have small cottages with their own living and bedrooms and a small kitchen facility, and then to share with a larger community a common dining room, assembly hall, and library. This form might be the prototype of the urban commune. All these possible living arrangements would require serious changes in the architecture of homes and communities. As they are built today, most living units assume the monogamous couple as the basic unit. We need houses and neighborhoods where this assumption is not built into the structure of houses. It will be crucial to have facilities where common life can develop, and at the same time have private homes for the individuals or couples whose privacy is sacrosanct.

The complete and permanent liberation of women will be a first priority of the transition period, and is likely to be accomplished within two to three generations of the revolution. In the transition every effort will be devoted to eliminating sex roles that have been developed for both men and women, in every area from jobs and education to personal relations.

In that period it is not unlikely that a strong independent women's movement will still function at every level of society to check on the progress in the battle to eliminate sexism and chauvinism. But after a few generations, this will be unnecessary. At that point, women will not be thought of as having any "group" characteristics that distinguish them from men, and much of what goes under the name of "masculinity" will also be transcended by men. Housework and child rearing will be completely shared, not because men think they "ought to help out" but because no one will see the slightest reason for women to have any greater role in these areas than men. There will be no economic dependence on men, and no assumption that a woman must find a man or else be thought of as strange or as a failure. In the transition period, many collective living arrangements will be composed only of women or only of men, although this is likely to seem less important once sex roles have largely disappeared. Women's passivity will be completely dethroned, and women will as likely be initiators of sexual contact as men, or as likely to shape the lives of their men as vice versa. Since decent human relations will become one of the main foci of life, there will be a marked reduction in competition for the affection and love of other people. Once love becomes superabundant, competition for it makes much less sense.

With nothing to compete for, love becomes the dominant mode of human relationship. Sexual love will become less neurotically necessary and more generally available, as people seek to give expression to their feelings for one another. What is possible then is a far cry from what goes under the title of "free love" in a capitalist society, in which the dominant mode of relationships is still "What's in it for me?" The injunction to free love in our society is usually the injunction that a woman should sleep with every man who asks. When there are no exploitative modes, when people have nothing in their lives pushing them to compete with each other, then love, including physical contact, becomes possible in a real sense. At the same time, not every physical contact becomes sexual in the genital sense; instead, sex becomes much less goal directed, and sensuality is spread to the entire body; the body is reeroticized. In this context, physical contact makes as much sense between members of the same sex, and what today is known as homosexuality disappears as a category but becomes a regular part of many people's normal experience. Expressions of love between man and man and between woman and woman will no longer be seen as aberrations but as perfectly normal and regular expressions of human love and solidarity.

One of the greatest beneficiaries of these possibilities will be children. No longer raised by parents who think of them as their own private property, children will have the opportunity to grow up in a more extended family where they come into contact with a variety of significant others, both adult and peer. Parents no longer will have the same need to make their children what they never could be, or to make their children feel and think like them. No longer will we be victimized by the desperate need of unhappy people to pretend that childhood is a utopian period full of innocence and free of frustration. It will thus be possible to see children for what they are. The mutual concern with and love for children expressed by the whole collective at once will give the child much more support and much more room for uniqueness and self-development, since there will be less consensus on "the right" path for him. Once the notion that children are not possessions is taken seriously, a variety of ways for them to become self-governing will develop, allowing them to maximize their own autonomy and to develop at their own pace, without in any way sacrificing the context of love and support. On the contrary, if children's ability to be independent and to define their lives for themselves is not considered a threatening sign of disrespect or lack of love for parents, the parent can begin to take pleasure in the child's development without feeling anxiety or rejection.

In talking about human relations I have suggested one style of relating which is likely to become common. But it will not be the only one. It is perfectly conceivable and even likely that there will still be many couples who like the monogamous family situation, and who want to live by themselves. This preference will also be respected. But its content and meaning for the individuals involved will inevitably be different from what it is today. In a context where other forms of living and relating obtain, no one will be forced to remain in the monogamous family for lack of an alternative. Hence monogamy is likely to be a free choice that can always be reversed without the tremendous pain and complications that attend divorce in modern America. Just as in questions of dress, appearance, art forms, work forms, etc., there will be plurality of life styles, each of which will be acceptable as long as it does not depend on some structural position which allows one person to exploit another. One of the worst aspects of the youth culture of the 1960s was its apparent totalitarianism: if you didn't live in a certain way, you weren't "one of us." This may have been inevitable in a capitalist society, in which there probably are antagonistic contradictions between one way of living and another. But it disappears in true socialism. A central guiding principle for our society is tolerance of differences in every area. This is impossible in a capitalist society, in which tolerance means that the oppressed should

318

tolerate their oppressors. But it becomes supremely important in our socialist society, when there is no more oppression, and people have a right to define for themselves how they want to live. It is precisely because one of our central aims in building a socialist society is to provide for the free development of each individual that a central concern of all is to prohibit, either in substance or in form, any development toward a "tyranny of the majority."

The same kind of principle will govern the existence of minority communities. Ethnic, religious, cultural, aesthetic, national, and historical differences embedded in common customs and traditions will be respected and there will be no attempt to uproot or displace them from the outside. Internationalism and human solidarity do not imply homogeneity. This point must be stressed again and again, not only because the reactionaries try to portray socialism as an extension of the trend, so marked in capitalist society, toward the suppression of individual and group differences, but also because some people in the New Left have given the most vulgar interpretation to what it means to fight "individualism." In the transition period especially, it is quite likely that minorities oppressed under capitalism will cling strongly to their culture as they join the general societal battle to smash the remnants of racism and other forms of prejudice. But even after racism and other prejudices no longer play any role in the consciousness or institutions of the new society, it is both probable and desirable that people take what is best in their cultural inheritance and build on it, rather than try to assimilate into one large homogeneous culture.

At several points in this account I have suggested forms of living, working, and community building that may not totally appeal to each reader of this book. Hence, it is important to stress that what I have tried to do is to outline a vision of what could be and what *I* would probably vote for and try to influence others to want. But I will have one vote, just like everyone else, and I will not have any more access to instruments of influence and power than anyone else, so the view that will win out will be the one that succeeds in convincing the largest number of people. There is no guarantee that every decision made will be the best one, but there is a guarantee that the mistakes will be *our* mistakes, made in good faith, and rectifiable by *all of us* when we decide to do so. That kind of guarantee is a world of difference from a society in which decisions about what to do, insofar as they are not simply given by the structure, are made on the basis of the need of a small group to maximize their own wealth and power. In capitalist society, rationality and truth have no efficacy unless they happen to coincide with the needs of vested interests. In a socialist society, free conscious activity is finally possible for all of us: we become the masters of our own fate.

CONCLUSION

The entire course of human development until the modern period has been guided by the need to deal with security. When people are hungry and cold and frightened of pain or imminent death, they have very little opportunity to develop the truly human dimensions of creativity, love, freedom, rationality, and benevolence. In order to conquer scarcity, many parts of human life have to be subordinated or even completely repressed. Most of life is directed toward survival and the attainment of a minimum level of comfort. For most of human history all this was inevitable. But now it is technologically possible to eliminate scarcity, so that life need not be governed by the struggle for survival or minimum comforts. On the contrary, it now becomes possible for every human being to develop his human potential and to spend very little time in production. It becomes possible to structure our society in a noncompetitive and loving way, in which people have real control over their own lives. As Karl Marx put it, it is the ascent from the kingdom of necessity into the kingdom of freedom.

We have been careful to stress that human freedom, the beginning of human history, is not the same as utopia. Socialism is the beginning of a long historical epoch in which people will experiment, make mistakes, learn from their mistakes, and try again. Far from being the end of history, a time for boredom and lack of challenge, it is the beginning: for the first time the people will decide what will happen, instead of being acted upon by outside forces over which they have virtually no control. Socialism is in one sense the entry into a period of permanent revolution; things will continue to change and develop in ways it would be impossible to predict beforehand. Talking about freedom, we know, is not the same thing as talking about a guarantee of happiness for everyone at all times; socialism does not guarantee that the man or woman you love will love you, or that everyone will find everyone else always making decisions they would like. Nevertheless, human freedom is likely to usher in an era of universal happiness that far exceeds anything we could imagine possible today, as human beings are finally allowed to loose the ties that restrain their natural inclinations to love and support their fellow creatures. The frustrations that remain in life will be so much more easy to deal with than those that flow from today's structures that the comparison will be almost hard to make; for, under socialism, there will be every structural aid possible to the realization of human potentialities, while today these potentialities are a threat to the established order and must be suppressed or actively combated.[3]

What stands in the way of all this is a tiny section of the American population which today controls the factories, banks, offices, and productive apparatus, and through that control is able to manipulate most people's understanding of the world and of themselves. The system that benefits these people has some benefits for those below them, and those benefits are continually drummed into people's consciousness, while the alternatives are portrayed as destructive and evil. People who talk sense are systematically undermined, and finally jailed or even killed. But the mechanism of control is not primarily through the brute strength of military technology, but through the elaborate ideological hegemony created by the media, the schools, and the rulers' control over a series of rewards. We have discussed how this works in more detail throughout this book, but the conclusion that wells up at every turn is how completely irrational the present system is and how desperately we need to change it.

We should emphasize that if this change does not occur within the next fifteen to twenty years, it may be too late. The ecological crisis may soon reach a point of no return. The madmen who run this country have already shown that they are willing to take us to the brink of nuclear destruction in order to preserve their own power, and it is quite possible that they will do so again. Whether through intention or oversight, these men may well destroy the world if the people do not move soon. We should not develop tactics that assume that a majority of Americans already understand this, because they would be self-defeating. On the other hand, we should not be overly patient either. It is our job to speed the development of that understanding.

If we do not succeed, we ourselves will be increasingly perverted and dehumanized. The attempt by the American government in 1972 to obliterate literally every factory, hospital, school, communications network, and power plant in North Vietnam and systematically to weaken the dikes in that country in hopes of causing flooding and terror is the most

[3] Still, socialism will not bring perfect happiness to everyone. It will not, for instance, eliminate death, which has profoundly influenced the emotions and thoughts of women and men in the past. Nor will it revive a God that everyone can believe in. The anxieties about the transcendent meaning of life will not be answered, although they are likely to play a much smaller role when people are allowed to create an immanent meaning for their own lives in the present.

obvious and obscene example of what is a perennial possibility as long as capitalism continues to function. Perhaps by the time you read these words, this whole period will be looked back on as "the past" and some liberal Democrat will assure you that now that he is in power things will be different. But even if outright genocide does not occur, there is no question that at the moment you are reading this there are tens of millions of people suffering unnecessary pain as a direct result of the continued operations of the capitalist system. What is equally shocking is that we have become so used to all this that it no longer bothers us. One of the greatest horrors of the modern world is that we have lost our ability to be horrified. Losing our sense of outrage at the brutalization and de-humanization we and our fellow human beings are subjected to, being able to do business as usual in a social system that degrades us as it murders others—this is the final triumph of capitalism. This tendency, the process by which we become accomplices in our own human destruction, is still just a tendency—but it suggests an appropriate sense of urgency that will not allow us to sit on the sidelines in the next several years, wait-ing to see if some new configuration of liberals will somehow do the job for us without any need for our personal involvement and struggle.

What happens in history is not independent of what people do. I am not talking about someone else, some mysterious "the people." I am talking about you and me. The choice is between freedom and slavery, between socialism and barbarianism, between a life that is fulfilling for all and a pointless and agonizing death to humanity. Let us choose life, by working to build an American democratic socialist revolution.

SUGGESTED READINGS

Alperovitz, Gar. *A Long Revolution?* Forthcoming.

Bookchin, Murray. *Post-Scarcity Anarchism.* Berkeley, Calif.: Ramparts Press, 1971.

Buber, Martin. *Paths in Utopia.* Boston: Beacon Press, 1958.

Goodman, Percival and Paul. *Communitas.* Chicago: University of Chicago Press, 1947.

Huberman, Leo, and Sweezy, Paul. "Peaceful Transition from Socialism? to Capitalism." *Monthly Review* 15 no. 11 (March 1964): 569–90.

Marcuse, Herbert. *Essay on Liberation.* Boston: Beacon Press, 1969.

———. *Counter-Revolution & Revolt.* Boston: Beacon Press, 1972.

Vanek, Jaroslav. *The Participatory Economy.* Ithaca, N.Y.: Cornell University Press, 1971.

Afterword

KEEPING UP AND DOING SOMETHING

SUPPOSE THAT YOU have read this book and have been successfully convinced by it to want to keep up with developments and perhaps get involved in some way. It is easier to know how to do the former than the latter, for the obvious reason that I cannot predict exactly what political developments will be occurring as you read this book, and what organizations will be doing good things.

Here are some things you can read to keep informed about what's happening:

Ramparts magazine is a must. It is published at 2054 University Avenue, Berkeley, California, and its yearly subscription fee is about $7. *Ramparts* used to be simply a muckraking journal, but it has recently been developing serious news coverage and good analysis.

Monthly Review is a much more specialized account of developments on the economic front. It often has important analyses of trends in the economy, and is edited by two of America's most respected radical economists, Paul Sweezy and Harry Magdoff. It is published at 116 West 14th Street, New York, N.Y. 10011. *Monthly Review* also publishes several interesting radical books each year.

New Left Review deals with more general philosophical issues as well as analyses of worldwide revolutionary developments. Some of the most talented leftists in the world publish articles in it. Write to B. de Boer, 188 High Street, Nutley, New Jersey. *Socialist Revolution,* published at 1445 Stockton Street, San Francisco, California; and *Liberation,* published at 339 Lafayette, New York, N.Y. 10012, have both been taken over by collectives of "total transformation now" people who tend to be extremely sectarian about their selection of material to print, who see their own political tendencies (e.g., educated labor and "cultural revolutionists" and the women's movement) as the only crucial elements in the revolution (to the point of believing that the only important struggles are against alienated social relations and authoritarianism), and who tend to be hostile toward the traditional working class, most concrete attempts at outward-directed political action (which is often labeled as "action for action's sake") and toward any political activists who do not accept their viewpoint in toto. Nevertheless, these magazines sometimes run insightful analyses on specialized problems, even though they usually will not print the views of people on the Left who have markedly different approaches from theirs.

The *New York Review of Books*, published at 250 West 57th Street, New York, N.Y. 10019, often has excellent articles on politics. Unfortunately, they almost never ask young radicals to do their book reviews. The radicals who publish in this journal are almost always superstars—the few radical intellectuals who have become well known and "acceptable" in liberal circles. Still, these radicals (e.g., Noam Chomsky, I. F. Stone, Dan Berrigan) write very important articles. Also, since the most intelligent and principled liberals write for and read this magazine, anyone who wants to carry on an intelligent debate with liberals should be reading it too.

Index

Index

A

Allen, Robert L., 92, 110
Alperovitz, Gar, 322
Anti-communism, 22

B

Berrigan, Dan, 324
Bettelheim, Charles, 68
Black Panther Party, 193, 200, 202,
206, 207–210, 218, 272–273
Blacks, 187
and busing, 133–134
exploited under capitalism, 87–
96
and nationalism, 195–197, 209–
210
as revolutionary agent, 192–211

Boggs, James, 111, 192–193, 194,
195
Bookchin, Murray, 322
Buber, Martin, 322

C

Capitalism
black, 38, 92–93, 194–195
and competition, 36–37
and consumption, 37–38, 43
effects on human relationships of,
17–18, 41–42, 225–226
and imperialism, 58, 66–70, 83–
84
and prosperity, 28–29
as sustainer of sexism, 105–106,
107, 215–217
and waste, 34–35
Chicanos, 87, 88, 97, 98, 187

T

U

V

W